F.W.J. SCHELLING

Philosophy of Revelation

(1841–42)

and Related Texts

Selected, translated, and with an introduction by

KLAUS OTTMANN

SPRING PUBLICATIONS
THOMPSON, CONN.

Published by Spring Publications
Putnam, Connecticut
www.springpublications.com

First Edition

ISBN: 978-0-88214-066-7

Library of Congress Control Number: 2020902851

Contents

Abbreviations

Works frequently cited are identified
by the following abbreviations:

EP = *Einleitung in die Philosophie,* ed. Walter E. Ehrhardt, Schellingiana 1 (Stuttgart: Frommann-Holzboog, 1989).

GPP = Friedrich Wilhelm Joseph Schelling, *Grundlegung der positiven Philosophie: Münchner Vorlesung WS 1832/33 und SS 1833,* vol. 1, ed. Horst Fuhrmans (Turin: Bottega d'Erasmo, 1972).

HKA = Friedrich Wilhelm Joseph Schelling, *Historisch-Kritische Ausgabe* (Stuttgart: Frommann-Holzboog, 1976–).

INITIA = Friedrich Wilhelm Joseph Schelling, *INITIA PHILOSOPHIÆ UNIVERSÆ: Erlanger Vorlesungen WS 1820/21,* ed. Horst Fuhrmans (Bonn: H. Bouvier u. Co. Verlag, 1969).

KG = *Kierkegaard's Journals and Notebooks: Volume 3, Notebooks* 1–15, ed. Niels Jørgen Cappelørn, Alastair Hannay, David Kangas, Bruce H. Kirmmse, George Pattison, Vanessa Rumble, and K. Brian Söderquist (Princeton, N.J., and Oxford: Princeton University Press, 2010).

PL = H.E.G. Paulus, *Die endlich offenbar gewordene positive Philosophie der Offenbarung oder Entstehungsgeschichte, wörtlicher Text, Beurtheiling und Berichtigung der v. Schellingischen Entdeckungen über Philosophie überhaupt, Mythologie und Offenbarung des dogmatischen Christenthums im Berliner Wintercursus von 1841–42* (The finally revealed positive philosophy of revelation or the genesis, verbatim text, assessment, and correction of von Schelling's discoveries about philosophy in general, mythology, and the revelation of dogmatic Christendom during the winter semester of 1841–42) (Darmstadt: Carl Wilhelm Leske, 1843).

SW = *Friedrich Wilhelm Joseph von Schellings Sämmtliche Werke,* ed. Karl F. August Schellling, 14 vols. 1. Abtheilung: 10 vols. [= I-X]; 2. Abtheilung: 4 vols. [= XI-XIV] (Stuttgart and Augsburg: J. G. Cotta' scher Verlag, 1856-61).

UF = Friedrich Wilhelm Joseph Schelling, *Urfassung der Philosophie der Offenbarung,* ed. Walter E. Ehrhardt (Hamburg: Felix Meiner Verlag, 1992). [Transcript of lectures presented in Munich in 1831-32.)

SpE = Benedicti de Spinoza, *Ethica,* in *Opera Quotquot Reperta Sunt,* ed. J. Van Vloten and J.P.N. Land, vol. 4 (The Hague: Martin Nijhoff, 1914).

Passages in Spinoza's Ethics are referred to as such: a (*axiomata*), d (*demonstratio*), e (*explicatio*), p (*propositio*), and s (*scholium*). The five parts of the *Ethics* are cited by Arab numerals.

DWB = Jacob and Wilhelm Grimm, *Deutsches Wörterbuch,* 32 vols. (Leipzig: S. Hirzel, 1854-1961).

BSB = Berean Study Bible.

ESV = English Standard Version.

KJV = King James Bible.

NAS = New American Standard Bible.

NIV = New International Version Bible.

N.T. = New Testament.

O.T. = Old Testament.

(Somewhat impatient of delay)
On the doorstep of the Absolute.
—T.S. Eliot

You say that theoretical reason is not able to comprehend a God. So be it; but call it what you will—assumption, knowledge, belief—you cannot get rid of the idea of God.
—F.W.J. Schelling (1795)

God, let me see you again in that [human] form.
—Bhagavad-Gita

Translator's Introduction

All philosophizing begins, and has always begun, with the idea of the Absolute come alive.
—F.W.J. Schelling, *Philosophy and Religion* (1804)

When Kant's *Critique of Pure Reason* first appeared in 1781, German academic philosophers were embroiled in the debate about the relationship between faith and reason, and the *Critique* was regarded as yet another contribution to the discussion of the latter. Not until the publication of Karl Leonhard Reinhold's *Letters on the Kantian Philosophy* in 1786-87 did the significance of the *Critique* become widely acknowledged.

Kant explains our *a priori* knowledge of the phenomenal world and justifies the beliefs in that which lies beyond all experience—God, freedom, and immortality—by distinguishing between a knowable phenomenal world and the things-in-themselves that we cannot know. Understanding cannot give us *a priori* knowledge of the things-in-themselves, only of appearances. Reason seeks to go beyond what is sensate but stops short of the intuition of the Absolute:

> All our knowledge starts with the senses, proceeds from there to understanding, and ends with reason beyond which no higher faculty is found for elaborating the matter of intuition and bringing it under the highest unity of thought.[1]

Kant may have claimed to have finally settled the debate about Reason and Faith with his *Critique,* but the discussions were far from over. The *Critique* led, on the one hand, to the metaphysical idealism of Fichte, Schelling, and Hegel,

1. Immanuel Kant, *Kritik der reinen Vernunft,* A298, in *Kant's gesammelte Schriften,* ed. Königlich Preußische Akademie der Wissenschaften, Erste Abtheilung, vol. 4 (Berlin: Georg Reimer, 1911), p. 191.

each of whom sought—on their respective idealist paths—to complete the Kantian program, each on his own idealist path; and, on the other, to a "non-philosophy" (*Nicht-Philosophie*) or "un-philosophy" (*Unphilosophie*) that claimed that Kant's critical philosophy had made room for a separate philosophy of faith alongside that of reason, discussed most notably by Carl August Eschenmayer, Johann Georg Hamann, and Friedrich Heinrich Jacobi.

In 1804, Schelling published *Philosophy and Religion,* mainly in response to Carl August Eschenmayer's *Philosophy in Its Transition to Non-Philosophy,*[2] with which Eschenmayer sought to accomplish for non-philosophy what Fichte and Schelling had for philosophy.

Schelling's path, on which he first trod alongside Fichte but by 1801 increasingly on his own, was that of a "speculative physics" or philosophy of nature that sought to solve the "riddle of the world" (*das Räthsel der Welt*)—the question: "how the Absolute could come out of itself and pose a world opposite it."[3] Answering this question of how the actual world can have its *positive* ground in the Absolute led directly to Schelling's declaration of constructing a positive philosophy on the basis of *actuality*—the *philosophy of revelation.*[4] It was this declaration

---

2. C.A Eschenmayer, *Die Philosophie in ihrem Uebergang zur Nichtphilosophie* (Erlangen: Walthersche Kunst- und Buchhandlung, 1803).

3. F.W.J. Schelling, *Philosophische Briefe über Dogmatismus und Kriticismus* (Philosophical Letters on Dogmatism and Criticism), *SW* I, p. 310. The question was first articulated by Leibniz—as "Why is there something rather than nothing?"—in his *Principles of Nature and Grace, Based on Reason* (1714), in *Leibniz: Selections,* ed. Philip P. Wiener (New York: Charles Scribner's Sons, 1951), p. 527. See also his earlier phrasing of the question in *On the Ultimate Origin of Things*: "You will never find a complete reason why there is a world at all, and why this world and not some other[...] it is evident that the reason must be sought elsewhere" (ibid., pp. 345–46); and Heidegger's rephrasing in his "Einleitung zu 'Was ist Metaphysik?' [Introduction to 'What Is Metaphysics?']": "Why is there Being at all, and not rather Nothing?" in Martin Heidegger, *Wegmarken* (Frankfurt am Main: Vittorio Klostermann, 1978), p. 381.

4. See Schelling's *Philosophie und Religion* (Philosophy and Religion), *SW* VI, p. 38: "If philosophy were able to derive the origin of the actual world in a *positive* manner from the Absolute, then the

that so excited Kierkegaard when he began attending Schelling's Berlin lectures in November of 1841:

> I am so glad to have heard Schelling's 2nd lecture—indescribable. I have been sighing and the thoughts within me have been groaning long enough; when he mentioned the word *actuality* concerning philosophy's relationship to the actual, the child of thought leaped for joy within me [...]. After that I remember almost every word he said. Perhaps here there can be clarity. This one word, it reminded me of all my philosophical pains and agonies.[5]

According to Eschenmayer, the question of how, in Schelling's system, the Absolute can come out of itself and become the actual world cannot be answered by philosophical reflection—only by a separate philosophy of faith. In response, Schelling proposed a new theory, that of the falling-away (*Abfall*) of the finite world from the infinite by way of a qualitative leap:

> There is no continuous transition from the Absolute to the actual; the origin of the phenomenal world is conceivable only as a complete falling-away from absoluteness by means of a leap [*Sprung*].[6]

But Eschenmayer remained unconvinced of Schelling's solution. He wrote to Schelling's friend Johann Jacob Wagner: "Schelling has no more saved himself with his idea of a falling-away (in 'Philosophy and Religion,' 1804) than he has with his other attempts."[7] Eschenmayer and Schelling

---

Absolute would have its positive cause in the same; however, in God resides only the cause of the ideas, and only those produce other ideas. There is no positive effect coming out of the Absolute that creates a conduit or bridge between the infinite and the finite. Furthermore: philosophy has only a *negative* relation to phenomenal objects; since it demonstrates less the truth of their Being than their non-Being, how could it therefore ascribe to them a *positive* relationship to God?" (emphasis mine).

5. KG 8:33, p. 229. However, Kierkegaard's enthusiasm did not last. He left Berlin early, when he realized the extent to which Schelling was willing to philosophize out of the Absolute. In a letter to his brother, he wrote: "Schelling spouts the most insufferable nonsense" (cited in KG, p. 661).

6. *Philosophie und Religion,* SW VI, p. 38.

7. Letter from Eschenmayer to Wagner, 26 November 1804, in

continued to be divided on one major point, which Eschenmayer summed up to Wagner in this way: "Here is the point where I part with Schelling. For him God is the Absolute, for me the Absolute is the afterimage [*Nachbild*] of reason, and God is beyond it."[8]

Despite the fact that Schelling's *Philosophy and Religion* having been largely ignored or even mocked,[9] it represented a new approach to the goal initially set in 1801 with his *Representation of My System of Philosophy,* the first system of philosophy he had conceived entirely on his own, independent of Fichte, after having seen "the light in philosophy," which led him to philosophize, as it were, out of the Absolute itself. In *Philosophy and Religion,* he tackled the problem of the manifestation of the finite world and human freedom by evoking Plato and Spinoza. By his own admission, however, he did not reach this goal "with complete determinateness" until 1809 when he published his *Freiheitsschrift*—the *Philosophical Investigations into the Essence of Human Freedom.*[10] The fundamentals of the system

---

F.W.J. Schelling: Briefe und Dokumente, vol. 1, ed. Horst Fuhrmans (Bonn: H. Bouvier u. Co., 1962), p. 320n.

8. Letter from Eschenmayer to Wagner, 5 April 1805, in *ibid.*

9. "Perhaps this essay will be granted the same respect and attention [*Achtung*] that [unbidden followers and opponents] showed the earlier related text, *Philosophy and Religion,* by completely ignoring it" (*Philosophische Untersuchungen über das Wesen der menschlichen Freiheit* [Philosophical Investigations into the Essence of Human Freedom], *SW* VII, p. 410n.).

"Anno 1804 God finally appeared to Herr Schelling, full-fledged, in his book entitled: *Philosophy and Religion* [...]. Here, philosophy stops with Herr Schelling, and poetry, that is to say, folly begins" (Heinrich Heine, *Zur Geschichte der Religion und Philosophie in Deutschland* [On the History and Religion in Germany] [Halle: Otto Händel, 1887], pp. 117–18).

10. "The author has confined himself to investigations into the philosophy of nature ever since the first presentation of his system (in the *Journal of Speculative Physics*), the continuation of which was unfortunately interrupted by external circumstances until a new beginning was made in *Philosophy and Religion*—which, admittedly, remained unclear due to the fault of its presentation. Therefore, the present essay is the first in which the author puts forth his concept of the ideal part of philosophy with complete

Schelling conceived during his *annus mirabilis* remained valid until his death. As Horst Fuhrmans writes, Fichte's work "challenged him to come into his own, to draw up *his* system, which, in all its transformations, he would never again abandon."[11] Schelling regarded the *Freiheitsschrift* as a synthesis of the *Representation of My System of Philosophy* and *Religion and Philosophy*; he would later write that it was with the latter work that he finally overcame the rigidity [*Starrheit*] of Fichte's philosophy.

It was not until 1831, when Schelling first began to lecture on the philosophy of revelation that he was able to make a conclusive case for the identity of the three principles that had informed his philosophy from its earliest beginnings through his last lectures—Freedom, God, and the Absolute—and to achieve the objective announced earlier, in *Philosophy and Religion*: to have philosophy "derive the origin of the actual world in a *positive* manner from the Absolute."[12]

With his philosophy of revelation, Schelling intended to complements the negative idealist system of necessity with a positive system of freedom to form a *complete* philosophy *in* God or the Absolute, one that begins and ends with God or the Absolute.

The philosophy of revelation is Schelling's *Godsong,* to borrow a term from the poet Amit Majmudar's new translation of the Bhagavad-Gita. Schelling's philosophy, like the Bhagavad-Gita, puts Man on an equal footing with God: "The Gita imagined a relationship in which the soul and God are equals."[13]

The *whole* of philosophy is now at stake:

> *Here*—even the novice will say—here, questions are to be answered for which there are no answers in all

---

determinateness" (*Philosophische Untersuchungen über das Wesen der Freiheit,* SWVII, pp. 333–37).

11. *Schelling: Briefe und Dokumente,* p. 231.

12. *Philosophie und Religion,* SWVI, p. 38.

13. *Godsong: A Verse Translation of the Bhagavad-Gita, with Commentary,* trans. Amit Majmudar (New York: Alfred A. Knopf, 2018), p. xiii.

> other sciences, and which sooner or later, but inevitably, unsettle every upright spirit; here, the veil is to be lifted, which until now has obscured—not individual matters but the *whole* itself.[14]

As Schelling had already declared in 1795:

> The beginning and end of all philosophy is—freedom [*Der Anfang und das Ende aller Philosophie ist—Freiheit*]![15]

Schelling's philosophy has always been first and foremost a *"science of the Absolute"*[16]—with freedom equal to the Absolute or God:

> Freedom is our highest principle, our godhood [*Freiheit ist unser Höchstes, unsere Gottheit*].[17]

With his positive philosophy, one arrives at the "last bastion [*letzte Linie*]," where one deals not with necessity but rather with free decision" and religious revelation is "not be merely a necessary result, but a manifestation of the uttermost free will of God."[18]

As Schelling declared in 1821, philosophy as a whole is "the most essential but also the most difficult":

> It is a battle of life and death, and Man is called upon to fight it. It is a battle that takes up all of our character, and in which we should strengthen and learn to know our strength, which is up to the task of all of infinity.[19]

---

14. *Einleitung in die Philosophie der Offenbarung oder Begründung der positiven Philosophie* (Introduction to the Philosophy of Revelation or Grounding of the Positive Philosophy), *SW* XIII, p. 3.

15. *Vom Ich als Prinzip der Philosophie oder über das Unbedingte im menschlichen Wissen* (On the I as a Principle of Philosophy or about the Unconditional in Human Knowledge), *SW* I, p. 177. See also Schelling's letter to Hegel, 2 April 1795, in G.W.F. Hegel, *Briefe von und an Hegel,* 4 vols., ed. Johannes Hofmeister (Hamburg: Felix Meiner Verlag, 1969), 1: 22: "The be-all and end-all of any philosophy is freedom [*Das A und O aller Philosophie ist Freiheit*]."

16. Horst Fuhrmans, *Schellings letzte Philosophie* (Berlin: Junker und Dünnhaupt Verlag, 1940), p. 278.

17. *Philosophie der Offenbarung* (Philosophy of Revelation), *SW* XIII, p. 256. See also *Philosophie der Offenbarung,* UF, p. 79 (Lecture 13): "Freedom is our and the godhood's highest principle [*Freiheit ist unser und der Gottheit Höchstes*]."

18. *Philosophie der Offenbarung,* UF, p. 409 (Lecture 50).

19. INITIA, p. 3.

For Schelling, this complete philosophy is neither a philosophy of faith nor a philosophy of religion but an "expansion [*Erweiterung*] of philosophy beyond its current limits."[20] It will "not be in any way dogmatic,"[21]but strictly based on philosophical principles:

> By no means does philosophy of revelation denote a philosophy that draws upon revelation, nor was it invented to prop up revelation; rather, it is independently called upon from revelation by the concept of philosophy itself. Consequently it is a strictly philosophical study originating from philosophical principles.[22]

The *Erweiterung,* in the form of the positive philosophy of revelation, was also not to be understood as a "sublation or contradiction of the earlier [negative] one" but as a consequence of it [*Folge*]; it is built onto the earlier one and relates to it like the ripened fruit to the blossom [*wie die gereifte Frucht zu der Blüte*]."[23] As Barbara Loer observes, the question about how the finite things can come out of the Absolute, first raised by Schelling in his *Philosophy and Religion,* became "the true driving force [*movens*]" of his philosophy.[24]

On the basis of newly discovered manuscripts and transcripts, both Loer and Walter E. Ehrhardt—who discovered and edited the so-called *Urfassung* (a set of transcriptions of Schelling's first lectures on revelation given in Munich

---

20. *Einleitung in die Philosophie der Offenbarung,* SW XIII, p. 145.

21. *Philosophie der Offenbarung,* SW XIV, p. 30.

22. J. Frauenstädt, *Schelling's Vorlesungen in Berlin: Darstellung und Kritik der Hauptpunkte derselben mit besonderer Beziehung auf das Verhältnis zwischen Christenthum und Philosophie* (Schelling's Lectures in Berlin: Presentation and Critique of its Main Points with Special Regard to the Relation of Christianity and Philosophy) (Berlin: Verlag von August Hirschwald, 1842), p. 68.

23. Manuscript of Schelling's 1827-28 lectures in Munich on the *System des Weltalters* (System of World Ages) (Universitätsbibliothek München, Sign. 4° Cod. ms. 1000), cited in Barbara Loer, *Das Absolute und die Wirklichkeit in Schellings Philosophie* (Berlin/New York: Walter de Gruyter, 1974), p. 280. See also INITIA, p. XVI n. 9: "The fruit was ripe; whoever stretched out his hand toward it, would catch it, and I have stretched out my hand toward it."

24. Loer, *Das Absolute und die Wirklichkeit,* p. 21.

in 1831–32)—have shown that the widespread notion of a decisive break between Schelling's early philosophy and his later lectures on the philosophy of mythology and revelation can no longer be supported. Schelling himself has always maintained this.[25] As Ehrhardt writes, "the continuing discoveries of transcripts of Schelling's lectures that were not included by Schelling's son, K.F.A. Schelling, in the *SW* [...] contradict the still prevalent view that Schelling's works were characterized by discontinuity, obscureness, and failure."[26]

Other Schelling scholars also emphasize the continuation between Schelling's early and late philosophies. Xavier Tilliette observes that the negative and the positive philosophy "are touching edge to edge; it is their concomitance that unites them. There is no 'transition' to connect them as two separate blocks," but "a relative duality that functions as a pivot around which the rational and the historical are arranged like the front and the back of the head."[27]

Because "a direct revelation of God is impossible,[28] revelation has to be accomplished by way of a "radical historicization"[29] of God—as an "epic composed in the mind of God":

---

25. "Some have wanted to explain my proposition of a positive philosophy as a change of mind. But since my studies of the Kantian philosophy, it has been clear to me that the latter could not be the whole of philosophy. I wrote in my "Letter on Dogmatism and Criticism" (1795) that a mightier, more majestic dogmatism would rise up against Kant's criticism, and this was the positive philosophy. Thus, *the notion of a positive philosophy* has been inscribed in me for a long time" (PL, p. 394, and below, p. 88); and *Die Philosophie der Offenbarung*, *SW* XIV, pp. 231–32: "I am taking the liberty on this occasion to point out that I have presented the philosophy of revelation since 1831–32 repeatedly in exactly the same manner as I do now [...] Nothing I have been presenting differs from what I have presented in the years 1831, 1832, and after. The lectures on mythology go back even further."

26. Walter E. Ehrhardt, "Afterword," UF, p. 730.

27. Xavier Tilliette, "Une Philosophie en Deux," in *Le Dernier Schelling: Raison et Positivité*, ed. Jean-François Courtine and Jean-François Marquet (Paris: Vrin, 1994), p. 57.

28. EP, p. 113: "An unmediated revelation of God is impossible [...] the world process is the revelation of God *per contrarium*."

29. Slavoj Žižek, *Absolute Recoil: Towards a New Foundation of Dialec-*

> God is the *absolute* harmony of necessity and freedom, and this harmony cannot be revealed in individual destinies but only in history as a whole; consequently, only history as a whole is a revelation of God—and then only a progressively evolving revelation [. . .]. History is an epic composed in the mind of God. It has two main parts: one depicting mankind's egress from its center to its farthest point of displacement; the other, its return. The former is, as it were, history's *Iliad*; the latter, its *Odyssey*. In the one, the direction is centrifugal; in the other, it becomes centripetal. In this way, the great purpose of the phenomenal world reveals itself in history.[30]

In Schelling, Jean-François Courtine observes,

> the idea of revelation, in its theological dimension, is without doubt intimately linked to an implicit conception of time and history: Revelation occurs at the time when it breaks with linearity and iteration: the Absolute, by its irruption into a time horizon, creates an event and inaugurates a specific history.[31]

Schelling's positive philosophy is no longer concerned with merely the concept or idea of God but with God becoming *actuality*—becoming an actual, "living God."[32] This *positive* relation with the living, actual God reveal what otherwise remains inapprehensible:

> The negative philosophy addresses what is apprehensible *a priori,* while the negative philosophy addresses what is inapprehensible *a priori*; but the positive philosophy concerns itself with it only in order to transform what is inapprehensible *a priori* into what is apprehensible *a posteriori*; what is inapprehensible *a priori* becomes apprehensible in God.[33]

Yet, as Wittgenstein has reminded us, something always remains that is nonrepresentable or inexpressible—beyond the boundary of language. In a conversation on Heidegger's

---

tical Materialism (London: Verso, 2014), p. 256.

30. *Philosophie und Religion,* SWVI, p. 57.

31. Jean-François Courtine, "Temporalité et Révélation," in *Le Dernier Schelling,* p. 9.

32. PL, p. 465, and below, p. 137.

33. *Einleitung in die Philosophie der Offenbarung,* SWXIII, p. 165.

Time and Being, recorded by Friedrich Waismann in 1929, Wittgenstein remarked,

> Man has the drive to run against the boundary of language. For example, think about the wonder at the fact that something exists. Wonder cannot be expressed in form of a question, and also there is no answer. Anything we might say could, *a priori,* only be nonsense. We nevertheless keep running against the boundary of language. This "running-against" was also seen by Kierkegaard; he even named it similarly (as a running against the paradox).[34]

Wittgenstein first describes this boundary in the concluding chapters of his *Tractatus*:

> The sense of the world must lie outside the world [...] There is indeed the inexpressible. This shows itself; it is the mystical.[35]

Because of Schelling's determination to philosophize *per contrarium,*[36] on the edge of the "originary abyss" [*anfängliche Ungrund*],[37] *i.e.,* in the face of the Absolute, his philosophy is associated—almost by default—with *failure,* with its own impossibility.

In wanting to complete Kant's philosophy, Schelling ended up failing philosophy altogether in an endgame of theory:

> As soon as the first [negative] philosophy has made possible or begotten the principle [of God], it already reached its end.[38]

Schelling attempted to philosophize out of the Absolute itself in spite of its impossibility. His *greatest* yet most *doomed*

---

34. *Ludwig Wittgenstein und der Wiener Kreis: Gespräche, aufgezeichnet von Friedrich Waismann,* ed. B.F. McGuiness (Frankfurt am Main: Suhrkamp Verlag, 1984), p. 68–69.

35. Ludwig Wittgenstein, *Tractatus Logico-Philosophicus,* trans. C.K. Ogden (London: Routledge & Kegan Paul Ltd., 1981), 6.41 and 6.522.

36. "However offensive term the term *per contrarium* or divine disguise [*Verstellung*], I confess that all of Christianity would be unintelligible without its premise." EP, p. 114.

37. *Philosophische Untersuchungen über das Wesen der menschlichen Freiheit,* SW VII, p. 408.

38. *Philosophie der Mythologie* (Philosophy of Mythology), *SW* XI, p. 562.

endeavor—to use Karl Jaspers's famous dictum[39]—was his monumental attempt to construct a complete philosophy at the event horizon of the Absolute or God. Leibniz's insight that the reason for our world must lie outside our world—the Absolute or God—led Schelling to position his philosophy on the very boundary of the "originary abyss," which Wittgenstein would later call the "mystical," in an attempt to retrieve what is unthought and in some sense inherently unthinkable.

Rather than execute a somersault that would land him safely on the ground, with one foot on reason and the other on faith—as advocated by Jacobi[40]—Schelling attempts a reverse *leap* into the Absolute within philosophy in order to initiate a "reverse formation [*Zurückbildung*] of difference into oneness"[41]—as a decisive leap in the face of certain failure.

It was this philosophizing out of failure, *i.e.,* the Absolute that become the driving force for his last, positive philosophy of revelation. As Mason Richey describes it, Schelling "is the Don Quixote of nineteenth-century German philosophy; his philosophy is not beholden to a rule [...] when his work succeeds it does so spectacularly, and when it fails it does so spectacularly."[42]

Schelling first developed the methodology for approaching his expansion of philosophy was first developed by Schelling in *Philosophy and Religion,* further refining it in his *Freiheitsschrift.* It represented the first step of a radical new approach in resolving the problem of the manifestation of the finite world and human freedom by asking not how Man becomes divine but how God becomes Man through freedom – a freedom that is as fragile as the God who is

---

39. Karl Jaspers, *Schelling: Größe und Verhängnis* (Munich: R. Piper & Co., 1955).

40. Friedrich Heinrich Jacobi, *Über die Lehre des Spinoza in Briefen an den Herrn Moses Mendelssohn* (Breslau: Gottlieb Löwe, 1785).

41. *Philosophie und Religion,* SWVI, p. 45.

42. "Translator's Introduction," in F.W.J. Schelling, *Historical-Critical Introduction to the Philosophy of Mythology* (Albany: State University of New York Press, 2007), p. xvii.

defined by it, who thus carries in himself the possibility of non-being. As Sartre would later write, "it is through Man that fragility comes into Being."[43] It is through Schelling's philosophy of revelation that fragility comes into the Absolute or God. It puts God on an equal footing with fallible man.

In his study of Schelling, Slavoj Žižek describes the philosopher as

> a kind of "vanishing mediator" between the Idealism of the Absolute and post-Hegelian universe of finitude-temporality-contingency, that his thought—for a brief moment, as it were, in a flash—renders visible something that was invisible beforehand and withdrew into invisibility thereafter.[44]

This description echoes Jean-François Lyotard's definition of the postmodern as that which "puts forward the unrepresentable in presentation itself [...] [and] denies itself the solace of good forms."[45] By understanding postmodernism as a condition rather than as a historically defined period of time, as Lyotard does, Schelling could arguably be regarded as a postmodern philosopher because he put forward the Absolute as the "unforethinkable," as the unground (*Ungrund*) or abyss of that prior to which there is no activity of thought (*das Unvordenkliche*),[46] in philosophy itself: "In presupposing a merely mediated knowledge of the Absolute (irrespective of how the mediation occurs), the Absolute in philosophy can only appear as something that is presumed in order that it can be philosophized about."[47]

---

43. Jean-Paul Sartre, *L'Être et le néant* (Paris: Librairie Gallimard, 1950), p. 43.

44. Slavoj Žižek, *The Indivisible Remainder: An Essay on Schelling and Related Matters* (London: Verso, 1996), p. 8.

45. Jean-François Lyotard, *The Postmodern Condition: A Report on Knowledge*, trans. G. Bennington and B. Massumi (Minneapolis: University of Minnesota Press, 1984), p. 81.

46. *Cf. Philosophie der Offenbarung*, SW XIV, p. 347: "That which has existence unforethinkably [*das unvordenkliche Existirende*] precedes all concepts."

47. *Philosophie und Religion*, SW VI, p. 27.

And as Jean-Luc Nancy, one of several philosophers who have recently entered into a discourse with religion,[48] writes (with a nod to Wittgenstein and Schelling):

> Language [. . .] addresses, appeals to, calls out to the unnamable, what is strictly the reverse side of all possible nomination. This reverse side is not the world's hidden face, nor a "thing in itself," neither Being [*être*] nor being [*étant*]. It does not exist: all existence opens itself starting from it and toward it.[49]

At the core of Schelling's positive philosophy is the Christian theory of *kenosis* (the *Entäusserung* or self-emptying of God during the act of Creation), which ultimately puts God outside of himself:

> This is Christ's reward, that he has a right to be outside of God in his own form; he is outside of God with God's will. Peter says to the Jews: "Therefore let all Israel know with certainty that God has made this Jesus, whom you crucified, both Lord and Christ!" He did not cease to be Man. We are in need of such an intermediate, for he is the eternal intermediate. Christ is outside of God by virtue of his eternal humanness, and he is outside of Man by virtue of his godhood.[50]

Schelling's concept of the God outside himself, results in a "pagan demiurge": "the becoming of the world is the becoming of God Himself, his self-creation and self-revelation, so that the human awareness of God is the self-awareness of God."[51]

With Christ's Becoming Human, a new beginning is made—a "second Creation":

> The *actus* of the revelation is merely the recurring and exalted [*gesteigerte*] *actus* of the Creation, taking place on a higher level.[52]

---

48. Most recently, this includes the 2-volume study *Auch eine Geschichte der Philosophie* by Jürgen Habermas (Berlin: Suhrkamp, 2019), a history of the intersection of faith and knowledge in philosophy, in which, however, Schelling is conspicuously absent.

49. Jean-Luc Nancy, *Adoration: The Deconstruction of Christianity II,* trans. John McKeane (New York: Fordham University Press, 2013), p. 2.

50. PL, p. 703, and below, p. 306.

51. Žižek, *Absolute Recoil,* p. 256.

52. *Philosophie der Offenbarung,* UF, p. 410 (Lecture 51).

This second Creation is to be completed by Man in and through history filled with, in Thomas Mann's words, "the divine freedom of the I [*mit der Gottesfreiheit des Ich*]"[53]—a history shared by God and Man, whose beginning and end are described by the philosophy of revelation.

Schelling's concept of the incarnated Christ outside of God is as unorthodox as it is crucial to his historicized philosophy of revelation:

> It is absolutely necessary for the understanding of Christianity—the *conditio sine qua non* of perceiving its true meaning—that we comprehend this being cut-off [*Abgeschnittenheit*] of the Son from the Father, this being in his own form and hence in complete freedom and independence of the Father.[54]

What Schelling ultimately failed to recognize, however, is that, as Nancy points out, Christianity's adaptation of the concept of *kenosis,* was the first step toward its destruction. Christianity has undone itself:

> It is no accident [...] that Christianity has desacralized, demythologized, and secularized itself in such a constant and irreversible way for at least six centuries—if not for far longer. (Should we not say: from the moment Christendom existed, it entered into deconstruction and dis-enclosure?)[55]

The world outside of God becomes the world without God. In Nancy's philosophy, "the Christian 'god' is atheist," and the fulfillment of "revelation" is not a return of Man to God's divinity but rather his abandonment of God. Ultimately, Schelling's God, actualizing himself in and through history, is less the "eternal intermediate" who is "outside of God by virtue of his eternal humanness, and [...] outside of Man by virtue of his godhood" and more like the Christ Child depicted in the Portinari Altarpiece by Hugo van der Goes (Galleria degli Uffizi, Florence, c. 1475), lying on the floor, naked and fragile like any human newborn, and

---

53. Thomas Mann, *Joseph and His Brothers,* trans. John E. Woods (New York: Alfred A. Knopf, 2005), p. 1158.

54. *Philosophie der Offenbarung,* SW XIV, p. 39.

55. Nancy, *Adoration,* p. 25.

forsaken like a God outside of himself—a depiction that does not follows the traditional view found in the Gospels of the adoration of the Christ Child in his crib but, rather, that of the revelations of the Swedish mystic Brigitta who envisioned the infant lying on a bare floor surrounded by supra-worldly rays of light.

> God effaces himself in that man: he is this effacement, he is therefore a trace, he is an impalpable, imperceptible vestige of the emptied and abandoned divine. Mankind is the abandonment of God: the trace upon him, the trace that he is, constitutes him as a sign of this abandonment. A sign of this: that the effacement of God is the sense of the world. The effacement of the Name, of Sense fulfilled.[56]

---

56. *Ibid.*, p. 30.

A Note about the Translation

Dealing with a text that is almost two hundred years old presents formidable challenges even to a native reader. In general, the following translation has sought to preserve Schelling's German, which is considerably richer and more nuanced than today's and suffused with the German of Martin Luther's Bible translation, without sacrificing readability.

Once stripped of its polemic apparatus of commentary and footnotes (as first done by Manfred Frank),[57] Paulus's transcription is the most complete record of Schelling's widely anticipated lectures on mythology and revelation given between 1841 and 1842 at the University of Berlin.[58] The lectures were attended by a large audience that includ-ing many distinguished names, such as Søren Kierkegaard, Alexander von Humboldt, Friedrich Engels, and Mikhail Bakunin. Word of these lectures traveled as far as New York where a translation of Schelling's 1841 inaugural lecture was published in 1843 in the Transcendentalist magazine *The Dial*.[59]

As is well known, Paulus's publication of his transcript was not authorized by Schelling, even though it was not the only one. Schelling virtually stopped publishing in 1809 after the publication of his *Philosophical Investigations on the Essence of Human Freedom* and the death of his first wife, Caroline, and he was well aware of the many transcriptions of his lectures circulating throughout Germany and beyond. Yet Schelling was so displeased with Paulus's publication that he went to court to stop its distribution, albeit unsuccessfully.[60]

57. F.W.J. Schelling, *Philosophie der Offenbarung 1841/42*, ed. Manfred Frank (Frankfurt am Main: Suhrkamp, 1977).

58. Most of Schelling's manuscripts and papers were destroyed during World War II.

59. "Schelling's Introductory Lecture in Berlin, 15th Nov. 1841," trans. Frederic Henry Hedge, *The Dial* (January 1843).

60. A detailed description of Schelling's legal battle as well as an analysis of the reliability of the transcript is given by Frank in his extensive introduction to his publication of the lectures.

Paulus transcription is not without errors and omissions. I have augmented Paulus's text with Kierkegaard's notes of Schelling's Berlin lectures, taken between late November 1841 and February 3, 1842, and Schelling's posthumously published *Philosophy of Revelation* (SW XIII and XIV), which was based on lectures given in Berlin between 1841 and 1847, whenever it felt necessary to help the comprehension of this often difficult text.

I have provided translations for Schelling's generous use of Latin, Greek, and Hebrew phrases and words in brackets and supplemented Schelling's sparse footnotes (indicated by symbols) with annotations of my own, which are numbered and meant to aid the understanding of references that are not easily accessible to contemporary readers. Unless noted otherwise, all translations of non-English citations in the footnotes are my own.

All text emphasized with letter-spacing (*Sperrdruck*) in the original has been converted to italics; and any text set in italics, to boldface. Additional italics have been added wherever words are capitalized for emphasis (*e.g.*, "*one* Being" for "Ein Seyn"), unless they are used as nouns (*e.g.*, "the First" for "das Erste.") Paulus's subheadings were retained, as well as his often idiosyncratic use of dashes (which may have meant to indicate pauses in Schelling's delivery).

Friedrich Wilhelm Joseph Schelling

Revelation and Public Education

Philosophisches Journal, No. 2, 1798

[*SW* I, pp. 474–82]

The following brief remarks were written on the occasion of the publication of Niethammer's *Doctrinae de revelatione modo rationis praeceptis consentaneo stabiliendae periculum* (1797)[1] (which should be wholesome reading for those newest theologians whose pseudophilosophy Niethammer enervates so rigorously). Whatever I have written here against this aberration of philosophy is for the most part taken from this treatise.—The rest should be ascribed entirely to my account.

* * *

It is time to stop regarding revelation as an *idea of reason* [*Vernunftsidee*] or even as a *postulate of practical reason* because the alleged practical necessity or acceptability of revelation is by now reduced to that of an external auxiliary means [*Hülfsmittel*] for morality (which revelation is supposed to be). Two things are thereby presupposed: first, that revelation is in need of such an auxiliary means at all—an idea that must be banned from true morals at long last and without mercy since it is incompatible with the freedom and purity of moral conclusions. There is no means [*Adjument*] of morality that is merely external; if something is an auxiliary means for morality, it is one not *by itself* but because we have made it one. In *this* sense, there is nothing in the world that could not become an means of morality. Thus (and this is the second presumption) if revelation were to be, first and foremost, such a means, then it would have to be such *by its nature, by itself,* not be dependent on our good will (our freedom). Clearly, it must be *such* because it exists; it must sustain morality as necessarily as breathing sustains our life

1. Friedrich Immanuel Niethammer, *Versuch einer Begründung des vernunftmäßigen Offenbarungsglaubens* (Leipzig and Jena: Friedrich Frommann, 1798).

functions. If it is used, as a means, as a function of our free decision, then this usage already presupposes morality for moral purposes; where such a means would be effective, it is not applicable, and where it is applicable, it is no longer required.

Hence the defender of the moral necessity of revelation sees himself driven to first demonstrate the *existence* of revelation. He is forced to drag this concept out of the hiding place of practical postulates into the open field of concepts of nature and put its reality, like the reality of every other object of nature, to the test of theory.

The dignity that the resolute theologians of old—who are far superior to today's half-philosophers [*Halbphilosophen*]—sought steadfastly to sustain is herewith restored to this concept. Even though they also considered moral arguments for the existence of a revelation, they nevertheless recognized that the reality of this theoretical attestation would be supported too weakly if they could not add to them.

What's more, the very philosophy (if this often misused word may be misused again here) that posits revelation as a practical postulate has completely false concepts about the nature and essence of moral postulates since a large part of those philosophers makes no secret of the theoretical reality of this concept not holding up well and being unconstruable by theoretical reason, *i.e.*, of being plainly unreasonable, and since those philosophers dream about a practical reality of this concept, they must be deluded in believing that what is highly unreasonable theoretically could be highly reasonable *practically* (what may they have been thinking?). One would ask in vain about their own reasoning; the only reason is that they believe that the essence of *Kantianism* (they do not want to lag behind the times, after all) is that what is thrown out of philosophy through the front door is re-introduced through the back door (the practical postulate). Now, among such contraband introduced from behind [*hinterrücks*] by those philosophers is the concept of revelation; and it seems to me that the main purpose of the aforementioned treatise is to make an end to that kind of clandestine trade [*Schleichhandel*], of which anyone whose activity of thought [*Denken*] is manly and brave can voice only one opinion.

It is evident that once such a concept is made into a practical postulate, one cannot go around providing a theoretical construct of it. Even though it is easy to analyze this concept, and to once again develop out of it the particular properties brought into it, such a maneuver can only prevent those who are shortsighted from asking about the final ground [*letzten Grund*] of the reality of this arbitrarily assembled concept. This final ground, however, can only be a synthetic construct (or originary bringing-forth) of this concept. In this respect, it asserts that there is a direct effect of God on the sensate world [*Sinnenwelt*] and on the human mind whereby, as is self-evident, the concept of God as an individual, personal being—namely, one who is effective in the sensate world—is presupposed, whereby those philosophers plunge into the greatest inconsequence because they posited the idea of *godhood* previously only as a practical reality, *i.e.*, as an object of doing and acting [*Thuns und Handelns*], not as a categorical *knowledge* (a knowledge that is directed at *Being*).

At the same time—if I may be allowed to add some of my own thoughts here—these philosophers presuppose a *receptivity* in the human mind that is contrary to its entire nature. Since the essence of the mind is activity, it is only capable of a kind of *being subjected to* [*Leiden*] that in another respect is a *doing* [*Thun*]. In other words, one cannot conceive of an *absolute passivity* in the human mind; any such presumption is false by its very nature.—(This is the touchstone for testing any transcendental statement.)—Now, revelation as defined in that philosophy, *i.e.*, as a real effect of the highest essence on the human mind, leaves nothing to the latter but absolute passivity. For the highest essence is absolute-active; but the necessary correlate of absolute activity is absolute passivity. That concept of revelation, according to the very principles of that philosophy, is therefore utterly false; for from the theoretical aspect, they admit that it is as little construable as, *e.g.*, the concept of witchcraft. But from the practical aspect (in relation to freedom), it destructs itself because it cannot coexist with freedom.

Nevertheless, those same philosophers want revelation to coexist with freedom because they stipulate a *use of reason in matters of revelation.* Were they capable of sustained consequential thinking, they would have learned long ago from another publication by the author—*On Religion as a Science*[2]—that this [usage] was unfathomable according to their concepts. It is no wonder that those who were still somewhat able to think consequently arrived at the concept of a *mediated revelation.* This concept, however, does not contain even a trace of what *revelation* meant *originarily,* and it is a hypocrisy unworthy of philosophy to want to retain and perpetuate the name of something after its concept has along ago disappeared.

They tried, of course, to gloss over this procedure. But as usual, the glossing over was worse than what was glossed over. *Lessing* posited revelation as a means to educate humanity. Those familiar with his spirit know what he meant by this. His spirit was removed completely from the kind of half-philosophy that was spun from this idea. In his biography, one finds excerpts from a number of his letters that should be a sword against the soul of those proponents of enlightenment who boast to have lived during Lessing's time and who from time to time still shed their dim little light on subsequent generations. "Should I begrudge the world," he writes, "seeking to enlighten itself further? Should I not wish from the heart that everyone may think about religion rationally? I would loathe myself if my writings had a different purpose than to further these great intentions. But let me do this in the way I believe is right for me. And what is simpler than this way? I do not wish the long unusable impure water to be retained, but I also do not want it to be poured away until one knows where to get purer water. [...] With orthodoxy, thank God, one was able to deal with rather well. A partition had been put up between it and

---

2. Friedrich Immanuel Niethammer, *Über Religion als Wissenschaft zur Bestimmung des Inhalts der Religionen und der Behandlungen ihrer Urkunden* (On Religion as Science for the Determination of the Content of Religions and the Treatment of their Documents) (Neu-Strelitz, 1795).

philosophy, behind which each could go about in its own way without impeding the other. But what is happening now? This partition is being torn down, and under the pretext of making us reasonable Christians we are turned into highly unreasonable philosophers. We are in agreement in the conviction that our old religious system is false. But I cannot say with you that it is a patchwork of bungler's and half-philosophers. I know of nothing in the world by which human acumen has more studied and strengthened itself. *The religious system, which one now wants to put in place of the old, is the patchwork of bunglers and half-philosophers* and with far more influence upon reason and philosophy than the old claimed for itself."[3]

One can hear when this passage was written. He would certainly be writing differently today, for why would one not be content with the way things have turned out? Had the partition remained, the superstitious ones would still be plying their trades quietly. Now that it is torn down, it *ought to* remain so; one must take care that the two roads, one leading from it to this world, the other to the world beyond, become *one* avenue [*Eine Heerstraße*] for all. Why not unmask those who deceive the public? One should not allow oneself to be misled by a rout of halfwits [*Halbköpfen*] who, because their service as candle snuffers* is coming to an end, curse the break of day. Should the sun not rise so that the fireflies keep on flashing or some rotting wood continues to glow?

One spoke of *deception* [*Betrug*]. Yet those who abolish the concept of revelation all agree that they must be needed by

---

3. Lessing to his brother Karl, Wolfenbüttel, 2 February 1774, in *Gotthold Ephraim Lessings Leben, nebst seinem noch übrigen litterarischen Nachlasse,* ed. K.G. Lessing (Berlin: In der Vossischen Buchhandlung, 1793), pp. 350–52.

* In the large concert hall in Leipzig, which is adorned with works by the allegorical painter [Adam Friedrich] Oeser, the *urge to enlighten* is demonstrated in the depiction, among others, of a *sprightly boy* who cleans the flame with candle snuffers, "in order to," as it is explained, "make the light of cognizance shine brighter in the eyes of all." (*Leipzig, ein Handbuch für Reisende* [*die ihren Aufenthalt daselbst sich angenehm und nützlich machen wollen* (Leipzig, a Handbook for Travelers Who Want to Make Their Stay Pleasant and Useful), 1892], by [George Carl] Claudius.

the public, if not as hobgoblin, then as *authority.* But it still is, and will continue to be, *deception*—deception in the holiest matters—to claim to be an authority on something of which they are convinced that it is nothing. Assuming that such a claim *was* useful *initially* (even though this is impossible because it abolishes the formation [*Bildung*] of independence [*Selbstständigkeit*]), would the end justify the means, and would these false means themselves not become subsequently destructive to the higher purpose? But the public [*Volk*] is itself a highly relative concept, one designated as having neither enough free time nor the ability to raise itself to the level of principles. But what are those principles? Your principles perhaps? But you have admitted to—and made no secret of—not being able to raise yourself to the level of principles that others deem rightfully to be the highest. Consequently, you would be counted by them according to their principles as *the public* with the same right that you count others according to *your* principles. You are outraged against it—you who are infinitely more blind than the blind you undertake to lead! What gives you the right to raise yourself above your brothers? Perhaps it is because they did not receive a higher education or memorize oriental languages or some philosophical compendium? You want to lead them on a leash when you have hardly the strength to lead yourself.

Every society with a religious purpose is perfectly egalitarian. No one is really a *teacher* or a *student,* much as this may break the parsons' pride [*Pfaffenstolz*]. Only truths supposed to be universally believed should be stimulated by collective confession (where one speaks in the name of all).† The State should not deny its citizens participation in such a collective nor should it stand in the way of any divisiveness, dispute, or consequent scandal from arising. For this reason only, not because you are deemed wiser than what you call *the public,* there can be no question of *examination,* of a

---

† I refer here to [Johann Gottlieb] *Fichte's System der Sittenlehre* [*nach den Prinzipien der Wissenschaftslehre* (System of Morals According to the Principles of the Doctrine of Science) (Jena and Leipzig: Christian Ernst Gabler, 1798)], p. 475f.), where the same is said and demonstrated.

returning to principles in such a society. What is learned therein is presupposed as universally accepted truth. Any instruction that is not based on principles is by nature *historical.* The ideas that animate religious gatherings with moral strength are presupposed among mankind (since ancient times) *as preexisting.* And it is a special stroke of luck for any cultured nation if a religious record from ancient times exists in which those ideas are laid down *historically.* The history of religion is then a progressive revelation or symbolic representation of those ideas; more generally, the entire history of mankind is therefore nothing but the progressive development of a moral world plan, which we have to assume to be predestined by reason (in as far as reason is absolute).

For—to say here what can serve also as an explanation of other assumptions—reason can generally be seen as having a dual function. Either one regards it as *absolute,* insofar as it is nothing other than the originary synthesis out of which all singular things evolve in infinite sequence, and so all phenomena of the external world and all historical events are nothing but various sequences wherein that originary synthesis unfolds *successively.* Or, to the extent that reason *ascends* conversely *from the individual evolutions to the originary involution,* its function is *empirical.*—The product of reason in its *absolute* function is the *actual* world; in its *empirical* function, it is the *ideal* world.

Now, since everything that exists in actuality unfolds *from absolute reason,* we must also find the trace of that *absolute reason* in history and especially in the history of the human mind, where it will appear to us empirically (merely *practically*) as *providence,* which has arranged everything in just the way we find it in actuality.

That which in us evolved consciously and completely we thus find evolved unconsciously and incompletely in the philosophies and religions of old, and it will be easy to recognize *our ideas* (*i.e.,* the general reason) in their monuments (if they are records of public religion).

I cannot understand what is said in the conclusion of the above-mentioned treatise on the rationality of revelation any other way.

As soon as the conditions of the construct of a concept are proven to be false or impossible, the concept must vanish from the system of concepts. Furthermore, the concept of revelation cannot claim *scientific* dignity. That much has been set forth irrefutably in the above-mentioned author's *On Religion as Science* by demonstrating that this concept, if raised to the level of a *principle,* would destroy all use of reason. But this is precisely how the question of whether a concept has scientific reality is put to the test, for any true and real concept (as well as any legal maxim for a general law of action) must be safely expandable to a general principal of knowledge.

Thus it will surely always befit a herdsman of the public to prevent the latter from being led astray by religious ideas through the careless degradation of positive teachings that were their vehicle. In contrast, he will not want to go as far in his eagerness (*ne quid detrimenti* [lest anything of harm], *etc.*)[4] as to impede the learned study of the untaught but rather to keep modestly within his boundaries, for, as Lessing says, a librarian is one thing, and another is a—pastor.[‡ 5]

---

4. Paraphrase of Sallust's "ne quid res publica detrimenti caperet (lest the Republic suffers any harm)." *Bellum Catalinae,* 29.

‡ How often will one even now try to parody those words!—When [Lessing], who was mentioned in this treatise more than once, let himself be inducted into the Freemasonry at the encouragement of his friends, one of them consoled him with the thought that he found nothing against State or Church therein. "God willing," the unforgettable replied, "I would have found *something.*" Others, *e.g.,* chief court preacher [Franz Volkmar] Reinhard in Dresden, complained bitterly to have found in the new philosophy much that is against State and Church. [It was Reinhard to whom Fichte dedicated the second edition of his *Versuch einer Kritik aller Offenbarung* (Attempt at a Critique of All Revelation) in 1793.]

5. Paraphrase of Lessing's "A parable with a small request and, if necessary, a challenge, to Pastor Goeze in Hamburg, 1778," in Gotthold Ephraim Lessing, *Philosophical and Theological Writings,* trans. H.B. Nisbet (Cambridge: Cambridge University Press, 2005), p. 113: "A pastor is one thing, and a librarian is another."

On the Historical Construct of Christianity

Eighth Lecture on the Method of Academic Study

(Jena 1802)

[*SWV*, pp. 286–95]

The real sciences are distinct from absolute or ideal science only by their historical construct. Theology, however, has another distinction apart from this general relation to history, one owing to its particular nature.

As the true center, wherein philosophy becomes objective in speculative ideas, theology is the highest synthesis of philosophical and historical knowledge. Presenting theology as such is the main purpose of the following observations.

I do not base theology's relation to history merely on the fact that the origins of religion, like every other type of cognizance and culture, can be understood in the context of the teachings of higher beings—in other words, that all religion has been, from the very outset, a product of tradition. As for other empirical explanations: according to some, feelings such as fear and gratitude gave rise to the first ideas of God or gods; according to others, it was a clever invention of the first lawgivers. The former understands the idea of God solely as a psychological phenomenon, while the latter explains neither how anyone thought of making himself a lawgiver in the first place nor how they could have come up with the idea of using religion as a deterrent [*Schreckmittel*] unless they already had an idea of God or gods as coming from another source. Of the falsest and most unoriginal writings in recent times, the so-called Histories of Mankind are at the top of the list.[1] Their view of the original conditions of our species are derived from travelogues that compiled the raw traits of savage tribes. Actually, there is no condition of barbarism that does not stem from a declined civilization. It is for future efforts of science to show how

1. See Friedrich August Carus's introductory overview of that literature in his *Ideen zur Geschichte der Menschheit* (Ideas for the History of Mankind) (Leipzig, 1809), pp. 5–46.

the savage tribes of today are simply the remnants of nations that were torn away from the rest of the world and scattered as a result of revolutions. Robbed of connections with each other and with their earlier cultural possessions, they regressed to their current state. I consider culture the earliest condition of the human race, occurring simultaneously with the founding of states, sciences, religion, and the arts or, more accurately, as one interpenetrating whole, as it will be again in the end.

Neither is the relation of history to theology grounded in the fact that the forms of Christianity through which the religion exists among us can only be understood historically.

What makes this relation absolute is that in Christianity the universe is regarded in general as *history,* as a moral realm, and this general view constitutes its fundamental character. This can only be fully comprehended in contrast to the religions of old, specifically that of ancient Greece. If I do not mention still older religions, such as the religion of India, it is because in this respect they form less of a contrast. The confines of this examination do not allow for a complete presentation of this contrast; I will deal with it only in passing. The mythology of the Greeks was a closed world of symbols for ideas that could be perceived as real only in the form of gods. Each god was ruled by pure delimitation on the one hand and undivided absoluteness on the other. The infinite was perceived only in the finite and was itself subordinated to the finite. The gods were beings of a higher nature—enduring, immutable figures. How different is a religion that has an unmediated relationship with the infinite, in which the finite is conceived of neither as a symbol of the infinite nor for its own sake but rather as an allegory of the former and subordinated wholly to it. The entity in which the ideas of such a religion become objective is necessarily an infinite itself—not an all-around complete and limited world. Its figures are not lasting but transient, not eternal beings of nature but historical figures in which the divine is revealed temporarily, its fleeting appearance held fast by faith yet never transformed into an absolute presence.

Where the infinite can become finite, it can also become a multiplicity; polytheism is possible. Where the infinite is only signified by the finite, it remains necessarily one, and no polytheism, no coexistence of divine figures, is possible. Polytheism arises from a synthesis of absoluteness and limitation so that neither absoluteness of form nor limitation is canceled. In a religion like Christianity, it cannot be rooted in nature for it does not conceive the finite as a symbol of the infinite or in independent signification. It can only have been taken from what falls within time, *i.e., history*; thus Christianity is, in the highest sense and in its innermost spirit, historical. Any particular moment of time is a revelation of a particular aspect of God in each of which he is absolute; what Greek religion had as simultaneity, Christianity has as sequence, although the time of distinction has not yet come.

It has already been pointed out earlier that nature is to history what the real is to the ideal; the same is true of the relationship between Greek and Christian religion. In the latter, the divine no longer reveals itself in nature and is recognizable only in history. Nature is generally the realm of things that have Being in themselves, *i.e.,* wherein those, as symbols of ideas, at the same time have a life independent of their signification on the strength of the imaginative formation [*Einbildung*] of the infinite into the finite. In nature, God therefore becomes exoteric, so to speak; the ideal shows itself through an Other than itself, through a Being [*Seyn*]. Yet only insofar as that Being is taken for the essence, and the symbol is understood independently from the idea, is the divine truly exoteric; in regards to the idea, however, it is esoteric. In the ideal world, thus particularly in history, the divine unveils itself; it is here that the mystery of the divine realm announces itself.

Just as in the symbolic images of nature, the intelligible world lay in Greek poetry as if in an unopened bud, veiled objectively and unspoken subjectively. By contrast, Christianity is the revealed mystery, and whereas paganism by its nature is exoteric, Christianity is by its nature esoteric.

In Christianity, the relationship between nature and the ideal world thus became reversed. Just as in paganism, nature was the revealed while the ideal world withdrew into the secret *Mysterium,* so in Christianity the more the ideal world became revealed, the more nature receded into secrecy. To the Greeks, nature as such was unmediated and divine as their gods were not supra- or extranatural. To the newer world, nature was elusive, for it was not grasped for itself but only as a metaphor for the invisible spiritual world. The most vigorous manifestations of nature, such as electrical phenomena and the chemistry of the human body, were scarcely known to the ancients or at any rate failed to arouse the enthusiasm with which they were received in the newer world. The highest form of religiosity, as expressed in Christian mysticism, holds the secrets of nature and the mystery of the Becoming Human [*Menschwerdung*] to be one and the same.

Elsewhere (in the *System of Transcendental Idealism*) I have shown that we must assume that there have been three periods of history: nature, destiny, and providence.[2] All three express the same thing, but in different ways. Destiny is providence as recognized in the world of real things; similarly, providence is destiny as viewed in the ideal world. Eternal necessity revealed itself as nature at a time of identity, when the opposition between the infinite and the finite was still concealed in the joint seed of the finite. Greek religion and poetry reached full bloom in this period. With its retreat from nature, eternal necessity revealed itself as fate as it found itself in a real conflict with freedom. This was the end of the old world, and for this reason its history as a whole is a tragic period. The new world began with a fall of Man, *i.e.,* a breaking away from nature. It was not the devotion to nature that was the sin but rather the Golden Age, as long it was without consciousness of the opposite. With consciousness, innocence is lost, and reconciliation and voluntary surrender are required; freedom, standing and falling at the same time, emerges from the struggle. This conscious

---

2. Schelling, *System des transzendentalen Idealismus* (System of Transcendental Idealism), *SW* III, p. 603: "We can assume three periods of this revelation, and thus three periods of history. The ground for such a division is provided by the two opposites, destiny and providence; between them stands nature, which effectuates the transition from one to the other."

reconciliation, which takes the place of the unconscious identity with nature and the conflict with fate and restores unity on a higher plane, is expressed in the idea of providence. With its prevailing view of the universe as history and as a world of providence, Christianity thus initiates the period of providence in history.

This is the great historical course of Christianity; this is why in Christianity the science of religion is inseparable from history, why indeed it must be identical with it. But that synthesis with history, without which theology would not be conceivable, demands as its condition the higher, Christian view of history.

The commonly made opposition of philosophy to history exists only as long as history is conceived of as a sequence of random occurrences or merely as empirical necessity. The former—to which the latter holds itself superior—is the most common view, but one is as limited as the other. History, too, comes out of an eternal unity and has roots in the Absolute, just as nature or any other object of knowledge does. To the common mind, the fortuitousness of events and actions is typically grounded in the fortuitous nature of individuals. But what is this or that individual but the very person who effectuated this or that particular action? There is no other definition of the individual. If the act was necessary, then so was the individual. What may appear as a free act, even from a secondary point of view, and thus objectively accidental, seems so merely because the individual tends to make a specific deed, out of what is predetermined and necessary, to be *his* choice, when for that matter the individual, in good and in evil, is an instrument of absolute necessity.

Empirical necessity is a way of prolonging fortuity by making necessity infinite. If we allow this kind of necessity in nature on the phenomenal level, should we not allow it even more so for history? Anyone capable of higher thought cannot be persuaded to believe that important historical events like the rise of Christianity, the migration of nations, the Crusades, *etc.*, have their true origin in the empirical causes commonly attributed to them. Even if these were the prevailing causes, they would have to be regarded as instruments of an eternal order of things.

What is true of history in general is particularly true of the history of religion, namely, that it is founded on an eternal necessity and, consequently, that a construct of it—whereby it becomes bound up most intimately with the science of religion—is possible.

The historical construct of Christianity can have only one point of departure, namely, that the universe is to be differentiated necessarily by two sides, and that this opposition, of the modern against the ancient world, is sufficient for the comprehension of Christianity's nature and characteristics.

The ancient world represents the nature side of history as the prevailing unity or the ideated Being [*Idee Seyn*] of the infinite in the finite. The end of the ancient era and the threshold of a newer, whose prevailing principle was the infinite, could only have been brought about by the true infinite coming into the finite—not to deify it but to offer it up as a sacrifice to God in his own person and thereby to reconcile the two. Thus the first idea of Christianity is necessarily that of God becoming human, Christ as pinnacle and end of the old world of gods. In him, too, the divine becomes finite, but the humanity he attracts is not humanity in its highest state but in its lowliness. He stands as the boundary between the two worlds, ordained by eternity yet a transient apparition in time. He himself returns to the invisible and promises not what arrives at the finite and remains in the finite but rather the Spirit, the ideal principle that leads the finite back to the infinite and as such is the light of the new world.

The other attributes of Christianity are bound up with this first idea. Due to its ideational orientation, it is impossible to represent the unity of the infinite and the finite in Christianity objectively through symbolism, as the Greek religion did. All symbolism falls back into the subject; dissolution of the opposition is perceived inwardly, not outwardly, and hence remains a mystery. The all-pervading antinomy of the divine and the natural is resolved only by the subjective determination to think of both in an incomprehensible way as one. Such a subjective unity is expressed in the concept of the miracle. According to this, every idea is a miracle; it is produced in time without having any relation to time. None can come about in a temporal manner; it is the Absolute, *i.e.*, God himself, that reveals each idea, and therefore the concept of revelation is as such a necessary concept to Christianity.

A religion that lives as poetry in the *genus* [*Gattung*] needs as little a historical foundation as outdoor nature.[3] Where the divine does not exist in enduring forms but makes only fleeting appearances, some way for them to be recorded and perpetuated through tradition is required. Apart from the actual mysteries of religion, there is necessarily mythology, which is their exoteric side and is grounded in religion, just as religion of the first kind was grounded conversely in mythology.

The idea of a religion that is directed at intuiting the infinite in the finite must be expressed chiefly in being, while the ideas of the opposite religion, in which all symbols belong only to the subject, can become objective only through human action. Here the originary symbol of any intuition [*Anschauung*] of God is history. History, however, is endless, immeasurable, and therefore must be represented by an infinite and yet limited intuition, which itself is again not real, like the State, but ideal and, as unmediated presence, unifies all individual differences without resolving them. This symbolic intuition of God is the Church as a living work of art.

Just as the action that expresses the unity of the infinite and the finite outwardly may be called symbolic, so the same action, when expressed inwardly, is mystical; more generally, mysticism is a subjective symbolism. Mystical writings have always been met with opposition, and sometimes with persecution, by the Church because they sought to make the esoteric elements in Christianity exoteric—not because the innermost spirit of Christianity is opposed to the spirit of mysticism.

---

3. See *Ueber das Verhältnis der Naturphilosophie zur Philosophie überhaupt* (On the Relationship of the Philosophy of Nature to Philosophy in General), *SWV*, p. 108: "Poetry, as long as it has not yet become the matter of a *genus* or at least generic to an entire race and the be-all and end-all of a nation, is only regarded in its relations."

If one considers the actions and customs of the Church as objectively symbolic because their significance can only be conceived mystically, then at least those Christian ideas symbolized in the dogmas of the Church did not cease to be of wholly speculative significance for their symbols have not achieved a life independent of meaning, like those of Greek mythology.

The reconciliation of the finite that had fallen away from God, through his birth into the finite world, is the first idea of Christianity and the fulfillment of its view of the universe and its history in the idea of the Trinity, which therefore is as such a necessary part of it. As is well known, Lessing, in his text *The Education of the Human Race,*[4] sought to reveal the philosophical significance of this doctrine, and his observations on this subject may be the most speculative of anything he has written. But his view lacks the relation of this idea to the history of the world, which consists in the eternal son of God who, born of the essence of the Father of all things, is the finite itself as it exists in the eternal intuitive cognition of God and manifests itself as a suffering God, subordinated to the vicissitudes of time. In Christ, the pinnacle of his apparition, [God] closes the world of the finite and opens the world of the infinite, *i.e.,* the reign of the spirit.

Were there time to go further into the historical construct of Christianity, we would recognize the necessity of every opposition of Christianity to paganism, as well as their prevailing Christian ideas and subjective symbols of ideas. It is sufficient for my purpose to have shown the possibility of such a construct. If Christianity as a whole, and in its most noble forms, is historically necessary, and if we connect this with a loftier view of history as an outflowing of eternal necessity, then it becomes possible to comprehend Christianity historically as a divine and absolute apparition and, consequently, as that of truly historical science of religion, or theology.

---

4. Gotthold Ephraim Lessing, *Die Erziehung des Menschengeschlechts* (The Education of the Human Race) (Berlin: Christian Friedrich Voß und Sohn, 1780).

Inaugural Lecture

(Munich, 26 November 1827)

[*SW* IX, pp. 355–64]

At last, as I stand before *you* to take up my duties as teacher at a public university, I see my dearest wish fulfilled. I confess that it was neither the honor attached to such a position nor the advantages of working in the *only* city in Germany with combined resources for science and art that led me to leave the quiet seclusion of a life of unconstrained research. Rather, it was the hope to once more enjoy the opportunity, as I did in my youth, to guide and mentor so many outstanding young men on their path toward a higher sphere of knowledge in science. If I have the strength to do justice to this most precious of all callings, I will be granted my most ardent wish. I neither sought nor pursued this position; I answered a call that in accord with my conscience I *could not* refuse—from a King of whose spirit and love of the sciences I had long ago predicted all that we see now largely fulfilled.[1] I was summoned to this higher institution in the heart of this state that has already become my home, and I have been welcomed as one of its own. I came here as a teacher before; alas, I soon fell silent, sooner than I would have wished. I did not teach in Bavaria proper, only in the adjacent province, but I have long had a deep regard for the Bavarian youth, their receptiveness, their fresh, unspoiled rigor, and their disposition toward penetrating inquiry. I have often spoken of the learnedness of the Bavarian people who could surpass even the most erudite in the German states. All that was needed was a sovereign who understood his people and who would initiate and maintain a vigorous public education system. I have often compared Bavaria to fertile soil that if tilled deeply enough

1. Ludwig I appointed Schelling in 1827 as professor to the newly established Munich University as well as the President of the Academy of Sciences and the General Curator of the Scientific Collections.

would yield a thousand-fold increase in crops. As Herder wrote to the Bavarian minister, Count Leyden, some forty years ago: "Do not let your youth sip reason and knowledge out of thimbles. Let them drink *ex pleno* [plentiful]." As long as knowledge was being dispensed in thimbles, as long as there were prescribed text books and a restricted curricula, as long as the relationship between students and teachers was not recognized as one of freedom and love, and as long as what was considered good for all in the sciences was not considered good for the Bavarian youth, I felt I could not teach here. My teaching is restricted in the sense that it must be unrestricted. It must be allowed to express itself with faith and confidence and be met with a free and self-assured desire of the heart and the mind for higher knowledge. Before an audience coerced in any way I fall silent. Coercion occurs where there is merely a *learning* of facts. There is, of course, a good deal of learning in philosophy—both in a material and in a formal sense. Philosophy requires a certain *proficiency,* but its true knowledge is altogether different from so-called facts. The sophists taught the Greek youth the nooses and snares with which to entrap their opponents during judicial or scientific argumentations. To this day, the enumeration of conceivable fallacies is an unsightly chapter in our logic; those who boast of having studied philosophy have been made to feel entitled to designate each of these captious conclusions with Latin names of their own invention, *e.g., captio aequivocationis, captio figurae dictionis, ignorationis elenchi, etc.* The ultimate goal of philosophical study cannot be reached by simply acquiring pieces of knowledge, which, while not without merit and to some extent even indispensable, are only the *means* to a higher end.

Only what is already completed, finished, and, as it were, laid aside, can be learned. For millennia, philosophy has been advancing gradually toward its true end, but until that end has been reached, it is only the forward progression that constitutes proper, living philosophy. Even when, for the first time, that end has been reached by one, it must be reached again in the same way by the next. As its name suggests, philosophy is unrestricted love; without it, it is dead. But can love be commanded or coerced? How can you treat something that is nascent, in continual motion, and never resting, as something that has died off, ended, or is already existing, as if it could be reproduced with a die stamp? Where the study of philosophy tends to be prescribed and restricted, one finds only a mediocre philosophy, one that avoids the outermost regions of thinking and allows for only average, unexceptional thought, both in regard to the thing itself and the way the major subjects of philosophy are discussed, thereby cheating the young of the true purpose of general philosophical study: philosophy demands decisiveness. Decisiveness implies going to the extremes of thinking; its very nature is to rise to the pinnacle of thought. Whenever it is impeded, whether by direct or indirect force, it resembles an eagle held captive, deprived of its true habitat, the mountain peak. In philosophy, one cannot capitulate or waver in the face of contrary philosophical systems without succumbing to a deplorable skepticism that destroys the spirit. A teacher forced to skip the major subjects of philosophy, the only ones truly worth studying, or to address them only middlingly and indecisively, cannot fulfill the proper purpose of philosophical instruction. The purpose of teaching is not to promise students knowledge that provides some answers to the questions that abound in philosophy. This is precisely how half-knowledge and semi-enlightenment are formed, which, in the absence of any deeper understanding, leads to judgments on the most profound subjects without the slightest inkling of what is required for truthful and enlightening pronouncements about questions pertinent to mankind.

One could argue that shying away from substantive and probing inquiries is compatible with a certain formal education. But this limitation to formalization would produce sophists, not philosophers. Our universities would then resemble the ancient schools of the sophist rhetoricians, who taught students to argue for and against everything with equal skill. But by no means should the foremost purpose of philosophical education be to produce more philosophers, any more than the purpose of mathematical education should be to produce more mathematicians or of philology to produce more philologists. It is certainly desirable that there be scholarly grammarians and critics, but it is far more important that there be those who are able to align and fortify themselves with the works of classical antiquity and penetrate their spirit. Most do not study philosophy in order to become philosophers but rather to obtain those grand integral convictions without which there would be no autonomous state of mind or dignity of life. At a time when everything else is swaying, when anything positive incurs disputation, a virile and profound philosophy—one that can navigate the depths of the mind and restore and reinforce the wavering foundations of all genuinely human beliefs—seems doubly important. Indeed, we have reached a turning point in this respect. Unworthy religious opinions have made room for deeper, more serious ones; one thinks differently about the dignity of humans and the meaning of life in general. However, any such turning point is largely the consequence of a philosophy that has apprehended life more deeply and asserted the true wealth of knowledge. If, in opposition, some are once again degrading philosophy by decrying it as a danger to religion, faith, *etc.*, they do so by employing means borrowed from philosophy in a false, overstated manner. However, the tolerance encountered by their anti-philosophical pronouncements is owed to the very philosophy they decry. We should not fear that the deeper contents of religion and the higher life, which are reconquered for scientific consciousness by the earnest labor and pensiveness of the German philosophers, will become easy prey for a few partisans who would like to turn them into a tool for the pursuit and attainment of certain exterior goals. The sanity and reason of our time ensure that the unhurried pace at which everything is initiated, and which will someday surprise the world with a result—the antithetical deductions are still a far cry from such a result—will not be disturbed and interrupted. But in times that are unclear, it is doubly necessary that the lessons of philosophy be delivered clearly and decisively, not with dubious terms that concede more than is due to the opponent but with determination and certainty, especially of the main points.

But can one say that such a philosophy should be mandatory? No, I would reply, especially not one like that. Because who can say that the true philosophy is here or there? By its very nature, philosophy ought not to, and cannot, exert influence except through free conviction; it must start over again with each student, stand the test for each anew, because no one person can believe for another or be convinced for another. And who would vouchsafe that a State would lend its seal of approval to a just and true philosophy, and not to some fantasizing nonsense? And would not any teacher coerced to communicate a particular conviction blush in front of his students? And would it not make the living words die on his tongue if the most beautiful and pure relationship, that between teacher and student, by its very nature a personal one, were to be mandated by the State?

Thanks to the King, our sovereign, and his eagerness for the truth, I am able to work freely and on my own accord—the only manner conceivable for me—and thus to repay my inculpable debt of many years to my country.

The abolishment of mandatory studies does not grant the Bavarian youth license to be unstudious, to neglect that which is not required or essential to earning a future living, *i.e.,* the higher and general education. On the contrary, it will kindle in them love and enthusiasm for science as they compete for the first time as equals with students from other universities. The abolishment of a mandate may, in rare cases, bring about a welcome effect of weeding out the few students who even in the years of the noblest sentiment and most vigorous pursuits have remained insentient and unreceptive to the sciences that elevate and liberate our inner self. These, as I said, are really exceptions, and while the mandatory system until now did not set them apart from their fellow students, the better students will recognize each other, and will be recognized also by their teachers. They will be drawn to the lecture halls of philosophical sciences neither by coercion nor by short-lived curiosity but by a desire of both the heart and the mind. These sciences are so tightly interwoven that studying one science out of true interest will propel a student to study them all. In principle, the subjects of philosophy are no different from those of the other sciences, but philosophy sees them in light of higher relations and comprehends those subjects—the world system, the plant world, the animal world, the State, the arts—as parts of a large organism that rises from the abyss of nature, wherein it has its root, into the world of the mind. Those who comprehend philosophy cannot let go of it until they have also glimpsed into the depths of nature and history. There are facts and appearances in nature that cannot be explained sufficiently by common sense alone; they require higher concepts. What would have been regarded as excessive speculation twenty-eight years ago now lies before us in the form of experimental observation. I am not speaking of the observations of ambiguous nature brought about by fraud and magic, which are embraced by the public as facts because *it* does not understand them, but of unquestionable scientific observations such as the chemical or electromagnetic effects of the voltaic pile.[2] It is not human speculation but nature itself that disturbs the peace of longstanding hypotheses. The progressively advancing observations in natural history, especially in earth science, are leading to undeniable facts that silence a merely material and external science. No less undeniable are facts manifesting themselves in human history that until now were obscured and made unrecognizable by insufficient theories. One need only present them in their raw nakedness to see that they *require* a philosophy that goes back to its deepest origins. In short, whenever we look at the vast realm of human cognizance [*Erkenntnis*] and science, we see signs of an approaching time, foreseen by the most prescient scientists, a time when by seizing upon the true structure of science's cognizance and knowledge, the innermost self of all sciences is revealed finally to humanity, millennia of unrest

2. The voltaic pile, the first electrical battery, was invented in 1799 by Alessandro Volta.

in human knowledge is put to rest, and age-old misconceptions of mankind are resolved.

Our time has been called great, but its greatest moment is yet to come. At *such* a time, will Bavarian youth show themselves to be weak? Far from it. With impatience, with forces until now shielded and restrained against their will, they will set out as soon as the trace and trail of true science have been shown to them, and the present barriers have fallen. With perseverance and steadfastness, they will follow the path and soon be indistinguishable from the best of the German youth in all branches of human knowledge. Once regarded worthy of freedom and choice, they will prove themselves worthy of the confidence of a King who wants nothing more than to light the fire of the spirit and see the richest, most active, and most developed scientific life flourish around him, especially at his university.

My activity begins at a great and important juncture in the history of the fatherland, in the development of the Bavarian people, and especially in the development of the science I have been asked to teach. As it has several times in its history, philosophy finds itself at a decisive moment. It no longer has to wrestle with the great and powerful antagonisms; these are subjugated to science, and there remains really only *one* question for philosophy. It is now *only* a matter of rebutting the last attempt to restrain the progress of this science toward absolute freedom and objectivity. It is a great advantage of our time to have brought the case for philosophy to a single point. The transformation of philosophy more than twenty-five years ago appears to have been profound, considering how many of the questions that were considered to be of great importance at the time—and had been discussed broadly and laboriously in course books and behind lecterns—have once and for all become meaningless and superfluous. At that time, philosophy was of interest only to academics entangled in trifling inquiries. Now it has returned to the truly great and general subjects, answers to the most learned world reason [*Weltverstand*]. The masses, which are accustomed to draw their wisdom from daily newspapers, still speak of the rapid change of systems. They do not recognize that a fundamentally new and materially different system has risen in the last twenty-five years, that living spirits have taken possession of it, and that what remains to be done is simply to improve on and complete what has been begun.

A major accomplishment of philosophy is that it is no longer opposed to philosophy but only to unphilosophy [*Unphilosophie*] and its advocates: those whose wisdom lies in the fact that one cannot know anything at all, or in their alleged freedom of thought, with which they stand up to a dominant or domineering philosophy, and which they claim to be a freedom from thought, a general freedom, or license not to think about anything that is worthwhile; those who are of the opinion that we must put an end to all scientific hardship and, in short, throw ourselves into the arms of some authority, who despair of any success of philosophy, or assure us that any modest philosophy must know its limits and be confined to the observation and enumeration of the inner facts of consciousness, in short, to a matter-of-fact psychology or anthropology. These circumstances—that those who claim to set themselves against the dominant philosophy know no better than to renounce any and all philosophy (which may be allowed to them), as well as the fact that the inquiry has narrowed and the ultimate decision on the meaning and future course of philosophy depends only on a single question, as mentioned before—proves that during its last crisis philosophy has reached a point below which it cannot sink and at which it is no longer concerned with unscience [*Unwissenschaft*] but only with the pure development of itself.

It is often said that interest in philosophy has diminished considerably in the last ten or fifteen years. Nothing has wronged our time more. One has only to follow the disputes arising in the religious realm, the struggle between supernaturalism and rationalism, to become convinced of the desire, the longing, for a philosophical judgment, and, consequently, for philosophy. And where there is desire, surely there is also interest in philosophy *as such,* albeit not for the kind of philosophy that shows itself *at random* and in a specific time period. In the last ten or fifteen years, there may have been no discernible interest in philosophical *manifestations*—not philosophy itself—as compared to the earlier period, and perhaps letting the matter rest for the time being was best. Perhaps, however, those more sensible realized that it was necessary to decide whether that which was claimed to be progress was progress at all or at least in some sense, and therefore they did not want to bother prematurely to learn about it. Thus, if I weigh the true and real longing of the time on one side and the position of science on the other, I cannot help but find a certain similarity between my first entry into philosophy and the present one, wherein it has become not just an inner but an outer duty for me to express myself clearly and distinctly.

When I was first summoned, almost thirty years ago, to actively engage in the advancement of philosophy, a self-assertive philosophy prevailed in the schools, one spirited inwardly yet removed from reality. Who would have thought that a nameless young teacher would become its master, the master of such a mighty philosophy that despite its empty abstraction closely followed some of the principal tendencies of its time? And yet this did happen—certainly not due to the teacher's merit and worthiness but rather by virtue of the nature of the things themselves, the power of the insurmountable reality that is in all things—and he will never forget the gratitude and joyful recognition that was bestowed upon him by the leading minds of the nation, even though nowadays few remember the extent to which philosophy had to be freed from barriers and impediments and how hard one had to wrangle to achieve the breakthrough into a free open field of objective science, this freedom and vivacity of thinking whose effect they now enjoy.

Now, once again, philosophy seems to find itself at a point it cannot rise above; meanwhile, what it has presented as the ultimate and outermost objective is irremovably in contradiction with a superior sentiment. For at the right time and hour, the spirit that invisibly prevails over all things calls forth sentiments that increase the strength to overcome any inhibition and makes minds receptive and docile when help appears. It is under such conditions of our country, our time, and our science that I step in *your* midst. I greet *you* with love. Receive me with love as well. I will live for *you,* act on *your* behalf, and work for *you* as long as it pleases God.

Philosophy of Revelation

The 1841-42 Berlin Lectures

Inaugural Lecture
Berlin, 15 November 1841
[*SW*XIV, pp. 357-67; PL, pp. 52-57]

Gentlemen, I very much feel the weight of this moment and the magnitude of what I am about to undertake. How could I not acknowledge—to myself or to you—what is conveyed by my presence here today. Surely, gentlemen, I would not be standing before you were I not convinced that I am providing an important service to philosophy, indeed, a greater service than the one I provided previously. This is what believe, but I am far from presuming—still less could I think of demanding—that this be the general opinion. I only hope to achieve this much: to not be regarded with ill will and to be given the time and room to answer to the question *Dic cur hic* [Say why you are here]?[1]—an answer I intend to provide in the course of these lectures. I myself have made room for others insofar as I have not prevented anyone else from pursuing the same goal in science. As far as my achievements, those that deserve to be brought to the attention of an assembly such as this—the path was open to all. No one can say that I have beaten him to it with undue haste.

It has been forty years since I turned over a new leaf in the history of philosophy; one page has been filled, and I would have left it willingly to another to draw conclusions from it and then turn the page and begin the next.

When I say that I have undertaken this task, rather than declined it, despite its magnitude and difficulty, I am articulating the consciousness of my chosen profession. But I have not imposed this task upon myself. It has not come to me through my own doing; but now that it has come, I cannot deny it or treat it lightly. I have not proposed myself as a teacher of this time. If I am such a teacher, time has made me so. I take no credit in the matter, for what I have done

1. A popular humanistic motto attributed to the German protestant educator Michael Moscherosch (1601-1669).

for philosophy has been done from a necessity imposed by my inner nature.

On this occasion, circumstances compel me to speak of myself, but not in vain self-praise. A man who, after doing his part in philosophy, thought it appropriate to retire from the stage and let others try; a man who suffered in silence every judgment passed on him and was not moved to break that silence by the undue advantage that was taken of it or even by the falsifications to the history of the newer philosophy; a man with a philosophy that accords insights yearningly desired and urgently demanded—not a philosophy that explains nothing, but one that extends the boundaries of human cognizance; a man of whom could be said that his day had *come and gone* but who now breaks his silence because he was summoned to do so, because it is clear that the time has come to speak the decisive word. Surely, this man has demonstrated that he is capable of self-denial, that he does not suffer from rash delusion, and that he is after something more than transient opinion, more than quick and fleeting renown.

I know all too well that for some I will be a nuisance. I have been accommodated; I have been interpreted; what was in me was known, but now the effort must begin anew to see whether there is something left in me that is not yet known.

The natural order of things would have a younger man in my place, one more equal to the task. If he arrives, I will make room happily for him. How many excellent younger talents have I seen struggling with means and forms that I knew would lead to nothing and from which there was nothing to be gained. How I would have gladly reached out to them! How I would have gladly helped those who wanted to know nothing of me! But now I see that I have to lend my own hand if the work I consider necessary—even demanded by the time, by the entire course of philosophy up to now—is to be achieved; and that I have been saved for this very task. Now that I have been asked to teach in this capital, where words of deeper import are uttered for all of Germany and are even carried beyond its borders, where a decisive effect can be achieved, where the fate of German philosophy must be decided; now, at this important moment, after God granted me a life long enough not to fail philosophy, which has been the guardian spirit of my life, I had to realize that this is a duty not to be denied. It was this thought, this clear conviction, that alone guided my decision.

I won't deny that there were many other reasons as well: to serve, if only briefly, a King[2] exalted no less by the qualities of his mind and heart than by the splendor of his throne, a man I revered long before he was adorned by the royal purple; to serve the land and people whose moral and political supremacy every true German has, since childhood, been accustomed to honor and has learned to honor anew in the ever memorable events of these latter years; to serve the city that is named first in any discussions of the advancements of science and culture in Germany and that, like a mighty sea, is not moved easily by every breath and is therefore slow to embrace new ideas (I remind you of the time when the philosophy of *Kant* found resonance in every quarter of Germany except the capital of his native land), but which also seizes and promotes whatever is recognized as worthy; to serve the circle of scientists, the most distinguished pillars of this city, some of them my friends since youth and others long revered by me, men with whom I always enjoy living and working; and finally, to serve this youth, known for being accustomed to answer the call of science, who when a worthy goal is set before them are not only undaunted by difficulty but leap forward joyously and outstrip their teachers wherever the trace and trail of true science is shown to them.—All these, gentlemen, were attractive and irresistible reasons, yet powerful as they were, they had to yield to considerations so obvious that I need not name them. Not until I realized that the unsought invitation contained a mandate that I could not and dared not resist without failing to fulfill my true and highest life calling, did I resolve to come. And, so resolved, I now step among *you,* with the conviction

2. Friedrich Wilhelm IV who appointed Schelling in 1841 to fill the chair of philosophy at the University of Berlin that had been vacant since Hegel's death in 1831.

that if ever I have accomplished anything, however much or little, in the service of philosophy, I will be capable of even more if I succeed in leading philosophy out of its current, difficult position and into a free and unrestrained movement. For these difficulties that philosophy must grapple with are evident and cannot be concealed.

At no time has philosophy encountered so strong a reaction from the side of life as at this moment. This is proof that philosophy has advanced to address those questions about life to which no one can be indifferent. As long as philosophy remains in its beginning stages, it concerns only those who make philosophy their business. All others wait for it to run its course; to the world it gains importance only through its results.

Only profound inexperience, however, would lead to the conceit that the world is willing to accept, indiscriminately, every conclusion that philosophy imposes upon it as the outcome of thorough and stringent scientific investigation, even one that might subject one to a doctrine that is essentially immoral or one by which the foundations of morality are abolished. But no one expects this of the world, and there has yet to be a philosopher who would. The world would not let itself be dismissed by the claim that it cannot understand the principles of philosophical inquiry, its artificial and convoluted proofs. The world would be unfazed by this and would insist that a philosophy that led to such results must be based on wrong principles. What Roman moralists have said with respect to the useful applies equally to the truth: *Nihil utile nisi quod honestum* [Nothing is useful that is not honest].[3] And what everyone acknowledges in regard to morals applies equally to all other convictions that together constitute human life, especially religious belief. No respectable philosophy will admit that it is going to end up in irreligion. At present, however, philosophy finds itself in precisely this position. It asserts that it is religious in its results while denying—in its deductions of Christian dogmas, which it alleges to be merely a smoke screen to the world—that this is so. This is acknowledged by even some

3. Cicero, *De Officiis,* III.3.

of its faithful, or unfaithful, disciples. Be that as it may; for now it is enough that there is suspicion about this.

But in the end, life is always proved right, and thus it is life that threatens to put the very existence of philosophy in danger. Already, there are those who pretend to strive against a particular philosophy but, in fact, are striving against all philosophy and saying, in the silence of their hearts, "Philosophy shall be no more." In this, I may have played a part, for assumedly providing the first impetus for this type of philosophy, which is now regarded an evil because of its religious conclusions. How will I now conduct myself? I would certainly not attack any philosophy on the basis of its results. No philosophic mind capable of judging first principles would do so. Besides, it is well known that all along I have been dissatisfied, and far from being in agreement, with the beginnings of said philosophy. It might be assumed that I would make it my main business to dispute a system whose results have created such an agitation against philosophy itself. Gentlemen, I will do no such thing. If I were capable of this, I would not be here. I do not think so little of my profession. I leave such joyless business happily to others. I say joyless because it is always sad to witness something that was created with exceptional energy to unravel itself. The intellectual and moral world is so divided, so inclined to anarchy, that one may well rejoice, if only for a moment, whenever a point of union is found. It is sadder still to destroy something when one has nothing with which to replace it. To those who only know how to criticize, it is said justly, "Do better!" Equally just is the saying of the man—who regretfully is no longer among the living—who, with admirable frankness, declared, "Men must have a *system,* and a system can be refuted only by another system. As long as that which stands is opposed by nothing tenable in the way of substitute, let it stand."*

With respect to systems, I agree with him: single truths no longer suffice. It is now understood that in this way nothing can be rightly known. Neither is he wrong in

---

* [Eduard] Gans, *Vorrede zu Hegels Philosophie des Rechts,* p. xiv. [In G.W.F. Hegel, *Werke,* vol. 8 (Berlin, 1833).]

expressing astonishment at reports that claim that the author of the philosophy of identity had strayed from his principle and sought asylum in a "faith not penetrated by science" and in history, under which he subordinated his new philosophy. I wonder that a man, otherwise so sagacious, did not take the trouble to ascertain whether what was said was founded in fact before expressing his astonishment. Were he still alive, he would learn from the course of these lectures how completely different the truth of the situation is from what he was made to believe.

Thus—what is called commonly polemics is not the aim of these lectures. Should anything of this kind appear, it will be only incidental. At the same time, I cannot make the course as instructive as I would like without referring to the past and indicating the progress of developments made so far. In order to advance into the promised land of philosophy, I will endeavor not to show where this one or that one has failed but rather to make it apparent where we have all failed and what we all fell short of. One who has erred more than another has dared more. If he has missed the goal, he has followed a path that his predecessors had not closed to him.

I do not come to exalt myself above another but to fulfill my life's calling.

The cognition of truth with its full conviction is so great a good that the public opinion and the vanity of the world are not to be weighed against it.

I do not wish to inflict wounds but rather to heal those that have been sustained by German science in a long and honorable conflict; not to expose spitefully the existing damage but to make us, where possible, forget them. I do not wish to incite but to reconcile and, where possible, step into a torn world as a messenger of peace. I am not here to destroy but to build, to construct a fortress wherein philosophy will dwell securely from now on. I will build on the grounds laid by earlier efforts. Nothing of what has been gained by genuine science since *Kant* shall be lost through any fault of mine. How could I renounce the very philosophy I had founded in my youth? It is not my intention to put a different philosophy in its place, but to add a new science to it, one thought impossible until now, in order to fortify the true foundations of philosophy, to return it to its previous position, which it had lost by transgressing its natural boundaries and by making a whole out of what are only a few lofty fragments.

Thus, during this time, philosophy has become a matter of general concern. The excitement alluded to earlier—the commotion of minds I have perceived around me—demonstrates that philosophy has ceased to be merely a matter of education and has become a matter for the entire nation. From its beginnings, the history of German philosophy has been intertwined with that of the German people. During the time of its great liberation, the Reformation, it vowed not to rest until its loftiest questions—which, until then, had been recognized only blindly—were taken up intentionally by cognitive reason, and therein found its place. At a time of the greatest humiliation, philosophy kept the Germans upright. Over the ruins of a perished glory, powerful men held up the banner of German science before the gathered youth. In the schools of the philosophers—who does not remember here *Fichte* and *Schleiermacher*?—many found in the fights for philosophy the resolve, courage, and prudence that would afterward be put to the test in other battlefields; and philosophy continued to play a role in Germany's heritage and glory. Shall this long and glorious movement end with a shameful wreckage, with the destruction of all great convictions and, consequently, of philosophy itself? Never again! I am here because as a German I have carried in my heart, and felt for, all the woes and suffering of Germany, as well as all its fortunes and well-being. For the salvation of the Germans is in science.

With such sentiments I come to this place, with no other weapon but that of truth, using no protection other than that which truth possesses in its own strength, asking for no other right for myself than that which I concede openly to all—the right to freely conduct research and to communicate its results unrestrainedly. So disposed, I enter *your* midst. I come with an earnestness of mind and heart. I am serious; may those who attend my lectures be serious as well! I greet you with love. Receive me with love as well. The teacher may achieve much, but he cannot achieve anything without his students. I am nothing without *you,* without your goodwill, without receptiveness, without eagerness on *your* part. I devote myself to the calling I have undertaken. I will live for *you,* work for *you,* and not tire as long as a breath remains in me, and as far as he permits, without whose consent not a hair can be released from our heads, much less a deeply felt word, a genuine product of the innermost being, "a ray of thought" [*Lichtgedanke*][4] in our mind as it struggles for truth and freedom, be lost.

---

4. A term coined by Friedrich Schiller in his 1802 poem "Die Gunst des Augenblicks" (The Favorable Moment): "Alles Göttliche auf Erden/ist ein Lichtgedanke nur (All that is divine on earth/Is but a ray of thought).

I. General Introduction

[PL, pp. 212–17]

The philosophy of revelation is usually last. It is the one with which I have concluded so far my series of lectures. I have described it as *the crown of a science that is advancing on its own course.* This time, however, many have requested that I present *this ultimate and highest science* first. Thus I need to begin with an introductory discussion of *everything that usually precedes it and leads toward this science.*

The *desire* for a philosophy that goes to the *heart of the matter* may never have been more apparent than it is today. There is a desire for philosophy to take a different position in regard to *the highest matters of reality* through a *new and unexpected* **deed** [*That*]. For human life is defined chiefly by two powers: State and Religion. How should philosophy relate to each one?

Undeniably, a great longing pervades our times. The old ways have perished and can no longer be restored! But should we give in to the opinions of those who are addicted to innovation?

There was a theory coming out of France, which also found followers in Germany, that something new need to take the place of Christianity. We confront this with the following question:

Do you truly know Christianity? What if only philosophy can unlock its depths?

Christianity cannot exist *alongside* another system. This other, *i.e.*, philosophy, has grown too immense for Christianity to exist beside it. *Christianity can subsist only by being All.*

For the time being, the title I have given this lecture, *Philosophy of Revelation,* is *just for now a pronouncement of words*; its meaning will emerge as we pursue the matter at hand. However, *I caution you not to understand herewith a philosophy that is under the authority of revelation.* Nothing is to be taken away from either—philosophy or revelation.

On the other hand, I also do not want revelation to be understood in the expanded sense of being an unexpected deed in the realm of the spirit. If it were so, it would be easy to doubt; as something that does not go beyond reason, it would also be of no interest. *Revelation must contain something that goes beyond reason,* but also something that one does not yet possess without reason.

First, *that which is factual* [*Thatsächliche*] goes **beyond** reason. But if revelation is a reality, then it is so in a historical connection; thus a higher historical connection, one that goes beyond itself, is required to comprehend it. Without this connection, revelation cannot be comprehended.

How then can a *philosophy* worthy of the name co-exist upon those premises? *Certainly no current philosophy is able to do so!* It has been attempted, but the relation between the two was always so tormented that it had to be dissolved. Any profound thinker preferred dissolution over staying in a coerced relationship. This is why it is necessary *to premise a purely philosophical discussion.*

There is no need to deal with the oppositions that animated philosophy at the time of *Fichte et al.*; but *one opposition* that remains *has been demanding a solution for a long time.*

We will therefore occupy ourselves *first* with the part of philosophy that contains *the uppermost principles.*

II. The Principles of the Science of Reason

[PL, pp. 217-31]

Special consideration must be given to the *relation of philosophy to actuality.* [1] There are two things that can be cognized or stated about all that is actual: *quid sit* and *quod sit* = **what** it is and **that** it is. [2] The former allows me to have a concept of it; the latter, to have knowledge of its existence so that I can cognize it. While it is possible to have a *concept without cognition,* the reverse is not true; there is no cognition without a concept. *To cognize* [Erkennen] is to recognize [*Wiedererkennen*] (that which is already contained in the concept).

The oldest philosophical definition is *arguably* επιστήμη τοῦ ὄντος [knowledge of that which has Being]; it is preeminent because it anticipates later developments.

---

1. See KG 8:33, p. 229: "I am so glad to have heard *Schelling*'s 2nd lecture—indescribable. I have been sighing and the thoughts within me have been groaning long enough; when he mentioned the word *'actuality'* concerning philosophy's relationship to the actual, the child of thought leaped for joy within me as in Elizabeth. After that I remember almost every word he said. Perhaps here there can be clarity. This one word, it reminded me of all my philosophical pains and agonies." Kierkegaard's allusion here is to Luke 1:41, when Elizabeth, pregnant with John the Baptist, learns that Mary is to give birth to the son of God: "The child leaped in her womb." (KJV).

2. Scholastic concepts connoting *essence* and *existence.* See also Schelling's *Einleitung in die Philosophie der Offenbarung oder Begründung der positiven Philosophie* (Introduction to the Philosophy of Revelation or Grounding of the Positive Philosophy), *S*W XIII, pp. 57-58: "Here, namely, should be noted that in all that is actual, two things are cognized, two completely different qualities are to be known about that which has Being: what it is, *quid sit,* and that it is, *quod sit.* The former—the answer to the question: *what* it is—affords me insight into the *essence* of the thing or makes me understand it, have a sense or concept of it, or have *it itself.* The latter—the insight *that* it is—affords me not only the mere concept but something that goes above and beyond the concept, which is its *existence.*"

But since, according to the preceding,[3] that which has Being [*das Seyende*] (τὸ ὄν) appears in two different ways, the question is whether philosophy pertains to both *quid sit* and *quod sit* and treats them as *one* science or whether each is treated separately.

Such a simple differentiation and its validity could be disputed. However, if one has apprehended the *What* or essence, one has apprehended *something that is actual*; in this sense, it is true that the concept does not have that which has Being outside of itself since by having existence nothing is changed with regard to the *content.*

Likewise, one can say: *Things exist as a result of logical necessity*; *e.g.,* the order of inorganic and then organic nature is a necessary one! But here we are speaking only of content. Nothing else is said than: *if* things exist, they exist in this order; but *that* they exist can be cognized only from experience. *What comes about in this purely logical concept by its immanent activity is not the actual world; it is only according to the* quid!

Does philosophy then not deal merely with the *essence* of things? And does it have nothing to do with their existence? And if it does, whose existence should it prove?[4]

There is no need to prove the existence of what can be experienced; and *philosophy does not engage in superfluous activities.* But if an *object* were to be found that goes above *all experience,* it would be the *special task* [*besondere Aufgabe*] *of philosophy to prove its existence.* If this object does not occur in experience, then its concept must be found purely in *reason,* and *necessarily* so.

---

3. KG 11:3, p. 303: "with respect to the above-mentioned duality."

4. KG 11:3, p. 304: "In consequence, philosophy became either a doctrine about essence, as we used to put it, or about existence, as some more recent [thinkers] have said." The last, possibly a reference to empiricism, is not found in Paulus's transcript. See also *Einleitung in die Philosophie der Offenbarung,* SW III, p. 62: "Experience therefore is not the *source* [*Quelle*] for the science of reason, as it was partially in the former metaphysics, but experience is its companion. In this way, Germany has empiricism (which has been venerated exclusively by all the other European nations for a hundred years now) without being itself empiricism."

In order to find this object in reason, its *entire content* of reason must be developed, and thereby one must proceed from the *unmediated content of reason.* In it must be found both a substance [*Materie*] for the development, a source for its movement and progression toward another object.

Reason, however, is nothing other than *the infinite potence of cognition.*[5] As such, it has content but without its intervention [*Zuthun*]. (Otherwise it would not be pure potence.) What is in reason then without its intervention is its innate *a priori content,* which is posited together with its essence before all actual cognizance.

What is this content? *Since all cognition corresponds to a Being, the infinite potence of cognition corresponds to the infinite potence of Being.* This is the *innate* content of reason, from which the concept of the object whose existence philosophy must prove, has to develop.

Insofar as reason in philosophy must be assumed to be self-acting, it is directed at itself and its unmediated content. Its activity is the *activity of thought* [*Denken*]. *The activity of thought,* however, as it is directed at this first content, *discovers its unmediatedly movable nature* and, soon after, a principle of movement. This determination of the infinite potence of

---

5. See *Einleitung in die Philosophie der Offenbarung,* SW XIII, p. 63: "Potence is the Latin *potentia,* power; it is opposed to *actus.* In the conventional use of language, one says, *e.g.,* the plant is in its seed as a mere potence, in *pura potentia,* while the actual grown or developed plant is the plant *in actu;* here potence is taken merely as *potentia passiva,* passive possibility, since the grain is not necessarily the potence of the plant; there must be other external conditions added to it—fertile soil, rain, sunshine, *etc.*—for this potence to become *actus.* As a faculty of cognition, reason appears of course also as *potentia passiva,* insofar as it is faculty capable of development and in that respect also dependent on external influences. Here, reason is not, however, taken, subjectively, as faculty of cognition but rather presumed to be the standpoint of reason from which it itself is its object—an object, however, whose limitations are being removed from the subject, cannot be anything other than the infinite potence of cognizance, *i.e.,* in its own and original content, without being dependent on anything, and is compelled to go forth into all Being, since only *all* Being (the entire fullness of Being) can equate to the *infinite* potence."

Being is the *ens omnimode* [*in*]*determinatum* [altogether indeterminate entity] of Scholastic philosophy—not, somehow, an already existing entity but the infinite potence of existing, of Being.[6]

But the infinite *ability to be* [*Seynkönnen*], the infinite potence of Being, is not merely the ability or readiness to exist; rather, it is *the infinite concept of Being itself.* By its very nature, *the potence is* therefore always and *necessarily about to become that which has Being, about to move or pass over into Being.* The infinite potence of Being is that which unmediatedly passes over into Being . Thus, as it is directed at the initial content of reason, the activity of thought discovers its movable nature unmediatedly, by virtue of which it cannot remain at the ability to be.

But this passing-over [*Uebergang*] should *not* be regarded as *a transition into actual Being.* It is only as a consequence of logical necessity that the infinite ability to be must pass over into Being—but *merely within the activity of thought* [*Denken*]! It is not a real process but merely a logical one; for here, Being is not extraneous to the concept. The passing-over is a Becoming Other [*Anderswerden*], but only in the sense of becoming a *quidditative* Being, not a *quodditative* one. It a *mere thought process,* not an actual one.

But with the infinite potence being the *prius* [the former or previous], which comes before all that emerges from the thinking subject [*Denker*] as a result of its passing over into Being, and with the infinite potence of cognition corresponding to the infinite potence of Being, *the activity of thought*—as a result of this beginning—gains the *a priori* position toward all Being and *therefore, without presupposing experience, can get, purely* a priori, *to the content of all Being.* Not

---

6. *Cf. Einleitung in die Philosophie der Offenbarung,* SW XIII, p. 64: "The mobility of its highest concepts distinguishes present-day philosophy from Scholasticism, which might appear to have had a similar beginning. In the former, the infinite *potence* of Being corresponds to the *ens omnimodo indeterminatum,* from which it originated: understood not as something that already exists in some manner but, as it says, that which exists in general." See also KG 11:3, p. 304: "In this respect, being might call to mind the old scholastic *ens omnimodo indeterminatum* [Being entirely undefined]—something not existing—not this or that existing thing, but the existing in general."

that *the activity of thought* can herewith *cognize* that this or that *exists actually*, but it can get itself progressively from the *a priori* content of reason to all *content* of Being. *It is only as a possibility*, not an actuality, *that the activity of thought catches a glimpse of the content that evolves from of the general potence.*

In the completed execution, therefore, the science that proceeds from this *prius* contains the *a priori* concepts of actually existing things; it is a science of concepts, and, like geometry, it has nothing to do with the actual and is therefore unconcerned with it! [7]

Thus, *we have an entirely* a priori, *closed-off, self-progressing science* that brings forth everything out of itself—a pure Science of Reason.

Kant's Critique laid the ground for this science; but it contained too much that was empirical, and it was too subjective. [8] Without it, philosophy is not certain of its subject; it is a science in search of its subject, and in that sense, it is philosophy: *philosophia prima* [first philosophy] or ontology. [9] In it, the activity of thought follows the movement of the infinite potence of Being whose entire content it also possesses as the infinite potence of appearance [*Erscheinens*]. This has occupied German philosophers since Kant and is, first and foremost, about whether it is *the* philosophy at all. [10]

But in order to be prepared to make a decision on this question, the *fundamentals of this science* must first be given.

We can see that the activity of thought, as directed at the unmediated content of reason, cognizes that it is made

---

7. KG11:3, p. 304: "The potency of Being, Seynkönnen, develops accordingly into being and into thought, but the whole movement is in the direction of the *quidditas* [whatness], not of *quodditas* [thatness]; this actuality remains, in another sense, a mere possibility. [Schelling] illustrated this by appealing to geometry, which has no interest whatsoever in any particular triangle."

8. KG11:3, p. 305: "K[ant] understood pure reason subjectively, not as it is presented here rather as the infinite potence of knowledge."

9. See Christian Wolff's *Philosophia prima, sive ontologia* (First Philosophy or Ontology) (Frankfurt and Leipzig: Renger, 1730).

10. KG11:3, p. 305: The question now is *whether it is philosophy but not* die Philosophie [*the* philosophy]; *or whether it is* die Philosophie; *or whether it is not philosophy at all.*

doubtable [*zweifelhaft*] of being subjected to the passing-over [*Uebergang*]. By its very definition, potence is subjected to the passing-over into Being. But once it has passed over, it is no longer the pure and plain power [*lautere Macht*] of Being; it has fallen to Being and is under its sway, a ϵξιστάμενον [one that is outside of or opposite to oneself] that has lost itself.[11] It does not cease to be, but it is no longer the potence of Being; it is de-spirited [*entgeistet*]. For spirit means *power* [*Macht*], *potence* [*Potenz*] *over Being.* By being subjected to the transition, it takes on an ambiguous, indecisive nature. Having passed over, it is despirited, senseless, boundless Being.

While we find in actual nature only an already formed Being [*gefasstes Seyn*], a Being that is *blind,* put out of its potence and thus *senseless,* lies underneath all Being that has already been taken over by form. Thus, the *first possibility originating* from the infinite potence is that of a *senseless, boundless Being.* This Being is necessary even if it is not the one we desire.

Rather, the infinity of the potence from which we proceed leads beyond this first possibility. Its freedom and infinity have infinite potence precisely because it (the first possibility) is not the ability to *unmediatedly* be but—without bringing the activity of thought to a decision—can be both *that which passes over into Being* and *that which does not.*

The *originary potence* [*Urpotenz*] (the infinite potence of Being) does not exclude any possibility, and it *allows for two contradictory conditions.* That which potentially [*potentiā*] has the ability to pass over [*Uebergehenkönnende*] can also remain

---

11. Kierkegaard transcribed it as ἐφιστάμενον: "If it becomes being, it is no longer power but is *ausser sich,* has lost itself [and] is an ἐφιστάμενον [motionless]" (KG 11:3, p. 305). See also *Einleitung in die Philosophie der Offenbarung,* SW XIII, p. 209, where he defines it as "that which is powerless to itself [*seiner selbst Ohnmächtige*], the insensate [*Besinnungslose*], τὸ ϵξιστάμενον, which is posited outside itself through a false ecstasy [*Ekstasis*] and exists in this bad sense"; and *Einleitung in die Philosophie der Mythologie* (Introduction to the Philosophy of Mythology), SW XI, p. 388, where it is "that which is posited *outside* itself, which has lost itself as a Being that is no longer in power of itself because it is displaced [*entsetzt*] from the potence it once was."

the same and identical.[12] (He who is potentially sick is also potentially healthy, and *vice versa*.) From the ability to be, the originary potence, no decided character can be gained, for, by its nature, it can be that which passes over into another, as well that which remains the same.

If these two possibilities are originally with each other and undecided, then the differentiation occurs only through the actual passing over of the first; the second is only thereby posited by it. For by its nature, it is not inclined toward Being but rather opposed to it. The *second possibility* is put *into* effect only by being excluded from that undecidedness.

Every passing-over *a potentia ad actum* [with respect to the ability to act] is the passing-over from non-desiring to desiring [*vom Nichtwollen zum Wollen*]. Let us therefore conceive of a will that has the ability to desire [*wollenkönnenden Willen*][13] and a will that does not have the ability to desire [*nichtwollenkönnenden Willen*].[14] The latter "is unable to desire" (by itself). But as soon as the former actually desires, it excludes the latter.[15] The latter can no longer be with the former *eodem loco* [in the same place]; it is excluded by the former and thus posited. In this way, the non-desiring will [*nichtwollende Wille*] becomes one that has Being for itself [*für sich Seyendes*]. *The second possibility* is thus of a kind that must first be brought into Being by exclusion; it is impotent for itself.

If now in the infinite potence the ability to pass over [*Uebergehenkönnen*] and the inability to pass over [*Nicht-Uebergehenkönnen*] do not exclude each other, then neither do

---

12. KG11:3, p. 305: "it does not cease to be, but ceases to be power to be. But potency is the power to be; therefore, inasmuch as it is, it ceases to be, and it is this ambiguity."

13. Kierkegaard has *Uebergehen-Willende* [having the will to pass over] (KG11:4, p. 306).

14. Kierkegaard has *Nicht-Uebergehen-Willende* [not having the will to pass over] (*ibid.*).

15. KG11:4, p. 306: "Capability is a will at peace. A transition *a potentia ad actum* [from potence to actuality] *is a transition from not-willing to willing.*" See Schelling's *Clara oder über den Zusammenhang der Natur mit der Geisterwelt* (Clara, or On Nature's Connection to the Spirit World), SW IX, p. 105, where he speaks of a "quietude of the will [*Ruhe des Willens*]."

they exclude a *third possibility,* which hovers freely between the ability to be [*Seynkönnen*] and the inability to be [*Nichtseynkönnen*]. *In general, the ability to be hovers between Being and non-Being*; however, the *first possibility* has an unmediated relation to Being, while the *second* has a mediated one. For it is only through exclusion that the latter becomes an ability to be. The *third* possibility is the most liberated from Being; it unmediatedly does not come into contact with it. The first possibility tends toward Being by its nature; the second is not intended for Being. The third possibility hovers between both; it is the *exclusum tertium* [the excluded third]. But the third cannot come about until the first two emerge from the undecidedness.

Thus, what is begotten from the unmediated content of reason is not an indeterminate set of possibilities but rather a closed totality, a totality of potences, as the organism of the objectively posited reason; for that is the infinite potence of Being. All Being must move among these three potences.

The infinite potence of Being is still *instar omnium* [equal to or worthy of them all]. Just as its indecision is being sublated and the First, deviating from its position, breaks forth, so it loses itself, finds itself outside of itself, and in order to be brought back into itself has to subordinate itself to something higher than the ὑποκείμενον [substrate].[16]

That which has the ability to *unmediatedly* be is the most accidental and therefore appears as the most ungrounded; it grounds its Being not in what precedes it but rather in what follows, by making itself, in relation to the latter, into a mere ὑποκείμενον, into *that which has relative non-Being* [*relativ Nichtseyenden*]. But it is in this way that it finds its grounding. It has lost it for itself; but since it is subordinated to some thing higher, it may become *suae potestatis* [self-dependent] again. Of that which serves as substrate [*Unterlage*] (ὑποκείμενον), one can say that *it is something,* but *it does not have Being.* This first substrate assumes the meaning of the *prima materia* [first matter] of all Being but does

---

16. See *Einleitung in die Philosophie der Mythologie,* SW III, p. 319, where the concept of the ὑποκείμενον is discussed in greater detail. See also Aristotle, *Metaphysics,* Z 1028*b*33-1029*a*7.

not become a determinate Being until it submits to a higher ability to be as its *substrate.*

Only by exclusion can this higher, second substrate be posited as that which has Being, by the first, with which it is posited together in the originary possibility [*Urmöglichkeit*], wanting to occupy the space for itself. Thus, the second substrate is excluded and thereby posited and elevated to the ability to be, that is, *by negation,* by being pulled out of its "state of being left to itself" [*Gelassenheit*].[17]

But since the negation is untenable, the second substrate must restore itself to its former state of being left to itself. It does not have the freedom to act or not to act; rather, it *must* act to negate the first of which it was negated. This second negation, however, can only exist in that which has passed over *a potentia ad actum* to be brought back *ex actu in potentiam* = to be given again to itself out of its *self-emptying* [*Entäusserung*].[18]

Thus we must go beyond the ability to unmediatedly be [*Unmittelbar-Seynkönnen*] by virtue of the infinity and freedom of the originary potence [*Urpotenz*], whose freedom lies in not being bound to a particular mode of Being. Were the infinite potence of Being that which has the ability to merely be [*Nur-Seynkönnen*], then there would be only *one* Being [*Ein Seyn*], namely that which is in the passing over *a potentia ad actum.* But the *ability to merely be is only the first possibility.* The second possibility, because it is second, cannot be that which has the ability to unmediatedly be [*Unmittelbar-Seynkönnende*]; on the contrary, it *only* has the *ability not unmediatedly to be* [*unmittelbar nur Nichtseynkönnen*].[19] But this ability

---

17. The word *Gelassenheit,* in the sense of being left to oneself, letting-be, or releasement, goes back to Meister Eckhart (1260-1327) and was most famously revived in the philosophy of Martin Heidegger. See also Schelling's *Clara,* where he speaks of a "state of being left to oneself and quietudef of the will [*Gelassenheit und Ruhe des Willens*]" (*Clara,* SW IX, p. 105).

18. See below p. 281n.2.

19. KG 11:5, p. 307: "The first potency of Nur-Seyn-Können is only the first; the second is Nicht-Nur-Seyn-Können. Schelling was asked how it could be posited in the original potency given that, according to his own explanation, it had of course been first posited

not unmediatedly to be can only be that which already goes above Being, which, without a trace of negation (for this would impel it to pass over), is that which *wholly and purely has Being* [*ganz und rein Seyende*]. That which *purely has Being* is therefore the *second* potence, which has pure Being, *i.e.*, without potence. (It is called *potence* only in opposition to that which has Being in actuality [*Wirklichseyende*].)

Is it thereby without the grounding of a potence, *it can nevertheless become a potence mediated by negation*. Namely, if the First—which, as long as it did not elevate itself, tarried in the originary possibility [*Urmöglichkeit*] without disturbing it—elevates itself so that instead of being a *mere subject* it becomes an object, one that has Being by itself [*Selbstseyendes*], thus driving that which purely has Being [*Reinseyende*] out of its "left-to-itself" Being ["*gelassenen*" *Seyn*] so that its unreflective state as *actus purus* [pure act],[20] from which it emanated purely, becomes suspended, and it steps back with necessity into its earlier state.

Not having the ability to pass over *a potentia ad actum* by itself, it cannot be brought *ad actum* through a transition within itself, only through a reverse transition. *It actualizes itself only by moving that which passed over into the actus back into its negation* ad potentiam. That which negates that *actus purus* has passed over from ability [*Können*] to Being, which can thereby be brought back from its self-emptying into its inner self (*potentia*). We thus see how the *first, boundless Being* (the ἄπειρον [infinite] of the Pythagoreans, the material substance of Plato)—which initially we could not desire but which imposed itself as the beginning [*Anfang*]—is brought back, step by step, into the ability. The First is posited to become forthwith the object of negation. Thus is understood *a priori* how a limited Being is necessarily put in place of the boundless Being, how *that de-spirited* [*entgeistete*] *Being,* brought back into ability step by step, becomes an owning of itself [*Sichselbstbesitzendes*], a being conscious of itself [*Sichselbstbewusstes*] *at the highest level.*

---

by the other."

20. A Scholastic term used by Thomas Aquinas and others to express the absolute perfection of God.

Thus a true infinity of possibilities, derived from that originary potence, again lies enclosed between both possibilities or potences (one should not get worked up over the expression "higher potence"; *to have the ability to be on a higher order is a higher potence*). A concrete entity emerges from the secondary potence positing *an interior and an exterior* in the primary boundless potence. *The growing together of material substance with a potence or a concept forms the concrete.* The possibilities enclosed within those two possibilities are *possibilities of the concrete world,* which are conceived herewith *a priori* out of the originary potence.

The *secondary potence surrenders* to the degree that *the primary potence, posited outside of itself, has become an ability to own itself*—an ability to return to itself (*any material body already contains and accommodates itself*)—and to the degree that it becomes more and more self-potent (this is most evident in the organic potence) as it progresses upward through the row of natural creations; for it does not exist for its own sake. It does not need to seek its own Being; it is that which wholly and purely has Being [*ganz und rein Seyende*]. *It only needs to negate again the* first *potence and save it from being lost to itself* [*Selbstverlorenheit*]. It suspends its Being-for-itself [*Fürsichseyn*] to the degree that it overcomes that which stands opposed to it, and *thus we see ourselves led also beyond the second potence.*

If a state of permanence is to be attained in Being, then in place of the first potence, which has been overcome completely by the second, a *third,* to which the second potence surrenders its power, must be posited. This third [potence] cannot be pure ability to be, nor can it be pure Being; for *these positions* have already been taken. It can only be that which in Being is *potence* and which as potence is Being, wherein the *contradiction* between potence and Being is posited in identity.

That which in Being is potence and does not cease to be potence, and *vice versa,* which is a potence that can pass over into Being without losing its power (over Being)—that which therefore can be and cannot be—constitutes that which is completely *free,* that *which can do anything it desires with its ability* because it does not cease to be potence in its Being, and to be such, it does not cease to effectuate [*wirken*]. It is **Spirit**, which is not at risk in Being and which even without effectuating does not cease to be potence.

Because this *third* potence is and should be in complete freedom against Being, it cannot effectuate unmediatedly. If it were to effectuate the first potence directly, it would not arrive in Being as that which is free, unmeddled with it, and unrestrained. It can only be realized by the second—the mediating potence. *This second potence negates the first in order to posit the third; the third is posited by the first, which has been overcome by the second.*

As long as it remains potence, the originary possibility is also spirit, freedom from Being; but the infinite potence was only materially, only essentially spirit, *potentially* spirit, and could also be the opposite (because it is *potential*). The second *must* effectuate. *As freedom,* the third alone has *remained unmeddled with Being, the spirit posited as spirit,* Being's crown, so that with its entry into Being (this is all to be comprehended *a priori*!), the completed Being is present, where the potence, posited originally out of itself, has now become self-owning, self-conscious ability.

As we know from experience, *it is in the self-conscious ability that the end of nature lies.*

But should this ability not give itself to a new movement, one that takes place only in and with consciousness, so that a second world, the spiritual one, rises above nature? The spiritual world is, therefore, the second, which is added on to nature and conceived within a single *a priori* science.

This is the outline of *the pure science of reason; it could not be considered in more detail. It's main principles have been reviewed only briefly since its fundamental concepts* will return *in a different form of philosophy* and derive *their reasoning and explanation* there.

What is most important are the general significance of this science and its conclusion. On this, then, some further remarks next.

III. Reflections on the General Nature and End Point of the Pure Science of Reason

[PL, pp. 254-58]

Thus far, science has been concerned with excluding everything contained in the unmediated content of reason that goes beyond it. Everything that passes over into Being actually ceases to be in reason and instead belongs to experience. Everything that is contained inevitably in the original nature of reason but is excluded from reason must be excluded by the previous scientific process.

From the outset, *the activity of thought* desires its [proper] content; but it cannot do so unless it removes everything that is only accidentally a content of reason, everything that is alien to it—when, after the complete exhaustion of all possibilities, only the potence that no longer passes over into another remains as the final content of reason, the potence as that which has Being by itself [*Selbstseyende*]!

The exclusion of content that can withdraw itself from the activity of thought should be continued until a single potence remains that can no longer pass over but is that which has Being [Seyende], that which has the ability to be [Seynkönnen]—Being [Seyn] itself. It can no longer empty itself [*entäussern*], but rather remains in itself. It is the essence [*Wesen*] that, unlike all that precedes it, *is not* subjugated to Being, *existentiae obnoxium* [dependent existence], but is above Being.[1]

The highest essence [höchste Wesen], which no longer has an other essence as prius and remains in Being as itself—and thus is Being in all its truth—therefore fulfills the highest

1. KG11: 6, p. 307: "The necess[ary] content of reason is potency—which does not have being outside itself [...] but remains in itself, is essence, das sich Entäußernde, which is not *existentiae obnoxium,* [but rather] what is called the highest essence, which does not have essence as something outside itself but is itself essence, which in Seyn remains what it was, which is at the same time potence and Aktus."

law of the activity of thought, since that entity is to be understood as both *potentia* and *actus,* both the ability to be *and* Being—the entity wherein the activity of thought is at the same time perfectly by itself and free.

Thus far, the course of the activity of thought has not been free but rather necessarily pulled away [*fortgezogen*], although it always returns to itself. In its final stage, however, *in the potence that remains arrested above Being,* it reaches the highest point, that which it has been desiring from the beginning.

The *starting point of this science* is to say, *I care nothing about Being; I desire the* αὐτὸ ὄν [this Being]. But it becomes the content of the activity of thought only in the final moment—no longer the merely undefined ὄν, also not merely the concept (potence = concept) of an Other, but rather the concept of itself, which remains in and by itself, the only one of its kind, intended to be achieved [*erzielt*] in the entire movement; in this sense, it is to be called *idea. Idea is thus that which is desired and intended to be achieved.*

Philosophy does not commence by haphazard [*auf das Gerathewohl*]; it is a science that is always conscious of its purpose and *already* contains *a desire* [*Wollen*]. We call that concept an *idea* also because it *remains concept* by nature and, at least within this science, *cannot be brought into existence.* The entire movement was intended to achieve this concept; but it is *actualized only logically, in the activity of thought* [*Denken*]. It could not be realized in an unmediated activity of thought. There, what first had to be excluded—that two-sided content that emerges from the originary potence—showed itself.

The previous science has been negative and critical, and it did not renounce its origin from Kant's *Critique.* One can call the *final* actualization, brought about by the entire movement merely logically, an inauthentic result. For a *result* is a succession of preceding actions. An *idea* is merely that which remains arrested [*Stehenbleibende*]; it is thus more of a negative concept. Just as it is for Kant, in his *Critique,* merely an end, so it is for us as well. But there is *one* difference. *In the science described by us* (here only a moment within a historical development that goes beyond it), *the concept of*

God is cognized and gained through methodological progression as the necessarily all-concluding fundamental concept, as the necessary content of reason. Kant's formal deduction is insufficient and merely an assumption.

This emphasized difference could create the *deception* by virtue of which this science *ascribed actual cognizance of God to itself* (*i.e.*, which at the same time was extended to God's existence). But *the final concept always has as its content only the pure* **What** (*quid*) *of the godhood.* Even though we call it *the potence of that which has Being* [*seyende Potenz*], it is *not the existing potence.*

It is important to understand precisely *the limits of this science.* One could call the system of this science a system of emanation, but one should be careful not to think of **God** as the principle of such a system. Rather, one would have to say: *God is himself only the final* (i.e., *merely logical*) *emanation of this system.* In this science, *God* can only be at the end and to such a degree that he can never become its beginning. *He is the final cause* to which everything in this system strives, but *he is not the effectuating cause.* He is a concept of regulative significance that can never be made into a (constitutive) principle. In the same line of progression (a limitation that *Kant* neglected to apply), there is nothing to be done with him since he is merely the end.

In this science especially, God does not, like everything else, have the ability to exist [*Existirenkönnende*], *i.e., the ability to be* [*Seynkönnende*] outside of the concept; he is that which remains in reason, unable to get out—the immanent concept of reason. If a potence elevated above all Being exists actually, then it cannot exist in such a way that the potence is the *prius.* All else exists in that way. If such a potence exists, the existence must be the *prius,* the concept of that which is later. Thus the final concept we have obtained is the reversed ability to be [*umgekehrte Seynkönnen*], which has Being as *prius* but not as *posterius.* It is said that God has existence necessarily; *i.e., if he exists,* Being, the *prius,* can only be of himself. *God, as necessary content of reason, cannot exist accidentally, as if his Being were the consequence of the potence.*

Since the progression in this science goes from potence to Being and, reversely, from Being to potence, this science reached its boundary with the final idea. This final reversal paralyzes this science and therewith also knows that it is completed. In a science that cognizes from the standpoint of that which is *before* Being, *a priori* (from its *prius* = potence *ad actum*), and because of what originates in that way, it refers to experience in order to prove its existence (to which, by the way, it is indifferent). If, in this science, *one also counts existence as content of the science, as that which is uncognizable,* since it is at the same time an object outside of all experience, then *only the idea remains* as the Last. Its existence could only be proven in another science, one that begins at the opposite end. Were there such a science, one could not deprive it of the name philosophy.[2] *This second science would have to decide forthwith to commence from that which is outside of reason in order to arrive at that which is beyond Being.*

---

2. KG11: 6, p. 308: "This philosophy could be called *philosophia secunda* [second philosophy] (an expression already used by Aristotle, though in his case to designate physics); it is indeed a true philosophy, and it would be difficult to show that the first is that. It is *the philosophy of identity.*"

IV. Assessment of the Philosophy of Identity

[PL, pp. 342-57]

The philosophy of identity[1] had the ambition to be *that pure science of reason.* It is the one we cognize again [*wieder erkennen*] in its fundamentals, stripped bare of the formulas that seemed needed at the time. At the same time, it will need to be shown how the philosophy of identity *failed* in this ambition.

So-called because it began with indifference and ended with the identity of subject and object, it came to the aforementioned expressions by way of *Fichte,* who *conceived the idea of elevating Kant's Critique to a science of knowledge that ought not to receive any more from experience but rather to posit everything self-determinately.* Fichte thereby missed to consider, right from the outset, the free status that reason ought to have since he demanded at the outset a Being that is unmediated and certain. This could only be the "*I am.*" Philosophy became that of every I [*Ich*]. From then on, all else could be tied in [*anknüpfen*] only through subjective reflection, however powerful the thought of a science that starts from itself.

Kant's *Critique* contained more that is objective since he allowed himself, unconcernedly, to be led by experience; with *Fichte,* reflection was only *accidental.* And however great *our* respect for this energy of subjective reflection, there was no discernible trace of objective cognizance in Fichte's doctrine of science.

Nevertheless, Fichte's starting point contained the seed of the subsequent philosophy.[2] *Fichte grasped Being in the act* [*auf der That*],[3] *in the act of the self-consciousness*; he grasped Being

---

1. Schelling's main philosophy between 1801 and 1806, which represented a significant break with Fichte and wherein Schelling posited the Absolute in the identity of subject and object.

2. *Einleitung in die Philosophie der Offenbarung,* SW XIII, p. 51: "It will always remain Fichte's great, unforgettable merit to be the first to have grasped within his spirit the idea of a completely *a priori* science."

3. See Johann Gottlieb Fichte *Grundlage der gesammten Wissenschaftslehre* (Foundation of the Entire Doctrine of Science) (Leipzig:

where it shows itself in the unmediated self-consciousness as a stepping out of the potence. The I is only in this act, and only in this act does it step out of the potence.

It required only one *step to cognize the essence of the* prius *of all Being. The restriction of positing oneself, as it appeared in the I, needed only to be dropped to find the absolute point of development.* In doing so, science would become independent from the subject.

Philosophy extricated itself from the restriction only gradually because the author of the philosophy of identity believed that they had to hold on to the continuity of philosophical development. It was a matter of turning his contemporaries away *from the subjective standpoint* and *perhaps even* free *Fichte* from it; alas, *we* never had that pleasure.

It was about finding *the subject-object enclosed in the I.* And nothing was easier than to cognize that *general* quality, the subject-object, in the act of the self-consciousness.

Even later, when Fichte's ideas seemed to be coming closer materially to the ideas of the later philosophy, he seems not to have grasped the method of the subject-object.

Because the I was allowed to remain the starting point for a while, the philosophy of identity was conscious of the fact that one must go back to the potence of the I in order to be raised from there to the higher level of the I. Only in this way did **nature** *become an object [Gegenstand] for philosophy.*[4] The potence, wherein the I is not yet posited as I, was the beginning, raised gradually to the I of consciousness. The system of transcendental idealism was conceived in this thought, wherein the subsequent

---

Christian Ernst Gabler, 1794), §1.6.*c*: "Thus the I's own positing of itself is its own pure activity [*Thätigkeit*].–The I *posits itself,* and it *is* by virtue of this mere self-positing: and conversely: the I *is,* and *posits* its Being by virtue of its mere being.–It is at the same time the agent and the product of action, the active [*Thätige*] and that which is brought about by the activity [*Thätigkeit*]; action [*Handlung*] and deed [*That*] are one and the same; and hence the *I am* is an expression of an enactment [*Thathandlung*]; and the only one possible–the necessary consequence of the entire Science of Knowledge."

4. KG 11:7, p. 308: "Identity phil. [by contrast] did not begin with the Ich [the I] but with the Ich as potency, and in this way nature entered philosophy."

philosophy was already cognizable, especially the objective method that was dormant in the object.

In this approach, the I started out from its deepest stage; what was won in the prior moment served the next as foundation. The I exists only in the act of self-consciousness; it is nothing outside of it. It is with the act. And because it is only in this act, it is not *before* the act and presupposes itself in this act as mere potence. The I thus contains in itself the general concept of the subject-object. *Subject, suppositum* of Being, is potence of Being, thus a transition *a potentia ad actum.* The general concept within the I is that of the subject-object—of the subject that which still has the *ability* to be, equal possibility [*Gleichmöglichkeit*],[5] indifference of subject and object. Having the ability to pass over into Being, it is equal possibility, indeed now a subject, but only in a way that in that moment it would also be an object, neither determined as one nor the other nor indifferent—according to its nature, uncertain and subjected to reversal.

The First in this science must *not be that which unmediatedly is certain,* from which there could be no progress. Indeed, Descartes began with *doubt*; however, this doubt cannot be brought to the object extrinsically. The truth of the object must be doubtable. The subject unmediatedly is that which not yet has Being [*Noch-nicht-seyende*] and thus is that for which Being lies still ahead—the ability to be in a transitory sense. Once it passes over, it has Being, but it is no longer Being itself in the substantive sense; it is the *μὴ ὄν* [non-Being] in the sense of Plato [as a relative or determinate non-Being].[6]

---

5. Schelling has used *Gleichmöglichkeit* synonymously with *Indifferenz* (indifference) and *Gleichgültigkeit* (equal validity); see, *e.g.*, Schelling's *Zur Geschichte der neueren Philosophie* (On the History of the Newer Philosophy), *SW* X, p. 145: "Equal validity (equal possibility, indifference) of subject and object"; and *Einleitung in die Philosophie der Mythologie, SW* XI, p. 366: "Equal possibility (indifference)."

6. KG 11:7, p. 309: "After it has made the transition, it is again non-being, but not in the same sense. This can be clarified by the distinction Plato drew betw[een] οὐκ ὄν and *μὴ ὄν*." See Plato, *Sophist* 256*d*.

But the correct explanation is already found in Plutarch: one needs to differentiate between μὴ εἶναι (non-Being) and μὴ ὄν εἶναι (Being that does not have Being).[7] Error and sickness do not exactly not have Being; the nature of that which does not have Being, like error and sickness, is not nothing. Like truth, both have reality, and the one has reality only through the other.

That which does not have Being [*das Nichtseyende*] must be cognizable to some extent as having Being.[8] This is the topic of Plato's *Sophist,*[9] which is a consecrating hymn [*Weihegesang*] to a higher science.

The concept of that which does not have Being is highly important. Here is another example: the reality of *sensate objects* that occurs in experience has been doubted all along; it is said to be *quodammodo* [in a certain manner], and it is only about the manner of this Being. This doubt stemmed from the *feeling* that sensate objects do not have Being in such a way that in them the truth, the subject, is asserted; yet they do not altogether not have Being. Sensate things are μὴ ὄντα [non-existent]; the potence of Being has not been taken from them. Only *actu* it is no longer within them.

Thus, the *philosophy of identity* put forward that the subject remained in things, that it was not, *as Fichte said,* absolute non-subject but rather subject turned object [*zum Object umgewendetes Subject*].[10] The philosophy of identity was called *the system of the identity of subject and object also in this sense. It did not acknowledge a non-being object as such.*

The subsequent course of this science was as follows: As soon as everything that posed as subject or potence passed

---

7. Plutarch, *Moralia* 15.115*d–f.* See also *Die Weltalter,* SW VIII, p. 221.

8. KG11:7, p. 309: "Thus error and sickness are not altogether nichts [nothing], not οὐκ ὄντα [not existing] but μὴ ὄντα [non-existent]."

9. Plato, *Sophist* 240*d*–e; 260*b*–261*b*.

10. KG11:7, p. 309: "But non-being always remains the subject, rather than, as Fichte maintained, the nicht-Ich [not-I]; the subject abides in things but in such a way that it is converted into the object. In this way, this philosophy preserves its subject-object character throughout. [R]elative-non-being is the real linchpin of identity phil., whereby it demonstrates that it has abandoned Fichte's subjective tendency."

over inevitably into Being, it was granted the status of an object; in its place, *an ability to be of a higher order* emerged. Thus one Being surrenders its claim to be a Being to a higher one and acquiesces to become an object opposite that higher Being. *That was the secret of this science's method.*

Articulating *the concept of that which has relative non-Being* [*relativ Nichtseyenden*] was arguably the greatest accomplishment of this system with respect to logic. Through a sequence in which every lower-ranking ability to be surrenders itself to a higher ranking one and professes itself as not having Being [*nichtseyend*], *the system advanced to the highest subject, which does not have the ability to be but* is *and ends as the pure and plain power* [*lautere Macht*] *of Being.* Whoever is given possibility only by a lower subject foregoing its Being can rightly be called a "higher potence." The lower subject is that which is subjugated to Being itself, not in power of itself, all the way up to Man, who fully is in power of himself and relatively above Being.

Only through the mediation of this second world can one advance to *that which absolutely has supra-Being* [*absolut Ueberseyenden*],[11] which is no longer outside of its concept but is with itself within it and which, insofar as it does not go beyond the activity of thought, is the identity of concept and Being—not longer equal possibility, indifference, but equal actuality [*Gleichwirklichkeit*], absolute identity of subject and object. Coming nearer to itself or to its actualization [*Verwirklichung*] from point to point [*Punct zu Punct*], yet never settling down completely, is the power that in the end, above and apart from all others remains in great solitariness [*in hoher Einsamkeit*].

Once cleared of the apparatus of formulas, which then still seemed necessary, the whole is the philosophy of identity. Originally, this was progress, but because of misconceptions, it has now become a hindrance. Returning it to its original meaning reveals the condition for any possible progress. In it, philosophy was given as *nothing other than the pure Science of Reason,* whose concept I have presented above.

---

11. That which extends beyond that which has Being and that which does not have Being in the sense of Plotinus's all-transcending One (*cf. The Enneads,* VI).

In its *nascency,* the philosophy of identity was too occupied with unmediated content; in it, *everything was hinging on the final One = omnia ex hoc uno* [everything out of the one]. No stillness, no endurance anywhere until this was reached. Everything became validated only by this final One. Thus left breathless, it could not look back at itself.

The worst misconception the philosophy of identity could have suffered was to be thought of having, like other systems, a self-true [*selbstwahres*] principle from which its truth would emanate to the other parts of the system. Therefore it was required to prove the truth of its principle. Nothing of the sort! Having *originated in the Kantian* Critique, it could have truth only as its concluding principle. Thus it was the *freest philosophy,* the purest flight [*Aufschwung*] of a *thinking that is also free of truth,* carried only by its own laws.

It was better understood by those who took it as a *poetic invention—a poem composed by reason itself. For reason is bound to nothing, therefore also not to truth; it excludes nothing, asserts nothing, and perceives everything.* If there were unmediated truths of reason, then reason would not be the completely free potence of cognition; it perceives that which has the ability to be all [*Allesseynkönnende*], that which can be true and not true.

Arguably, philosophy, as a desire [*Wollen*], unmediatedly desires not that which "*is*" and "*is not*" but that which *actually is,* and it would like to unmediatedly grasp that which genuinely has Being [*wahrhaft Seyende*] at the very first thought. There, reason throws itself against philosophy by putting before it that which genuinely does not have Being [*Nichtwahrhaftseyendes*] nevertheless exists to some extent; that the same substance is in one as well as in the other—unchanged in the one and altered in the other; and that it has that which genuinely has Being only in differentiation from that which genuinely does not have Being.

Reason pits its indifference and its inherent ability to have infinite Being [*Unendlichseynkönnende*] against the impetuous desire [*ungestüme Wollen*]. It does not relieve science of any of these possibilities but rather impels it to go through all of them by awarding, in the end and for that reason alone, that which truly has Being as prize. Science therewith gains the *a priori* position by having as unmediated content (not: object) only the *equal possibility or absolute indifference.* Only then does philosophy become a pure science of reason.

The philosophy of identity was the purest, entirely free flight of the activity of thinking. It could only fall away from itself by wanting to be something more.

The philosophy of identity did not therefore originate from that which is true but rather from that which has its truth only in the end—just as it also did not arise from an unmediated certitude [*Gewissen*] but rather from that which is *doubtable,* which receives its last determination *only in the final outcome.* All things up to the last only had *relative truth,* with the subsequent always having been the truth of the earlier one. Each had its truth only by professing itself to have *relative non-Being* opposite each subsequent one and, finally, the highest one.

It was thus the ascending method—from the lowest Being, which was posited outside of itself, and in which the trace of being was covered up the most, rising up toward the Being wherein it was cognized the most. However, this method could *also* have been called *descending*—by making that from which one started out merely the stage of a higher subject (καταβολὴ [what is made into its substrate]) until at last that which has no longer an ability to empty itself [*nicht mehr Entäussern-könnende*] remains as *the Being* in unified splendor [*Glanz*].

But all of it was accomplished only in thought [*Gedanken*]—even the *Last,* God, who, however, had a sanctuary in thought, a throne above all others. The actual course of the system cannot be a thought process except by complete reversal. In that method, everything became moment; each subject that passed over into Being moved center stage only to be pushed to the side. Each was held in place only long enough to become an object during the activity of thought, *i.e.,* an object of possible cognizance, so that *the science assigned the actual cognizance of the same to another science.* Everything was brought only to the gateway of actual cognizance, to cognizability [*Erkennbarkeit*].

In this science, each element admitted to Being gained only *the* truth it had in relation to what alone is thought of as *that which has genuine Being* [*wahrhaft seyend*]. All were of *one* material, like the iron filings between the negative and positive magnetic poles, which are identical with respect to their material yet different with respect to their direction and position.

This philosophy was accused of: *Everything in it is one and the same* [*einerlei*]! [12] And *as long as it seemed necessary to argue against Fichte,* it was necessary to emphasize the one-and-the-sameness [*Einerleiheit*] of object and subject (*i.e.,* everything in it is of the same material, substance). After all, the system had only just taught this particular distinction.

In any case, what will remain of this philosophy is *the thought of an* a priori that encloses in itself a content of the actual (in nature and history) that is seemingly far removed from thought and the method found herewith.

We have thus presented this science as a purely *a priori* science. *Kant* called any cognizance *a priori* that is drawn merely from the faculty of cognition. With even greater justification, *we call any cognizance* a priori *that develops from the infinite potence of Being. Through pure reason, we can see in each thing what results from it; thus, the pure science of reason arises from the general* prius. A priori *cognition does not mean to cognize from the existence so that the existence of the object is thereby presupposed.* Its starting point is rather that which is the **prius** *of all Being.* Everything derived from it possesses this science not only as an actual existing but as concept. What can be explained merely by *actus* can no longer be apprehended logically.

But *this Science of Reason* regards everything only as it flows out of the nature of having an infinite ability to be. *It is a science that is merely logical.* One might otherwise put forward that in the mere activity of thought the progression creates nothing but tautological or analytical sentences.

---

12. KG11: 8, p. 310: "this is true in the same sense that everything is einerlei in the voltaic pile, a discovery that was, remarkably, contemporary with this philosophy—everything in it is of one substance, one material." See also Schelling's reference to the voltaic pile in his inaugural lecture in Munich, *SW* IX: p. 362, and above, p. 24.

Kant called that which goes beyond the nature of things synthetic.[13] However, that which goes beyond can only be an accidental. Thus, with things whose existence does not result from their nature, *i.e.,* are accidental, their existence would be that which goes beyond their nature. Accordingly, a science that does not step out into existence would contain merely tautological, analytical propositions. But the nature of that which is presupposed by us is that it passes over into an *Other,* into an object, and *thus here the synthetic and analytic progression are identical—something Kant sought in vain.* Yet this Other remains within thought, as the image of one that does not yet have Being, as a future Being, without the activity of thinking needing to stride over into actual existence.

This science contains only *a priori* concepts of these things. Only through the transition of that which is possible *a potentia ad actum* is existence only accidental. But therefrom existence does not let itself be understood *a priori*; this only applies to essence, concept, and content.

The philosophy of nature does not wish to deduce any actual plants; any actual existing plant is here and now. But just as in the ideal [*vorbildlichen*] world, everything ought to be contained only γενικῶς, *according to genus,* so pure science contains only genera and types. It has *sensate things* only *by having the ability to be outside the activity of thought,* not by having Being. The Last has it only insofar as it is unable to get outside of the activity of thought. By never going beyond the activity of thought, this science is, in this way, quite an *immanent, not transcending science*—so purely *a priori* that it were true even if nothing existed, just as geometry were true even if no triangle existed.[14]

---

13. See Immanuel Kant, *Critique of Pure Reason,* trans. Norman Kemp Smith (New York: Palgrave Macmillan, 2007), p. 48 (A6-7/B10-11): "In all judgments in which the relation of a subject to the predicate is thought [...] this relation is possible in two different ways. Either the predicate B belongs to the subject A, as something which is covertly contained in this concept A; or B lies entirely outside the concept A [...] In the one case, I entitle the judgment analytic, in the other synthetic."

14. See Descartes's fifth *Meditation*: "I find within me countless ideas of things which even though they may not exist anywhere

Insofar as this science, as an *a priori* science, has as its object that which is to be cognized, it found itself once again in the same place as Kant's *Critique* of the cognitive faculty; but it might better call itself the science of that which is *cognizable* [*Wissenschaft des Erkennbaren*]—a name that proclaims its objective position.

While the *philosophy of identity,* understood properly, led to the same result as the Kantian *Critique,* it nevertheless differed from the latter in that its author first elevated it to a *necessary* science. But it should not, for that reason, be confused with a *dogmatic* science since it did not assert anything without being therefore the ἐποχή [suspension of judgments][15] of the academics. It did not go beyond the activity of thought by way of assertion, and it still had the entire content of the purely logical correlation of things. It was not assertive because it kept itself independent of all existence, of that which is positive.

This philosophy, in its wavering [*Schwanken*],[16] *should have been called negative philosophy.* Nothing is diminished by determining its limits; only in them can it truly find conclusion. It was appropriate to call it a *philosophy* because it sought the highest object of all cognizance [*Erkennens*] and found it only at the end, *bringing any other object as far as their cognizability* [*Erkennbarkeit*] *and at the same time leaving it unmediatedly to the actual cognition of another science.* The highest object remains in it as uncognizable; but therein it comes

---

outside me still cannot be called nothing. When, for example, I imagine a triangle, even if perhaps no such figure exists, or has ever existed anywhere outside my thought, there is still a determinate nature, or essence, or form of the triangle, which is immutable and eternal, and not invented by me or dependent on my mind." *The Philosophical Writings of Descartes,* ed. and trans. John Cottingham, Robert Stoothoff, and Dugald Murdoch (Cambridge: Cambridge University Press, 1984), vol. 2, p. 45.

15. Advocated by the non-dogmatic skeptics at Plato's Academy in Athens.

16. See KG11:8, p. 309: "The phil. of identity did not presuppose truth but arrived at it, beginning not with unmediated certainty but with wavering: everything betw. beginning and end was understood to have only relative truth."

to an end, and *at the same time the prospect of a positive philosophy is offered.* Whether these two philosophies form only *one* philosophy is a question to be set aside for later.

It was not enough that this science was a **negative** *philosophy; it also had to profess to it. But here is where it fell short, for a* **positive** *philosophy had not yet been declared separate from it.* It could not exclude the *positive* in the just explained sense (*existence*) without first positing it outside of itself.

The concept of a negative philosophy demands a positive one. But the progress of the human mind is slow, so both sides of an object are not always brought to light at the same time; rather, *one half of the conception* [*Erfindung*] becomes obscured because the other is not yet present. Only when the science of reason cognizes itself to being merely negative will a positive be there as well. *However, the positive is undeniable, and the actual presses for an explanation.* Thus it happens that the logical progression is mistaken for the actual one.

One could then believe to have apprehended the actual God in the logical concept of God. This philosophy was therefore accused of *having God in it only as the end, not as the creator of the world!* And in doing so one assumed that *it spoke of the actual God.* It could reply: *I believe that I know as little about the actual God as about actual things.* As theoretical science has done after Kant, so the negative philosophy must say about God that it does not know *whether or not there is a God, just as it does not know it of actual things.*

Misled by the general accusation that his philosophy was *idealism,* i.e., *the assertion that things do not exist independently from us,* Kant added a *refutation of idealism* in the second edition of his *Critique of Pure Reason.*[17] In the pure science of reason, that question cannot present itself. The philosophy of identity could call itself absolute idealism since there can be no talk at all about existence. (Relative idealism *denies* the existence of things independent from us.)

The philosophy of identity would never want to speak of the actual God; nevertheless, one continued to be convinced that it did. But if one presupposed the actual God in

17. See Kant's *Critique of Pure Reason,* pp. 244–45 (B 274–75).

it, *then it appeared to be a doctrine that apprehends God as a result of the world,* either as the result of a principle that is independent from it or as the *process* that mediates itself through the world and its various stages, wherein God is still conceived incompletely; for it did not matter whether God was in the process or was himself the process. Both, however, went beyond the task of philosophy.

There was nothing philosophy had to stay clearer of than being taken for a doctrine that speaks about an actual course of events or a system for implementing a particular contention; it could be as less a system as *geometry.*

Whether one is looking at the beginning or the end of *the philosophy of identity,* it will come across as the *determined opposite of Spinozism.* For *Spinoza,* God was principle, beginning; for the philosophy of identity, God was to be merely the end. For Spinoza, all things are *logical emanations* of the divine nature; for *the philosophy of identity, the idea of God is the highest emanation of a merely logical process.*

If one were to allow that an actual course of events is charted in this philosophy, God would have to be presupposed at the earliest stages—*in a state of only incomplete actualization. God would essentially be all*; indeed, this philosophy could then be regarded at last as the completion of Spinozism.

It was Spinoza who first brought the *confusion of* (what we call) *the positive and negative* into philosophy. He made God into a principle that *necessarily and blindly* has existence. He then lets things follow unmediatedly from God's nature, just as the laws governing a triangle follow from the latter's nature. This monstrous connection of a merely logical consequence with something presupposed as existing is the power that Spinoza wielded over the many who had lost their free spirit opposite this system.

Besides, Spinoza merely *assured* us that things result from the nature of God with *logical necessity.*[18] Here that

---

18. KG 11: 9, p. 311: "but never demonstrated it."

philosophy seemed to be able to meddle in it [*in's Mittel zu treten*] only if it allowed the infinite potence—out of which everything arises with logical necessity, defined as God's nature—to emerge victoriously from all stages as the final conclusion. Therewith, the gap in Spinoza's demonstration was filled in. *Thus, the philosophy of identity let itself be turned into Spinozism.*

The temptation was great since the positive would not let itself be dismissed and intruded from all sides. The purer the nature of the negative, the stronger the positive had to assert itself from the other side. *Negative philosophy contains the demand for a positive philosophy; thus the former, as long as the latter is not yet established, must turn into it.*[19]

A future edition of my collected works will describe the stages of my development all the way to the positive philosophy. *I did not dare* put the philosophy found thus far forward as an absolute system.

---

19. *Einleitung in die Philosophie der Offenbarung*, SWXIII, p. 92: "At its conclusion, negative philosophy itself contains the demand for a positive [philosophy]; any philosophy conscious of itself and comprehends itself fully *has* the desire to posit the positive outside of itself. In that sense, one could say that the negative grounds [*begründe*] the positive, but not the other way around."

V. Hegel and the Philosophy of Identity

[PL, pp. 358–97]

It was another philosopher who brought about the conclusion of the *system* with the greatest energy. Not to speak about him would be unworthy of me and would do little to honor his memory. I have always been outspoken about *Kant* and *Fichte,* both of whom were teachers of mine even though I did not attend their lectures (actually, I did attend one of Fichte's lectures for *one* hour, but I was already a fellow teacher). Should I now shy away from speaking about *Hegel*? So many have sought philosophical laurels yet only earned a crown of thorns. I do not mention them. That I mention Hegel shows how highly I regard him.

I recognize how *Hegel alone has saved the basic thought of my philosophy for a later time* and has cognized and preserved this thought in its purity, in particular, in his lectures on the history of philosophy.[1] While *we others* allowed ourselves to be diverted by the material aspect of the gained insight, he adhered to the *method* in its purity. No one could have completed the earlier philosophy better than he did.

He himself made the philosophy of identity into a positive philosophy and thus elevated it to an absolute philosophy in the first place, one that leaves nothing outside of itself.

We can speak here without any polemics; history will decide for itself. The decision lies in Hegel's statements. Hegel did what was obvious to him; I cannot not criticize him for that. The philosophy of identity could not keep itself within its limitation of having the ability to exist [*Existiren-Könnenden*]. *Hegel believed that the given system was the philosophy,* but he also could not allow it to stay within a limitation that excludes all existence. We best follow his expositions

---

The reflections on Hegel follow closely Schelling's 1833–34 lectures in Munich, published as *Zur Geschichte der neueren Philosophie* (On the History of the Newer Philosophy), SW X, pp. 126–61.

1. See Georg Wilhelm Friedrich Hegel, *Lectures on the History of Philosophy,* vol. 3, trans. E.S. Haldane and Frances H. Simson (Lincoln and London: University of Nebraska Press), pp. 512–45.

against the immediately preceding philosophy. (I have nothing in common with the other enemies of Hegel's.)

I agree completely with *the Hegelian definition of philosophy: it is the science of reason insofar as it becomes conscious that it is all Being.*[2] This explanation is not strictly applicable to positive and negative philosophy but nevertheless *expresses perfectly the essence of the science of reason.* In it, reason becomes conscious that it is all Being, *provided that Being is not also understood to be the real, actual one* but rather in the sense that reason comes forth in the science of reason as all that has Being according to its material substance [*der Materie nach*].[3] *That reason becomes conscious of its content in the philosophy—as* **the content** *of all Being—is the explanation of the science of reason.* This distinction should not be omitted! Whether *Hegel* withheld this distinction tacitly or was not aware of it will be shown in due course.

Insofar as Hegel did *not* believe in having to presuppose the Absolute *through intellectual intuition* [*Anschauung*], but rather sought to find it in the science as a result of the same, he believed that in elevating himself along with the former philosophy *to acknowledging the Absolute,* he diverged from it.[4] *The Absolute* is cogitated here for the first time[5]—a *word* that since the philosophy of identity has been *in omnium ore* [to be renowned].

The philosophy of identity started out with *the indifference of subject and object.* This indifference is *the infinite potence, the infinite ability to have Being,* the latter posited as unmediated

---

2. Georg Wilhelm Friedrich Hegel, *System der Wissenschaft: Erster Theil, die Phänomenologie des Geistes* (System of Science: Part One, the Phenomenology of Spirit) (Bamberg und Würzburg: Joseph Anton Goebhardt, 1807), p. 164: "Reason is the certainty that consciousness has of being all reality; in this way idealism enunciates its concept."

3. KG1:9, p. 311: "one must simply bear in mind that alles Seyn [all Being] is not actual Seyn; reason reveals itself der Materie nach [according to its substance] as Alles Seyn."

4. KG11:10, pp. 311–12: "Concerning the whole of his work, Hegel remarks, in a matter-of-fact fashion, that he did not merely want to presuppose the Absolute as existing with respect to intellectual intuition, but to achieve it scientifically."

5. *Ibid.*: p. 312: "The Absolute is here named for the first time in these lectures, and we shall now approach what it might mean."

content of reason. This infinite potence was *a kind of Orphic unity wherein all that was to evolve from it lay still concealed*: first, the unmediated ability to have Being; further, that potence that does not pass over but remains in itself. The latter alone could be defined as the *Absolute* since it was *that which is absolved from the necessity to pass over into Being*[6] *and cleaves to the eternal freedom opposite Being.*

Meanwhile, that Orphic unity could also be called the *Absolute,* as the *quod omnibus numeris absolutum est* [that which is absolute in all respects]. For it is the potence of the non-Absolute—those potences that are finite opposite each other and mutually exclusive (each of them being infinite in itself, *e.g.,* that which purely has Being; but opposite the other potence, having the ability to be [*Seynkönnende*], it is finite again, namely when it steps into the opposition)—as well as the potence of the Absolute posited as such, which has the non-Absolute already outside itself.[7] (For it is absolute precisely because it has the non-Absolute outside of itself!) But to us, the indifference is the absolute potence of everything. Only the material, exponentiated Absolute, the genuine Absolute, is at the end.

This discussion leads to the question: *What kind of Absolute does Hegel speak of?* Even the philosophy of identity could desire the Absolute, designated as an end, only as a result. Hegel must think that the philosophy of identity has *the Absolute not only in substance* (as the pure content of reason) *but also as a result of existence*; to this end, it presupposed indifference as existing but demonstrated the existence only "in a bad way [*auf die schlechte Weise*]," through *intellectual intuition.* If absolute indifference were to have existence, then everything that emerged from it would also have existence, where there is not only the world of the finite but also already the Absolute, which is contained in the indifference, that which has existence.

Hegel assumes unsuspectingly that the previous philosophy wanted to be above actual existence and *demonstrate the*

---

6. *Ibid.*: "for it was freigesprochen [absolved] from making the transition."

7. *Ibid.*: "[The Absolute] is equally the potential for the one (the not-Absolute) and for the other."

existence of the Absolute, but it did so in a bad, merely subjective manner through the intellectual intuition. That this is generally not the case has already been shown.

"But *intellectual intuition* had to have played a major role during the foundation of this philosophy!"—I will comment on this simply by saying: While "intellectual intuition" is not found in the *first* presentation of the philosophy of identity (*the only one certifiably acknowledged by the author as authentic,* in the *Zeitschrift für Physik,* volume 2, issue 2), it is mentioned in the first volume of said publication.

To explain this, one has to go back to *Fichte's intellectual intuition. Fichte* called for *an unmediated certitude* [*Gewisses*], the I [*Ich*], *of which he believed to assure himself through the intellectual intuition as an unmediated certitude.* He impelled everyone who practiced philosophy toward this intellectual intuition. Its content, expressed with unmediated certitude, was: *I am* [*Ich bin*]. *Intellectual* intuition was set against *sensate* [*sinnlich*] intuition because in the former, subject and object were not differentiated from each other.[8]

I did not seek to break with Fichte but instead to find a path from his position to a more general concept of the indifference of subject and object (in the text mentioned above). The transition was as follows: Not the I, as it is in intellectual intuition as unmediated certitude but rather as gained through abstraction from the subjective in the intellectual intuition, a general concept removed from intellectual intuition and thus no longer an unmediated certainty. *Thus removed,* it became a matter of pure thought. *It no longer involved the I,* whose *existence* Fichte invoked in the intellectual intuition, *but the absolute subject-object.* It did not involve existence but rather the general nature (*quid*) of intellectual intuition.

The explanation given at the time—that one had to draw the *concept* of the subject-object from the intellectual intuition—is proof that it was not about Being but rather about pure content. Had I not been clear about this, Hegel could

8. *Ibid.*: "This expression belongs to Fichte. He called for an intellectual intuition, the content of which was: Ich bin [I am]. The expression was chosen in contra-distinction to sensible intuition, in which subj[ect] and obj[ect] differ."

have misunderstood me. I shall repeat: This philosophy has nothing to do with that which is in actuality [*Wirkliches*], but with *the innate absolute content of reason.* Hegel, in contrast, sublates the desire for *immanence.*

This philosophy could not desire indifference as that which is true, as that which has existence, except gained by development. If it were there in the beginning, philosophy would not be free of Being, would not be pure thought.

Viewed from different perspective: Ought *the prius of all existence* have Being itself? So it is shown by Hegel, *who starts out from Being, not from the ability to have Being,* which impels his philosophy in the direction of an existential system [*Existential-System*]—through its beginning, which according to him ought to be an improvement.

Since that which has existence is that which is not immanent [*Nichtimmanente*], the method rests on a passing-over that takes place in that which is not immanent rather than in the pure activity of thought. The demand to pull back from the standpoint of pure reason, which Hegel also made, requires pulling back from everything—except the activity of thought—and therefore also from Being. *If I grasp something merely as the content of the activity of thought, I need not care about Being.* The infinite potence is in reason, not outside of reason. The activity of thought is there by itself, alone with itself. We have the infinite potence as the unmediated content of reason, as only objectively posited reason.

Had the earlier philosophy invoked *intellectual intuition,* it would have earned blame for trying to prove existence altogether. Thus, I have to reject intellectual intuition in the described sense. If it is understood as an intuition that corresponds to the subject-object, then one can speak of an intellectual intuition, not of the subject but of reason itself. However, intellectual intuition then occurs as that in which reason grasps itself and finds in itself the infinite potence of Being. *There reason is both that which beholds* [*Anschauende*] *and that which is beheld* [*Angeschaute*].

I ask those who oppose all intuition to consider the following: How does *the infinite potence of reason* relate to the activity of thought? Merely as matter [*Materie*], not as object. *The true* prima materia *of the activity of thought* cannot be that which is thought [*das Gedachte*] since that is its singular form. It is merely the underlying [substance] [*das zu Grunde liegende*] and therefore relates to the actual activity of thought only as "*that which is not unthinkable* [*Nicht-Nichtzudenkende*]." If the activity of thought is occupied with a particular thought, then it thinks of the definition of the concept, which it posits into this substance. This is the *non-thinking activity of thought, and it may well be intuition.*

Hegel asserts that *the existence of the Absolute has been proven by a separate science,* i.e., *logic,* whose purpose is to prove the existence of the Absolute, and only then move on to the philosophies of nature and mind.—The fact that logic is only one part is evident from its position toward philosophy, for, strictly speaking, all of philosophy ought to be *logical.* Putting logic first, in order to prove the existence of the Absolute, is rather wondrous, as one has the Absolute as a result twice.[9] The second time, it is at the end of the system—at the end of logic already as resulting existence. That, at least, seemed to be the intent of Hegel's logic.

In the immanent activity of thought, there is no question of Being, *only of essence* [*Wesen*]. Hegel takes *Being* and declares: this is the indifference! Thus one asks whether his understanding of Being might be different from ours. *With Hegel,* Being is perceived as *actus, i.e.,* as the *opposite of potence.* He refers to Being as an unmediated certitude, which can only be *actus,* not potence. He defines Being as that which is the farthest removed from the concept, as the opposite of all that is subjective and conceptual. But wherein no concept and nothing subjective is contained, there is no potence. The pure Being includes all of Being; it is *actus purus.*

The further proceedings are as follows: Definitions of concepts are posited into pure Being, whereby pure Being

---

9. KG 11:10, p. 313: "Hegel did not have, as he himself said, the bad [form of] intell[ectual] intuition. On the contrary, he has logic as the science that must prove the existence of the Absolute, at which point he proceeds to another science. The fact that this science is a portion of science in its entirety is already suspect. Hegel is therefore in the position of having proven the Absolute twice, first in logic; for already there he arrives of course at existence, and then in the second science."

is sublated. *It is the idea, so to speak,* that has the infinite purport [*Bedeutung*] of feeding on the pure Being. After it has absorbed the pure Being into itself, it is *actualized idea.* It has Being as its substance. I can only think about logic that way. This idea, actualized at the endpoint of logic, is, like the Absolute, defined at the end of the philosophy of identity as a *unity of the ideal and the real.* But for Hegel, *the Absolute* has the meaning of the now existing idea, which is therefore free *to decide for nature.* The idea is brought into existence and can then decide to go into action [*Handlung*]. *To decide is an* actus. *Therewith another philosophy begins. With the merely logical conclusion ends also rational philosophy.* With the decision of the actually existing idea, rational philosophy is surpassed. In this way, the *preceding* philosophy has become *a dogmatic system.* (For the physicians of old, *system* was synonymous with *stagnation* [*Stockung*].)

That earlier philosophy did not have to formally become a system; it was born with the system, and the system was born in it. Whether the external representation was following the official doctrine [*schulmässig*] did not matter. But a system in this sense, *i.e.,* one that is not assertive, is not how most understand it. Everyone likes to be assertive. One desires a dogmatic *positive* philosophy. In this demand for a dogmatic philosophy can be seen the need for a philosophy that satisfies this desire—*to have a positive philosophy alongside the negative* [*philosophy*].

By first treating the logical from a completely abstract standpoint and then letting it emerge from within it, *Hegel* became the author of a system and therewith assumed a burden that was increasingly oppressive and unbearable. Logic does not lay claim to contain anything actual. It wants to be merely a subjective activity of thought. The activity of thought is alone with itself; it does not even have the world as its content—only itself. The abundance of the concrete world, says *Hegel,* is still outside of him [*ausser ihm*]. The preceding philosophy had the content of nature as a concept, and its result was the logically actualized world and nature. Hegel's logic has the actualized existing idea as its end.

The preceding philosophy had *a priori* concepts (*i.e.*, concepts that were already formed in relation to the actual). In the subsequent philosophy, all relation to something real is taken away; its concepts are *empty* concepts. The preceding philosophy had the actual world as its content. The First, which the ability to have existence determines itself to be, was an actual, *e.g.*, substance [*Materie*]. It had the real *a priori* as concept. The concept was assisted by intuition; it had experience as its guarantee [*Gewähr*] and possible emendations [*Berichtigungen*] at its side and in this way distinguished itself from the pre-Kantian metaphysics. As its general basis (ontology), the latter had a science that only had concepts as concepts for its content.

With the *falling-away from metaphysics that began with Bacon,* ontology lost all meaning;[10] the Germans had to be freed from it by *Kant.* After Kant, they held on to metaphysics but interwove it with experience; *this is the philosophy of nature. The joining of thought to nature is the true accomplishment of the European philosophy of nature.*[11] It corresponds to the tendency of the European spirit in its emancipation from metaphysics. The truly objective logic was laid down in the philosophies of nature and spirit; any logic treated differently was merely subjective.

The *philosophy of nature* was a child of that newer spirit that demanded the real. *The gloomy* spirits took offense at that. Hegel wanted to be *reconciliatory,* but he approached the activity of thought with logic without sensate substrate. The acclamation was understandable, but the philosophy of nature can neither approve it nor consider it an improvement.

One might perhaps object: Somewhere in a complete system, there must also be *concepts as concepts.* Where does

---

10. KG11:11, p. 314: "The metaphysics of pre-Kantian phil. had as its content only the concepts *qua* concepts (ontology), but, since Bacon's fell away from ontology, such a metaphysics lost its significance; all the nations have turned to experience."

11. *Ibid.*: "After Kant, loyalty to metaphysics was maintained, but this did not exclude experience; the phil. of ident. joined thought to nature; thus it had objective logic (Hegel himself of course calls his subjective); for it had a relation to the object. Hegel excluded nature from logic."

the earlier philosophy make room for the treatment of concepts as concepts? It had no place *for those concepts that have the real still outside themselves; it traversed all of nature up to the point* where **the self-possessing subject, the I**, comes to light and no longer finds nature in itself, only its concepts. This is related to the doctrine of innate ideas. Thus, consciousness operates with them as a free possession.[12]

In this way, one could hear in the *first* lecture of this system at which point it arrived at the concepts. There one could find *logical forms derived like natural forms. Here, where the infinite potence itself first became objectified, where it unfolded its objectively set apart organism subjectively as an organism of reason*—here was the place for concepts as such. No different from the corporeal world, these can only be objects of the *a priori* philosophy. The development of a philosophy that attaches itself to a natural progression has the concept itself as something actual, objective; by contrast, *with Hegel the concepts are only subjective. But concepts exist only after nature, not before*; *abstracta* cannot be prior to that from which they are abstracted.

When Hegel wants philosophy to begin by entering into the pure activity of thought, he has expressed accurately the *essence of rational philosophy.* But with Hegel, this withdrawing into the pure activity of thought is only in relation to logic; he does not mean the things, as they are *a priori* in the activity of thought but rather their concepts as such (as subjective concepts). But there is no actual activity of thought with mere concepts. Where the actual activity of thought ought now to begin (at the end of logic), there it is already finished [*ganz am Ende*], for, as Hegel says, the concept loses its power.[13] What does the world gain from

---

12. *Ibid.*: "It has no place for concepts that have the real outside themselves, but, in its successive advance, it must come to the point where it has the concepts as *impressa vestigia* [footprints] in what went before, up to the point where the concepts show themselves as the free possession of consciousness."

13. *Ibid.* "Hegel assigns pure thought to logic, which is thus thought about thought; but such thought finally cancels actual thought. He is either concerned with concepts that are not actual and do not have actual content–and, when he moves on to nature, he then says that

your activity of thought if nothing is produced? It is truly an activity of thought only if something comes of it.

Lest anyone believes that the work itself is to be condemned and the merit of the author denied, it might now be desirable to go *to the core of Hegel's logic* to emphasize the methodological arguments and the acumen manifested in its particulars. *I criticize only the fact that his logic omitted the philosophy of nature and the philosophy of spirit.* His was an absolute logic, an ideal of the pure science of reason. *I understood only much later—and not independently from Hegel—that this entire science had to dissolve into the logical.*

Here *logic* comes into question only as the *science of an actual existing idea,* by which Hegel seeks to get across into existence and which (according to him) has seized the existing Absolute better than the intellectual intuition. Hegel wants to let the Absolute result from science before using it as a principle. *What it thus results in* and becomes is not objective. The objective becoming of the idea begins only after it has become self-conscious. But as one that has existence actually, it is already at the limit of the logical. Also, there is no moving forward with it; else one finds oneself outside of the logical, so that it must leave its position as result and pass over into the illogical, indeed into the world that is directly opposite.

This directly opposite world is nature. It is no longer *a priori* nature, which would have been dealt with in logic, but rather empirical nature, which can no longer be grasped conceptually but requires to be explicated. But there is no movement by which the idea could progress within itself or fully break away from itself. That which is unfinished and unconscious of itself moves necessarily, but *the idea is subject-object, as ideal-real, and does not have a desire to become anything further.*

If it is assumed that the idea is seeking another reality, then only because nature is still there. Against the complete idea, nature is something superfluous, accidental. No such thing should exist in the philosophy of reason; there

---

the concept has lost its power; thus he really has actual thought nowhere."

everything should be *modo aeterno* [in the mode of eternity]. When Hegel says that the idea, in its infinite freedom, decides to *empty itself* [*entläßt sich*], etc. (see §244 in the third edition of his *Encyclopedia*),[14] this could be a timid expression for the idea positing itself as Being-Other [*Andersseyns*] (*release* is an expression of passive emanation). In any case, here the doubt sets in: Did Hegel understand idea as existing in actuality? Obviously, a mere concept cannot "make a decision."

We have no hostile intentions, but the difficulty of a transition from logic into the philosophy of nature cannot be concealed. I'd like to show *a way out.* There ought to be no talk of the actually existing nature and its explication [*Erklärung*][15] in the pure science of reason but rather only as it is *a priori. The explication of that which has existence is to be left to another science, the positive one.* Yet the science of reason retains a powerful content: *that of the entire actual world of possibilities.* At the beginning of his philosophy, *Hegel* himself was not so far from the significance assigned to the Absolute by the negative philosophy. Consider the last §§ in the first edition of the *Encyclopedia.*[16] But even before those §§, he denoted

---

14. Georg Wilhelm Friedrich Hegel, *Encyclopädie der philosophischen Wissenschaften im Grundrisse,* 3rd ed. (Heidelberg, 1830), §244: "Yet the absolute *freedom* of the idea is that it does not merely *pass over into life* [...] but rather, that it *decides* in the absolute truth of itself *to empty itself* freely out of itself as *nature* [sich als *Natur* frei aus *sich zu entlassen*]."

15. *Cf.* Immanuel Kant's *Kritik der Urteilskraft* (Critique of the Power of Judgment), §78 (*Kant's Werke* [Berlin: Georg Reimer, 1913], 5:412): "To explicate [*erklären*] [*e.g.,* in the judging of nature] means to derive from a principle, which one must therefore cognize distinctly and able to declare."

16. Hegel, *Encyclopädie der philosophischen Wissenschaften im Grundrisse,* 1st ed. (Heidelberg, 1817), §476: "This appearance is sublated in *the second syllogism,* wherein the spirit is the mediating agency;—a syllogism that is already the standpoint of the spirit itself, which *presupposes* nature and joins it together with the *logical.* It is the syllogism of *reflexion* in the *idea;* science appears as a subjective *cognition.*"

Ibid., §477: "These appearances are sublated in the idea of philosophy, which has *self-knowing reason,* the absolutely universal, for its *middle,* a middle that divides into spirit and nature, making the

nature as a *falling-away* [*Abfall*] *from the idea.*[17] (In my writing, this expression appears only in the 1804 *Philosophy and Religion,* where it was meant to express a different conviction than the one expressed in the 1802 *Bruno.*)[18] A third publication was supposed to resolve the contradiction between them. *Alas, it did not happen!*[19] It was indeed the contradiction between the negative and the positive philosophy that then began to stir;[20] and therein, just as in the "deciding" of the idea, Hegel's philosophy already contains a fragment of "historical" philosophy.

Meanwhile, the idea has now thrown itself into nature, not to remain there but rather to become, through it, spirit again.[21] *The*

---

former the presupposition, and the latter the general extreme. As such, nature is posited unmediatedly, just as spirit is in itself, not the presupposition but the totality that has returned to itself. In this way, the middle, the knowing concept, as such has those conceptual moments as its reality and is as the universal in its determinateness the knowledge that adheres to itself unmediatedly."

17. *Ibid.*, §193: "Nature in general has been defined, with reason, as the *falling-away* [*Abfall*] of the idea because in the elements of outwardness it has the definition of its own inadequacy [*Unangemessenheit*]."

18. *Philosophie und Religion* (Philosophy and Religion), SWVI, pp. 11–70; *Bruno oder über das göttliche und natürliche Princip der Dinge* (Bruno or On the Divine and Natural Principle of Things), SWIV, pp. 213–332.

19. "When I published *Bruno or On the Divine and Natural Principle of Things* in 1802, it was meant to be the beginning of a series of publications in the form of philosophical conversations whose topics were already proposed therein. For some time now, a second conversation has been lacking only its final redaction; however, external circumstances have not permitted its completion" (*Philosophie und Religion,* SWVI, p. 13).

20. "It seems to me that we should further discuss the institution of the mystery cults and the nature of mythology. And it seems perfectly appropriate that Bruno [...] speak about the kind of philosophy he believes to be taught by the mystery cults [...] And then [...] spell out the allegories and actions that might be used to represent such a cult. And finally let one of us, or all of us together, [...] tackle the discussion of poetry and mythology" (*Bruno,* SWIV, p. 234).

21. See Hegel, *Encyclopädie* (1st ed.), §476: "The logical *becomes* nature, and nature becomes spirit. Nature, which stands between the spirit and its essence does not divide them into extremes of finite abstraction, for the syllogism is *in the idea,* and nature is defined essentially only as point of passage [*Durchgangspunkt*] and negative

human spirit, however, is only the arena where the spirit, through its own doing, is working off its subjectivity and *at last becomes the absolute spirit, which absorbs all moments and is God.*

Here again, the peculiarity of Hegel stands out nowhere sharper than by comparison with the *earlier* philosophy, which was *reproached* for *having defined God as substance, not as spirit.* I will not dispute whether, as a result, *the Absolute* was called spirit in the previous philosophy. The word *spirit* surely would have had a more edifying ring to it. For the matter at hand, it was sufficient for *God* to be the *subsisting subject-object.* For he was thus also ὁ ἑαυτὸν νοῶν [that which thinks itself], *spirit by essence,* not substance as one that blindly has Being [*Blind-seyendes*].

One cannot overlook that it is only as substance that the spirit can be posited in the pure science of reason. The word *spirit* was reserved for the actual spirit. The God *who is only an end,* who has no future, and who cannot say, "I will be!"—who is only *final cause, not principle*—that God is spirit only by nature, by essence. He is spirit only in substance.

Also, when Hegel kept within the boundaries of logic, only a substantial meaning could remain, since he could not get away from the end, taking in all prior moments only conclusively [*beschliessend*] in itself. Setting out from logic, where everything follows only *aeterno modo* [from the perspective of eternity], Hegel arrives at empirical nature. Therefore, he does not have *the idea of God at the end of the movement but instead the actual God as a real result of the movement*—as a result of the entire movement pervading nature and spirit. One is obliged to say: What emerges at the end is already *a* or *the* beginning. *However, God must be one at the beginning and another at the end.* At the beginning, he is only the beginning; at the end, he is the end of himself. *The whole is the process of self-realization* in the sense that in the early stage he is still incomplete and subjected to an external [*aussernhafte*] development.

---

moment; but the mediation of the concept has the external form of the passing-over [*Uebergehens*] and science, that of a *Being.*"

Philosophy burdened itself by needlessly taking what was *merely* a logical progression for a real one. Hegel then asserts, in the second edition of his *Logic,*[22] that the Last [*das Letzte*], wherein everything becomes grounded, is rather *that* from which all comes forth, so that the absolute spirit, as the most concrete and highest truth of Being, surrenders itself and, emptying itself freely at the end of the development, is thought to resolve itself into the creation of a world, which contains everything that fell within the development; if such an inversion were possible, Hegel would be positing a *second* philosophy alongside his philosophy. One would then have to descend the same steps one otherwise would have ascended. But since Hegel himself makes possible the free self-emptying [*Entäusserung*], the free effectuating [*Wirken*], only at the end of the development, he thus has it at the end not yet as one that effectuates but only as an end cause of the entire movement, as a cause not by its own effectuating but by the fact that everything gravitates toward it.

---

22. Georg Wilhelm Friedrich Hegel, *The Science of Logic,* trans. George di Giovanni (Cambridge: Cambridge University Press, 2010), p. 49 (21.57): "It must be admitted that it is an essential consideration—one that will be found elaborated again within the logic itself—that *progression* is a retreat to the *ground,* to the *origin* and the *truth* on which that with which the beginning was made, and from which it is in fact produced, depends.—Thus consciousness, on its forward path from the immediacy with which it began, is led back to the absolute knowledge that is its innermost *truth.* This truth, the ground, is then also that from which the original first proceeds, the same first that at the beginning came on the scene as something unmediated.—It is most of all in this way that absolute spirit (which is revealed as the concrete and supreme truth of all being) comes to be known, as at the *end* of the development it freely externalizes itself, letting itself go into the shape of an *immediate* being—resolving itself into the creation of a world that contains all that fell within the development preceding that result and that, through this reversal of position with its beginning, is converted into something dependent on the result as principle. Essential to science is not so much that a pure immediacy should be the beginning but that the whole of science is in itself a circle in which the first becomes also the last, and the last also the first.

Conversely, it follows that it is just as necessary to consider as *result* that into which the movement returns as to its *ground.*"

The Last is, of course, *also the highest final cause,* but the entire movement is only a steady sequence of final causes. If we go back, then the inorganic nature is the final cause for matter—the organic for the inorganic, the animal nature for the plant world, and Man for the animal world. If now, by inversion, the Absolute becomes the effectuating cause, then the animal world would appear as the effectuating cause for Man, *etc.* We do not know how far Hegel would have wanted this to be pursued.

It would also be rather illusory to transform, by inversion, the first philosophy into one that teaches a free Creation of the world. About the last point, Hegel always expressed himself cautiously *in order to avoid the misfortune of becoming popularized.* The latest that is now *circulating* is that it is actually God, the absolute spirit, who empties himself into the world. With this, the realm of pure rational science has been left behind. The self-emptying is a free act that herewith approaches a *historical* philosophy. But it is canceled again by being an eternal act [*ewiger Act*]. God is free to empty himself into nature, but free to immolate his freedom. From this point on, he is in *process,* or *he himself* is *the process.* He is the God of eternal doings [*Thuns*], but he does only what he has always done; his life is in a cycle of forms [*Gestalten*] in which he keeps emptying and withdrawing himself.[23]

In the last version, this theory tends to be explicated as: while God is by itself the Absolute, even beforehand [*zuvor*], in order to become self-conscious, he empties himself, posits the world as another before him, ascends from the lowest stage of self-emptying to that of Man in whose consciousness of God [*Gottesbewusstsein*] he has the knowledge of himself. *This is really the lowest grade of popularizing.* This going on about his ideas [*Breittreten*] does not redound to Hegel's honor. There is barely a trace of his original mind left. Now theology is to be reformed with these *disfigured* doctrines.

---

23. KG 11:13, p. 317: "This account seeks to assume historic form, but when it adds that 'it has always happened and always will happen,' it is once again annulled. God is free insofar as he always sacrifices his freedom; he is im Proces and is Selbst-Proces, who always does what he always has done—a cycle."

God the Father, before the Creation, is the logical concept; he has to reveal himself, empty himself, and is the world (God is the Son), but God must again sublate [*aufheben*] this self-emptying and return to himself; this happens through the human spirit, which is also the divine spirit. Few would be inclined to accept those deductions; at the least, they are not commensurate with the content of Christianity. The philosophy of reason ought to be neither un-Christian nor Christian. It is to be rebuked for trying to be Christian; it simply does not require it.

An aside to the just mentioned deduction needs to be touched upon: *art, religion, and philosophy were designated in it as moments through which the spirit that emptied itself into nature returns to itself.*[24] In the philosophy of identity, similarly, art and religion are designated as the last moments. Hegel accuses it of having regarded *art alone as the Absolute, which is only the Absolute in the sensate idea.* That toward the end art is also joined by religion is not mentioned. But how could this philosophy, which has been considering so many things, not have considered *religion*? Already the *System of Transcendental Idealism* (1800) proves otherwise.[25]

"But the philosophy of identity has neglected to posit philosophy as the Last."—Surely, this is not an extraordinary thought, one even I can be trusted to have, *that philosophy would posit itself in the final reflection.* But in what way could art, religion, and philosophy occur in the earlier philosophy? The philosophy of identity arrived, through nature, at the world of individual actions and the universally free movement of humanity (history); and here it was pushed toward the idea of a power [*Macht*] that does not lose itself

---

24. "Art, religion, and philosophy, these are the three spheres of human activity, in which the highest spirit as such manifests itself." *Zur Geschichte der neueren Philosophie,* SW X, p. 119.

25. See Schelling's section on "Religion within the transcendental idealism" in his *System des transcendentalen Idealismus* (System of Transcendental Idealism), SW III, p. 601: "If reflexion [*Reflexion*] rises up to that Absolute, the mutual ground for the harmony between freedom and intellect, then the system of providence, *i.e.*, religion, in the only true sense of the word, emerges."

to Being and does not descend into the process—"*that which has supra-Being [das Ueberseyende]*"—God.

At first, this concept was called for only in the sense, as in the entire line, of being the last concept only as concept. Nothing yet stepped out of line. But this concept is not like any other. In view of it, nothing can occur in experience;—here we find only the potence of Being transformed into Being. Yet we are not indifferent to this concept; rather, in view of it, existence is being called for [*gefordert*]. A subjective or moral necessity presents itself [*einfinden*], which is no reason for rational philosophy to go beyond itself. It cannot regard it as a proof of itself. It remains within itself, but the consequence of this moral necessity is that while keeping within its limitation, it calls for externally what it cannot have internally. And here comes as the First whereby Man actualizes for himself "*that which has supra-Being* "—*religion, art, and philosophy; however, only philosophy can be the positive one.*

Rational philosophy still cognizes *different possibilities to assure itself of the existence of that which has supra-Being.* The first [possibility] is that Man makes that which has supra-Being for himself exist in his practical life by abolishing all contingent Being in him. This possibility is actualized only in subjective religion, which is linked fully to the individual and cannot be separated from the askesis that stands in opposition to all sciences and does not comprehend the objective appearance of religion.

Rational philosophy does not know of the rational religion that is sometimes *evoked* by rationalists without ever representing it, especially one that would be a science. Religion appears in it but as a transgressing moment, and only in that subjective form that does not require science but rather is only askesis, praxis, *etc.*

This first possibility for seizing the existence of that which has supra-Being is opposed by the other, which conjures up that spirit that is raised above all matter, indeed is empowered to create all matter in order to reveal itself with objective creations, with real productions. This spirit first reveals itself in the fine arts. The highest truth of the plastic arts is in their having been brought forth by the creative spirit. Of all the arts, poetry is the truly creative one. In it, the spirit that remains *above* Being announces itself. In tragedy, in the darkening storms of passions, *etc.,* the poet appears as the wise providence that can lead contradictions to a conclusion. *Rational philosophy* may acknowledge as necessary those striving for actualizing that which has supra-Being not merely logically but actually transgressing; but it treats art as objective,[26] as being outside of itself. It does not view it as identical with itself or as something it itself desires. That which it desires for itself and views for itself not merely as possibility (which it would have to surrender to the other spheres for actualization to remain identical with itself) can only be *a second philosophy,* one that posits rational philosophy *not outside itself* but *above* itself.

In the philosophy of reason, religion and art occur only as possibilities to rise to a *third,* which it views no longer as a mere possibility but assumes to be identical with itself—*a second philosophy,* which recognizes it as a task and only then resolves itself. Thus *negative* philosophy ends in a demand for a *positive* philosophy, one in which that which has supra-Being is actualized both objectively, as in art, and subjectively into unmediated certainty, as in religion.[27]

Hegel's exposition ends with three stages: the religion of art, revealed religion, and philosophy.[28] Revealed religion is included

---

26. *Zur Geschichte der neueren Philosophie,* SWX, p. 118: "If art is the most objective side of human activity, then *religion* is the subjective side of it, insofar as the latter does not, unlike the former, move toward positing a *Being* [*Seyn*] but rather in relation to that highest subject, toward positing all that has Being as not having Being [*alles Seyende als nicht seyend*]."

27. KG 11: 4, p. 319: "Positive philosophy is therefore required by negative philosophy. Negative philosophy posits positive philosophy outside itself."

28. Hegel, *Encyclopädie,* 1st ed. (1817), heading above §456. See KG 11: 14, p. 319: "(In the second edition of the *Encyclopädie,* however, the expression 'religion of art' is changed to 'art' alone; and in any case it is only in an improper sense that this expression can be justified.) The difference, then, is that 'religion' appears twice here."

in rational science, but *revelation presupposes a real relationship of the human consciousness to God prior to the actual God. Rational science cannot include this revelation even as a possibility*—just like subjective religion, of which Hegel knows nothing.

The philosophy posited last by Hegel is simply the one from which he came from. But rational science has already been transgressed with art and religion; how could it fall back from there into itself? Philosophy does not merely posit itself again in its demand for a second philosophy; instead, it posits something different from it, something both *outside of itself* and *identical with itself.*

When a *positive* philosophy was first announced in my lectures, some believed they had to come to the defense of the negative philosophy, as if I had taken *Hegel's philosophy* for a negative one. *In fact, I have always taken it for a positive philosophy. After all, it ascribes to a full cognition of God.* I have only fought against the kind of a philosophy that inflates itself into a positive one and boasts of borrowed riches rather than honorable poverty. The negative philosophy will receive its due and no longer encroach on the territory of a positive philosophy.

Some have wanted to explain my proposition of a positive philosophy as a change of mind. But since my studies of the Kantian philosophy, it has been clear to me that the latter could not be the whole of philosophy. I wrote in my "Letter on Dogmatism and Criticism" (1795) that a mightier, more majestic dogmatism would rise up against Kant's criticism, and this was the positive philosophy.[29] Thus, *the notion of a positive philosophy* has been inscribed in me for a long time.

The old metaphysics was *dogmatizing,*[30] and it was destroyed irrevocably by Kant; however, Kant does not reach

---

29. *Philosophische Briefe über Dogmatismus und Kriticismus* (Philosophical Letters on Dogmatism and Criticism), *SW* I, p. 303: "Anyone who has read attentively what the *Critique* says about practical postulates must surely admit that it leaves an open field for dogmatism to erect its edifice safely and durably."

30. KG11:14, p. 319: "In the Kantian period, the expression 'dogmatism' was used. Subsequently, this fell in Verruf [into disrepute].

all the way to the actual dogmatic philosophy. The old metaphysics was a positive rationalism that Kant's *Critique* dissolved. This dissolution held out the prospect of a *pure rationalism* (not a negative one since it can only be negative in contrast to a positive one), one that was already contained materially in Kant's *Critique.*[31] *It leaves to reason only the concept of God,* and it also makes no exception with the concept of God, so that it also only contains the *What.* Trying to get to existence by way of syllogisms is a futile endeavor. Kant grants reason only the science that embraces the essence of things; it takes the place of metaphysics. But he also extends what was said about reason to philosophy. *Whether, however,* after the demolition of the old metaphysics, *the other, positive element is negated completely or instead becomes free and independent within its own science, was the further question.*

Surrounded by much that was accidental, that pure rationalism was only indirectly contained in Kant's *Critique.* The more decisively all that is positive was excluded, the more that which was incited by Kant was completed. The first to be summoned to represent this pure rationalism had to put it forward as a purpose. And yet this was only done so that reason would be freed from that element with which it was forced together in the previous metaphysics.

But once I had the system of pure rationalism in front of me, the thought of a free science, which would shape the positive element, had to fall upon my soul. I abandoned that rational system, leaving it to others to throw themselves at an orphaned system. For me, that philosophy had merely been a transition. With a pure heart, I sought the next possible philosophy after Kant; I was far from accepting it as the whole of

---

A distinction must be drawn, however, between a dogmatizing and a dogmatic phil. The older metaphysics was dogmatizing and therefore never achieved what it aimed at, a rational demonstration of existence; therefore, it remained merely dogmatizing. This was destroyed by Kant, fully and forever."

31. *Einleitung in die Philosophie der Offenbarung*, *SW* XIII, p. 46: "By destroying the old metaphysics, Kant became at the same time the creator of an entirely new science since, under the modest name of a critique of pure reason, he claimed to have established a complete and exhaustive theory of the human faculty of cognition."

philosophy, as Hegel had done.[32] In my *Memorial to Jacobi* (1812),[33] the beginnings of a positive philosophy were given; the bold paradoxes found therein point to it.[34] With my silence, I allowed the other direction of thought the freedom to develop.

The main argument of Hegel's defenders is this: a rational philosophy is necessary, especially for the grounding of a positive philosophy.—Philosophy completes itself through both rational philosophy and positive philosophy, but in positive philosophy there is a very different *modus progrediendi* [mode of progressing]. Also, its grounding takes place only if the negative philosophy passes on its subject as already cognized to the positive philosophy. But the Last remains uncognized. The negative philosophy does not have to prove the object as one that has existence; the end of one is not the beginning of the other. The negative philosophy passes on its *Last* to the subsequent philosophy only

32. *Ibid.*, p. 86: "The more purely the negative philosophy was posited, the more forcefully the positive had to rise up in opposition to it, and it seemed as if nothing was being done until the latter had been found as well. This might explain how, almost unmediatedly after the first presentation of the system that emerged out of the *Critique,* it was abandoned, as it were, by its author and left for the time being to those who stood ready to appropriate it, who, as Plato would say, were drawn by the luster of the vacated position to leap at it avidly."

33. Schelling's polemical reply to Friedrich Heinrich Jacobi's book *Von den göttlichen Dingen und ihrer Offenbarung* (*Of Divine Things and Their Revelation*), published in 1811 as *F.W.J. Schellings Denkmal der Schrift von den göttlichen Dingen des Herrn Friedrich Heinrich Jacobi und der ihm in derselben gemachten Beschuldigung eines absichtlich täuschenden, Lüge redenden Atheismus* (F.W.J. Schelling's Memorial to Mr. Friedrich Heinrich Jacobi's Writing on the Divine Things and to the Accusation Made Against Him Therein Regarding an Intentional Deceiving and Lying Atheism), *SW* VIII, pp. 19-136.

34. *Einleitung in die Philosophie der Offenbarung, SW* XIII, p. 86: "And if I allowed the positive philosophy, even after it was found, to be revealed at the most through hints, through the well-known paradoxes of a polemical essay against Jacobi, then I believe that also this restraint was to be praised more than to be reprimanded."

as a task, not as a principle. The positive philosophy has to acquire the means to be adequate to the task itself.

The former rises to the demand only to complete itself. As a science that is itself a desire [*Wollen*], positive philosophy can begin without it. *Its beginning is of a kind that is incapable of founding* [*Begründung*]. By its very concept, its beginning is an absolute beginning while the beginning of the negative philosophy transforms itself into an Other; it is exposed to a necessary overthrow. It is not *principle.*

This *duality of philosophies* has long been present in the rational system, which sought to posit difference into one. What difficulties have arisen from that very fact to give a sufficient definition of philosophy! Withdrawing into pure activity of thought is what the negative philosophy does; *however, existence demands to be explicated as well.* Neither side ought to be suppressed, nor should one become commingled with the other. Besides, it can be proven that both lines have been present in philosophy from the beginning, and wherever a conflict arose between them, they persisted alongside each other.

VI. Historical Examples of Negative and Positive Philosophy

[PL, pp. 397-408]

Aristotle may have understood "theologians" to mean those *who were still under the influence of divine inspiration*[1]—the *Orphics* or authors of the παλαιῶν λόγων [ancient discourse].[2] There is *one* place, however, where he also speaks of theologians as being philosophers.[3] Those can only be *positive philosophers who derive the world from an actually existing God.*

The *Ionian physicists,* Heraclitus *et al.,* derived everything from reason. The idea that "all things flow" can only have come from a science of reason. What is subject at one moment becomes object the next: "All things give way."[4]

The Eleatics, who sought to *explicate* everything through logic, *also belong to this rational philosophy.* Aristotle said that the Eleatic philosophy only excites fraud, since mere movement in thought excludes all reality. When the logical tries to *explicate* that which is actual, this philosophy appears to be fighting actuality and remains in *one* place.

Already *Socrates* directed *dialectic,* which for him was only an implement of destruction—far from being something positive—not only against the Sophists but *also against the rational pseudo-knowledge of the Eleatics.* In *Plato,* Sophists and Eleatics are very closely related. *Socrates's dialectic* was directed as much against the shallowness of the Sophists as against the *bombast of the Eleatics.* The means to that were for him his questions, which intended to make those inflated by

---

1. Kierkegaard writes this as "oracles, etc" (KG11:15, p. 320).

2. See Plato, *Timaeus,* 21*a*: "It is an old tale, and I heard it from a man not young" (trans. W.R.M Lamb).

3. Aristotle, *Metaphysics,* A 982*b*: "The myth-lover is in a sense a philosopher, since myths are composed of wonders" (trans. Hugh Tredennick).

4. Plato, *Cratylus,* 402*a*: "Heraclitus says [...] that all things move and nothing remains still" (trans. Harold N. Fowler).

the Eleatics' and Sophists' diet of pseudo-knowledge receptive to true knowledge. When Socrates said, in regard to his relationship to others, that "all others were as ignorant as he was, but unlike them, he knew that he was ignorant," he was *not* denying himself *all* knowledge; rather, he was not accepting as actual knowledge the kind of knowledge that the others (the Eleatics) were boasting of. *The activity of thought is not yet knowledge; it only becomes knowledge when it passes over to the object. The knowledge that does not have knowledge [nichtwissende Wissen] is cognitive knowledge [Denkwissen],* just as geometry, according to Plato, is διάνοια [thought], not ἐπιστήμη [knowledge].[5]

Socrates posits *a positive science that has knowledge [wissende Wissenschaft]* apart from the logical science, which seeks to explicate reality. And therewith the confession of his ignorance gains a *positive* meaning. There is still a veil over the person of Socrates (this is not the place to lift it!), who stood at the boundary between the logical and the positive sciences! Averse to common mythology, he sought a historical connection that is higher than one that solely contains actual knowledge.[6]

---

5. According to Plato, understanding lies between opinion and reason. See *Republic,* 511*d.*

6. *Einleitung in die Philosophie der Offenbarung,* SWXIII, pp. 99–100: "Evidently, Socrates presupposes a knowledge to which the mere science of reason relates only as not-knowing [*Nichtwissen*]. Here, however, is not the place to demonstrate fully the actual desire [*Wollen*] of this most unique man who has, not without reason, incurred the hate and aversion of Sophists of all time, all the way to the present. There is a veil over his inner glory that has not yet been fully lifted; however, from what has survived, one can conclude that his spirit lingered precisely at the boundary between the merely logical and the positive. One indication not to be dismissed is how he used to give everything in his *doctrine,* or whatever deserved the name of a doctrine (*e.g.,* continuity after death), not merely a mythical, *i.e.,* historical, interpretation; averse to common mythology, he sought instead a *higher* historical context, as if only *the latter* contained actual knowledge." See also *Philosophie der Mythologie,* SWXII, p. 284: "Socrates's greatness was that he was conscious of the fact that certain questions do not allow for rational answers, merely historical ones. He would have quite happily posited actual

Plato, who at the culmination of his philosophy (in the *Timaeus*) becomes *historical,* more than anyone attested to this position of Socrates. Here he breaks through to the *positive,* if only by force. However, it is more of a breaking free from the dialectic than an actual transition. The attitudes of Socrates and Plato toward this *positive* were prospective in nature only.

However, *Aristotle*—with whom philosophy has purged itself of all its prophetic elements—turned away from the logical and toward the empirical, whereby the "*That*" became the First and the "*What*" the Second. He turned away from the merely logical, insofar as it wants to be explicatory—thus positive. He reproached those who by being only ἐν τοῖς λόγοις [in theory][7] wanted to nonetheless comprehend actuality. He even extended this reproach to Plato's *Timaeus* and the μέδεξις [participation].[8] When used to explain actual origination [*Entstehen*], the μέδεξις is empty. It is only applicable with respect to a possible explication; and it was for this reason Aristotle called this activity κενολογεῖν [empty talk].[9] He countered that getting from the logical form to reality, from the general to the individual, was a big leap; he accused them of reversing the formal principles of Being and confusing the actual path with that of science.

Nothing so agrees with the position of the negative philosophy as understood by us as Aristotle's philosophy. The *a priori* character of the philosophy of reason relates to that which has Being and, at least according to its content, goes above the empirical. That which has passed over into Being becomes relinquished as content of the activity of thought; it is excluded from being the possible object of an empirical cognizance that exceeds the activity of thought. In the philosophy of reason, that which is excluded serves as a step

---

history in place of myths had he not lacked much of the necessary data we now possess."

7. See Aristotle, *Metaphysics,* Z1938*b*.

8. A term used by Plato for the sharing and participation of things in ideas (see Plato, *Parmenides,* 132*d*).

9. See KG11:16, p. 322: "[Aristotle] criticizes Plato's doctrine of the participation of things in the idea, calling it κενολογεῖν." See also Aristotle, *Metaphysics* A991*a*.

toward a higher level, until finally the necessary activity of thought—which is in a mutual interrelation with necessary cognizance (experience)—arrives finally at the object with which the activity of thought sees itself freely.

The *a priori* excludes the empirical as little as the empirical is free of the *a priori*; rather, the empirical stands with one foot in the *a priori*. (The essence of everything belongs to it.) *Just* as *there is a path from the logical to the empirical, there is also a path from the empirical to the* a priori. This path was followed by *Aristotle* in the broadest manner. He developed an actual application of the general *categories*, which treated the entire history of philosophy as an object of his analytical cognition and explored nature in all directions; thus he ascended step by step to the first philosophy.[10]

The Aristotelian philosophy is of a spirit that has been cleansed of all elements of nature and the human mind by the fire of the purest analysis. Following this path, Aristotle had to converge eventually with the negative philosophy. In an ascending progression, he begins with the potence wherein all opposites are enveloped; from there, nature rises step by step toward the end to which it is attracted. On each step, the sequence has the subsequent final cause as its goal. For the sequence, he says, cannot continue on into infinity; there has to be a final goal. The potence (ὕλη [matter])[11] is cast aside in the same proportion as it is approaching the goal. The Last is τὸ ἐνεργεία ὄν [in actuality], the potence surpassed wholly by the *actus*, which is the highest expression of the whole and is beyond having being for itself.

For Aristotle, the Last is therefore that which has existence in actuality, but only because for him all of science is grounded in experience. For him the whole world is the actual; however, for him it is not about the actual but about

10. KG 11:16, p. 322: "Aristotle walked this path, ascending step by step to his first science, or first philosophy. For both names appear (πρώτηἐ πιστήμη, πρώτη φιλοσοφία [first science, first philosophy])." See Aristotle, *Metaphysics* E 1026*a*.

11. KG 11:16, p. 322: "ὕλη, matter (which, in Aristotle, is potency and must not be understood as merely physical; thus there is mention of matter in a [logical] conclusion)."

the *What.* The Last is thus to him only that which according to its nature (not according to existence) is the *actus purus.*[12] For this reason, Aristotle does not make use of the Last as one that has existence in actuality. He takes it only as αἴτιον τελικόν [final cause], not as ποιητικόν [motive cause], so that he does try to make it again a beginning that effectuates; for him, it remains an end. All is only movement toward this goal; when he tries to explain the movement of the heavenly bodies, he explains it through ὄρεξις [desire], a longing that the lower causes feel toward the highest. This is an ἐρώμενον [object of desire] that moves while it itself is not being moved,[13] cut off as the thoroughly immobile heavy bodies. God is ἄπρακτος [inactive], incapable of externally directed effect and only able to think everlastingly and only of himself. Thus he is the subject-object who is, remains, and no longer moves away from himself.

Those who see only arbitrariness in the course of philosophy have not noticed how, after thousands of years, the same concepts reappear. *The author of the philosophy of identity knew very little of Aristotle at the time.* This proves the necessity of such concepts.

Properly—that is, separately from the νόησις [activity of thought]—God is to Aristotle no longer νοῦς [intellect or mind]. It was only with the help of various intermediate concepts, *e.g.*, that this highest essence [*höchste Wesen*] had to be *the most blessed,* that Aristotle succeeded in positing this *actus* as an *actus* of the activity of thought. *Of all* actus, *however, the most blessed is the activity of thought.* But now, *what does this highest essence think?* To think of another would be beneath its dignity; hence it thinks of *itself.* This should express only the infinity of the *actus,* how onward into infinity, it encounters nothing extraneous, only the *actus,* the activity of thinking. With this, Aristotle attempted to express the absolute exclusion of all potentialities.

---

12. KG 11:16, p. 322: "Nevertheless, it is not das [that] but was [what] that principally occupies his mind."

13. See Aristotle, *Metaphysics,* Λ 1072*a*26-*b*3.

The summit of ancient philosophy—a peculiar combination of the logical and the actual—was reached with Aristotle. Not until the *Neo-Platonists,* who belonged to a new age, was another attempt made to restore that tendency, to proceed from Plato in particular toward a positive philosophy.

Even today, the path of Aristotle—a progression from that which has existence to the logical—would be the only path for philosophy if the God of Aristotle were enough for us.[14] But we have a deeper consciousness of God, not just because of Christianity but also because of mythology. For Aristotle, *mythology* had no value. That he did not concern himself with it shows that he did not find in it—nor in any other religion—a source of truthful experience.

So why were Charlemagne's academies founded on the writings of Aristotle? Aristotle did not know of God as a principle, and he excluded any effectual providence.[15] *Providence exists only to the extent that everything moves toward God and nothing happens that has not been determined by this final goal.* The reason those academies were not founded on Plato's philosophy lies in *the indeterminateness of the Platonic ideas.* In fact, nothing less than pure Aristotelian philosophy was taught in those academies.[16] The negative philosophy assimilates Christianity no more purely than Christianity can be combined with an Aristotelian philosophy without altering it.

Scholastic metaphysics took the place of Aristotelian philosophy. In it, at least, there was *reason.* It presupposed three sources of cognition: (1) *experience*; (2) the κοιναὶ ἔννοίαι, which are *partly innate concepts*—the *ens universale* [universal Being], being the highest among them—and partly *the prin-*

---

14. *Einleitung in die Philosophie der Offenbarung,* SW XIII, p. 107: "To reach an *actually* existing God, in the absence of a positive philosophy, Aristotle's path would still be, even today, the only way to start out from the empirical to that which is in experience, insofar as it exists, to the logical, to the content of Being."

15. *Ibid.,* p. 108: "Aristotle, however, knew of no other God than the one that could be used as a principle from which to explain the world."

16. KG 11:16, p. 323: "There is, however, another answer, and Aristotelian philosophy has never been taught in its pure form."

ciples that have the character of universality and necessity—causality being the most important and necessary among them; and (3) *syllogism of reason*[17] [*Vernunftschluss*]. The latter was for the Scholastic philosophers a special and highest source of cognition insofar as the syllogism comes forth by taking an existential fact as basis if an universal principle is applied.

In this philosophy, *rationalism* was restricted to formal functions. Neither rationalism nor empiricism could emerge freely. It was an artificial composite of disparate concepts held together by the authoritative power of the Church.

The freely emerging empiricism[18] denied the truth of universal principles (*Locke* and *Hume*). *Therewith, all dogmatic rationalism was impossible* (even before *Kant* began its methodical destruction) *because experience and universal principles became doubtable.* Syllogisms also became eliminated. Here we see apostasy from dogmatism for unconditional empiricism—an apostasy only Leibniz was still able to hold off until, at last, *Kant* put an end to that also in German philosophy.

---

17. KG 11: 17, p. 323: "*ratiocinium* [reasoning]."
18. KG 11: 17, p. 323: "after the Reformation."

VII. The Relation of Rational and Positive Philosophy to Empiricism

[PL, pp. 408-15]

Ever since Kant, a pure empiricism (coming from other nations) has opposed the pure rationalism in Germany. But if one goes back to the source of this empiricism, one notices something more profound at its core. How else to explain the religious conscientiousness and persistence of these examinations and the importance with which seemingly insignificant facts are ascertained than with, at the least, a dark awareness that there is more to these facts than the facts themselves,—with a feeling that tells the enthusiastic naturalist that this self-purifying empiricism will at some point encounter a higher system, one that represents itself as resulting equally from the activity of thought and from experience?[1]

Ultimately, an *objective reason* (*logic*), which pure rationalism will strive to seize upon in the activity of thought, will impose itself on this empiricism. There must be a point where the *potences* thus removed of human knowledge, *thinking* and *experiencing*, interpenetrate and form *one* indomitable whole. This was also Bacon's last thought. Now, of course, the true philosophers of England and France are their naturalists. *German rationalism, on the other hand, is not exclusionary; it encompasses both the facts of nature and the great thoughts of history.*

What is the current relationship of empiricism to the positive philosophy? In the context of philosophical empiricism, *experience* is usually understood as *the certainty we obtain of the external world through our external and internal senses.* However, if empiricism becomes exclusionary, then it denies all

1. *Einleitung in die Philosophie der Offenbarung,* SW XIII, p. 110: "Anyone who looks at this eagerness of the exploration of *pure* facts, especially in the natural sciences, cannot help but recognize in it something higher, even if only active on an instinctual level, a thought that stands in the background, a drive that goes beyond an immediate goal."

universal concepts, even moral ones (*e.g.*, as accustomed through education). But it would be wrong to connect all this necessarily with empiricism.[2] *There is another empiricism, one that does not dispute universal concepts and is not restricted to that which is under the purview of the senses* [*das Sinnfällige*].

A freely desiring and active intelligence does not fall under the purview of the senses; yet it is cognizable empirically—indeed *only* empirically. It is from their expressions and actions, more than anything else, that what defines humans can be extrapolated. Providing that we are dealing with an intelligence that is set before the world, it will be cognizable only through its actions, which fall into the realm of experience.

Empiricism does not exclude extrasensory cognition; *there is also a metaphysical empiricism* (not merely a sensualism).[3] *E.g.*, the doctrine that asserts that all philosophy must be grounded in divine revelation (which is now called *Christian philosophy*) is to be regarded as empiricism; then the doctrine that, by transgressing any merely external historical fact, reduces all convictions of God's existence to a *feeling* by asserting that all reason leads to atheism.[4]

As metaphysical empiricism of an even higher order are to be considered those doctrines that pretend to possess the secret

---

2. *Einleitung in die Philosophie der Offenbarung*, SW XIII, p. 113: "as Hegel does in his *Encyclopedia of the Philosophical Sciences* [*Encyklopaedie der philosophischen Wissenschaften im Grundrisse*, 2nd ed. (Heidelberg, 1827), p. 213], when he declares as a necessary consequence of empiricism that legal and moral regulations and laws must appear as something unintentional and that their objectivity is abandoned."

3. *Ibid.*, p. 114: "as we would like to name it for the time being; for this reason, there are still other systems to be subsumed under the *general* concept of philosophical empiricism, other than the sensualist ones that limit all cognition to sensory perception or even deny the existence of anything extrasensory."

4. *Ibid.*, p. 116: "As is generally known, this was the earlier doctrine of *Jacobi*, which was attacked many times over because of its mysticism. He later sought to make peace with rationalism, which he did in a rather unique way by positing reason in place of the earlier individualized feeling and then proposing something quite strange, namely that reason in itself, in a substantial manner, absent of all *actus* and thus also *before* all science, is that which posits and knows God."

of the divine nature and the emanation of things out of God through ecstatic contemplation (theosophy), which is a theoretical or speculative mysticism that gives itself scientific form, laying claim to objective cognition.

All these *oppose dogmatic rationalism* and even form a powerful opposition *to the rationalism that has not yet been surpassed.* For it can be surpassed only by the positive philosophy.

The mystical empiricism that manifested itself in the Middle Ages as well as after the Reformation demonstrates that until now philosophy has not been able to achieve in a scientific, universally enlightening, and rationally convincing manner what these doctrines had achieved unscientifically, mythically, and incomprehensibly. This empiricism takes the place of the positive philosophy, which does not yet exist.[5]

Since *the positive philosophy is opposed to rationalism,* it must not, according to conventional language usage, refuse the name of empiricism. But all those empiricist tendencies originate from something that occurs in experience, be it the miracles and appearance of Christ, an exuberant feeling, or immediate intuition of the divine. *Positive philosophy, on the contrary, no more originates from something merely existing in the activity of thought than it does from something that occurs in experience.* It is not empiricism insofar as it does not originate from experience. *Its principle occurs neither in experience nor in the pure activity of thought. It can therefore originate only from the absolute-transcendental,* which is above all experience, just as it is above all activity of thought, and *precedes both the activity of thought and experience.*

The beginning of positive philosophy will not be *merely a relative prius,* like the beginning in the pure activity of thought (the potence must by inherent necessity pass over into Being, and thus the activity of thinking itself is subjected to a necessary movement!), but it will be *the absolute prius,* which does not move into Being necessarily and

5. *Einleitung in die Philosophie der Offenbarung,* SW XIII, p. 120: "For precisely this reason, these doctrines contain the demand, albeit not yet satisfied, for a positive philosophy."

therefore is also not the *prius* of Being (otherwise it would have to pass over into Being as well!). It can only be *prius* of the concept, so that *the progression must not be from the concept to Being but from Being to the concept, as Being precedes the concept.* Concept as opposed to Being = potence.

It can thus also be said that the progression is from Being to potence, whereby potence has the meaning of *one that necessarily has supra-Being* [*Ueberseyenden*].[6] This was the final concept of the negative philosophy, until now only shown in the distance. But there is no necessary transition from Being to potence, as there is from potence to Being. Whatever follows from the absolute *prius* as a consequence does not follow necessarily. It can only be the consequence of a free *act,* which *overcomes* Being and the unmovable, and can be cognized only *a posteriori.* While the positive philosophy does not begin with experience, it can move *toward* experience and demonstrate its *prius a posteriori.*[7]

The negative philosophy has experiential Being [*das in der Erfahrung Seyende*] only as an object of possible cognizance. Its convergence with actuality is *accidental.* It would be true even if nothing were to exist anywhere. It is *the logic, the apriorism of empiricism.* The positive philosophy, however, *concretizes* with experience. It originates not merely from the relative *prius* but rather from the absolute *prius,* and it derives the *a priori* not necessarily but freely, originarily [*urkundlich*], so to speak.[8]

---

6. KG 11:17, p. 325: "Concept as opposed to Seyn is potency; the transition is thus from Seyn as prius to the concept as *posterius.* Potence is thus *posterius,* but potence thereby becomes the Ueberseiende."

7. *Einleitung in die Philosophie der Offenbarung,* SW XIII, p. 128: "and prove *a posteriori* that its *prius* is God, *e.g.,* that which has supra-Being [*das Ueberseyende*]. For it is *a priori* that from which it originates—it is not God *a priori*; it is God only *a posteriori.* That it is God is not a *res naturae* or self-evident; it is a *res facti* and can therefore only be proven factually. It is God. This does not mean that the concept of this *prius* = the concept of God, but that this *prius is* God, not according to its concept but according to its actuality." See also KG 11:18, p. 325: "With respect to the world, pos. phil is thus *a priori*; with respect to the concept, to God, it is *a posteriori.*"

8. In the sense of *ursprünglich,* as used, *e.g.,* by Jacob Boehme ("aus dem ersten principio Gottes" [out of God as the first principle]), GWB 24.2464.

Progressing only within the free activity of thought, the positive philosophy requires experience as proof. Although the absolute *prius* does not require proof, that which is derived as its consequence must be proven and demonstrated factually.[9] Experience thus becomes co-active [*mitwirkend*]. *Positive Philosophy is* a priori *empiricism.* The experience toward which it moves is the *entire experience.* Positive philosophy is nothing more than steadily progressing and accruing proof; just as actuality is never concluded, neither is proof. This entire philosophy (in the sense of *philosophia,* because it seeks wisdom) is continually progressing cognition, and it is proof only for those who desire to think forward [*fortdenken*].[10]

To it belongs not merely an activity of thought but also *a desire* [*ein Wollen*]. Only *fools* say: there is no God.[11] The proof is never concluded. Not even the presence is a limit; it opens a future for the positive philosophy, which again will be nothing other than a progressing and growing proof. While the negative philosophy is a completed system, the positive philosophy is not a system in that sense.[12]

If, however, by "system" one understands a fixed assertion, then the opposite is the case.[13]—In view of the world,

9. *Einleitung in die Philosophie der Offenbarung,* SW XIII, p. 129: "it must be proven factually, and thereby the *godhood* of that *prius*—that it is *God,* and thus that *God* exists."

10. GWB 4.13: opposite of *zurückdenken* (to think backward).

11. KG 11:18, p. 326: "In positive philosophy, the proof of God's existence is only there for the willing; the wise alone learn from experience. The demonstration [evinced by positive philosophy] thus lacks the necess[esity] that would allow it to more or less compel the stupid." See also *Einleitung in die Philosophie der Offenbarung,* SW XIII, p. 132: "Therefore the proof is only a proof for the *wise,* unlike a proof in geometry, with which also the mentally impeded, even the stupid, can be coerced, whereas I cannot coerce anyone to become wise through experience if they do not want to, and this is why the psalm says: 'The fool hath said in his heart/There is no God' [Psalms 14:1 (KJV)]."

12. *Einleitung in die Philosophie der Offenbarung,* SW XIII, p. 133: "The positive philosophy cannot, in the same sense, be called a system precisely because it is never absolutely completed"

13. *Ibid.*: "This second sense, under which one understands a totality of knowledge that serves as the basis for a magnificent

the positive philosophy is an *a priori* science since it begins with the absolute *prius*; in view of the concept, it iscan *a posteriori* science. But, as said before, it is the authority of *all of experience,* not merely of revelation but also of the appearance of the world and humanity.

Thus the positive philosophy is toto coelo [by the whole extent of the heavens] *different from Christian philosophy.* If it were to call itself *religious* philosophy, then it would imply that negative is *irreligious* philosophy; *rather, the true concept of religion is only to be found through it.* Christianity, of course, has to appear in the whole of philosophy, and therefore this philosophy has to expand its concepts beyond their initial limitations, like, *e.g.,* a philosophy that wishes to apprehend all of nature. However, the content of our philosophy would not be philosophy if it were not independent from Christianity.[14]

---

declaration—in this sense, the negative philosophy—is not a system. In contrast, the positive philosophy, as the preferentially asserting one, is in this sense eminently a *system.*"

14. KG11:18, p. 326: "If, by contrast, positive phil. wished to lay claim to being religious, it would be far too vague a definition to really mean anything. It would have to characterize itself more specifically as Christian, Catholic, Protestant, etc., something that can only occur to those who desire a philosophy with special privileges. But in opposition to this, however, one could point to the dependence of all philosophy on Xnty [Christianity]; one could say, 'Never would philosophy never would have come so far without Xnty'; but then philosophy could just as well be called empirical, as phil. would have come into being without the existence of this world. But Xnty ought not be conceived engherzig [narrow-mindedly] as merely historical fact. Ever since the world's beginning, Christianity has been much more than that. I would express this relation between philosophy and revelation figuratively. As is known, Jupiter's four moons are visible only through a telescope, though some can see them with the naked eye, and still others, unable to see a fixed star with the naked eye, can only do so after they have seen it through a telescope, there is much that philosophy would have been unable to see without revelation but that it now can see with the naked eye. In recent times, Xnty has been assimilated by philosophy, but it is so distorted in neg. phil. that it is scarcely recognizable. But by emphasizing Xnty in this fashion, we return to the point where the opposition between neg. and pos. phil., which history in its entirety displays, again becomes conspicuous."

Thus we see ourselves being pushed from all sides toward a *duality* [*Zweiheit*] *of philosophies.* The most striking proof of this is still [the one provided by Kant.][15]

---

15. In Paulus's transcript, the sentence remains incomplete. Kierkegaard has: "The most striking example of this opposition is provided by Kant" (KG 11: 18, p. 326).

VIII. Kant's Antithetic of Pure Reason

[PL, pp. 415–18]

Kant's four antinomies are nothing other than four expressions of this opposition between the negative and the positive philosophy. According to his view, Kant could have named his antithesis a "thesis," but his better sense allowed him to see its true character.[1] For him, *the thesis* is really *the positive.* This is even evident in his mathematical antinomies, which relate to space and time. To articulate the absence of any limits in the world is *to assert or posit nothing*; but setting limits is something positive. The antithesis only transfers to the actual world that which is asserted about the world as an *a priori* possibility. By its nature, by its possibility, the world is infinite, indeterminate; there is nothing in its nature that determines its magnitude. The error occurs when the antithesis (the impossibility of setting limits to the world) is posited as assertion and transferred to the actual world. The fact that the actual world in itself has no limits prompts the demand for a cause to limit it. However, the negative philosophy does not have cognition of a positively effecting cause. Reason is predominant in the assertion of the antithesis; the thesis, on the contrary, begins with that which has existence in actuality.

Since thesis and antithesis each speak of a different world, there is actually no contradiction. The antithesis, *e.g.,* the negative philosophy, is not able to set limits, as Kant shows about the infinity of the world in regard to space and time: the flow of empty time is an impossibility, and

1. See Kant, *Critique of Pure Reason,* p. 393 (A420–21/B448): "If thetic be the name for any body of dogmatic doctrines, antithetic may be taken as meaning, not dogmatic assertions of the opposite but rather the conflict of the doctrines of seemingly dogmatic reason (*thesis cum antithesis*) in which no one assertion can establish superiority over another. The antithetic does not, therefore, deal with one-sided assertions. It treats only of the conflict of the doctrines of reason with one another and the causes of this conflict."

therefore the world cannot have a first beginning. *But the positive philosophy will show that a first beginning can be thought of without the necessity of time having to flow first.* Likewise, the other antithesis supposes that the world, if it were limited, could only be limited by empty space.[2]

One other remark: It is curious that Kant finds the contradiction only in cosmological ideas since it takes place wherever the negative raises itself toward the positive. When it takes place, it passes through all of Kant's "transcendental ideas."[3] Already the *cosmological antinomies* have significance for theology and psychology; or else the question about the limits of the world would be irrelevant for theology. Kant distinguishes mathematical and dynamic antinomies. Both are of great significance for theology and psychology. Whether the causality according to the laws of nature is the only one from which to explain the appearances of the world, or whether there is another causality, one of freedom, is a question almost more at home in psychology and transcendental theology than in cosmology.

The fourth antinomy is almost theological. In transcendental [theology], the propositions "Man's soul is eternal!" and "Man's soul is mortal!" are posited as being just as contradictory as the propositions "The world is infinite!" and "The world is finite!" If one makes the error rebuked above in the cosmological propositions, then the immortality of the soul can be denied. The logical eternity of the soul is (by definition) independent from the conditions of time.

If one makes something positive out of the limitations of the negative philosophy, then one can prove that the distinction between this world and the beyond is an illusion.

---

2. *Ibid.*, p. 457 (A520/B548): "The first and negative answer to the cosmological problem regarding the magnitude of the world is that the world has no beginning in time and no outermost limit in space.

For if we suppose the opposite, the world would be limited on the one hand by empty time and on the other by empty space."

3. *Ibid.*, p. 323 (A334/B391): "In general, all pure concepts are concerned with the synthetic unity of representations, but those that are concepts of pure reason (transcendental ideas) are concerned with the unconditioned synthetic unity of all conditions in general."

Furthermore, do the assertions *God is a blindly acting essence* and *God is only the immanent cause, etc.*, not stand as much in opposition in theology as the cosmological antinomies?

If Kant did not see this, it is because of the artificial symmetry of division and also because he regarded this system too much through the eyes of school metaphysics [*Schulmetaphysik*] and did not pay enough attention to Spinozism. In fact, this metaphysics took more liberties with the world and the soul than with God; with respect to cosmological questions, metaphysics allowed the antithesis to enter. Reputable theologians of the Wolffian school declared that it is of little interest whether or not God has created the world under the aspect of eternity or whether it was posited eternally with God.[4]

Thus the antithetic of pure reason is the opposition of positive and negative philosophy. These two lines of philosophy have always been separate. Kant acknowledged the existence of the opposition, but he could not conceive the possibility of a positive philosophy, even though his philosophy ended with a demand for transcending the science of reason. Are we willing to let this opposition of two philosophies stand?

---

4. See, *e.g.*, Johann Gustav Reinbeck, *Betrachtungen über die in der Augspurgischen Confeßion enthaltene und damit verknüpfte Göttliche Wahrheiten, welche theils aus vernünftigen Gründen, allesammt aber aus Heiliger Göttlicher Schrifft hergeleitet, und zur Uebung in der wahren Gottseligkeit angewendet werden* (Observations on the Divine Wisdoms contained in and associated with the Augsburg Confession, which are derived partially from rational grounds, but entirely from the Sacred Divine Scriptures, and applied to the exercise in true Godliness), in 9 parts (Berlin and Leipzig: Ambrosius Haude, 1731–47).

IX. The Relation Between the Negative and the Positive Philosophy

[PL, pp. 418–23]

To answer the question asked above, we must return to a position above this opposition: *Philosophy is the only science that determines and acquires its own object*; doing so is its first business. By seeking its subject, it cannot exclude anything in advance but rather *must inspect all others to arrive at the one that is its proper object.* But it may not acquire these subjects randomly, as experience offers them up, not let them be given to it from the outside. It has to assure itself of the complete order [of things].

It can only do so if *it originates from the unmediated content of reason.* It discovers how everything arrives at Being from the universal possibility, whereby everything is handed over to that which follows, as if by relay. *What this science of thought* [*Denkwissenschaft*] brings to cognizability, *it hands over to another for the cognition of actuality. Thus progressing, it will arrive finally at a* Last [*ein Letztes*] above which it can no longer continue, and *which it has not brought to cognizability,* for it does not pass over into Being and cannot be outside of Being.[1] However, that *which in it is uncognizable* is τὸ μάλιστα επιστετόν [the most knowable], and not only "that which is most worthy of knowing" but also that which is knowable as the purest knowledge because it alone is that

---

1. *Einleitung in die Philosophie der Offenbarung,* SW XIII, pp. 148–49: "This Last is that which stands above Being, no longer passing over into Being. It is what we have called that which has Being itself. It is no longer merely that which has Being [*das Seyende*] but rather Being itself that which has Being itself [*das Seyende selbst*], in its truth [*in seiner Wahrheit*], and thus that which truly was desired [*eigentlich gewollte*] from the beginning—not merely *cognoscibile* [cognizable] (since all else is this as well) but rather the *maxime cognoscendum* [the most cognized], that which is most worthy of cognizance."

which purely has Being [*rein Seyende*]; all else[2] is a composite of knowing and not-knowing, potence and *actus*.

The potence that remains arrested is absolutely transparent to reason, παντελῶς ον, παντελῶς γνωστόν [that which entirely is knowable] (Plato). All else is only admitted [*zugelassen*] to Being in relation to the Last, which cannot be left uncognized by philosophy; nor can it be handed over to another science. Rather, it must hold onto it as its proper subject, the subject for whose sake it regarded all else as nothing, in order to reach—though not in the same line—actual cognition with it. Thus ends its function—one that does not posit *actual knowledge* in itself but rather *posits it in the very sciences of which it is the science of all sciences*—whose hierarchical orders can contains and represents according to an infallible method.[3]

By drawing that Last to itself and determining it as that which is necessary to be cognized, it no longer posits knowledge outside of itself; it is *no longer negative* but rather *positive* science.[4] Even though it seeks—as one or the other—*preferred knowledge,* it is nevertheless a positive philosophy in the truest sense because it brings only the highest object of cognizance to its actual cognition. *That which has supra-existence [das Ueberexistirende], must not only pronounce itself as the highest idea but as that which has existence.*[5]

A science that has truth only as an end cannot be the true science; but it is therefore not false. As opposed to true

---

2. *Einleitung in die Philosophie der Offenbarung,* SW XIII, p. 149: "that which passes over *a potentia ad actum.*"

3. *Ibid.*, p. 150: "As the science of all sciences, philosophy has the peculiar characteristic of positing *actual* knowledge not in itself but in the very sciences of which it is the science. To this extent, philosophy is also a not knowing and, in this sense, a negative science."

4. *Ibid.*: "From here on, however, philosophy no longer posits knowledge outside itself but rather within itself. It is no longer not-knowing but is rather itself knowing and, thus, positive science."

5. *Ibid.*: "Before moving completely away from the opposition discussed up to now, the following can be stipulated, according to these determinations, about the difference between both philosophies.—In the negative science, everything that lies between the beginning and the end is only a relative truth, thus not the genuine truth, *truth itself*; every moment is quite true as a point on the way to the truth, but it is not *the* truth, Being itself."

science, which itself is within truth, the negative science may not make a claim to being a philosophy.[6] This is a very important point, which will *sublate the duality of the philosophies.*[7] Opposite the positive philosophy, the negative philosophy will have to content itself to be called πρώτη επιστήμη [first science], which, as the science of all sciences—indeed, to philosophy itself—it is already, and recognize the positive philosophy as the highest science. That from which the negative philosophy proceeds is the *primum cogitabile* [first cognizable], whereas the positive philosophy is the *summum cogitabile* [highest cognizable]. All other sciences are situated in-between these two philosophies, in a way that the negative philosophy is brought to a close by the positive philosophy.

Herein lies its difference to Kant:[8] *with Kant,* even though the negative philosophy ultimately dismisses everything that is positive, it posits the positive in a different cognition. Now the semblance of a duality[9] has disappeared. *The negative philosophy is philosophy only insofar as it posits the positive philosophy.* The negative philosophy ought not therewith to lose its independent status and be reduced to a mere introduction; rather, as a pure philosophy of reason, woven from human reason, it takes *the place of the school philosophy* [*Schulphilosophie*]. It is the self-seeking positive philosophy and cannot by itself pass for philosophy. *It is negative because it deals only with ablation* [*Wegschaffen*].

What is its content? Nothing less than *the constant overthrow of reason* [*der fortwährende Umsturz der Vernunft*]. And its result? That reason, insofar as takes itself as principle, is *incapable of actual cognition*; for it does not attain any cognition of experience, and even with that which remains, it can begin nothing for itself. To the extent that the positive philosophy brings to cognition that which stays on in the

---

6. *Ibid.*, p. 151: "It becomes worthy of this name only in its final moment, through its relation to the positive science."

7. *Ibid.*: "For the negative philosophy is, by itself, not yet philosophy but is so only in relation to the positive one."

8. *Ibid.*: "as well as to the philosophy of identity."

9. *Ibid.*, p. 152: "which indeed would have to be called a scandal of philosophy."

negative philosophy, it straightens up reason that is stooped [*gebeugte*] in the negative philosophy.

By itself, the negative science would have no result and, as science, be null and void; but, insofar as it is a science of the positive philosophy, which it posits and calls for, it has content. Thus there is only *one* content. In the positive philosophy, the negative triumphs; for it is the science in which the activity of thought liberates itself from all necessary content. In its truth, it is therefore itself positive since it posits the positive outside itself and strives toward it.[10]

The first inclination of the newer philosophy was directed toward positive science. Early on, the human spirit concerned itself with representations that appeared transcendent from a rational point of view; this evoked criticism in the form of the negative philosophy.

The positive science could begin for itself because it *starts with an absolute beginning,* and if it presupposes the negative, it is by its own will. The negative philosophy could also exist for itself if it were to renounce all actual cognition. But actual cognition is the objective of all science: how could philosophy renounce that? As philosophy, will it be able to resist the demands of humanity? Will it say: *God* is only a creation of emotions and the power of imagination? Consequently, *Jacobi* ought to have expressed himself that way.

Will one find the other explanation any better, that God exists only in the evolution of human spirit? This is the consequent *avowal* of the negative philosophy, especially against those who wish to achieve the ideas of Christianity with the negative philosophy. *The negative philosophy can be comprehended only through the positive philosophy. The former is a philosophy for the academy, the latter for life.* There the minor, here the major mysteries.[11] (In this way the Neoplatonists had already compared Aristotle to Plato.)

---

10. *Ibid.*, p. 153: "Thus, in its truth, *i.e.*, to the extent that it is *philosophy,* the negative is itself positive since it posits the latter outside itself; thus, there is *no more* duality."

11. *Ibid.*, p. 155: "As is well known, the Eleusinian Initiations distinguished between the Lesser and the Greater Mysteries, whereby the former were regarded as a preliminary stage to the latter."

X. The Transition to the Positive Philosophy

[PL, pp. 423–40; 447]

The negative philosophy does not end with that which in actuality has existence but with that which has the *ability to have existence* [*Existirenkönnenden*]. The Last, the *ability to have existence* [*Existirenkönnen*], *is the potence itself—which has Being in its purity* since all else is no longer Being itself but Being overlaid with accidental Being—while said potence itself is *actus*—an *actus* that does not becloud it [*nichts sie Trübendes ist*]. Thus the Last is the potence that has Being [*seyende Potenz*] but firstly only as *concept*.

One can now see *a priori* in what way the potence alone can be that which has existence. It does not exist as *potentia ad actum*. If it exists, then only *antecedenter* [preexisting] *a priori*; it can have Being only as a *prius* (the reversed ability to be).

Metaphysics also advanced to this point, albeit within a misunderstood ontological argument.[1] Insofar as it was to be a proof of God's existence, it had been dismissed by Anselm and Thomas. But the real error in this argument was not *even* seen by *Kant* and those after him. With Cartesius, the argument is: the highest essence (the highest potence) cannot exist by accident and thus must exist necessarily—*i.e., if* it exists![2] It does not follow necessarily *that* it exists. The paralogism can be proven as follows. In the major premise, there is talk only of necessary existing, thus of a manner of existence, so the conclusion can therefore be only this: God exists necessarily only *if* he exists.[3]

---

1. *Ibid.*, p. 156: "It is called ontological because it is to be derived from the mere essence of God *a priori*, without including anything from experience."

2. The main statement of the argument appears in Descartes's Fifth Meditation.

3. *Cf. Einleitung in die Philosophie der Offenbarung*, SW XIII, p. 156: "God, if he exists, must be that which has existence *a priori*; he cannot exist in other ways. But from this does not follow *that* he exists."

The ontological argument could no more prove the existence of God than it could have led, if understood correctly, to the beginning of positive philosophy. God cannot exist accidentally, *per transitum a potentia ad actum* [by means of a transition from potence to actuality]; thus *if* he exists he can only be that which has Being by and for himself [*An-und-vor-sich-selbst-Seiende*][4] (*i.e.*, that which exists prior to his being God). If he is that which exists prior to his being God, then he *precedes* as Being his and all concepts. As such, he is *that which blindly has Being* [*das Blindseyende*], *that which necessarily has Being* [*das Notwendigseyende*].

One can see *a priori* that *if* he existed, he would be that which has Being by and for himself. However, since this is doubtable, I cannot start out in the positive philosophy with the sentence: God is that which has Being by and before himself! *I can only start out with that which blindly has Being,* by letting go of the concept of the godhood to see if I can get from one to the other.[5]

In order to prove the godhood, I have to start with the *prius,* that which has Being blindly. I can also arrive at the ability to be from the negative philosophy—but from the wrong end, from the concept, the *posterius.* If I wish to bring it into actual existence, I need to begin with the *prius,* with Being; but this is not possible without *beginning anew, i.e.,*

---

4. See also Schelling's footnote in *Einleitung in die Philosophie der Offenbarung,* SW XIII, p. 158: "To say 'by and for itself [*an und für sich*]' (so that the 'by itself' and the 'for itself' denote different concepts) is not correct (as was already mentioned earlier: in the *Philosophy of Mythology* [SW XII], p. 28 n.1). This is counter to the genius of the German language, which, in such manners of speaking, loves to combine synonyms but not disparate expressions."

5. *Einleitung in die Philosophie. der Offenbarung,* SW XIII, p. 158: "In the positive philosophy, therefore, I do not start out with the concept of God, as the ontological argument and the former metaphysics had attempted to do. Rather, I must do away with this concept, the concept of God, in order to start out with that which simply has existence [*dem bloss Existirende*], in which nothing at all is thought other than mere existence, to see whether one can get from it to the godhood."

without beginning a new science. We do not arrive immediately at the personal God but rather at Spinoza's blind Being, which conceives all thoughts prior to that which has existence.[6]

One observation on Spinoza! Since the Scholastic philosophy, a positive strive has been notable in the new construct of philosophy. Although his character is revolutionary, *even Cartesius* directs his first question not to the concept, the potence, but rather to that which has Being without doubt [*unzweifelhaft*], which is how the "I am!" presents itself. But he treats *this unmediated certainty* merely as a subjective starting point and therewith resuscitates the ontological argument. The truth in this argument, however, is the thought we have seen.

With Spinoza, the true content of this argument is also the beginning of a new philosophy; but he grasps this beginning only in order to fall back at the same time into the necessary activity of thought. Although Spinoza had only ascertained this logical necessity, it nevertheless made an impression on philosophy, which it could not surpass again.[7] Every thinker *since Leibniz* has been accused of Spinozism; according to *Jacobi,* even Kant is said to have abetted it.[8] But how was Spinoza especially supposed to

---

6. See SpE IIp1d: "Therefore an attribute belongs to God whose conception is involved in all singular thoughts, and through which they are conceived). See also SpE IIp1s: "This proposition is evident also from the fact that we can conceive of an infinite thinking being."

7. See *Einleitung in die Philosophie der Offenbarung,* SW XIII, p. 157: "While one must concede that Spinoza was correct in that the only positive from which one may begin is precisely that which simply exists, his error lies in the fact that he posits this being immediately equal to God without having shown, as true philosophy must, how one can get from that which simply exists as *prius* to God as *posterius,* that is, he had not shown how that Being which simply exists (to the extent that it is not God, indeed, not *natura sua,* for this is impossible), but that it is effectively, as *actu,* according to its actuality, God *a posteriori.* Spinoza had, to this extent, arrived at the most profound foundation of all positive philosophy, but his mistake was that he did not know how to move on from there."

8. Schelling most likely refers here to Friedrich Heinrich Jacobi's infamous footnote in the first edition of his *Über die Lehre des Spinoza*

have articulated the beginning of the positive philosophy? Think about it! How else could his doctrine have had an effect on so many religious minds than through that principle that precedes all concept. Jacobi, even if battling the abyss [*Abgrund*], is connected to it.[9] Likewise the deep, visionary

---

in Briefen an den Herrn Moses Mendelssohn (Concerning the Doctrine of Jacobi in Letters to Herr Moses Mendelssohn) (Breslau: Gottl. Löwe, 1785), p. 123n.3, where he cites two passages from Kant's *Critique of Pure Reason* as being "entirely in the spirit of Spinoza," together with passages from Spinoza's *Tractatus de Intellectus Emendatione* and *Cogitata Metaphysica*. It should be noted that Jacobi revised his footnote in the second edition of 1798 to say that "the following passages of Kant may serve to aid in the comprehension of the concept [Spinoza's doctrine of immanence]. It should not be necessary to explain to a reasonable person that by this the Kantian philosophy is not accused of Spinozism" (p. 173n.3).

9. See also Schelling's *Philosophische Untersuchungen über das Wesen der Freiheit* (Philosophical Inquiries into the Essence of Human Freedom), *SW* VII, pp. 348–49: "Everyone is now warned against the abyss; it was laid out openly for all to see; the only means that still seemed possible were taken; that audacious word could bring about the crisis and make the Germans shy away from the ruinous philosophy altogether, and lead them back to the heart, to inner feeling, and belief [...] And here then, once and for all, our definite opinion of Spinozism! This system is not fatalism because it allows things to be contained in God; for, as we have shown, pantheism at least does not make formal freedom impossible; Spinoza therefore has to be a fatalist because of a different reason, independent of pantheism. The error of his system lies by no means in positing things in *God,* but that they are *things.*"

KG 11:20, p. 330: "Jacobi himself struggles in vain with the abyss into which Spinoza hurls him." See, *e.g.,* Jacobi's mention of the "abyss" in his novel *Woldemar,* part 1 (Königsberg: Friedrich Nicolovius, 1796), p. 299; and his letter to Johann Georg Hamann, 16 June 1783: "I cannot describe to you what happened to me when I first became aware of this hole, and saw nothing else than a horrendous abyss before me," in Friedrich Heinrich Jacobi's *Werke,* vol. 1 (Leipzig: Gerhard Fleischer d. Jüng., 1812), p. 366.

The abyss subsequently became linked to Jacobi's much misunderstood concept of a metaphysical *salto mortale* (literally, a mortal somersault or leap whereby one flips head over heels in the air), which Jacobi mentions several times in his Spinoza book, when, for example, telling Lessing, "I extricate myself from this problem through a *salto mortale*" (*Über die Lehre des Spinoza,* p. 27), and later in the book imagining Lessing to say, "Therefore if I want to speak of the pleasure of this highest essence, I must not elevate it above all concepts, but

doctrines of Boehme.[10] He is the beginning of the reaction of *orientalism* against occidentalism within our philosophy, which has remained essentially Aristotelian.

The negative philosophy was an *a priori* science because its activity of thought preceded all Being. *The beginning of the positive philosophy is the Being that precedes all activity of thought.*[11] *It moves from Being, which is not preceded by a concept, toward the concept, toward "that which has supra-Being"* [*"Ueberseyenden"*].

Instead of "*that which straightforwardly has Being* [*geradezu Seyende*]," I could also say: *that which necessarily has Being* [*das nothwendig Seyende*]; but through long usage, this expression has been identified with the concept of *God,* of whom, however, one should steer clear. By that which necessarily has Being, one thinks of *one whose necessity to exist was imposed by a preceding concept,* and by this, according to the ontological argument, one means *God.*

---

must expel it audaciously from all concepts. My astute friend Mendelssohn was right to call this a leap that goes beyond itself. It was a *salto mortale,* to which I responded *on the spot* with a *salto mortale* of my own, and therewith I stood again next to the man with whom I was conversing" (p. 353). This led Friedrich Schlegel to describe Jacobi's *Woldemar* (in his review for the journal *Deutschland*) as "an invitation to make God's acquaintance" that ends with "a *salto mortale* into the abyss of God's mercy." Friedrich Schlegel, *Kritische Ausgabe seiner Werke,* vol. 2: *Charakteristiken und Kritiken,* ed. Hans Eichner (Paderborn: Ferdinand Schöningh, 1967), p. 72.

Jacobi later clarified his concept in a letter to Johann Neeb, 30 May 1817: "With me there can be no talk of plunging from a cliff into an abyss but of swinging from even ground across cliff and abyss and landing firmly and soundly on my feet on the other side." Friedrich Heinrich, Jacobi's *Auserlesener Briefwechsel,* vol. 2 (Leipzig: Gerhard Fleischer, 1827), p. 466.

10. KG 11: 20, p. 330: "The relationship between Spinoza and Jakob Böhme has never really been illuminated." Jakob Boehme [1575–1624], was a German contemplative who exercised some influence on Schelling's thought. It is said that while he was looking at a pewter dish in the sunlight, he saw the "Being of beings, the Byss of the Abyss." Quoted in *The Encyclopedia of Christina Literature,* vol. 1, ed. George Thomas Kurian and James D. Smith III (Lanham: The Scarecrow Press, 2010), p. 215.

11. KG 11: 21, p. 331: "Das geradezu Seyende was thus the point of departure for pos. phil. In neg. phil. Seyn precedes thought."

The sentence: "God can only be that which necessarily has existence [*das nothwendig Existirende*]" cannot prove his existence, but it does express that if he does exist, *the necessary existence* is his *prius*, the prius *of the godhood.* He is *that which only as the ability to necessarily be* [*nur-nothwendig-seyn-Könnende*]. But even *that which necessarily has Being* is in itself the *potence of that which has Being as the highest essence* [*das-höchste-Wesen-Seyns*]. *That which has the ability to be as the highest essence,* or the highest essence, *has the necessary existence as part of its potence.*

One could rebut this line of thought with the old expression: *in Deo nihil potentiale* [In God, there is no potentiality]![12] But this expression could also be understood partly in relation to his nature alone (for us God is also, according to his nature, pure actuality), not in relation to his existence; partly, that expression means *authentic potence,* which can pass over into Being. But *what we* call the potence of God is the opposite; it is *Being, in which there is no potence.* We therewith exclude all that is potential. God *in potentia* is *actus purus.*[13] The last ability to have existence [*Existirenkönnen*][14] is the pure potence that has Being [*seyende Potenz*]. But potence cannot be preceded by potence, only by *actus.* And for that very reason, *we must begin with the Being that precedes the potence* in order to reach God.

The negative philosophy also leads to that which *necessarily* has Being, *i.e.,* that which precedes all concept. It leads to it through its final conclusion, the correctly understood ontological argument. But it is *simply with that which blindly has Being* [*dem Blindseyenden*] *that philosophy has arrived*

---

12. See Thomas Aquinas, *Summa Theologica* I, q. 3, art. 4c: "Since in God there is no potentiality [*in Deo nihil sit potentiale*], [...] it follows that in him essence does not differ from existence. Therefore, his essence is his existence."

13. KG 11:21, p. 331: "To this might be answered, it is a question here not of God's nature—according to his nature, God is sheer actuality—but of existence. Here it is a question not of potency's transformation into Seyn but of *purus actus.*"

14. In the *Urfassung* (UF), pp. 86f., Schelling distinguishes between that which *can be* [*seyn Könnendes*], that which *must be* [*seyn Müssendes*], and that which *ought to have Being* [*seyn Sollendes*]."

at that which needs no reasoning. One cannot get to it from anywhere. It is its essence to be independent of all ideas. *The concept of that which blindly has Being* detaches itself from having the negative philosophy as a premise; and *the positive,* by dropping the concept and *merely keeping that which blindly has Being, is entirely independent* and can thus begin from there. *Spinoza began from that which infinitely has existence. That which blindly has Being is that* which quells everything that is derived from the concept, everything *before which the activity of thought falls silent. That which blindly has Being* therefore *has a relation to reason* independent from a preceding idea. This shall now be explained.

That which blindly has Being does not exist; *it is existence itself,* αὐτὸ τὸ ὄν [that which genuinely has Being]. One cannot, therefore, attributively ascribe Being to it. As existence itself, it is *pure* quid, *whose concept contains no* quod.[15] It is a concept of reason that does not posits reason before Being but rather posits Being before reason. This Being, which reason posits *before* itself, can only be posited absolutely outside of itself in order for it to be retained *a posteriori. Within it, it is absolutely "ec*static [*ek*statisch]."[16] (Thus the ecstatic in

---

15. KG11:21, p. 331: "Seyn cannot be used attributively of it. One is reminded of the ancient Indian saying that it weder ist noch nicht ist [neither is nor is not]; it is a pure *quid* [what], not a *quod* [that]."

16. See UF, p. 29: "But all first and originary beginning of Being [*Seyns-Entstehung*] occurs only through an originary ecstasy [*Ekstasis*]. Ecstasy is a *vox anceps* [two-faced expression]. There is a kind of ecstasy, whereby a subject is posited outside itself, alienated from itself; then there is another kind of ecstasy, whereby that which is alienated from itself is given back to itself. The last is the better ecstasy." *Cf.* Schelling's earlier Erlangen lectures, where he substitutes *Ekstasis,* as "stepping out of itself" [*sich heraussstreten*], for intellectual intuition (the "non-knowing knowing" [*nichtswissende Wissen*]), as the beginning of philosophy in a moment of wonder: "It was named *intellectual intuition* because one presumed that in the intuiting or *beholding* the subject loses itself, is posited outside itself. It is *intellectual* intuition because the subject is not lost here in an actual object but is lost, by abandoning itself, in what *by no means can be an object* [...] Rather, to describe this situation, one should use the word *ecstasy* [*Ekstase*] [...] Only in this self-abandonment can the absolute subject emerge in the subject—the self-abandonment we also see in the *wonder* [*Erstaunen*]. This is the somewhat gentler expression,

Spinozism and all doctrines that begin with that which necessarily has existence.) That which purely has Being before all concept is the concept of reason placed *outside itself.*

The *potence,* however, was the concept of reason pulled back into the pure activity of thought. This was, after all, the condition of the negative philosophy. The positive philosophy has no conditions other than that reason not objectify itself in it. Here it is *reason left to itself* [*die gelassene Vernunft*].[17] Insofar as the concept of reason of the negative philosophy is conditional, the necessarily-existing is the unconditional [*unbedingte*] concept of reason, in which reason frees itself from itself, from the necessary movement, toward the free activity of thought.[18] Only within the free activity of thought can one can get away from that which necessarily has existence.

Against the *cosmological proof,*[19] *Kant* asserts: The simply necessary concatenation [*Verknüpfung*] of appearances are only an idea, which does not fulfill this conclusion. Of course, one may not arrive at that which necessarily has existence by conclusion. Otherwise I would grant the accidental as premise, as *prius,* to that which necessarily has existence; but precisely that which necessarily has existence necessarily all premises. Or let us take the formal proof of the fourth antinomy:[20] Who is going to ask for proof of the existence of that which is itself that which has existence necessarily? But hereby one foists the idea of God on the concept of that which necessarily has existence. *We,* however, have *dropped all concept* and kept only that for ourselves which necessarily has existence.

---

which the milder Plato makes use of when he says, 'Before everything there is the affect of the philosopher—the wonder, τὸ θαυμάζειν,' and adds, 'for there is no other beginning for philosophy than wonder' [see Plato, *Theaetetus* 155*d*]." *Erlangener Vorträge* [Erlangen Lectures], *SW* IX, pp. 229–30.

17. KG 11:21, p. 332: "Das unbedingt Seyende [that which unconditionally has Being] has no condition other than a negative one, that reason is left to itself [*sich läßt*]."

18. KG 11:21, p. 332: "This is the unconditional concept of reason and transforms itself into thought."

19. See Thomas Aquinas's cosmological argument in *Summa Theologica* I, q. 2, art. 3.

20. See Kant, *Critique of Pure Reason,* A452–53/B480–81.

No other concept has been so spoiled by the former metaphysics. Thus it is *utterly absurd to ask whether that which necessarily has existence can exist.* For it necessarily has existence precisely because it *excludes* all potential, all potence.[21]

No less absurd is the question: "What could the nature of that which necessarily has existence be?" When *Kant* says: The task of dogmatic metaphysics involves finding a concept for the absolutely necessary, and *vice versa*; and that reason cognizes as necessary only that which is necessary by its concept! I counter: only what is not preceded by a concept is necessary as such. However, to find a concept for that which is absolutely necessary can mean:

Either that a concept ought to be found from which that which necessarily has existence can be *deduced.* (This is what Kant meant!) However, if the necessary existence could be deduced from a preceding concept, then it would therewith be relinquished. Therefore one cannot arrive at the necessary existence through a concept of God. And even if one moves in the negative philosophy through the concept of God to the necessary existence, one must nonetheless let go of the concept of God. One can only arrive again at the concept as the *posterius* from that which purely has Being [*Reinseyenden*], so that what is proven *in the positive philosophy is not the existence of God but rather the godhood of that which has existence* [*Gottheit des Existirenden*].

Or is it the second meaning, that one can arrive at the concept from that which has Being purely? This is the task of the positive philosophy.

The first meaning contains impossibilities, and *Kant* was right to point out that it is impossible to find the necessary existence for a concept unmediatedly. But he should have separated the complication of that which has Being necessarily from the concept of God and posited *that which necessarily has Being free of all concept.* This last is so much closer to Kant since he acknowledged that which *necessarily*

---

21. KG11:21, p. 332: "The question has been raised whether one, with respect to Etwas existirende [something that has existence], could prove that it is a necess. existence—a foolish question because in saying 'Etwas,' one has already designated a particular."

has Being as a concept of reason, one that even overpowered reason. He was right to inveigh against spoiling the concept by placing it within the concept of the highest essence. Thus, however, Kant placed the highest immanent concept of the highest essence alongside the absolutely transcending concept of that which *necessarily* has Being. The latter is at the end of the negative philosophy; the former, at the beginning of the positive philosophy. In this way, they border each other. Kant posited them side by side as necessary concepts of reason.

That which *necessarily* has Being is the absolutely transcending concept. With that concept, the old metaphysics wanted to get beyond it and into Being. If I wanted to *infer the existence of the highest essence from its idea,* then this would be transcendent. *However, by positing Being before any idea, I am excluding all ideas.*

The transcendence of the old metaphysics was merely relative, halfway, hesitant; *that of the positive philosophy is absolute and resolute, but* precisely for that reason it is not a transcendence in the sense that Kant disallows. Once I make myself immanent in the idea, then of course I become transcendent. *But if I were to begin with the transcendent, like Spinoza, then I would not be transcending anything. Kant* disallows transcendence only in the dogmatizing reason, which originates out of itself; but he *does not disallow going from the concept of that which necessarily has existence to the highest essence, as* posterius.

Reason posits that which blindly has Being outside itself absolutely but only in order to make that which is outside and above reason again the content of reason by being *a posteriori* the concept of godhood. That which blindly has Being is the content that is not identical with the activity of thought (in contrast to the beginning of the negative philosophy), but it can *make toward* it. The negative philosophy has as its content the *a priori* comprehensible Being, while *the positive philosophy has the* a priori *incomprehensible Being as its content, so that it becomes comprehensible* a posteriori. And it is in God that it becomes comprehensible. *The uncognizability of that which blindly has Being becomes comprehensible in God.* It becomes *a content that is immanent to reason in God.*

Thus the positive philosophy can also be called a science of reason. In the negative philosophy, reason is only by and for itself; it is not-yet-knowing; it is knowing philosophy only in the last moment. In the positive philosophy, reason, having been chastised by the negative philosophy, is raised up again to the cognition it always seeks.

Whoever moves toward a future is well advised to first conclude the past. The positive philosophy is a future for the now largely prevailing philosophical consciousness. *We had to ensure that nothing is left behind that could henceforth raise itself against it.* Its relation to the philosophy so far had to first be made clear and its positions set out. The torn thread of historical development had to be retied. This resulted in *the necessity to distinguish between the positive and the negative philosophy.* Now we commence with the *general part of the positive philosophy.*[22]

---

22. KG 11: 21, p. 332: "The introduction is herewith complete."

XI. The "Unforethinkable Being" and the Possibility to Proceed from There

[PL, pp. 447-76]

Any potence that precedes Being cannot be the true principle. A principle is only that which undoubtably is immune to all only subsequent possibility; that which has existence, and remains at the top. *That which is most doubtable [Zweifelhafteste] is that which has the ability to be [das Seynkönnende]* (the δυάς [dyad] of the Pythagoreans, while that which is always equal to itself is the μόνας [monad]).[1]

The Being that precedes the potence can be 1) regarded merely as idea, and thus is at the end of the negative philosophy; or 2) something *we* **desire** *to have existence.* Here we can only start from Being and from there arrive at the potence, which subsequently is immune to any overthrow [*Umsturz*], because it *does not* have Being *before* but *after, as something that has been overcome* [*Ueberwundenes*], as past. *Hence the beginning of the positive philosophy is the Being that has never been* potentia; *it has always been* actu.[2]

It could say that what precedes all potence, also precedes all activity of thought [*Denken*]! We must also, however, name the Being that precedes all potence *the unforethinkable* Being [*"unvordenkliche Seyn"*],[3] the one that *precedes*

1. *Cf.* KG11:22, p. 333: "The Pythagoreans distinguished between δυάς [dyad] and μόνας [unit, monad] and set them in opposition to one another. By the first, they meant more this double movement, this fluidity, and by μόνας, true being. In true science, positive science, *monas* [unity] must come before *düas* [duality]."

2. *Ibid.*: "the *Seyn* that never moves *a potentia ad actum,* but that immediately is *actus* and always *actus.*"

3. *Cf. Einleitung in die Philosophie der Offenbarung,* SWXIII, p. 161: "That which merely has existence is precisely that which quells everything that desires to originate from the activity of thought, before which the activity of thought falls silent, and to which reason defers to"; *Andere Deduktion der Principien der positiven Philosophie* (Another Deduction of the Principles of the Positive Philosophy) *S*WXIV, p. 345: "Posited at the end of the negative philosophy

all activity of thought. What is the beginning of all activity of thought is not yet the activity of thought; it is the First, *quod se objicit cogitanti* [that which is an object of cognition].[4] which therefore ought to be *overcome,* at the beginning, *outside of the activity of thought, opposing it.*

It would be wrong to object that we could imagine an actuality that precedes all possibility! What is brought forth by humans can be imagined prior to its actuality, but there are also things whose possibility is imagined only through their actuality. Only the latter we call original or originary. No one calls original that which is brought forth from an existing concept. *Initium philosophiae est admiratio* [the beginning of philosophy is wonder],[5] or even more precisely after Plato: τὸ πάθος τοῦ φιλοσοφοῦ ἐστι τὸ θαυμάζειν [the pathos of the philosopher is wonder].[6] This affect [*Affekt*] of the philosopher now has a place in positive philosophy.

One could also say: This which is prior to the activity of thought is without concept—the unconceivable! But philosophy makes that which is inconceivable *a priori* into something that is conceivable *a posteriori. In the inconceivability of his existence. God is not the true God. The true essence of God is his conceivability.*

The main point is to say to oneself: that this which purely has Being [*Reinseyende*] is also to be taken merely as that which has Being in a verbal sense, as that which has existence [*Existirende*] *in actu puro existentiae* [in pure, actual existence], and that its essence [*Wesen*] is precisely this, to be

---

outside of itself, reason, confounded, as it were, decides to originate from the Being that is prior to all activity of thought because it sees that in this philosophy it does not possess its *true* content as an actual content."

4. *Cf. Einleitung in die Philosophie der Offenbarung,* SW XIII, p. 162: "The beginning of the activity of thought is not yet the activity of thought. Any actuality that precedes possibility, however, is also an actuality that precedes the activity of thought (*quod se objicit*)."

5. See Aristotle, *Metaphysic,* A 982*b*: "It is through wonder that men now begin and originally began to philosophize" (trans. Hugh Tredennick).

6. See Plato, *Theaetetus* 155*d*: "This feeling of wonder shows that you are a philosopher" (trans. Harold N. Fowler).

that which purely has existence [*rein Existirende*]. It has no essence besides Being.

I remind you of the old formulation: *In Deo essentia et existentia unum idemque sunt* [In God, essence and existence are one and the same],[7] *i.e.*, in the current thinking. (Once one no longer speaks of God by and for himself, another meaning arises!) God's essence, and thus also his concept, consists precisely in this, that he *exists*; this shall here be the only concept.

Another formulation says: *est ipse suum esse* [he himself is his own Being], which can be reversed to: *suum esse est ipse* [his own Being is he himself],[8] *i.e.*, his Being by and before himself is he himself, his essence. *In Deo non differunt esse et quod est* [in God, Being does not differ from what it is],[9] *the What of God* [*das Was Gottes*] consists in Being. There is also the formulation: *a se esse* [aseity],[10] *i.e.*, to exist by itself, *ultro* [of one's own accord], *sponte* [willingly], without anything prior, without a prior potence, to simply exist. This has been recognized all along as the *primum, quod de Deo concipi potest* [the first, which can be conceived from God].[11]

Spinoza's influence came from the fact that he highlighted the *a se esse* of the divine nature. But his mistake was that he could not get past this concept. The same can be said of his formulation of God: *Quod cogitari non potest nisi existens* [that which cannot be thought unless it exists]. God is that

---

7. See SpE Ip20c2: "God's existence and essence are one and the same"; and Thomas Aquinas, *Summa contra Gentiles* I, chap. 22: "In God, Being and essence are the same."

8. Thomas Aquinas, *De spiritualibus creaturis*, art. 1, rep.

9. See Thomas Aquinas, *De ente et essentia*, chap. 6: "Hsis essence is not something other than his existence."

10. KG11:22, p. 334: "*Aseitas* [aseity] therefore always recognized as the highest." See Thomas Aquinas, *Summa Theologica* I, q. 4, art. 2: "God is Being itself subsisting as such"; and Anselm, *Monologium* 6: "The supreme nature could be created neither by itself, nor by another; nor could itself or any other be the matter whence it should be created; nor did it assist itself in any way; nor did anything assist it to be what it was not before"; and Exodus 3:14: "I am that I am" (KJV).

11. *Cf.* SpE Ip15: "Whatever exists, exists in God, and nothing can exist or be conceived without God."

which cannot be anticipated by the thought of a non-Being [*Nichtseyns*].[12]

The more decisively the essence of God is posited here in Being, the less it seems possible to proceed from there; *the* actus purus *cannot begin anything; it is rigid and unmovable; without potence, there is no moving forward, and yet we must try to get past it.* The unforethinkable Being is the real First. Once *there was nothing except that which* purely *has Being,* but since other things exist *besides it,* there must be a means to get past it. Let me put it this way: here, in the beginning, it is only an attempt.

We have rejected the potence that at the outset *precedes* Being. Thus that which purely has Being cannot be potence beforehand; *i.e.,* before it is, but from this—that it is not potence beforehand—it does not follow that Being cannot have *the ability to be* afterhand [*nach der Hand*], *post actum, after it is,* hence *a posteriori.* However, Being, the *actus,* must precede it. Yet nothing is preventing that which purely has Being (and it would not contradict its nature) from being presented with *a possibility to be an Other* afterhand, *to be different from when it is unforethinkable.* It finds itself in the first without its doing. Let us assume that the latter occurs. (More *later* on the rectification of this hypotheses.)

Thus an Other shows itself, not in itself as God but as an Other than that which unforethinkably has Being [*unvordenklich Seyende*]: in this way Being is elevated to *potentia potentiae* [the potence of the potence; potence itself] to a potence that has as its object potence itself. It would see itself set at liberty from its unforethinkable Being and elevated to that which genuinely and actually has Being [*zum Wahrhaft- und Wirklichseyenden*].

The first naked potence (in the negative philosophy) can only pass over into Being; the other potence cognizes Being as its *prius* under whose power it is, irrespective of whether it passes over into Being or not. On the other hand, that which is prior to all potence is that which genuinely has

---

12. KG11: 22, p. 334: "indeed, God himself cannot even precede himself with the thought that he is not."

Being, which has the ability for existence because it is certain of its originary Being [*Urseyn*] as a truly *a priori* Being, independent of any prior possibility, and therefore sees itself fully at liberty *to accept or not accept that other Being* (which is nothing other than its godhood, since it is godhood precisely through the possible elevation above the *actus*). For itself, *that which has Being* is completely indifferent to accepting or not accepting Being; it is the Being that is prior to all concept and all potence. It is indifferent to adopting or not adopting Being. *The possibility exists only if it desires it.* The possibility of that Other, different from the originary Being, shows itself, presents itself, appears only as possibility, and not if that which has Being does not want it. *This possibility* appears to Being as something that has not been before, something new, unexpected, something that exists only after Being. But from then on it *appears to it as something that is, for all eternity.* For we call *eternal* that which cannot even be preceded by a thought, that which straightforwardly has Being [*geradezu Seyende*]. *The eternal Being of God precedes even his own activity of thought.*

Eternity is one of the attributes of God theologians call negative. All these attributes, eternity in particular, apply to God in and for himself [*an und vor sich*], without which he is not God, but with them, he is also not God.[13] *Substance is also eternal, but it is not God.* This ungrounded [*grundlose*] eternity, which forestalls any thought, this *"abyss"* [*Abgrund*], which the activity of thought becomes engulfed in, is only *terminus a quo* [the point of origin]; science does not dwell on it and posits it only in order to get away from it.

Even though that possibility is unexpected, it is not unwelcome; for only by showing a Being to that which has Being [*dem Seyenden ein Seyn*], which it can have by desiring it, does it give to that which has Being purely a Being that it can desire (it cannot desire itself), namely, *having the ability to be and not to be* [*ein Seyn-und-nicht-Seyn-Könnendes*], i.e., *an accidental.* By showing the object of a possible desire to that

13. KG11:22, p. 334: "Spinoza's substance is also eternal in this way, but nevertheless not God."

which is enclosed in the pure Being, it becomes conscious now as *lord of a Being [Herr eines Seyns] that is not yet* and thereby frees itself from its unforethinkable Being whose lord it is not. That which has Being [*das Seyende*] first gives *itself* (*dativus*) the appearance of that originary possibility [*Urmöglichkeit*] by freeing itself of the steadfast holy ανάγκη [necessity][14] of Being—all the more so as it imagines, in the Being it sees before itself, *that it will* free itself of its unforethinkable Being. *After all, it is lord of a Being that is the opposite of the unforethinkable Being.* Thus it sees itself, at the same time, as lord of the unforethinkable Being [*Herr des unvordenklichen Seyns*].

Imagine, gentlemen, this lord of a Being that does not yet have Being except as possibility—and when it does, only accidentally—as actually desiring this Being. If you imagine this accidental Being as having come into existence in actuality, it will necessarily encounter the originary Being, that which did not come into existence. Only then will the originary Being receive the character of being ungrounded or without beginning (before it was in a state of completely being left to itself [*Gelassenheit*]). And further: this accidental Being cannot come into existence in the same place without having an effect on the eternal. The accidental becomes at the same time the unequal; once it comes into existence, B will be in the place where otherwise there is nothing other than the pure A, and the *actus purus* [pure actuality] (A^0),[15] which before was not restrained or driven back into itself by anything, has an opposite, is displaced and raised up, like a part of the body that was previously undisturbed becomes raised up by an infection underneath.[16]

---

14. In the ancient Greek mythology, Ananke was the goddess of necessity, see, *e.g.*, Aeschylus, *Prometheus Bound*, 217f.

15. *Cf.* Schelling's seventeenth lecture in Erlangen on the Absolute as pure actuality (INITIA, pp. 81-83).

16. KG. 11:22, p. 335: "If we now call unvordenkliche Seyn 'A' and the accidental 'B,' then being becomes lord over B in positing B, over which it is lord, but it is also A's lord. In positing B, it ushers A out of its Gelassenheit and becomes its lord. Now being has a negation within itself, and no longer is pure being, but only der Potenz nach [with regard to potence] is it *actus purus*."

And in this way a mobility comes into the immobile Being [*unbewegliche Seyn*]; it gains a negation within itself, and while it does not cease to be *actus purus,* it is *actu* only according to its essential nature [*Wesen*], only *potentia actus purus* [potence of pure actuality]. It is hindered in its *actus purus* and is no longer a pure Being without potence. But by having gained a negation, a potence, within itself, it has been become a self-possessing Being, set back into itself and become itself. The one who is lord *of positing that which is accidental has become empowered with his originary Being* in order to elevate the *actus purus* to a potence.

We are traversing *untrodden paths* here—*thoughts alien to our time.* All of it can only be introduced piece by piece. Therefore I count primarily on your participation, gentlemen, that you yourselves may tie together all that is being said about one and the same concept at different times.

As we have seen, it is possible that a potence comes after Being, *i.e., it is not contradicted by the nature of that which has Being*; for *only that which purely has Being can have the ability to be.* The *potentia pura* [pure potence], the beginning of the negative philosophy, even lacked the power to be potence and could not sustain itself as such. Only that which purely has Being is powerful enough to be potence, and since it cannot be potence of the *actus,* it is already *potentia potentiae* materially. Whichever always has its Being beforehand is that which, in the proper sense, has the ability to desire and begin something—by having its Being independent from itself, by having its Being beforehand, and by being certain of it. One says about someone who becomes confined by his Being that he is unable to start anything and thus must remain still. That which *a priori* has Being—which does not first have the ability to have Being, and only then *is*—is the only true and actual potence. Therefore that which purely has Being can have the ability to be *afterhand* (*post actum*). **Indeed**, if we needed a predicate for this which has existence (*loco subjecti* [in place of as subject]) then there would none better than this: what comes into Being is that which has the ability to be [*Seynkönnende*]—just not beforehand!

But for now this is merely a possibility. In order for it to have the ability to be in actuality it must first be shown *a posteriori* through its success. *A priori* we can only know **that** what necessarily exists *is* [**dass** *das nothwendig Existirende ist*]; and it is only possible *a priori* that it has the ability to be afterhand. The preliminary assumption of a potence that is seen *post actum* is hypothetical and remains to be proven. The thesis is that what purely has Being, simply *is*. The antithesis or hypothesis is that it has the ability to be only afterhand; for the time being, this proposition can only be elaborated hypothetically. The subsequent potence can only be posited in the free activity of thought, since the positive philosophy is not compelled by the necessary activity of thought.

Let us assume then that *the possibility* were to appear to Being (*loco subjecti*)—or were to appear to that subject or essential nature identical with Being and *unable to get Being away from it* (essential nature not distinguished here from Being)—that it is *different from what it is according to its unforethinkable Being*. As a consequence, that which has Being becomes an object for its unforethinkable Being only with the appearance of *another* Being.[17] Prior to this appearance, that which has Being purely has the unforethinkable Being only *by itself* [*an sich*]. Human beings have virtues or vices, but they are not objectively apparent to them; their will has no power over them! Being, however—*i.e.*, the *actus* of having existence—is therefore necessary with Being in the identical nature (*identischem Wesen*] only insofar as it has Being in itself, so long as having existence has not become objectively apparent; and herewith a second proposition results. As it becomes objectively apparent to it, *it becomes withdrawn by the appearance of another possible Being from its originary Being* [*Urseyn*] and also distinguishes itself from its *actu* and, in this respect, from *that which necessarily has existence only by*

17. *Cf. Grundlegung der positiven Philosophie*, GPP, p. 415: "That which we have called a merely essential Being could you also be called 'subjective,' a Being that *has Being* only in itself [*nur in sich seiende Sein*]; and that which objectively has Being [*Gegenständlich-seiende*], the purely objective Being."

accident, as that which necessarily has Being according to its nature.

This distinction between that which necessarily has existence according to its nature and that which necessarily has existence *only by accident* is important. The nature of that which necessarily has existence (the concept from which we began) implies that it exists *actu* before it knows itself. Even the *actus* of having existence precedes it; *it has Being before it conceives itself* [*sich denkt*]. It thus *has Being in an unforethinkable fashion,* and to that extent, however, Being is necessary for it, *existentia ineluctabilis* [inescapable existence],[18] for which and prior to which it is incapable of anything. No *posse* [ability] precedes this Being, but it does not follow that because it is incapable of anything prior to this that it is incapable of something after and beyond it. It is found in that **blind** *Being,* before it thinks and knows itself, and to that extent it is accidental to it. Here the difference emerges between our philosophy and that of *Jacobi* who *equates God with consciousness.* Instead, *we must assume an originary Being of God that even precedes God himself.*

The *a se esse* [Being by itself] is not to be confused with the *causa sui* [cause of itself]:[19] *causa* belongs to the general concept δύναμις = potence.[20] In that case, God would have to be first potence, then *actus.* The act of having existence is not foreseen and willed by God. Objectively, therefore,it is by absolute necessity, but *in relation to God it is accidental because it precedes its concept.* The *actu,* that which according to its concept necessarily does not have existence, is that which has *necessity by accident.*

---

18. *Cf.* Virgil, *Aeneid* 8.334: "Irresistible Fortune and inescapable Fate have planted me in this place" (trans. Robert Fagles).

19. *Cf.* SpE Id1: "I understand something to be self-caused when by its nature it cannot but exist."

20. KG11:23, p. 336: "*a se esse* may not be translated as von sich seyn [being by itself]; it will either lead to the concept *causa sui* [cause of itself] (just as Descartes and Spinoza understood it, notwithstanding the fact that in Spinoza it is a deceptive word; for thereby he comes into the contradiction with himself that God as *causa sui* becomes potency, δύναμις [power], and in consequence God comes as potency to precedes himself as *actus*)."

The accidental in that which unforethinkably has existence was to be shown.[21] It precedes that which exists, that which has existence itself, so that it is not even posited *as* essence but rather is *posited altogether ecstatically, outside of itself,* is straightforwardly [*geradezu*] that which has Being. The essential nature has not emptied itself [*entäussert*]; rather, it is emptied before it thinks itself [*sich denkt*].[22] It is the *antipodal to all idea,* but in this opposition it is itself idea on account of this complete reversal.

This *actus purus* has not become itself again by an *actus*—if it had, it would have to be a potence first. Rather, it is the inaccessible Being [*unzugängliche Seyn*], wherein the activity of thought renounces all *prius,* and hereby renounces itself. *That which unforethinkably has Being* [*Unvordenklichseyende*] *has Being by itself* [*an sich*], in the declared sense; it is therefore that which has Being by itself [*Ansichseyende*]. But then what is it? It cannot be any other than that which necessarily has existence according to its nature. But since it exists prior to itself, its necessity is not determined by its nature; it exists only *actu* [in actuality], *i.e., only blindly, which accidentally has existence.* (*Cf.* Aristotle's *Metaphysics* on the accidental).[23]

The unwanted or unforeseen is also *accidental,* prior to that which has existence is incapable of anything,[24] which it

---

21. KG11: 23, p. 336: "[U]nvordenkliche Seyn thus manifests itself as the accidental. When I sow a seed in a particular place, I do not find it strange that it sprouts there, because I have a concept of it prior to its being; if, by contrast, a plant comes up in a place where I have not sown, I am surprised, because in relation to me it is accidental."

22. KG11: 24, p. 337: "Das unvordenkliche S[eyn] is not existence but precedes it. Its essence is not as essence; it is altogether ecstatic; it has nicht sich entäußert, but is entäußert [it has not emptied itself but is emptied]."

23. KG11: 24, p. 337: "This is not the place to elaborate the many meanings of the accidental; rather, I refer to the portion on the accidental in Aristotle's *Metaphysics.* Here only a comment: the unwilled and unforeseen is accidental, but something unforeseen is that blind being *prae quo nihil potest* [before which nothing is possible]." See, *e.g.,* Aristotle, *Metaphysics,* Δ 1025*a*: "'Accident' means that which applies to something and is truly stated, but neither necessarily nor usually" (trans. Hugh Tredennick).

24. KG11: 24, p. 337: "Here only a comment: the unwilled and the

must first remove in order to put itself in a position of ability, of freedom. One may also declare the *blind Being* as that which did not know its possible opposite. If I have to choose between +A and -A, and choose +A, then this is desired. But if I am +A, without desiring it, then -A is not forever excluded; *it can show itself afterhand.*[25]

We have said about the *potence of the other Being* [*andern Seyns*][26] that it can come before, but not after; therefore it can also not be *overcome* in the act of the unforethinkable Being. Thus there is accidentalness that is not excluded [*nicht ausgeschlossene Zufälligkeit*]. A doubt remains, arises *post actum* and demands from the blind Being to prove itself as necessary—for which it did not yet have time—by *overcoming* its opposite. It will also prove itself as necessary if another potence is set against it. For even that which has divine existence must be strong enough to prove itself as being perpetual and necessary against any opposite.

It will first prove itself, but first it must prove itself. This then is the final ground of the opposite potence.

It is demanded by the *highest law of all Being, which wants nothing to remain untried, and everything to be open, clear, and decided.* The law is, in that sense, above God; the law posits God only in freedom against his unforethinkable Being.

---

unforeseen is accidental, but something unforeseen is that blind being *prae quo nihil potest* [before which nothing is possible]."

25. KG11:24, p. 337: "If I choose between +A and -A, and I choose +A, then -A is absolutely excluded. But if I thereby become +A *actu,* then -A is indeed excluded, but not absolutely." *Cf.* INITIA, p. 82-83: "Since we could not posit eternal freedom, the first A^0, as such, the 2nd, that which it posits outside of itself, becomes *that which has Being as eternal freedom,* and the latter we are designating symbolically as $+A^0$, the former as $-A^0$. Thus $-A^0$ must posit $+A^0$ outside of itself. Eternal freedom is first only the $-A^0$. Thus we found it without looking for it, involuntarily. But now one must posit also the $+A^0$."

26. Kierkegaard has *Andersseyn* (Being-Other). (KG11:24, p. 337): "Das Andersseyn, as we have shown in the foregoing, is not vanquished; it can arise subsequently. A doubt can come afterward, *post actum,* and render un[vordenkliche] S[eyn] accidental, require of it that it show itself as necess[ary], something for which, if one dare put it this way, it has not yet had the time. It will indeed manifest itself as necess[ary] if this opposite steps forth."

The law wherein we see the sole ground of the appearance of those opposite potences is God's own law. It only seems accidental, outside of God because of the nature of the unforethinkable Being, which precedes all freedom. The idea of godhood [*Gottheit*], which is above that which has Being *actu,* reveals to that which is, as it were, prevented from Being, the *accidental nature of its existence; at the same time it reveals to it the means to free itself from the unforethinkable Being.* The idea for itself would have no power; the *actus* must come before. Because Being comes before, and the idea is excluded from its blind *actus,* the latter becomes something real, that has Being in actuality [*Wirklichseyenden*]. The idea reveals to God the potence by which he frees himself. It is not a power alien to God—the law should not be understood in this sense. It is only his idea that it subjects itself to, if he assumes the *possibility*; for the law forbids anything from remaining in doubt. *The law of the real dialectic of the world* [*Weltdialektik*] *desires that nothing doubtful remains anywhere.*[27]

Hegel has re-asserted the concept of dialectic in philosophy. For Plato it is the royal art, *i.e.,* a divine one.[28] But one ought not to apply it merely to the logical, negative science, as Hegel does. Aristotle used διαλεκτικῶς and λογικῶς synonymously, but he did so because, for him, the logical presupposed the actual.[29] In the negative philosophy, dialectic has at most a formal significance. *Actual*

---

27. KG11:24, p. 337: "[T]his law is indeed the ultimate ground of everything [...] This law is indeed not above God but freely posits God over against his unvordenkliches Seyn. Thus it is the divinity's own law, and it is only because das unv[ordenkliche] S[eyn] precedes all thought that this law appears as something foreign to God. It is only God's own idea that promulgates this law."

28. See Plato, *Republic* 534e: "Do you agree then [...] that we have set dialectics above all other studies [...] and that no higher kind of study could rightly be placed above it?" (trans. Paul Shorey).

29. See Lorenzo Valla, *Dialectical Disputations,* ed. and trans. Brian P. Copenhaver and Lodi Nauta, 2 vols. (London: Harvard University Press, 2012), 2:211 [Book III, chap. 1]: "Aristotle called dialectic a 'means of inferring through what is probable,' and logic '[...] through what is true and necessary.'"

dialectic is found only in the realm of freedom: it alone *is able to solve all riddles.*

God is so just that he acknowledges the once acknowledged principle of the opposite Being until all contradictions are exhausted. [This principle] is applied in order to question everything. *Set against his unforethinkable Being by God, it wrenched God away from his rigid eternity* and set him free *opposite his blind Being.*

I have tried *to demonstrate the accidental nature of that which first has existence* because the possibility of progress, which the rigid Being denies, is based solely on this *accidental. With this accidentalness is posited the possibility of a potence that sublates [aufheben] the unforethinkable Being.* Do not see herein a pleonasm when I speak of the possibility of a potence that sublates said Being. That which blindly has existence, through its accidentalness, is the very (material) potence of that contrary potence. The formal potence is somewhere else entirely. Through that which is accidental, the potence of another Being is admitted; the accidental allows another Being as possibility.[30] The other Being is not only excluded by that accidental Being; it gives it space, but it does not yet appear as actuality.

This possibility is perceived by the Being (= essence) that is overtaken by Being in the unforethinkable *actus* of its existing, from the point of its existence (from eternity), as one that is *in sua potestate* [in its power], *i.e., it sees itself as the ability to be an Other than that which unforethinkably has existence [das-ein-Anderes-von-seinem-unvordenklichen-Existiren-Seynkönnen]; as an ability to be* by its mere will. *Only* as will *does it become godhood*—by being an Other than its unforethinkable existence.

God is the ability to be as the Other (B) [*das Andere* ***(B)*** *Seynkönnende*]. But he is the *ability to be as* ***B*** only in so far as he is preceded by the blind Being. And to the extent of his godhood is grounded in that ability to be, his godhood is already *mediated* here in so far as he looks beyond his

30. KG11:24, p. 338: "[T]he accidental is material potence, and thereby an Andersseyn is zugelassen as a possibility."

unforethinkable Being as that which has the ability to be the Other.[31]

Here the concepts become reversed; the blind Being shows itself as the impotent, the negative; and the ability to be, which was preceded by that Being, as the positive. The strength of God is in this ability to be, αὐτοῦ δύναμις καὶ θειότης [his eternal power and godhood]; which manifests itself in the creation of the world.[32] *Therewith, his godhood begins.* In his ability to be, he is already that which has supra-Being [*Ueberseyende*], already God. *The* principium divinitatis *is the ability to be.* An essential being [*Wesen*] that has to remain in its originary Being [*Urseyn*], wherein it is by itself, could only be rigid [*starr*] and motionless, dead and unfree. *Even Man must tear himself away from his Being* to begin a free existence. The higher the power of this self-abnegation and self-emptying (the objectification of the involuntary Being), the more productive, independent, divine humans appear to be. *To liberate oneself from oneself* is the task of all formative education [*Bildung*]. Those who do not get away from themselves remain deficient.

The true God is the living God; living means to dispose of one's Being freely; the living God goes beyond himself by his own power and becomes something Other than his unforethinkable Being, different from the Being in which he is *a se* [by himself]. To think of God without this power means to rob him of the possibility of any movement. Then things would have to either emanate (with Spinoza) from God (bad pantheism); or one would have to assure, on the assumption of a free, intelligent demiurge, that Creation is inapprehensible! (stale theism).

Pantheism is only really *"overcome"* by the genuine apprehension of a free world creation, as *God is the creator of a Being different from his own.* However, that vacuous theism is the limited content of the religious doctrine wherein *Jacobi* and the *common rationalists* concur entirely.

---

31. KG11:24, p. 338: "His divinity begins with the S[eyn]-K[önnende]; he thereby is able to transcend the unv[ordenkliche] S[eyn]."

32. Romans 1:20.

With such a coming out by God, one could object that the potence of a ungodly Being is posited in God and that therewith one falls into material pantheism (*naturalism*); in this way God is allowed to pass over wholly into nature. —Indeed, if one does not posit in God anything but that potence of Being-Other [*Andersseyn*]! God, however, is an infinite *potentia existendi* [existing power] (*a Being outside of itself* [*Aussersichseyn*]), but he is 1) not a potence that passes over blindly, since the *actus of blindly existing comes before,* and thereby God is just as free opposite that potence of Being-Other as the latter sets him free; 2) *God contains this potence of an ungodly Being only as raw material* [*Stoff*], *matter* [*Materie*] *of his divine nature in order to be the opposite Being by negation, as spirit, as the actual God.* For this is the concept of God. As mere presupposition of his actual Being-God [*Gott-Seyn*], *potence* is to him only a means to get away from a rigid state and be the actual God.

We have shown the possibility of *sublation of the unforethinkable Being* from the perspective of Being in order to arrive at that which is above Being (the foremost purpose of the positive philosophy following the negative philosophy). If viewed another way, the same possibility of sublation manifests itself. For that which has existence in said manner *actu* unmediatedly is nevertheless in the proper sense, according to its self, not the *actu,* that which accidentally has existence, but that which necessarily has existence [*Notwendigexistirende*]. It is that which *natura sua* [by its nature] has existence. By virtue of its necessary existence, it already projects beyond the *actus* of his unforethinkable Being. It transcends it and is free toward this existence. In this *actus,* it finds itself overtaken by it; for that which *natura sua* has existence has not moved (otherwise it would have come before as possibility). Nothing can be thought prior to God's Being; it is unmediatedly actual. If that which *natura sua* has existence were to precede that which has existence *actu* necessarily, then it would have to be necessitated by the preceding (just as the plant is necessitated by the seed). Rather, this *actus* is *a se esse, a voluntary, spontaneous Being.*

(The best example of this *a se esse,* which was our starting point, is the concept of innocence. *Innocence* is *a se esse,* not posited first by anything prior.)

Hence that which is necessary *natura sua*—even though it is, in the proper sense, the self of that which has existence *actu*—is not the cause of this existence, even though it is posited implicitly in the *actus.* But just as now *that which unforethinkably has Being* is shown its non-excludable *accidentalness,* so that which genuinely is necessary emerges as its essence and self, namely as that which has no need for this *actus* of existing since it is that which is necessary *natura sua.* It is that which exists necessarily also without the *actus,* indeed even with the sublation of this *actus.* From then on it sees itself as that which has the ability to also go *beyond* this *actus,* to have existence beyond; it sees itself as free to allow *an Other opposite the unforethinkable actus,* one that is entirely in its power. Only now does that which unforethinkably has Being sees itself as *that which necessarily has existence beyond the actus, as lord* 1) of the Being that is to be posited against the unforethinkable Being, which it can assume by its mere volition and 2) of the unforethinkable Being itself, albeit not as the lord who posits it, since the unforethinkable Being precedes it and thus cannot be sublated by it absolutely. It sees itself as not posited by it but with its *actus* posited by its essence it sees itself as lord; the *actus* sublates its accidentalness in order to transform it into a necessity according to the law of the world [*Weltgesetz*].

Hence the *actus* of existing in its accidentalness is being sublated! That which unforethinkably has Being [*Unvordenklichseyende*] perceives along *with* the first possibility (**B**), *the second possibility,* namely *that the pure Being is being elevated to a potence and, put into tension, reproduces itself through this negation.* For now, Being cannot simply be sublated; however, it can be shifted from its place, lifted up, and *put into tension.* Previously, it was that which moved outward; now, *it encounters itself by way of negation* and becomes that which has Being [*Seyendes*], one that is in possession of itself [*Sichselbstbesitzendes*]. Into its incapacity comes a potence; Being left to itself [*gelassene*] becomes one *that by itself has Being* [*ein*

Selbstseyendes]; and only now, by way of negation, Being appears as incable of being sublated, its accidentalness no doubt extinguished. And now it proves itself as the *that which does not have non-Being* [*nicht-nicht-Seyende*] (for this purpose it must first be posited as that which has non-Being) in order to reveal that it is not simply *actus* but the Being of that which necessarily has existence *natura sua,* hence that it is divine Being. That first possibility (B) becomes a means *to prove itself as that which does not have non-Being.*

The expressions *God* and *divine* can certainly be used here since we recognize the lord of Being in that which has Being unforethinkably, to the extent that the potence is oppose to him and it is hindered from its pure going-outward [*reine Ausgehen*]. *The godhood consists in the lordship over Being, and it is the highest task of all philosophy to get from that which merely has Being* (τὸ ὄν) *to the lord of Being. Cf.* Newton's famous *scholium in philos.-princ. math.*: *Deus est vox relativa, includens dominationem* [God is a relative term, including dominion].[33]

From whence this Being, over which God is lord, if not from his own unforethinkable existence? *The unforethinkable Being becomes heightened by becoming potence in order to be not merely* actu *but divinely necessary.* It is therefore assumed that the *actus* of the unforethinkable existence is posited *ex actu* by the newly created Being and its exclusionary nature. Thereby the unforethinkable Being is posited back in itself as mere potence. *But potentiality does not become him*; it can well be *actu,* but by its nature it cannot cease being *actus. The necessity to effectuate is imposed on it in order to restore itself in the* actus purus.

It must again negate the added external Being and return it to its originary nothingness, to its potentiality. Thus the prospect of life and process is offered *together with the appearance of the first possibility. Thus that which is lord of the first potence sees itself at the same time as lord of a second possibility to transform the unforethinkable Being, to make it for*

---

33. Isaac Newton's *Philosophiae Naturalis Principia Mathematica* Book 3: "Nam deus est vox relativa [...] & deitas est dominatio dei (For God is a relative term [...] and Deity is the dominion of God)."

itself into an accidental, to make it into a potence, and therewith cast it away. In the first unforethinkable existence there is not merely Being but also an enswathed essence [*eingewickeltes Wesen*]. Pure Being, which by means of the negation it has experienced has Being for itself and autonomously, now excludes necessarily that which has been in this Being as essence, also positing it for itself, separately, but liberated from Being, as essence [*Wesen*].

To that which is lord of the first possibility is put herewith the *third* possibility, to posit itself as an entity that is free from that which necessarily has Being, *as having and not having the ability to be* [*sein- und nicht-seynkönnendes*]*—as spirit.* Thus that which unforethinkably has Being is given, with that first possibility, the means to posit itself as spirit. Spirit is that which is free to effectuate or not to effectuate [*wirken*] that freely posited essence, having the ability to be, which remains to have command over it in Being, which in Being (which is open to it) retains itself, remains the same, thus has the ability to be.

This possibility, which occupies the third place, cannot be that which has the ability to unmediatedly be . This place is already taken (B). Excluded from that which has the ability to unmediatedly be, it can also not be *that which must have Being* [*Seynmüssende*], for this is the *actus purus* posited as having Being. It is thus *that which has the ability to be as that which must have Being* [*das als Seynkönnendes Seynmüssende*], the necessary essential Being that does not lose itself—or the *spirit.*

This third possibility appears to that which unforethinkably has Being, which through the first possibility was already posited as lord, as *that which ought to have Being* [*Seynsollende*], from which therefore the conclusion can be drawn that there is no other possibility aside from those three and that in them is contained all that has the ability to be, and thus all that is in the future [*das Zukünftige*]. (This entire development is heading toward a future.)

What is left for that which unforethinkably has Being, which now is *lord of its Being and its essential nature and is able to empty itself of both*? Nothing other that to elevate itself from that which no longer has Being *actu* to that which necessarily has Being *sua natura*. It has cast out all else from itself. (The *actus purus*, the foundation, is only the *potentia potentiae*.) It has elevated itself in actuality to that which by its nature necessarily has existence, posited implicitly in the *actus purus*, to the degree that the *actus purus* of his existence has dissolved into mere possibility (potence). It knows itself as lord over its essential nature and Being, as that which now is necessary *natura sua*. This *knowing itself as independent* [*sich-unabhängig-Wissen*] from that unforethinkable *actus* gives it the freedom to posit in place of the first Being a free Being. *God is this absolutely free spirit who abounds above* [*schwingt über*] *that wherein he is spirit, who as spirit is neither bound to itself nor treats himself only as a potence: only this is the supra-abound* [*das Überschwängliche*].[34]

In the Christian doctrine, God is thought of as spirit; and yet *the* spirit is only a potence in him. God is spirit, who likewise is all other potences, yet none for himself but all of them in untorn unity.[35] Even though the relationship of that which *natura sua* is necessary to the *actus purus* is that of the essence or concept, it does not precede it; it emerges as nothing else than having supra-existence [*überexistirend*], and therefore Being comes before essence.

Once that which unforethinkably has Being has been shown its entire essential nature as sublatable, it ascends in its idea; only now it is God since, as that which merely unforethinkably has Being, it is only *potentia*, implicitly God, not *as* God. That which unforethinkably has Being ascends in its idea, once it ascends to that which exists *natura sua* necessarily. *Only that which as essence* [*Wesen*] *does not require existence is God.*

---

34. See *Einleitung in die Philosophie der Offenbarung*, SW XIII, p. 126: "the existence of an supra-abound feeling [*überschwenglichen Gefühles*] in us that can only be satisfied by the existing God or originate from an unmediated beholding of the divine."

35. KG 11:25, pp. 339–40: "God is not only spirit; he is more than spirit; he is not necess[ary] spirit, but the absolutely free spirit. Thus Xnity [Christianity], too, teaches that spirit is a person, and yet God is spirit. The same applies to essence; for essence manifests itself prior to existence, but [also] after it, because it shows itself as the überexistirende."

We have herewith arrived at the Highest [*zum Höchsten*], beyond which there is nothing to think of. *Only the most exhausted dialectic is able to go from that which has Being* actu *of Spinoza to that which has Being according to its nature.*[36] From the beginning, for that matter, we could only desire that which presents itself as unmediated and in the first instance. *We have posited that which is necessary* actu, *as it were, blindly. That which we called the unforethinkable Being was only the* actus *of the* actus purus, before which the *actus purus* itself had not been seen. Now that the *actus* has been sublated, the *actus purus* is sustained as essence [*Wesen*]. God is the *actus purus* as essence, and therefore an essential being that is *beyond* essence (in the sense of potence), the supra-essential essence [*überwesentliche Wesen*] of the Greek theologians.[37] Now the above formulation means *in Deo essentia et existentia unum sunt* [In God, essence and existence are one]![38] In God, *the actus of Being* is precisely the essence.

Allowing the *actus purus* itself *precede* its *actus*—which only then was to be cast off, and for which we should have been reproached least by those who assume negative attributes in God—was unavoidable. *God can only be* that which is the Eternal as such [*das Ewige schlechthin*], the One as such[*das schlechthin Einzige*]! one ought to say with regard to the negative attributes. It is not necessarily God. There is no necessary transition from the negative to the positive

---

36. KG11:26, p. 340: "Unv[ordenkliche] S[eyn] raises itself to the Idea and is now actually God; previously, it was God only substantially or according to possibility. Only now is it actually God."

37. KG11:26, p. 340: "Necess[ary] existence *natura* has the same relation to necess[ary] existence that is merely *actu* as essence does to Seyn, and concept to Seyn, but in such a way that it does not precede Seyn but exists as überexistirende [that which has supra-existence] and consequently is more than essence, is überwesen [supra-essence], in the common understanding of the word. For this reason, and quite correctly, dogmaticians early on called attention to the fact that, when the word "essence" is used of God, it must be borne in mind that he is more than essence, is υπερουσια [above essence]." See Pseudo-Dionysius the Areopagite's *On Divine Names*, chap. 1, where he speaks of ὑπερούσιος θεαρχία (the supra-essential godhood).

38. KG11:26, p. 340: "*in deo essentia et existentia non differunt* [in God, essence does not differ from existence]."

attributes, through which only now God becomes God (grace, providence). The theologians have not yet found a necessary transition because it is impossible. Theology has not been able to cope with pantheism precisely because they have yet to comprehend this thought.

Without the preceding blind Being, God could not be God, could not be that which has supra-Being. And as such, we have *achieved* our goal. "Lord over Being" is the concept of *personality*; lordship over Being in and of itself is *absolute personality.*[39] But what is *beyond* Being cannot be *before* him, *only after* him. *The existence of God cannot be proven, only the godhood of that which has existence, of that which has Being* actu *by itself and eternally,* though that, too, *only a posteriori.*

However, the Being that comes before all, which God possesses without any doing on his part [*ohne sein Zuthun*], is *only a momentary thought,* presupposition in substance, not in time. Just as he is within the unforethinkable Being, he knows himself *at the same time* not to be in need of this *actus* of having existence, as that which is necessary by its very nature; and it is precisely in this transcendence over the originary Being that he is God. From all eternity, he sees himself as Lord, capable of suspending his unforethinkable Being in order to become, by means of a necessary process, that Being that desires itself [*zum selbstgewollten Seyn*] and becomes only now the divine Being. Before the actual, he already knows himself as lord.

Until now everything has been possibility. How is God able to bring this possibility into actuality?[40]

---

39. KG11:26, p. 340: "Without unv[ordenkliche] S[eyn], God could not be; for he could not be lord, nor could he be personality; for lordship over Seyn is precisely what personality is; absolute personality transcends Seyn schlechthin [Being as such]."

40. KG11:26: p. 340: "*We now come to something new.* Why does God suspend this unv[ordenkliche] S[eyn], why does he actualize this possibility, given that he is, already, lord?"

XII. How God Posits a Being Other Than His Own in Actuality

[PL, pp. 476–86]

A dialectic that stops short might say: God assumes that opposite potence in order to transform, through negation, the blind affirmation of his Being into a desired Being. But *for whom* ought he to do this? He already knows that the Being that in actuality [*actu*] is eternal will prove and create itself. A *purposeless* process for his own sake, which for him cannot be an end? He would only decides on this process because of something outside of himself (*praeter se*).[1] He would only decide on the *suspension of that Being that is eternal Being* actu because of an Other outside of himself, which to him would be the means to actualize those potences. *Only as the lord of a Being other than his own is God entirely removed from himself, absolutely free and blessed* [*selig*].[2]

This assertion should attract the attention of those who know God only as that last concept of the negative philosophy, the eternal, absolute subject-object, or, according to Aristotle, *that which always only thinks itself.*[3]

But in this necessity, to eternally think oneself, lies an enormous limitation; one no mortal would want to take on. To always only think oneself would be, for any healthy nature, a most embarrassing condition. Human beings are not self-involved. *Johannes Müller* writes: I am only happy when I produce.[4] *Goethe*: I only think when I produce.[5] In

---

1. *Philosophy der Offenbarung* (Philosophy of Revelation), *SW* XIII, p. 283: "praeter Deum [outside of God]"; *ibid.*, p. 352: "Man [...] has posited the world outside of God, not merely *praeter* but *extra Deum*; he can call this world *his* world."

2. KG 11:26, p. 341: "Arist[otle] locates God's happiness precisely in this [thinking of self]."

3. See Aristotle, *Metaphysics*, Λ1074*b*: "Mind thinks itself [...] and its thinking is a thinking of thinking" (Hugh Tredennick).

4. The anatomist and physiologist Johannes Peter Müller (1801–1858), an early devotee of Schelling and Goethe.

5. Goethe to Karl Ludwig von Knebel, March 1799 (*Goethes Briefe*

the act of producing, human beings are not involved with themselves but with something *outside of themselves,* and for that reason, God is the most blessed one [*der grosse Selige*] (Pindar).[6]

However, this process, which is mediated for God by the potences that manifest themselves in him, is one of suspension; yet it is a restoration of the Being that *actu* is necessary. Between these two instances lies the entire world. *The world is* the suspension of that which has existence *actu* in the godhood; it is *the suspended* actus *of the divine Being.* The essence is to be elevated only in itself by the suspension of the *actus.*

God does not empty himself [*entäussert sich nicht*] into the world. Rather, he elevates himself within his godhood; he is emptied of himself unforethinkably. He goes within himself by suspending the *actus.* At the same time, God suspends the *actus* of his necessary existence to posit a Being other than his own in place of the first existence. In that unmediated, mere ability to be, which is present in him from eternity and which is something only if he *wills* it, God has as real principle the same indifference toward the ability or the inability to be. We have seen this in the pure science of reason as *prima materia. With the ability or inability to be, God now has the real ground on which he leads to actuality that which is contained in the negative science of reason as mere possibility.* The same potences that occur in the negative philosophy *a priori* recur here; not as preceding Being but as having Being *ahead* of them [*vor sich*] and held together *through Being posited as essence, as a supra-material spiritual oneness* [*übermaterielle geistige Einheit*]. It is held together through this oneness, even when it has become actual and placed through this oneness into *tension* [*Spannung*] and difference.

This unity is not material but spiritual, indissoluble, and held together *uno eodemque loco* [in one and the same

---

in 4 Bänden, ed. Karl Robert Mandelkow [Hamburg: Christian Wegner, 1968], 2:369): "I can only think to the extent that I produce."

6. *Cf.* Schelling's "Über einige Oden Pindars" (About Some Odes by Pindar), in HKA II.1.1, pp. 187-201; see also Schelling's reference to Pindar in his *Andere Deduktion der Principien der positiven Philosophie* (Another Deduction of the Principles of Positive Philosophy), *SW* XIV, p. 352.

place], which is *only* possible *through process*. The disunited potences are held together through the cause of the processes, through that *supra-material unity*.[7] If we imagine the outcome of this process beforehand, it becomes an actuality that encompasses and comprehends all *a priori* possibilities; it will be πᾶν [all], namely, a world from which the accidental is not excluded but is subordinated to that which is necessary so that it appears on the one hand as real (not logical) and on the other as logical since the accidental is here subordinated to the necessary, to that which must have Being.[8]

This connection of that which is real and that which is logical has all along been one of the most difficult notions to comprehend, so much so that Kant attributed that which is accidental to the uncognized thing by itself [*Ding an sich*] but that which is necessary to the logical part of cognition. The accidental lies rather in what we have called that which has the ability to be and not to be [*Seyn-und Nichtseynkönnenden*], that which is necessary, cannot be sublated in or by anything, and continuously realizes itself *in the suspended* actus *of divine existence,* which is compelled to create itself in the *actum* (that which must have Being [*das Seinmüssende*]).

But it is to be demonstrated that a Being that is different from God can arise out of the *process* that has been shown as possibility. The point with which *the entire process* ties in is the other Being, which emerges *ex improviso* [*suddenly*] and has not previously existed. The necessary Being finds itself then in the Being that is not preceded by a potence. This Being could not be posited by the overcoming [*Überwindung*]

---

7. *Philosophie der Offenbarung,* SWXIV, p. 354: "The potences represent only that which materially exists; the *purus actus* posited as *essence* is raised above the mere materiality of Being, that which is supra-material [*übermaterielle*], thus an indissoluble and insurmountable unity, which, *e.g.,* does not let the just arisen–and indeed *ex improviso* [unexpectedly] arisen Being–and the originary Being–which is negated by it and hence is in discord with it–come apart and coerces it to be *uno eodemque loco* [in one and the same place]. In this way, it becomes the material cause of a process whose supramaterial cause it (the unity) is itself."

8. KG11:26, p. 341: "This connection of the real and the logical is truly the most difficult to comprehend."

of an opposite potence. An opposite potence did not have time to show itself. But because this potence *has not been overcome* by the *actus,* it can show itself afterhand [*nach der Hand*]; a possibility cannot be excluded, only an actuality. Only the *unforethinkable* Being [*das unvordenkliche Seyn*], which is prior to any activity of thought and which therefore we have called *potentia potentiae,* gives it the possibility to show itself. It could not show itself before this Being; thus, it has found in the unforethinkable Being a position it had not previously been in. It can turn not to that which exists but to that which necessarily is enclosed within it, which is therefore also free to sublate the originary Being [*Urseyn*] through adoption of the opposite potence, not according to its essence but according to its *actus.* Only from this essence, which has Being beyond the *actus* of having existence, can that possibility be assumed, *adopted* (after one's own children). The potence we are speaking of is in itself an objective possibility, given as possibility only through the unforethinkable Being. But it cannot pass over in itself *ad actum* [to actuality]; *it is only there for God. It can only become actuality if God desires it,* but it is because of its inability to pass over *a potentia ad actum* [from potence to actuality] that it *calls forth in God a will* so that it becomes *the material potence of a divine will.* God may or may not direct his will toward it. It can only be posited into this intent [*Vorsaz*] of God as a means, just as the unforethinkable Being must have also been posited into this intent, wherein God has the power to transform the opposite Being into whatever he desires it to be *finaliter* [in the end].

Thus, God's Being and essence become mere potences of a future Being other than his own. By nature, he is desireless, necessary essence, *natura necessaria.* As the supra-abound [*Ueberschwängliche*], having posited his own essence and Being outside of himself, God is the invincible [*unbesiegliche*] because he is no longer a material but a *"suprasubstantial"* [*übersubstantielle*] *unity,* through which the contrary Being [*conträre Seyn*] and the unforethinkable Being negated by the former, are held together so that *a process* becomes necessary. Though the unforethinkable Being is posited *ex actu* [from actuality] by the contrary Being, it cannot be sublated absolutely, as it has its roots in eternity; however, its actual Being [*actu-Seyn*] can be sublated. [The unforethinkable Being] itself becomes posited rather through inhibition, negation, as infinite potence of the *actus* so that it *must* effectuate in this way in order to produce itself in its *actus purus* through the overcoming of the opposite Being.[9]

How then is one to think of *the overcoming of the opposite Being*? That which has true Being within that contrary Being is a will called forth in God; and in this respect, it is an accidental (blind) will, which he directs at that first appearing potence.

We have in this first Being, which is at work in a divine will, that which has Being through the divine will alone and is also regarded as πρῶτον ὑποκείμενον [the first material substrate] in the general doctrine of Creation. It is said of it that it is created out of *nothingness,* i.e., *it has Being in the divine desire alone.*—Nothing, however, is superable, and nothing can withstand as a will. Will is *originary Being,* matter, out of everything.

In fact, a will can be superable. If an accidental desire arises within our unperturbed [*gelassenen*] inner self (= *actus purus*), we feel our will perturbed, confined, and impeded. Where it was before, there is now an Other. The originally unperturbed will is placed peripherally; but because it is negated by an extraneous will, it gains the power to negate and overcome the opposite will, which then lets the unperturbed will emanate again. Thus, another Being that has been allowed to be actualized can be overcome because it came into Being through a will.

The overcoming could happen suddenly; but since the contrary potence has been granted Being, it can only be

---

9. KG11:27, p. 342: "God is by virtue of being lord over his substantiality and the unity in which unv[ordenkliche] S[eyn] and contingency are held together. Unv[ordenkliche] S[eyn] is indeed posited *ex actu* but is not, however, absolutely annulled; for not even God is capable of this. Der *actus* is annulled, and thereby it is itself posited as the potency of *actus* and must work to place itself back in *actus purus*."

dispelled step by step. With respect to the contrary principle, the gentle *Plato* used this expression: *it must be persuaded.*[10] The will, which is the true energy of the opposite accidental Being, is self-contained and autonomous; it is overturned incrementally by the self-producing *actus purus.*[11]

But there must be a principle that determines the steps, a principle that is independent of the contrary Being as well as the incrementally beseeching principle. For the former has, by its nature, only the will to endure unconditionally; the latter has the will to overcome it.[12] That determining principle is given to us in the third potence, *the spirit,* the essence that is free from Being, which does not bother with Being but arrives in Being without affect and unengaged. It can exercise power over it precisely because it is not mixed up in it. The third [potence] is thus the regulating principle so that different moments and steps remain.

We thus have *three potences* within the process (they are *very important* for the entire succession even though they appear in *different forms*).

1) The initiating cause of the whole movement, the other Being, *which is in opposition to the originary Being* (**B**), whose energy we have found as an accidental will, posited out of the bounds of mere ability, boundless [*schrankenlos*], blind, mindless [*gesinnungslos*]. This Being now acts exclusionarily on the *originary Being,* [and] completely exclusionary in the beginning, so that what is now pure *actus* must be thought by us of as purely sublated.

---

10. *Cf.* Plato, *Timaeus,* 48*a*: "For, in truth, this Cosmos in its origin was generated as a compound, from the combination of Necessity and Reason. And inasmuch as Reason was controlling Necessity by persuading her to conduct to the best end the most part of the things coming into existence, thus and thereby it came about, through Necessity yielding to intelligent persuasion" (trans. W.R.M. Lamb).

11. KG11: 27, p. 342: "With respect to overcoming the accidental, an analogy appears in hum[an] life. Anger posits a foreign will in an individual, but then it acts in such a way that the individual's true will reacts and the subject feels his freedom."

12. *Ibid.*: "the first wants unconditionally to endure; the second wants unconditionally to oppress."

2) In the deepest negation also appears that *potence* which likewise is foreseen and posited into the divine will and which we shall call *mindful* [*besonnen*]. For that which is mindful has its seat not in will; rather, excluded from Being by the opposite potence, it gains from the strength of its originary Being the power to repel the boundless will and put it back in its place, *i.e.*, back into the potence. Once this has more or less been accomplished, and an ability has been created in the boundless Being through the effect of the second potence, something has been posited that is not only the work of that *first* will but also of the other unperturbed will, which only now has become effectual—a third, apart from the other two.

Creation breaks down into two moments: (*a*) the positing of the unbounded Being in order to be returned immediately into inwardness, into the potence and boundary; (*b*) internalization as a result of the creation of a potence in Being.

Creation is not something simply positive, not a positing outside of itself. Rather, the originary Being—which so far has Being in itself and possesses itself by bringing forth in it the ability—is put in its place; thus, that which emerges is self-potent, a veritable third opposite both potences, a thing, namely, a concrete thing as joint product of both potences.

The second potence (A^2) is that which is negated originarily, posited from actuality [*ex actu*], which actualizes itself only insofar as it negates the other. As an originarily actual, it could not actualize itself; this requires negation. Thus, this capacity to actualize itself, the potence and power of the second principle, is one that is given him. The second potence is not that which has the ability to unmediatedly be but that which does so *secundo loco* [secondarily].

It must be preceded by *the first possibility* (B). After B has ceased to be a potence, it comes to the *actus purus* to have the ability to be. *Raised to a potence, it is* A^2; through this, the boundless will is overcome.

Once this process is accomplished, A^2 no longer has an opposite; thus, nothing that is actual in the true sense remains in the end. It is only then that

3) *the third potence*, A^3, steps into *actuality*. The final goal of this process is that the Being, which is to be overcome, is brought to its *expiration* and becomes the *last breath* of the *third essence, the spirit,* to which *Being alone belongs*. But to a certain extent, B is nonetheless subjugated by the second potence (A^2). (I am using this terminology to keep a connection to my earliest presentation on the subject.) [13]

B relates to A^2 as its ὑποκειμενον, as *the matter into which it actualizes itself*. To the same extent that A^2 has carried out its work, A^3 has been given space, as A^3 already prevailed in the process as the organizing principle. *It is the spirit that puts measure and goal to it and determines the boundary of the overcoming for the victorious potence.*

Each of the three potences is now exclusionary; they coalesce only in the product, which thereby is independent. Each potence is still *potentia pura et ab omni concretione libera* [Pure potence and free from all materiality], [14] pure cause, and right here is the proof for the *triad of causes*: [15] B is the *causa materialis* [material cause]; [16] A^2, the *causa efficiens* [efficient cause]; [17] and A^3, the *causa in quam or secundum quam*

---

13. *Darstellung meines Systems der Philosophy* (Presentation of My System of Philosophy), *SW* IV, published in 1801 in *Zeitschrift für speculative Physik*, vol. 2, no. 2 (see esp. §§58ff.).

14. *Cf.* Jean Bodin, *Methodus ad facilem historiarum cognitionem* (Amsterdam, 1650), p. 98: "The human body, however, is encompassed within the elements, the blood in the body, the spirit in the blood, the soul in the spirit, the mind in the soul: although the last is free from all materiality, it is still very much contaminated by the effects of this association."

15. *Cf.* Aristotle, *Physics*, II.3.194*b*16-195*a*3. See also *Philosophy der Offenbarung*, *SW* XIII, p. 342: "This is in accordance with Basil the G[reat], probably in regard to the earlier mentioned Aristotelian classification of causes, or rather already that by Pythagoras, into the *causa materialis*, *formalis*, and *finalis*."

16. *Cf. Einleitung in die Philosophie der Mythologie*, *SW* XI, p. 394: "The first, merely material cause is not really a cause; being an undetermined nature that, for that reason is in need of determination, it is really only passively [*leidend*] a cause."

17. *Ibid.*, p. 395: "The second cause, which gives determination and acts toward the substance as determining cause, *is a pure cause* because it desires nothing for itself."

omnia fiunt [the cause according to which everything happens].[18] The two other potences are already oriented toward the third during the process of bringing forth or creating; they have the third potence in mind as *that which genuinely ought to have Being* [*eigentlich Seynsollende*]. The other two potences look at it as their model [*Muster*], but they also obey their own will; they decide between both. The third is the only one that B obeys when it acquiesces to the measure (potence) brought forth in it by the second. The third is also the only one that the other potence obeys when it lets up on the partially overcome B. The third is the one that through its desire alone keeps all that is becoming at the stage determined for it.

Regarding this, it is said about God in the O.T.: he commands and it stands fast, *i.e.,* remains in place.[19] The final intention of the process is the overcoming of B, to posit in its *expiration* the Highest, which rises above a world of manifold Being as overpowering, All-resolving [*Alles beschliessende*] power.

If the third potence is defined as that which ought to have Being, then the thought might occur that the first potence is that which ought not to be [*Nichtseynsollende*] and

---

18. *Ibid.,* p. 395: "What can be thought above both, or rather, what *must* be thought above both in order to come to an end? Clearly, something that is both substance *and* cause, determinable and determining, thus a self-determining substance that, undetermined, contains an ability but is elevated through Being above the danger it is affiliated with."

19. KG11:27, p. 343: "It is therefore said, 'He commanded and it was there,' not in the sense of coming into existence, but of remaining in place." *Cf. Philosophie der Offenbarung,* SWXIII, pp. 341–42: "as it is written in the Psalm: he commanded and it *stands*; not (as I had already remarked earlier): it stands *there* (the usual translation), but it stands, *i.e.,* remains in place; it does not develop further because the way a thing remains in place and doesn't move on, beyond its stage, requires no less an explanation than how it comes into being. There is a will associated with remaining in place just as there is one with continuing to move. While *that* will may be the will of one and the same absolute person, the one will is nonetheless different from the other." The reference is to Psalm 33:9: "For he spoke, and it came to be/He commanded, and it stood fast" (BSB).

that therefore *a kind of evil principle* has been let into the process. It is important that *the principle necessary for Creation* not be understood *as evil.* But on account of it being called *that which ought not to have Being,* it is regarded as a means. However, being a means does not make it reprehensible; it can be a means willed by God. The divine world governance [*die göttliche Weltregierung*][20] acts mostly through means, namely, mostly δί ἐναντίου [in opposition]. *For now, the opposite Being* [*entgegengesetzte Seyn*] *is, properly speaking, that which ought to have Being, but only in order to be negated in the following moment as that which ought not to have Being.* But once it is declared as such, that view changes; were it to inflame itself against the divine will, *then it would be evil.*

---

20. *Cf.* Johann Gottfried Fichte's essay "Ueber den Grund unsers Glaubens an eine göttliche Weltregierung [On the Ground of Our Belief in a Divine World Governance]," in *Philosophisches Journal einer Gesellschaft Teutscher Gelehrter,* vol. 1 (Jena and Leipzig, 1798).

XIII. The Ultimate Goal of Creation

[PL, pp. 486–96]

We have now arrived at an overview of the content of the process and at the potences that are presented *a priori* to that which has Being. The necessary result of the process is the bringing forth of a Being that, according to its substrate [*Unterlage*] is accidental but in actuality [*actu*] is subjugated to necessity, that is spread across different stages and yet is not incommensurate but moving toward a final goal, *the bringing forth of a κοσμος, a world of all possible things posited as actuality. Moreover, if the unforethinkable Being is a necessary precondition for its godhood, then it is nonetheless not God; rather, God is God only as Lord and Creator who brings the potences into actuality.*

Without potences, God would not be God. He is potentially always God; according to his nature he is already substantially free in the unforethinkable existence opposite Being, This is precisely what is imparted to him by the originary potence; the latter liberates him from his unforethinkable Being.

The assertion articulated here—*that God is only God insofar as he sees himself as lord of the world-creating potences*—must be differentiated from the assertion that God is not God without the world. *For as lord of said potences* (even if they are only possibilities), *he is already God; he does not need to go through the world in order to first come to self-consciousness in Man or in world history.* God is *lord over the world before it is,* both posited and not posited; whether to exist one way or another is all the same to him with regard to his Being, he is completely indifferent to it.

But there is also no coercion [*Nöthigung*] with regard to his godhood, even though by positing the world in actuality a purpose has to be achieved. Our concept of Creation is therefore essentially different from the assumptions that the world is a logical consequence of divine nature and that God decides freely on emptying himself in order to become himself the process. *For us, the world also comes into being through a divine process but one above which [God] stands as absolute cause, as* causa causarum, *which puts the potences into tension [Spannung], and as the cause that persists outside the mutual exclusion.* Certainly no one has applauded those unfortunate theories just because another explanation could not be found. One certainly cannot be content with saying that Creation is incomprehensible.[1]

If the world were now to be a freely posited creation of the divine will, then there would need to be something in the middle, between God's eternity and the world. The world as a possible world must have been contained in the divine will. In the *originary possibility* [*Urmöglichkeit*] inside him, the Creator had the means to imagine the successive Being as a possibility. It liberates him from his unforethinkable Being; it gives him the possibility to use this Being as a means to *overcome* the opposite Being, *to posit itself as liberated from Being, as pure potence, or as spirit.*

The opposite Being is *overcome* at different stages, and the second potence can thus actualize itself in different degrees. This also holds true for the third potence, for it exists by overcoming the first. An infinite diversity of possible positions of the potences that oppose each other is given through this relationship, and it is for the lord of these potences to try out all possible positions and to pre-visualize them [*vor sich im Bilde vorüber gehen zu lassen*]. Here the *ideas,* the originary images [*Urbilder*], gain real significance.

'Ιδεα is *vision* [*Gesicht*]; it contains both the vision itself and its pre-visualization. The ideas are mediations [*Vermittelungen*] between the things (the modified units) and the godhood as the highest unit. Omniscience is too general, γνωστα παντα τα εργα αὔτου: *the ideas are the visions of the Creator.*[2]

1. KG 11:28, p. 343: "Creation necessarily requires an explanation."

2. *Cf. Philosophie der Offenbarung,* SW XIII, p. 294: "God knows all his works from eternity. They exist as visions of the Creator before they become actual." *Cf.* Thomas Aquinas, *Quaestiones Disputatae de Potentia Dei* (Disputed Questions on the Power of God), q. 3, qrt. 17:

As far back as human lore reaches, *that originary potence* [*Urpotenz*] has been celebrated as the origin of all the kinds of Being different from God. It was worshipped in Praeneste as Fortuna Primigenia, in whose arms the future lord of the world lay.[3] Fortuna is that which does and does not have the ability to be [*das Seyn- und Nichtseynkönnende*], the *originary accidental* [*das Urzufällige*], which can only be *subsequent to* that which is necessary, not *prior* to it, which does not really belong to divine nature and yet cannot be separated from it. Rather, it makes itself a representation of God and retains only the nature of "something that is adscititious" [*etwas Angenommenen*].[4]

Fortuna was celebrated as the *wet nurse of the world* [*Weltamme*]. *Mater* [mother] and *materia* [matter] are factually related; for [Fortuna] is the *ὑποκείμενον* [underlying substance] of the future Creation. She is the *maya* (related to power, possibility, potence [*Macht, Möglichkeit, Potenz*]),[5] which spread the web of (mere) semblance before the Creator in order to trap him and impel him toward the actual Creation.[6]

This potence is most pointedly expressed in the Proverbs of Solomon—as *wisdom* (*chokhmah*) [חָכְמָה]: "Jehovah" (the name of the one who is the *Lord of Being*) possessed me at the beginning, etc.[7] But what should this potence, this *wisdom*, which sees God only as potence of a blind Being, be

---

"God's work is eternal and the world was made from eternity."

3. KG11:28, p. 344: "in whose arms Zeus lies." *Philosophie der Offenbarung*, SW XIII, p. 294: "in whose arms the future Lord of the World Zeus lies as a *child*."

4. *Philosophie der Offenbarung*, SW XIII, p. 294: "and remains an *adsciti quid* (something that is adscititious)."

5. KG11:28, p. 344: "The Maya of the Indians is related to the German Macht and to the Machia of the Persians."

6. See also *Philosophie der Mythologie*, SW XII, p. 481, on the Vedic scriptures: "'Everything has its movement through the proper mixture of the three attributes: the creating, the preserving, and the destroying.' Elsewhere the divine effectuality [*Wirksamkeit*] is compared to that of the spider, which extrudes and retracts the silk for its web."

7. *Cf.* Proverbs 8:1: "Does not wisdom call out, and understanding raise her voice?" (BSB).

called?[8] This principle is not regarded here in its Being-outside-of itself [*Aussersichseyns*] but in its possibility, before its actual Being. Here it is, however, subject, *prius*, presupposition of all future movement, that which imparts its knowledge of the future movement to the Creator. (Here, where everything is gained not through necessity but through free will, nothing should be considered completed until that which is the Last [*das Letzte*] has been added.)

There is something unsatisfactory in the development so far: according to the preceding, it seems as if that principle (the *originary* possibility) is simply overcome and is retreating into non-Being, so that the process would be without purpose. However, that which has returned from Being has gone through Being once and is brought back out of Being into itself. It has become self-conscious. *God cannot unmediatedly bring forth consciousness; consciousness can only arise from unconsciousness.* That principle has gone through all *the joys and pains of the process*; it is the beginning, middle, and end of the process; it is knowledge that comprehends the latter; and that is *wisdom.*

This was the purpose of the process, and only for the sake of such a partaking knowledge [*mitwissenden Wissen*] could God want such a process. This knowing was the purpose of the process. Having knowledge, the [originary] potence was able to foresee its beginning, and it is around this potence that everything revolves. Now it is not unusual for a principle to be named at the beginning after what it becomes in the end. Thus, *that which is without understanding* [*das Verstandlose*] has understanding [*Verstand*], that which it

8. *Cf. Philosophie der Mythologie,* SW XII, p. 482: "The Vedanta is in fact nothing other than the most exalted [*gesteigertste*] idealism or spiritualism that in the end amounts to nothing other than to concede that the material world is merely a semblance of existence [*Scheinexistenz*] [...] For that which was to be brought forth had to be presented first as possibility. This possibility is the *maya.* That which is based only on a possibility, which is summoned to existence through free will, cannot be compared to that which is by itself (*a se*). In that sense, the world is also for the Vedanta an illusion. This is the *maya* = magic = possibility [*Maja* = *Magie* = *Möglichkeit*]."

becomes, as its beginning. On the lower levels, nature takes only an imprint [*Gepräge*] of understanding, but in Man, it has broken through and is understanding entirely. All actual understanding shows itself only by overcoming that which is without understanding. *Insanity* [*Wahnsinn*], which is potentially buried in the depths of the human soul, is that which ought to be overcome but by some cause becomes effectual again. It is the actuality of the principle that is outside of itself.

This principle underlies even the highest level of understanding, as one that has been overcome: in its subduing, not in its absence, the creative force reveals itself. *Where there is no insanity to rule and subdue, neither is there effective understanding.*[9] *Imbecility* [*Blödsinn*] consists in the absence of this originary substance, on which understanding wants to prove itself.

One tends to pit understanding against will and rightly so insofar as will cannot have any bounds within itself when it abstracts from understanding. For this reason, however, the will that has itself under control is also in itself understanding. Thus, will and understanding are again the same; *the originary potence emanating from itself, a blind desire* [*blindes Wollen*], *is understanding when it comes into its own.* The will is the subject of understanding in the proper sense, *quod subjectum est* [that which is the subject];[10] that which is the subject of understanding, however, is potentially [*potentiā*] already understanding.

In that originary potence is contained the understanding of divine life. Understanding = forestanding = originary standing [*Verstand* = *Vorstand* = *Urstand*] (Jacob Boehme) sig-

---

9. *Cf.* Schelling's *Die Weltalter* (The Ages of the World), *SW* VIII, p. 338: "Since Aristotle, it has become common to say that without some addition of insanity [*Wahnsinn*] no one could accomplish anything great. We would like to say instead that without continuous solicitation from insanity, which has to be subdued but should not be absent [. . .] Where there is no insanity, there is also no proper, actual, and living understanding [*rechter, wirklicher, lebendiger Verstand*]."

10. *Cf.* Boethius, *In topica Ciceronis* (*Patrologia Latina,* ed. Migne, 64:1130): "Every simple proposition consists of subject and predicate; the subject is what the predicate is said of, and the predicate is what is said of the subject) [*quod subjectum est*]."

nifies that from which something comes forth.[11] That originary potence, however, is actually the originary standing [*Urstand*] that ties in with the whole process. And if this potence is then brought back from its movement into a state of rest, then it is the actual understanding, the actual subject (the *substanding* [*Unterstand*], *id quod substat* [that which stands under]) of the explicated divine existence. For the Being that God gives himself by *adopting* the opposite Being is an explicated [*explicites*] Being, and the actualized originary potence, posited as such, no longer relates to this Being as understanding or originary standing but as substanding. Ἐπιστήμη [understanding], from ἐπισταμαι = εφισταμαι, *I remain standing. Understanding is nothing other than the originary potence brought to a standstill* (originarily that which is the unsteady [*Unstäte*]), that which came back from the movement and is now the self-possessing principle of movement. To understand = to be able to remain standing [*bestehenkönnen*]. Bacon: *scientia est potentia* [knowledge is power]. *Thus, that which is the science of all Being, wisdom, is also the potence of all Being.*

All that was cited previously from the Proverbs about wisdom is consistent with the nature of the originary potence, as posited by us, which first imparts the Creation to the Creator. "The Lord possessed me at the beginning of his way,"[12] *i.e., when he moved out of the unforethinkable Being;* before his deeds.—This line demonstrates that it is about something that is not an act of God. That originary potence is not brought forth by God. While it is not *before* him as

---

11. *Urstand* commonly signifies the originary condition of the first humans, Adam and Eve, before the fall from Paradise. In Boehme, it is synonymous with *Ungrund* [unground] or *Abgrund* [abyss] and with God, the origin, originary standing or condition, or primal moment from which Creation comes forth. See Boehme's *Psychologia vera, or Forty Questions about the Soul* (*Jacob Böhme's Sämmtliche Werke,* ed. K.W. Schiebler [Leipzig: Johann Ambrosius Barth, 1846], p. 27): "The first and greatest mystery is the abyss [*Abgrund*], where into nothingness a will is introduced, which is called Father, or the originary standing [*Urstand*] toward something. Creation originates out of [*geurständet*] the mystery of the Father through nature."

12. Proverbs 8:22 (KJV).

potence of Being, it is there as he is; it presents itself to him *as something he can either desire or not desire.* Although not God, it is also not his creature, and it is therefore between God and the creatures. The Lord possessed it; he overcame it because it had not been there before, but *afterhand, after he is, after he established himself* [*sich einstellte*]. He had it as a possibility not of himself but of all else.—"I was established [*Ich war eingesetzt*],"[13] i.e., *princeps constituta sum. Princeps* means that which is the originating one [*das Anfangende*]. (Varro, in his grammatical reflections on mythology, calls the heavens and the earth the gods that founded all, but he distinguishes *principes deos* [the first gods], *penes quos sunt prima* [those who have dominion over the first things], from *summi, penes quos sunt summa* [those who have dominion over the highest things].)[14] In this sense, wisdom is from eternity posited by the Creator as *that which originates all* [*Alles anfangend*], who ties it to *the process of becoming.—"I was established* when there were no watery depths," *etc.,* when he laid his compass on the earth, *i.e.,* during the origins [*Entstehung*] of the worldly system.[15]

But even after it was completed, I remained at his side as a child, as a *nursling* [*Pflegling*] (not as a craftsman), *nutritius* [being nurtured], thus also as an adopted child.[16] (Plato speaks of one that was brought up [*Mitaufgezogenen*]

---

13. Proverbs 8:23 (BSB).

14. *Cf.* Terentius Varro, *De lingua latina* V.57: "Principes dei Caelum et Terra" (The first gods were the Heavens and the Earth); and *Philosophie der Offenbarung,* SW XIII, p. 302: "As Varro in his partly grammatical, partly philosophical reflections on mythology says: *principes dii coelum et terra* [the first gods are the heavens and the earth], the gods who originated all, with whom the mythology of all peoples began, are the heavens and the earth. Varro also distinguishes *principes deos* [the first gods] from *summis* [the highest]. The former are to him *penes quos sunt prima* [those who have dominion over the first things]; the latter, *penes quos sunt summa* [those who have dominion over the highest things]."

15. Proverbs 8:24 (BSB).

16. Proverbs 8:30: "Then I was a skilled craftsman at his side." (BSB). KG 11:29, pp. 345–46: "The following must be translated 'like a child,' not, as usually happens, 'als Werkmeister [craftsman]' (the Hebrew word means both)."

together with the divine nature, wherein there was much disorder at the beginning.) The potence was not yet set out [*hinausgesetzt*]; thus, it was like a child in his father's house. This originary possibility, it continues, was welcomed by the Creator. I was the *model* for the Creation; it showed him what was possible if he wanted to create. I showed him "day after day,"[17] *i.e.*, all the moments of the future Creation.

(The Brahmins used to put the missionaries on the spot with the foll*ow*ing question: What did God do before the Creation? If the missionaries had picked up their Bibles more diligently, they would have found the answer in this passage.)

"My delight was to show the Creator the future Man."[18] For that originary potence, the *subjectum ultimum* of Creation, was intended to gain consciousness and thus become a knowledge partaking of the divine Creation.—

This passage is truly inspired, but I would judge it the same if it had come from the pen of a profane scribe.

Thus far, we have considered the Creation only as a possibility. It is not *a priori* discernible that the Creator will give this possibility reality, as is the case with any act of free will. Seeing such an accidental world before us, which more and more is transformed into understanding, as it ascends from the intermediate stages to human consciousness, *is proof through experience that God genuinely and by his deeds has Being necessarily*—a proof that strengthens more and more. In the end, this fact even becomes an unmediated object of the human consciousness.

If, however, *the actual positing of the potences and its processes* is a matter of indifference to God, if it is the same to him whether he leaves these potences in the unity of the originary design or intention, or lets them come forth in the

17. Proverbs 8:30: "I was filled with delight day after day, rejoicing always in his presence" (NIV).

18. See Proverbs 8:31: "I was rejoicing in his whole world, delighting together in the sons of men" (BSB). KG 11:29, p. 346: "'I played before him,' showed him (the father) all that could come about, because it is all-possibility; 'my joy was in the children of men.'"

tension and exclusion, *what then moves him to posit the actual world*? For we are convinced that this happened by *the epitome of the accidental Being in the place where before there was nothing other than that which necessarily and unforethinkably has existence [das notwendige unvordenkliche Existiren]*.

Even though he knows himself as Lord of Being, God lacks something, namely, to be cognized. This desire to be cognized belongs the most to the noblest characters; we should therefore not hesitate to posit this desire into the nature of God, which in itself is desireless. The main purpose is *to cognize* that God desired this process, which was shown to him *a priori*; the potence that was posited outside of itself was to become that which is knowledgeable of the entire Creation, that which posits God proper and is the seat and throne of the godhood.

XIV. Monotheism

[PL, pp. 515–28]

God is Lord only as lord of the three potences, which he holds together in inseparable unity. The three causes are joined together in him. There are no other causes except for *the absolute cause that stands above them* and effectuates and actuates all. *The Creator is not the One* as such [*der schlechthin Einfache*] but the All-One [*All-Eine*], for this plurality is a closed totality. We have thus arrived at *the concept of monotheism,*[1] *the transition from the positive philosophy to the philosophy of revelation.*

The most profound Christian dogmata, such as the trinity and the incarnation, have long been questioned philosophically without coming to terms with monotheism. Monotheism is a δόγμα κατ' ἐξοχήν [doctrine *par excellence*]; it contains more than the thought of the *one and only* God who, if he is God, cannot by definition have another god beside him. This *one-and-onliness* [*Einzigkeit*] is one of the negative attributes of God and holds true for the unforethinkable Being since divine Being, the *actus purus,* precedes all possibility. It has no equal because it is not potence.

Furthermore, *that which has Being purely* does not *have Being in actuality* [*actu*]; only that through whose Being an opposing potence is *overcome* has Being *actu.* It is Being in itself = essence = substance. If monotheism had this absolute singularity as its content, then Spinoza would have had to be a perfect monotheist.[2]

Even *Hegel* speaks of monotheism*s*;[3] one can see from this that he has not turned his attention to this concept. It is only curious how some develop a doctrine to overthrow

---

1. KG11:29, p. 346: "He can be creator not as one but as one in many. And this he is, for he is *causa causarum,* unity of *causa materialis, efficiens, et in quam.* Here we have arrived at monotheism."

2. KG11:29, p. 346: "Pure *S*[*eyn*] ([B]eing) is Spinoza's substance, but in this way Spinoza did indeed become a monotheist."

3. See Hegel's 1817 *Encyclopädie der philosophischen Wissenschaften im Grundrisse,* §573.

Christianity based on a system that never even debated this concept. This is not a matter of a doctrine but of a *world-historical* concept. On that basis, the critique ought to have held out the true sense to the *Christian dogmatists.* For they do not know it and count it under the negative attributes; thus, one of them relegates it to the *addendum.*[4]

The negative attributes describe God as substance. Theologians are therefore only able to understand the *One and Only* as infinite substance. If one does not get beyond God as he is in and for himself, then one can *only* determine *God as absolute substance.* Theism should also be called atheism.[5] God is the One and Only by virtue of his Being, which precedes his godhood. One is therefore to understand under such a theism a doctrine that conceives God merely as infinite substance. But therein (God merely *potentiā*) lies the demand to proceed to the one who exists *as* God; and so far as theism does not fulfill this demand, it can be called *atheism.* Our older theologians use the words *theist* and *atheist* almost synonymously.[6]

Every doctrine must address God's relationship to the [world of] things. If one now proceeds to the world but continues to cling to a bare theism so that the things are merely qualifications of the divine substance, then *pantheism* arises. A doctrine that is theism must progress to pantheism.[7] *Theism, at its conclusion, must become pantheism.*

---

4. See Friedrich Schleiermacher, who discusses the doctrine of the trinity only at the conclusion of his two-volume doctrine of faith, *Der christliche Glaube: nach den Grundsäzen der evangelischen Kirche im Zusammenhange dargestellt* (The Christian Faith: According to the Principles of the Protestant Church, 1822).

5. KG11:29, p. 346: "The one God is infinite substance. If one cannot go further, one can continue to insist that one is a monotheist and resign oneself to being called an atheist, both with equal justification.

6. KG11:30, p. 346: "Monotheism's general thesis does not go beyond the mere concept of God, does not arrive at the one God; this is theism, not monotheism."

7. KG11:30, p. 347: "Theism, therefore, is by no means the true contrary of pantheism, because theism itself, as soon as it wants to address this question, must define itself in a pantheistic direction."

Monotheism is the doctrine that defines God or his godhood. *But what is this godhood actually based on?* It is said that the true God is a living God. However, a living God is only one that can step forth from his unforethinkable Being, can make it into a moment of his own, and, *freeing his essence* from it, can posit it as *spirit,* by means of which he is also given *the possibility to be Creator by his pitting another Being against the unforethinkable Being.*

This is no longer just that simple unity of substance; *the substantial unity has disappeared into the potences, and a suprasubstantial [übersubstantielle] unity has taken its place.* In actuality, *the potences* are the *forces of the movement* in which God moves as the living God. *Thus God is the All-One, according to the forms of his Being not One but many; he is necessarily One only according to his godhood* since he effectuates in all those forms. *Apart from his godhood, God is not One but many.* The unity asserted in monotheism is, in fact, a contradiction. God is not singular in the way a principle, *e.g.,* one of our potences, is One. In this sense, God is, in fact, not singular.

John of Damascus, from whom most of what is still philosophy in theology is derived, has the sense to say: God is not so much the one and only [*einzig*] as he is *supra-one-and-only* [*übereinzig*].[8] In the Mosaic Law (5 Moses 6:4),[9] it is written: "Hear, O Israel, Jehovah our Elohim is the one Jehovah." If by this was intended only oneness in the customary sense, then it should have been written without the repetition of Jehovah אֶחָד (*'echâd*) [one]. It also did not say "a single Elohim," since *only as Jehovah is he the true godhood.* Apart from that, he could be more than one. In the beginning, when monotheism was the world religion, there was cause to not

8. See *Saint John of Damascus, Writings,* ed. Frederic H. Chase, Jr., trans. S.D.F. Salmand (New York: Fathers of the Church, 1958), p. 167: "Now, we both know and confess that God is without beginning and without end, everlasting and eternal, uncreated, unchangeable, inalterable, simple, uncompounded, incorporeal, invisible, impalpable, uncircumscribed, unlimited, incomprehensible, uncontained, unfathomable, good, just, the maker of all created things, all-powerful, all-ruling, all-seeing, the provider, the sovereign, and the judge of all."

9. Deuteronomy 6:4: "Hear, O Israel: The Lord our God, the Lord is One" (BSB).

emphasize the deeper concept; *thus, monotheism could shrivel into this meaningless sentence.*

It is only in the sense given by us that monotheism is opposed to pantheism. According to pantheism, *God is that which has Being merely; the godhood, however, rises also above its necessary Being.* Pantheism has, as its whole content, that which in true Being is but a moment. The true concept of God is not the concept of the infinite Being but that to which it is *subjected.* But it is precisely for that reason that what has Being unmediatedly or merely is the presupposition for the true concept and only makes it possible. *For only the necessity of this Being gives God the freedom to have this Being be subjected to him.* Nothing has ever had power over the human mind that was not subjected to this concept of monotheism. The steady polemic against *pantheism* only shows that it has *not been overcome.*

Theism pronounces a death sentence on itself when it calls itself *moral theism.*[10] The metaphysical is impossible to obliterate from the concept of God. The necessary Being of God is the fundamental concept of all religion. It has a magical effect on the mind. Where this moment is missing, there can be no monotheism. Monotheism and pantheism are more closely related to each other than each of them is to the empty theism. For it does not matter that any God is recognized but only that *the* God is recognized.

Theism is a concept of God that posits him only in regard to his substance, as θεός, not as ὁ θεός.[11] Theism is therefore to be understood as *a way of thinking that has not progressed to the cognition of the living God.*[12] Thus, those who have not

---

10. See Kant's *Vorlesungen über die philosophische Religionslehre* (Lectures on the Philosophical Doctrine of Religion), ed. Karl Heinrich Ludwig Pölitz (Leipzig: Taubert'sche Buchhandlung, 1830), pp. 16–17: "What to call a theology that regards God as **summum bonum**, as the highest moral good? It has until now not correctly been discerned, and thus it has not been given a name. One can call it **Theismus moralis**, where God is the originator of our moral laws."

11. *Philosophy of Mythology,* SW XII, p. 70: "Theism is that concept in which God (θεός) is posited only in general, not as the definite God (ὁ θεός), the God who *is.*"

12. See Kant's *Vorlesungen über die philosophische Religionslehre,* p. 15: "Theism consists in believing not merely in a God, but also in a *living*

arrived at true monotheism are sincere when they call themselves theists. However, if theism opposes this progression, then it is the wrong system. Insofar as theism is lacking determination and positive content, true scientific philosophy cannot remain with it and must move on necessarily toward either pantheism or monotheism. *Theism* is undetermined; it can potentially be either pantheism or monotheism. Both assert more than a mere empty oneness [*Einheit*].[13]

Spinoza's pantheism also had to assume—in addition to the oneness, to that which blindly exists before all—an allness [*Allheit*], and therein Spinoza rises above the abstract elements of the *Eleatic* philosophy. He posits substance as extended and thinking. It is none other than Being that, having passed over *a potentia ad actum* [from potence to actuality], has lost itself as potence (our first potence, which has the ability to be). The thinking substance could be compared to our second potence, which is modifiably [*modificabel*] subordinated to the first.[14] But this second potence, as autonomous principle, was modeled after Descartes, and Spinoza posits both attributes as equal. To him, they are merely mediated by the substance; thus, where we have the spirit, Spinoza falls back into the dead universal substance. Spinoza's all-oneness [*All-Einheit*] is dead and lifeless.[15]

God, who has produced the world through knowledge and free volition."

13. KG11:30, p. 347: "Jacobi boasted of being a pure theist and agitated against pantheism, defining the word as the doctrine of Allheit, εν το παν [one and all]. This, however, is also monotheism [...] The distinction is that panth[eism] thinks of only one principle, blind being, from which no system can be formed; alongside Einheit [oneness], he places an Allheit."

14. *SW*XII, pp. 68-69: "Pantheism itself, in its mere possibility, is the ground of all godhood and all true religion. Therein lies, as previously remarked, the spell that pantheism has cast over so many, a spell that cannot be reversed by the speeches of those who do not go back to this originary concept [the true concept of God]. Monotheism is nothing more than pantheism that has become esoteric, latent, and inward; it is pantheism that has been overcome."

15. KG11:30, p. 348: "[Spinoza's] error [...] is not his doctrine of Alleinheit but the fact that his Alleinheit is dead. From two sides, opposite charges can be brought against him—that he is not a mono-

Theism is an inept doctrine that has nothing to set against pantheism. Only an assertion can be refuted, but that is precisely what *pantheism* lacks; it *does not progress toward an assertion* but rather remains with the mere concept, *i.e.*, with theism. Both lack what ought to be asserted.

Jacobi had no choice but to agree theoretically with pantheism. Against it, he posited his insuperable faith in a personal God and called himself first a believer [*Gläubigen*] and later a rationalist believer [*Vernunftgläubigen*].[16] But in common parlance, one does not call someone who *recognizes the impossibility of something and yet believes in it* a rationalist! If the newer philosophy posited a living doctrine in place of the dead doctrine of all-oneness, then it would also be called pantheism, like everything that goes beyond pure theism. Deeper theologians are also familiar with the depth of pantheism and know that it can only be overcome by positive knowledge. But those who pride themselves on being the purest theists (rationalism is only an improved deism), who warn against pantheism in their writings and from the pulpit—those may be hiding *a fear of monotheism* behind the fear of pantheism, *whereby something positive is reached in the cognition of God.*

Theism can only position itself against atheism, which, if it is an actual atheism, is, like the Epicurean system and the clumsy French materialism, no less hostile toward pantheism than toward theism. For that matter, *the better theism* sets out to cognize in that which has Being *a priori* not only *the bruta existentia* [brute existence] but also that which is free of Being; then it should not be difficult to progress toward true monotheism.

---

theist, and that he is more than a theist, that his God is not empty. The latter is of course the objection of theism."

16. On the so-called Pantheism controversy (*Pantheismusstreit*), which lasted from 1785 to 1789, see Gérard Vallée, *The Spinoza Conversations between Lessing and Jacobi* (Lanham: University Press of America, 1988).

XV. The Trinity: The Further Development of the Theogonic Process

[PL, pp. 528–33]

The concept of monotheism provides entry into the specifics of the Christian doctrine; it is the point where philosophy first enters into a relationship with the highest idea of Christianity.[1] *The concept of all-oneness has its more specific expression in the triune God.* Since I do not take the deduction of Christian ideas as lightly as has been done previously, as I prefer not to state any vague concordance, I will say right away that with the doctrine of all-oneness the doctrine of the Christian Trinity is not yet given.

But how does the one differ from the other? And what has to be added to the concept of all-oneness to arrive at the content of the Christian Trinity?

Even before the Creation, in the *preconception of the Creation, God had three potences as possibilities of a future Being.* In the Creation, these potences are put into effect. Here is a multiplicity of potences and effectuating causes, which, however, are not yet self-sufficient; rather, one is effective in all, and thus is *alone the self-sufficient absolute personality.*

A *multiplicity of persons,* each of which is God, *constitutes the Christian Trinity.* If one wanted to designate *the absolute personality* with a Christian expression, one would have to call it, as the originator and beginner of the process, ὁ θεός καὶπατὴρ [the God and Father].

Toward the end of the process, it may be possible to designate *that absolute possibility* even more specifically as *Father* and as that which turns the *actus purus*[2] from actuality [*ex actu*] into potence. Now there is no other expression than *to beget* [*zeugen*] for an activity, in which what had Being pre-

1. John 17:3: "Now this is eternal life, that they may know you, the only true God, and Jesus Christ, whom you have sent" (BSB).

2. In scholastic philosophy, *actus purus* (literally "pure act") is the absolute perfection of God.

viously *takes away* something that belonged to it, *i.e.*, posits it as an other from itself, yet not as an actual but in a way that it is compelled *to actualize itself unrelentingly. The second potence is thus the begotten potence.*

If we now think of B as having been actually *overcome* by the second potence, then the latter is the Lord of Being in the same way as the Father; but as Lord of Being, it is no longer simply potence but personality, like the Father already before. It is the Son, of the same glory [*Herrlichkeit*] as the Father, through the lordship over Being (B), which was originarily with the Father but is now *given* to the Son by the Father. Just as the glory over Being is the same in both, so is their godhood.

As we know, God, being the third potence, posits his own essence, which is freed from the unforethinkable Being and therewith negated. Only when B is overcome by A^2, and A^3 has lordship over B, can the essence of God—freed from the unforethinkable Being and thus posited as potence—be instated in Being as Spirit. The third potence is thus no less lord of the same Being, whose lord is also the Son and the Father; hence, it is also personality in equal glory with Father and Son.

And in this way—and only this way, namely, *through continued development—is the Christian doctrine of Trinity to be understood from the idea of all-oneness.* The beginning potence B is not the Father but *only the begetting force of the Father,* the potence of the Father; *the Father remains outside of the process.* He is Father only in the actualized Son, and is the latter only in the completely *overcome B.* Father and Son thus come into actualization together. Before the Son is actualized, the Father is the one who effectuates, but only invisibly. The Father is only Father once he has Being again within himself as that which has been brought back. Here, thus, where Being is that which has been brought back into possibility, it is a shared [*gemeinschaftliche*] Being of Father and Son, and *the same holds true for the Spirit.* The Father is no sooner Father than the Spirit is posited as personality. There are not three gods because *Being,* and thus also *the glory of Being,* is *one shared by all.* Therefore, where the opposition of potences ends, there are no longer potences *but personalities.* They are potences only during the process. *Father, Son, and Spirit are actualized in the overcome* **B**.

Therewith our consideration has been elevated to another level, indeed to another world. We see in the potences only *the genesis of the concrete world.* With the personalities, we are entering the divine world, and only here does *the higher meaning of the potences* become manifest. *Being is originarily only with the Father,* as possibility; then it is given to the Son (to whom the Father has given life, namely B, for *life is within it*). Then the Son gives the *overcome* Being again to the Father, so that he possesses it again as potence, possibility, into which it has been brought back. This is the higher meaning of the process: that the Father gives Being to the Son, and together Father and Son give Being to the Spirit. He who loves me will be loved again by my Father, and we shall make our μονὴν [abode] with him, *i.e.,* he himself rests and no longer partakes in the process.[3]

Here a higher divine history arises; and we can be confident we are now at the point at which a philosophy of revelation is possible. I only want to put you at the point from which to grasp the content of revelation. I will proceed quickly. *For now, I will only expose the world, the site at which the great history of revelation has come to pass.* The detailed history will be explained *later.*

This is not about speculative dogmatism, or any dogmas at all, not about demonstrating the truth of Christian religion, but only about understanding! Its acceptance is another matter; it requires heart and courage.

3. John 14:23: "Jesus replied, 'If anyone loves me, he will keep my word. My Father will love him, and we will come to him and make our home with him.'" (BSB).

XVI. From Potences to Personalities
[PL, pp. 533-36]

This, as has been shown so far, is what happens at the end of Creation: the *tension* [*Spannung*] *of the potences* moves throughout all of nature. Every thing is in relation to [the tension]. None represent their complete oneness. Any thing that is originating (*Entstehende*) is a fourth element between the three potences. But this tension lasts only to the end of nature, which is ruled by tension; each thing in nature has a relation only to the potences.[1]

Originary Man, in whom the tension of the potences subsides, has a relation to the personalities; in him is expressed *the last moment* of actualization, *where the potences have become actual personalities.*

In the first book of Moses, only the one Elohim[2] speaks until the story transitions to the plural counsel of Elohim. Here that one Elohim says: "Let us make Man in our image," *i.e.,* after our likeness and unity.[3] At the end of the process, there is a plurality of personalities. There is not yet the true Son; being begotten, he is only in the end.[4] The same is true for the Spirit. Now there are *three,* each a lord over his Being, but only the *Father* as the *originary personality* is ἀγένητος [unbegotten]. To the Son and the Spirit have been bestowed the glory and personality. If the godhood is therefore complete and absolute only in the three personalities, then the process is, in regard to the things, a process of creation and, with respect to God, a theogonic process. The process strives toward the realization of the godhood and its *eternal relations.* In that sense it is to be understood as *theogony.*

---

1. KG11:32: p. 350: "nature is related only to potences."
2. The Hebrew name of God: אֱלֹהִים (Elohim).
3. Genesis 1:26.
4. KG11:32, p. 350: The Son is indeed present in the process, but as potency, not as personality.

Dionysius the Areopagite calls the Father the *God-begetting godhood* and the Son the godhood that is *begotten by God.*[5] Basil of Caesarea lines up all three as *αἰτία προκαταρκτικὴ* [the original cause], *δημιουργητικη* [the creative cause], and *τελειωτικη* [the perfecting cause].[6] Same in Paul: *ἐξ οὗ, δι' οὗ καὶ εἰς ὅν τὰ πάντα.*[7] I don't have time to demonstrate the shallowness of the exegetical attempts to wipe out this reference to the triad.

Where now is the unity of this trinity? It is in the godhood that all three personalities share. Theologians have long rejected the view that there is a fourth; it can only be possible in said manner.

In the final stage of the process, *the difference between the potences is sublated. The personalities appear as such,* and Man, who finds himself immediately after the Creation in a place of joy, in a space surrounded and cared for by the godhood, is enclosed by the three personalities, by the [plural] Elohim. (Not only the German word *Garten* and the many names of towns that end in "gard," but also the Hebrew word *gan* [גַּן, garden, enclosure] denotes a *guarded space*). Through Man as the end goal of nature, everything else was taken into by the godhood as well. Here is nothing outside the divine [*Aussergöttliches*]. As the Pythagoreans have said about the world, Man is enclosed by God as his custodian.

---

5. *Ibid.*: "θεογονος θεοτης [divinity born of god]."

6. Basil, *De Spiritu Sancto,* 16.38: "And in the creation bethink you first, I pray you, of the original cause of all things that are made, the Father; of the creative cause, the Son; of the perfecting cause, the Spirit; so that the ministering spirits subsist by the will of the Father, are brought into being by the operation of the Son, and perfected by the presence of the Spirit" (translated by Blomfield Jackson. *From Nicene and Post-Nicene Fathers, Second Series,* vol. 8, ed. Philip Schaff and Henry Wace [Buffalo, N.Y.: Christian Literature Publishing Co., 1895]).

7. Romans 11:36: "For from him and through him and to him are all things" (BSB).

XVII. The Origin of the Extra-Divine World

[PL, pp. 536–49]

By the very fact that nothing extra-divine [*Aussergöttliches*] is presenting itself to us as yet shows the limitations of the development thus far. In that originary state, where Man does not have a relation to any of the potences but is in an unmediated relation to the godhood, there was more than a revelation. Previously, the Creation was only a *quid praeter Deum* [what is beside God], not *extra Deum* [outside of God]. As conceived so far, the Creation was by all means immanent. We have not yet arrived at the world as it is now.

The present world is extra-divine. We must ask for it to become comprehensible to us as such. We are called upon to do so by our sense of freedom, which can only be satisfied in a free relation to God. Man is free not only in relation to God but also in relation to the world. There would be no salvation [*Erlösung*] if our world were divine because then any striving to liberate oneself from it would be foolishness.

Our development has been inconsistent with reality in another respect as well, and it is therefore not completed. It has found its conclusion thus far in the assumption that *the Creation has been brought to a close in Man.* But we can see now how the circle of events opens again. A new world rises above nature and its monotonous cycle, which, by comparison, has become a mute and apathetic past. Instead of Man, we find a human race, a spiritual life [*geistiges Leben*] that recreates itself continually. Where did this new world rising above nature come from? It could not have been in the unmediated intention of *the Creation whose objective was in Man.* The cause of this new movement that rose above nature could only have been in Man himself.

The intent of the Creation was to have Man **rest** [*ruhen*] *in God.* This prompts us to explain how it was *within the power of Man to question everything at the very moment when everything was meant to enter into unison.* We have to explain how *Man himself was able to bring about a new tension* in order to make himself the beginning of a new process.

A second question would be: what changes took place in the Being brought about by the Creation from this overthrow and how were they possible? *How was an extra-divine world, namely paganism, possible?* This external world cannot be explained without breaking apart the divine unity, something that could not possibly have originated from God. Where did Man get this power? And certainly this only happened with the intention to bring about a higher manifestation of the divine.

Man was the creator of this external world. All along, nothing has evaded research and impeded an all-comprehending system as much as the efforts to *reconcile Man's freedom of will with divine causality,* which was taken to be unconditional. God's infinite power of causality can only allow for an infinite passivity in his creation. That which is determined by the *one* cause cannot find in itself any possibility other than that One.

A solution suggests itself: the Creation is not a single act but rather two distinct moments, one negative and one positive, neither of which posited unmediatedly by the same cause. They presuppose two independent causes, one sublating the effects of the other. That which comes into Being is the result not of a single cause but rather of several causes, *each of which is in itself infinite, yet finite opposite the other.*

From eternity, the Creator finds in himself a *potence,* a will ignitable [*entzündbar*] by his desire to be elevated to an *actus*; this will is infinite by nature but thereby *impotent* and merely matter [*Stoff*]. It is confronted by the unforethinkable Being of God posited from actuality [*ex actu*] by *that other Being.* The same cause that posits matter cannot also posit form. Matter is boundless and requires a cause independent from it, as form. The Creator, however, is the one who prods all causes into working in unison. Consequently, that which appears as the final result, wherein *all three causes* come into unity, comes between them as one that is free from the first cause through the second and, by having B as its substrate, is free from A^2. It is like the tongue of a balance scale [*wie das Zünglein in der Wage*]; it stands between both and at the same time contains a relation to the third potence (which is not the effecting one but the final cause) and to which only a free relation is possible. *This is the only way to explain how freedom is created.*

The final result—into which the tension among the potences settles and which comes to rest among the three personalities—is pure mobility, freedom, without any substrate or materiality (because those exist only in the conflict of the potences). It can only be life, pure mobility, spirit in the sense of how God is spirit.

This explains the age-old *doctrine of the supra-material nature of the human soul.* Spirit is not a created thing but pure breath [*Hauch*], pure freedom and mobility.

Yet this freedom is always a conditional freedom but only insofar as Man remains in this position of unity and concordance with the potences. Man has been put into this unity as absolute freedom and mobility and therefore has the possibility to posit himself outside of it. It was therefore necessary for Man to maintain the unity. He had a law that God did not have. God could set the potences into tension and remain insurmountable even within the tension. He is lord over both actual and possible potences. With Man, it is different. He possesses that B as his ground since the Creation. However, since he only possesses it as part of the Creation, he only possesses it as possibility. Creation is meant to posit this principle as possibility. This possibility may present itself to Man as the potence of another Being, which is within his power. In fact, the *very law* that tells him *not to move* **B**, *the ground of the Creation,* reveals to him the possibility to up-heave this ground of the Creation again.

For Man, B is *that which ought not to be* [*das Nicht-seyn-sollende*]. B is given to him for preservation, and with the knowledge of the possibility of setting it into motion again, the lure [*Reiz*] of re-actualizing it was planted in him. *It requires a supra-natural will to resist this temptation.* However, the consequence is entirely different from what is expected. *Man wanted to do what God did, set the potences into tension to rule with them as lord.* But this is not given to him; on the contrary, with the attempt to be like God, the glory [*Herrlichkeit*] of God is lost to him, στερούμενος τῆς δόξης τοῦ θεοῦ [he is lacking in the glory of God]. For Man was lord of the potences as well in order to keep them (on God's behalf) in indissoluble unity. He believed to be as powerful as lord over the principle that was the cause of the tension in the Creation (and which in him was the complete reverse when it again became active) as he was over himself in his potentiality.

God is also the All-One prior to the Creation; in this self-concept [*Selbstbegriff*] before the Creation, the first potence, which is the posterior B, is the deepest, most inward, most negated. What is posited in actuality and willed in this self-concept before the Creation is the *third potence* wherein God posits his essence as Spirit, as one who potentializes his unforethinkable Being and posits himself as Spirit. The contrary potence is the outermost one; the others, which by their nature are mostly positive, are the most negated ones at the beginning of the Creation. *God turns outward that which he intends to turn* **inward** (and he already practices this irony in the Creation)

In Creation, there is also a reversal [*Umkehrung*] of the unity, just as there is in the divine self-concept. The world is the *unum versum* [turned toward one point], and the act of this reversal is the *universio* (Lucretius). Man believed to be as powerful in this *turning outward* as God is in the *universio*. He thought to obtain therewith *indissoluble* life, like God, and to initiate, like God, an eternal motion. But that principle, as the ground (basis) of human consciousness, is handed over and subjected to the same if it remains in itself. When it is set into motion, it becomes a power that transcends and subjugates human consciousness.

This principle is no longer a divine principle, as it was in Creation, but an *extra-divine [aussergöttliche] power, even an anti-divine [widergöttliche] power.* It was within the power of Man to keep the world in God. *But because he put himself in God's place, he posits the world for himself but outside of God. This world* of Man is divested of its glory; *it no longer has a point of unity in itself, which Man was supposed to be.* Having failed to maintain that inwardness, the world has been given to externality—where the individual has lost his momentous position and appears accidentally, and without meaning, outside the Other.

The true meaning of every thing lies in the unity of the human consciousness. But *instead of all that has been created entering into an eternal consciousness,* it fell victim to the untrue Being, as we now perceive it. The *one Man who lives on in all of us* can rightly be called the author of this world—a world that searches for its final goal in vain and brings about that wrong time, one that never ends but emerges continuously.

One can give credit to the scientific philosophy, which has often been accused of bringing itself only as far as an immanent Creation, for calling the phenomenal world a world outside of God while also teaching an immanent Creation. On the other hand, it will not be easy for a philosophy to return the bad form of outside- and besideness [*Ausser- und Nebeneinander*] to the Absolute.

Man thought to gain eternal life with the help of that principle. Since he could not sublate the substance of the world, he altered the form of its Being into one that is fragmented and outside of God. He could no longer sublate the substances, only their meaning and unity. *And therewith a new tension is established.* Only this time, it is posited by human will, not by divine will. "Behold, the man has become like one of us," *i.e.,* he is no longer resembles the godhood but has become *One of us.*[1]

But which of the potences has Man made himself alike? The potence that he has elevated in himself to his will is the one he had already preserved for safekeeping; thus, it would not be too bold to say: *Man has seized the fatherly, begetting power in that prehistoric act. But to be lord over the activated principle is not given to him*; he succumbs under its rule, which now takes on, against his consciousness, the attributes it had before the Creation. In this quieted principle, the second and third principle was also actualized. *The second potence,* which had made itself the lord of that principle, *was thereby de-glorified* [*entherrlicht*]; not that it could cease to be personality in itself, but in the human consciousness and opposite *the same activated principle, that which ought not to be* [*das Nicht-seyn-sollende*], the second will again behave like

1. Genesis 3:22 (BSB).

a potence. No less the spirit, which, excluded from Being, again becomes potence, *i.e.,* only cosmic spirit (as it was during the Creation).

The position of the second potence given to it by Man is especially important to us. Here one first discovers an *incompleteness in our development of the triune doctrine.* If *from the point where we have seen three personalities of equal glory and godhood,* we immerse ourselves deeper into the particular historical circumstances of the persons, namely as they are further determined in Christianity, then we see that its entire content is not yet conveyed in our development. When the *Son* speaks of his obedience to the Father, he ascribes to himself, at least as possibility, *a will of his own, an independent Being.* The Becoming Human is presented as a voluntary degradation that he could have eluded. This free relation could no longer happen at the end of the Creation. *In the Creation, there was only One personality, that of the Father. At the end, the Son also became a divine personality, but he shares lordship over one common Being with the Father.* He is God but only in and with the Father, and without being able to confront him, as he will be able to in the later history of their relationship.

We thus need to proceed to this further point in the historical *development.* At the end of the Creation, that unity remains only as idea. *Man* is brought back to himself, to *the self-possessing* B. Having possessed B only as possibility, he could now elevate it again to actuality. That he actually did that cannot be determined *a priori*; it can only be cognized empirically from the state of the world. *By reawakening in himself a principle that was meant to be in a state of rest, the personalities became potences* and excluded from the consciousness now ruled by B. Their Being is therefore *independent from the absolute cause*; *they owe their Being to Man. They are self-subsistent powers outside of God* who, when they restore themselves to the glory and godhood, will *not merely be in and with the Father but be equal to him by virtue of their own, self-acquired godhood,* which they owed previously only to the Father.

Giving special attention to the *Being of the Son,* which is now as *suspended* by the action of Man as it was during the Creation by the Father. *Thus, the Son no longer has a position given to him by the Father but one that is independent from the Father. Through the action of Man, he has been posited outside his godhood and separated from the Father, therefore without being able to cease in his consciousness to be a divine personality and be one with the Father.* He is a divine personality by his originary nature, *but he is extra-divine because of being posited into a Being independent from the Father. He is the son of Man and the son of God—ὁ υἱὸς τοῦ ἀνθρώπου* [the son of Man]*—not in the sense of genus* but rather as used by Christ in an individual sense.[2]

One could see herein an argument for *the idea that Christ should be regarded the originary, archetypal Man.* This view recommends itself because in this way one would not have to grant Christ more than mere humanity, and, on the other hand, he could be elevated *as the One and Only.* Aside from any objections to this we might otherwise have, this view is contradicted by the fact that "Son of Man" has been used in the N.T. not as a title of glorification[3] but of *denigration*. The strain of melancholy painted on Christ's face when he calls himself thus contradicts any explanation that sees an elevation in this name.

After the Son has been posited again as potence—by the same principle that already opposed him in the Creation—he must *overcome* the antagonistic principle. Thus, in relation to the human consciousness, from which he is excluded by B, a process emerges that is not willed by God but posited against God's will. In general terms, a world has come into Being that is not willed by God, an extra-divine world, as required by us earlier.

However, it cannot be said with absolute certainty that God did not will this extra-divine world, because if his will was *against* this world, then the Father, having foreseen this

2. See Matthew 9:6–8: "'But so that you may know that the Son of Man has authority on earth to forgive sins' [...] when the crowds saw this, they were filled with awe and glorified God whom had given such authority to men." (BSB).

3. KG11:34, p. 354: "Since Kant's time, this expression has been understood to refer to the primal human being, the human being *par excellence,* but in the N.T. it is used not as a title of honor, but as a title of denigration."

overthrow [*Umsturz*], would not have willed the world at all. *Yet, at the same time, he foresaw the Son as an independent personality. Indeed, the same overthrow gave him the Son as an independent personality.* In itself, the action of the Father could not proceed beyond the begetting of the unity that brought about the Creation. *And once the unity was broken, God could not restore it*; he could only create the first world. It could only be restored by the Son who has now become self-subsistent. Only by foreseeing the Son's self-subsistent personality could the Father have willed both the Creation and its overthrow.

Only a world of fixed, inalterable, and eternal Being was possible by virtue of the Father and the Son conceived in him as Demiurge—[but] not this world of free movement, the truly creative Being, the world of Man. The latter was only possible by virtue of the Son with foresight [*Hinaussicht*] of him (ἐν αὐτῷ ἐκτίσδη τὰ πάντα, he was anticipated before the Creation).[4] The Father creates the concrete manifold Being only to pass it on to the Son as self-subsistent personality (πάντα μοι παρεδόθη παρὰ τοῦ πατρός).[5] Without the foresight [*Voraussicht*] toward the Son, without the resolution (πρόθεσις [setting forth]) made in the Son before the world, without the resolution of the Son as self-subsistent personality, there would be no freedom, no world as we know it.

While speaking *of an extra-worldly god* [*ausserweltlichen Gott*] may seem precarious and should be done *with caution, one must speak of an extra-divine world* [*aussergöttliche Welt*] *whereby freedom alone is possible.* If ever there was such a world, it would have been unavoidable for this Being to have fallen away from God. Therefore, the Father has loved the Son before the world was created because otherwise there could be no freedom, no world. He values freedom so highly that he makes the fate of his Creation dependent on its freedom. The Father hands the world over to his Son and has no more claim to it.

---

4. Colossians 1:16: "In him all things were created" (BSB).

5. Matthew 11:27: "All things have been entrusted to me by my Father" (BSB).

But if the world has now been posited by the action of Man outside of God, how does it persist? The world and the potences that created it are posited originarily only in the will of the one who wills all things.[6] However, this will also remains in effect after the estrangement has come to pass but without thereby willing that which is estranged. *The originary will of God* continues to operate but as an *unwilling* [*Unwille*], as divine wrath. All human beings, both Jews and pagans, are by nature children of the divine wrath.[7]

As we can see, *the second potence has gained, a self-subsistent position* and is therefore able to follow Being in its extra-divinity [*Aussergöttlichkeit*] in order to *bring it back into godhood* and posit it as such. Only in the foresight toward his Son could the Father will a Being that he knew beforehand would remove itself from him. The substance of Being and the world persists despite the catastrophe. But it could not have persisted in substance if not God's will in B remained in Being. But it remains in Being against God's will. Only the substance of the world is affected by him, not the form insofar as it is extra-divine. It is estranged not from his power but from his will. His will is turned away from it. He has an effect [*wirkt*] on it but no longer as Father, and a relation to it as Father is only possible again through the Son. *This is the great depth of the doctrine of the wrath of God.* The will that is in B, and within which the world remains, is one that, at the end of Creation, has been ignited and incited out of its state of calmness.

Of course, it would have been within the power of the Creator to just take back all of Being (for everything was figured on Man [*denn auf den Menschen war Alles berechnet*]). However, he would then not have willed the Creation in the first place. He wanted the Creation only in anticipation of, and in relation to, *the personality that, even bereaved of his godhood, would not let go of Being and restore it back into its essence.* It is therefore in accordance with divine will that *the potence*

---

6. *Cf.* 1 Corinthians 15:28: "And when all things have been subjected to him, then the Son himself will be made subject to him who put all things under him, so that God may be all in all" (BSB).

7. Ephesians 2:3: "Like the rest, we were by nature children of wrath" (BSB).

that negated B retains its relation to the same *in order to overcome that anti-divine* [*widergöttliche*] *principle and atone for the unwilling of God* [*den Unwillen Gottes zu sühnen*].

According to this, we must differentiate two ages:

1) *The Age* or the Eon *of the Father,* when Being is entirely in the hands of the Father, and the Son is still within the Father.

2) *The Age of the Son,* which spans this entire world *since the Creation.* Since that time he is a self-subsistent personality outside of the Father, who has given all Being over to him.

The following is *only the history of the second personality,* within which *two personalities* must be differentiated. *When Man has fallen under the power of B,* and this principle of the divine unwilling has become revealed and still dominates the human consciousness with unbroken force, the mediating personality is in the deepest state of negation and restriction. It is in a state of suffering (in the Paulinian parlance, πάσχειν [suffer] as opposed to δοξάζεσθαι [glorify]). If one part suffers, every part suffers with it—if one part is glorified, *etc.* [8]

The second personality is posited out of its δόξα [glory], which it possessed in and with the Father, into suffering, wherein it no longer had a place in the human consciousness—excluded entirely from Being, therefore unfree, so that it is as *that which must have an effect* [*das Wirken-müssende*] not according to its will but according to its nature. However, the more it gives itself this suffering, the more self-conscious it makes itself.

But first it must again make itself the lord of the undivine [*ungöttliche*] Being by means of a merely natural and necessary effect [*Wirkung*], through a process wherein it is an unfree, naturally effecting potence. This time of the merely natural effect of the mediating personality is *the Age of Paganism,* a process in which it must effect not according to its will but according to its nature. This time of suffering

8. 1 Corinthians 12:26: "If one part suffers, every part suffers with it; if one part is honored, every part rejoices with it" (BSB).

is most determinedly hinted at in the O.T., for example, in Isaiah. There, the Messiah (the name of the second personality in the O.T. as the one designated as King and Lord of all Being from the beginning, indeed before the foundation of the world, *not in the future*), is presented as *suffering* through the entire time of prevailing darkness. The Messiah is compared to a tender shoot of rice [*eben erst aufschiessenden Reis*].[9]

By the end of this *process, however,* when this potence has once again made itself the Lord of Being, it finds itself in a position to make use of it freely according to its will, whether to keep all Being for itself or to return this bought-at-a-price [*teuer erworbene*] Being to the Father.[10] It now acts of its own free will. This is the time of its appearance in Christ. The content of this voluntary deed is the content of Revelation.

Herewith is given the position, scope, and path of our further development.

---

9. Isaiah 53:2: "He grew up before him like a tender shoot, and like a root out of dry ground" (BSB). KG 11:35, p. 355: "The Messiah is the Lord's Anointed, but the Anointed is still not king."

10. 1 Corinthians 6:20: "You were bought at a price" (BSB).

XVIII. Sketch of the Philosophy of Mythology

[PL, pp. 549–58]

The General Significance of the Mythological Process

When Man reawakens the principle meant to be at rest—which the potences had to overcome in order to elevate themselves to personalities—the higher potences become de-actualized [*entwirklicht*] and excluded from the consciousness in which only the first [potence] now rules. Inwardly, they retain their divine significance; but outwardly, being under the tension of the process, they are extra-divine powers [*aussergöttliche Mächte*]. This process is to be defined in greater detail as follows.

1) If it is objective by its nature, then it occurs only in the human consciousness. For *all of Creation was about consciousness*; the Creator is indifferent to all else. *Consciousness must be healed again* by way of a second analogous process.

2) The process is a natural one, from which the divinity is excluded. Being under tension, *the powers that are divine by their essence behave like natural potences.* Even though God has no part in it, it is a theogonic process, one that generates God within the consciousness without excluding B, insofar as the originary consciousness's positing of God is restored through it. For in the human consciousness, B is, in itself and ideally, that which posits God. As the *ὑποκείμενον* [material substrate], it is that which originarily posits God [*das ursprünglich Gott-Sezende*]. He is the *τὸ σπέρμα τοῦ θεοῦ* [the seed of God]—and John says (in the first letter): "He in whom the *σπέρμα* remains does not sin (*ἁμαρτίαν οὐ ποιεῖ*)."[1]

In the O.T. and N.T., that *ἁμαρτία κατ' ἐξοχήν* [sin *par excellence*] is Paganism. Paganism is the falling away of consciousness from the true God and has its origin in the

1. 1 John 3:9: "Whosoever is born of God doth not commit sin" (KJV).

God-positing principle not continuing to inhabit human consciousness, which led to a suspension of its intended unity. By re-appearing, that theogonic ground effects an overthrow of the divine unity, whereby the lowest becomes the uppermost; yet, mediatedly, a theogonic process that restores the unity is therewith posited. In its reappearance, *B is that which sublates the divine unity*; but in stepping outside of itself, the God-negating principle becomes, *by stepping back into itself, the God-positing principle, namely, that which posits God in actuality* [*actu*].

But this *bringing back* would have been impossible, and the human consciousness would have remained ecstatic, had not the potence, which by its nature overcomes B, held out or persevered [*ausharrte*] within the process. Now lord of his Being by his own action, not by divine intervention, he can do with Being anything he wants, even opposite the Father.

Consciousness is thus falls to the potences in the mythological process (a new theogonic process, from which God is excluded). "You were without God in the World," said the Apostle [Paul]; it is the opposite of being in God, *ἄτεοι εν τῳ κοσμω* [without God in the world].[2] Humanity fell to the cosmic potences, to the powers outside of God, *ἀπηλλοτρομένοι τοῦ θεοῦ* [alienated from God].

Here is the transition to the philosophy of mythology. It must precede the philosophy of revelation. For the mediating potence that was excluded from Being must first make itself lord of Being and consciousness, in accordance with the divine will that remained within it. Its doings [*Thun*] are the content of revelation. Revelation, however, requires deeper, historical mediations; and to those, without which revelation would remain incomprehensible, mythology belongs.

---

2. Ephesians 2:12: "remember that at that time you were separate from Christ, alienated from the commonwealth of Israel, and strangers to the covenants of the promise, without hope and without God in the world" (BSB).

However, it is not necessary for our purpose to present it completely. One needs only to establish the *principal moments of the mythological process* and the causes (potences) that create mythology.[3] They are found in the *doctrine of the mystery cults* [*Mysterienlehre*], which forms a corollary [*Corollarium*] to mythology and thus the unmediated transition to the philosophy of revelation.

The motive [*Anlass*], as well as the mediating [*Vermittelnde*] and the goal [*Ziel*] of the second process and all of its potences, are the same as in the first theogonic process, which repeats itself in the human consciousness.

The last product of Creation was absolute movable, which therefore could *turn over* again and, indeed, had to. When we survey all the moments traversed thus far, we must say that the great law hovering above the whole presses on *toward this world, through which God drives all Being away from himself.* All of the moments traversed thus far are real, yet they are only moments in thought [*Gedankenmomente*] insofar as there are no stays [*Aufenthalt*] until our present world was reached. Man carries the mediating potence with him into the necessary process so that it goes into the extra-divine [*aussergöttliche*] process because it cannot let go of Man.[4]

This second process takes place within the consciousness. Although independent from the freedom of Man, it can only express and announce itself through mental pictures [*Vorstellungen*], through processes within the consciousness. *These mental pictures* are precisely the *mythological,* which, as has been demonstrated by result of all hypotheses about their origin, etc., are not invented speculatively or poetically; neither can they be explained by a merely accidental confusion or even a previous revelation. Rather, *they are a necessary product of the consciousness that has fallen under the power of the potences, which, in their tension, are only cosmic forces.* They do

3. KG11:36, p. 356: "His deed as free act is the content of revelation. The deeper presupposition of revelation is mythology. A philosophy of mythology can present the mythological representations, as well as the causes of these representations."

4. Kierkegaard has "widergöttliche Process" (anti-divine process) (KG11:36, p. 356).

not come into the consciousness from the outside, through individual inventors but are products of a (false) life process [*Lebensprocesses*] of the consciousness. Otherwise, they could not remain so closely interwoven with it.

Also, they are not accidental products but *rather the substance of the consciousness.* The principle of human consciousness coming forward again is put back, as it were, into its prehuman Being. This also explains the belief in those mental pictures by mankind as it is caught within this process. For the process was an objective one, independent of freedom and the activity of thought.

The forces at work in the process were not imagined by the mind but rather *the actual theogonic potences;* it was not just the development of the idea of God but *the actual theogonic potences taking possession of the consciousness.* For the same world-begetting potences that are at work in nature are at work here. The connection is not an artificial one but rather a natural one.

With this view of an involuntary process, the history of mankind has gained *a completely new fact,* one that fills out the prehistoric void. What occupied mankind during that time? Time was consummated with those enormous upheavals of human consciousness that accompanied peoples' mental pictures of the gods. The external history of peoples begins then; only then, when the world stepped out of that inner process with its completed mental pictures, did it devolve to externality [*Aeusserlichkeit*].

The migrations of the peoples was then only defined by that inner process. For so long, mankind was in an ecstatic state; only then did it pass over into a reflective state [*Besonnenheit*]. Fully taken in by these mental pictures, mankind did not yet have a sense of external relations; or they were, as in the case of the division of peoples [*Scheidung der Völker*],[5] defined only by inner conditions.

The moments of the theogonic process were distributed like roles among different peoples. With each newly divided people, the process advanced further; the various peoples

---

5. Genesis 11:1-9.

entering history represent parallel moments of the theogonic process. The mythologies of all peoples originated from the same causes (potences), and since each later people takes up the process where an earlier people let go of it, the mythologies of different peoples look similar. It need not be assumed, as it was by Creuzer and others, that the mental pictures arose in an originary people [*Urvolk*],[6] from which it was transmitted to the *Indians* (which, against all analogies, have been declared to be the most ancient people). The mythologies of peoples are the integrated parts of the same myth-generating process. To show these different moments in the successive mythologies is the subject of the philosophy of mythology.

The principle that ought to rest within Man as an intensive ability to be [*Seynkönnen*], the theogonic ground, could do nothing on its own account, only on account of the will of Man. If one holds that this possibility by itself is impotent, then the presented possibility can appear to Man only as feminine. The originary possibility [*Urmöglichkeit*] is a female being that shows itself to the Creator. It appears as an alluring and enticing female drawing the will toward itself; thus, it is also depicted this way in mythology. If it remains inward, it is equal in essence; if it steps out, it equals that which is accidental. But after its entry, it is blindly necessary. With the Greeks, it is *Persephone* who steps out of the essence and into the accidental realm. The Pythagoreans equated her with the *Dyad*.[7] She has a dual nature, first wholly internal, then after leaving her essence, she surrenders to the necessary process. But she does not constitute the beginning of mythology but rather arrives at consciousness by reflecting on it.

---

6. Friedrich Creuzer, *Symbolik und Mythologie der alten Völker* (Leipzig and Darmstadt: Karl Wilhelm Leske, 1810). See also Carl Daub's "Einleitung in die christliche Dogmatik," in *Studien*, vol. 5, ed. Carl Daub and Friedrich Creuzer (Heidelberg: Mohr and Zimmer, 1809), p. 154. Both Daub and Creuzer argued that an *Urvolk* predated the Babelian division of languages and peoples.

7. The Pythagoreans identified the monad with the male principle and the dyad with the female.

The beginnings of mythology are itself hidden from the consciousness, which is surprised by it. It becomes aware of this principle only at the end of the process; thus, *Persephone* now appears as the principle that carried the process from its beginnings to its end.

I should also expound here *on the story of Genesis,* but I cannot do so without relating it to the condition of the consciousnesses we have presupposed in the entire organization of the O.T. It suffices to say that what is talked about here is also an *enticement,* so that the side of Man that is susceptible to being enticed is presented as *actual,* and *the seducing principle* is imagined as a *serpent that coiled into itself is a picture of tranquility but uncoiled causes perdition.*[8]

The serpent is generally seen as a dualistic principle. In the Greek mystery cults, it was *Zeus who,* as founder of a future time, *approached Persephone in the shape of a serpent.*[9] Persephone herself is introduced as an unapproachable fortress.[10] Zeus will make her into the birth mother of a new principle; for remaining entirely on the inside, she is pure and chaste, but once she steps outside, she becomes the mother of the [mythological] process.

By tying the beginning of the mythological process to the first of all events, we explain the mythological process also as a general fate to which mankind was subjected. Mythology

---

8. KG11: 36, p. 357: "Genesis teaches something similar. 3 things are especially noteworthy: (1) humanity's first sin is leading astray; (2) woman is the accessible side; (3) the seductive principle is the serpent. The serpent is an image of eternity, which becomes corruptible as soon as it is broken, which is suggested by the serpent's upright gait, by its standing on end. It is *nature anceps* [of dual nature]." SW XIII, p. 384: "Thus, the serpent is referred to commonly as a symbol of that dual nature (that *natura anceps*), which, when it turns from the inside to the outside, occasions the Fall."

9. Ovid, *Metamorphoses,* 6.114: "As a spotted serpent [Zeus seduced] Deois [Persephone]" (trans. A.D. Melville).

10. SW XII, p. 158: "What is called in the myth of Persephone, as well as by the Pythagoreans, a divine fortress or custody is named similarly in the narrative of the O.T.; [...] here also the originary humans are not posited into the vast and boundless space—to which they are only expelled later—but [...] into a garden, which is nothing other than closed, custodial space."

cannot be explained by [reading] poets, philosophers, etc. It loses itself in that originary fact [*Urthatsache*] or unforethinkable deed, without which there is no history. That originary event [*Urereignis*] makes history possible in the first place.

Posited outside of their unity, the potences can only return into unity through a new process. Now to be considered are the moments and epochs of the mythological processes.

XIX. The Epochs of the Mythological Process

[PL, pp. 558–75]

First Epoch. The presumed process can only begin with the exclusive lordship of that which unboundedly has Being [Unbeschränkt-Seyenden] of B, which has risen up again. By this principle being the power over consciousness, the essence of Man is returned to the beginnings of all nature, indeed, *into the time before nature.* That principle is the *prius* before nature. In its boundlessness, it is to some extent also anti-nature [*das Naturwidrige*], which desires to have nothing to do with nature. For it is nature only as one that has limits. In its limitless omnipotence, it is that which sublates all nature. It is *that forepart [Vordere], that face of God before which no man can subsist and live.* It is the adversary of all that is concrete.

In the originary consciousness—as pure, idle potence—it is purely spiritual, the point of attraction for all potences. However, once it steps out of itself, it excludes the higher potences. Nevertheless, it wants to assert its centrality, its spiritual position, which it possesses only in itself, in its latency. By stepping outside of it, it must peripherally and materially become ὑποκείμενον [substrate] against the next higher potence. Now, however, it wants to assert its spiritual nature. It does not want to be de-spirited [*entgeisted*], in a passive state [*leidend*], materialized against the higher potence. It strives to assert itself as supra-material [*übermateriell*] against the higher necessity, which thereby degrades it to the status of matter.

The battle unfolds in consciousness in the same moments we witnessed during the originary becoming of nature; when the consuming boundless principle was torn and scattered in the face of the subordinating potence. Each of these elements desires to be spiritual in itself, desires to be at the center and not material, while posited at the periphery by the higher power.

In this wrestling between spirit and materiality, in which lay the transition to the future nature, *the system of the world was formed.* And the moment corresponding to this stage of the mythological consciousness is *astro-theology,* humankind's most ancient religion—*Sabianism.* It worships a heavenly host [*himmlisches Heer*], which over time became understood as a spiritual realm surrounding the throne.

The object of this most ancient form of worship was not the corporeal, merely accidental aspect of the stars; *the heavenly body itself is supra-corporeal* [*überkörperlich*]. Sabianism concerned itself only with the *astral,* the cause of the indwelling sidereal movements, not with the sensate perceptions and the impressions of the sun. But the most ancient humanity could not be elevated by either the unmediated sensate perceptions or by thought; rather, *the most ancient humans, who worshipped the spirit that inhabits the world as a whole,* were immersed in the essence of the astral movement by the necessary and inner movement of their consciousness. They fell to the sidereal principle, which corresponds to the *nomadic* life of the most ancient humans (not yet [organized as] peoples) who roamed like the stars. The pattern of their consciousness was also the pattern of their lives. *In the stars, they saw a model of their own lives,* which was restless and uniform: *nomads of the sky in the ether's desert.* A *king of the heavens* took the place of the true God in their consciousness; it held on to it in order to not lose God entirely.

The oldest religion was a monotheism insofar as the object of its worship was a single principle; but their god was one-sidedly one and thus still subjected to destruction. Polytheism emerged from its destruction. However, it was this one God who held prehistoric humanity together until the time of humanity's crisis and division.

A. *The first epoch* is thus the exclusive, albeit already contested, *rule of the blind principle of nature, which is outside of itself, whereby **B** still asserts itself against the higher potences.*

B. *The second epoch* [is] the actual subjugation of the principle prevailing up to now under the next higher potence—in a way that the former makes itself only accessible by the higher potence, yet still conquerable. Before this subjugation, the Siderian principle appeared to consciousness—which found itself spellbound by the circle of necessary mental pictures [*Vorstellungen*]—as a *male* principle, as Lord of the Heavens, Uranos. Just as it begins to become passive, presenting and subjugating itself as matter of a potential overcoming, it turns into a *female* principle through a natural movement of the mental picture. *The King of the Heavens becomes Urania,* and contained in this idea is the first transition, the first foundation of mythology. In itself, Sabianism is not yet mythological. *Mythology arises only through a successive polytheism.* Even though that god of the heavens is the first link in a future succession of gods, he is not yet posited as such. Sabianism is still a *prehistoric* religion.

That first god is followed by a second, which, however, *is not Urania herself*; she only forms the transition. We find Urania especially in the consciousness of the earliest peoples, wherein Sabianism already leaned toward the worship of the material stars. With the *Persians,* there is still a memory of the ancient religion since they worship the revolutions of the heavenly bodies, as well as the sun, the moon, and the elements (the astral matter). *In addition,* they learned to sacrifice to Urania, according to Herodotus ([*The Histories*] 1.131 and 1.199), the first evidence of the emergence from pure Sabianism. Aside from the Persians, it is especially the Babylonians and Assyrians, the Arabs (the inhabitants of Happy Arabia,[1] according to Herodotus), who signify this transition. With the *Babylonians,* Urania is worshipped under the name *Mylitta.*[2] With the appearance of Mylitta, the acquiescent [*nachgiebig*] first god, the second potence has also taken a place in consciousness; indeed, the feminization of the first god is the coming of the second god, A^2. It appears clearly in the usage of the Babylonians mentioned by Herodotus.

Otherwise, a transition of the consciousness from the old god to the new one is, in these ancient times, also represented as adultery. Furthermore, among the Arabs, the

---

1. *Arabia felix;* the formal division of Arabia into three regions—Happy, Stony, and Desert Arabia—is first found in Ptolemy (*Geography* 17 and 19).

2. Herodotus ascribed the name Mylitta for Venus to the Assyrians, not the Babylonians.

second, spiritual god is qualified *as the son of Urania.* By becoming female, the first god posits the second. Herodotus calls this second god *Dionysos.*[3] I will use this name as well, without referring specifically to the Greek god. *He is determined by his overcoming of that first wild and self-estranging principle* and by leading consciousness back to humanity. He is the liberating god and executes this work of his in the consciousness only successively. His relation to that which is to be overcome is therefore different in each moment. The contradictions can be explained in this way. A^2 is one when it is just born into actuality, another when it begins to work, and yet another once its work has been applied. The time of Urania is the time of two deities existing together, still ineffectively (for example, with Herod's Arabs). But is the determination of Dionysos to establish thew foundation for the genuinely human life. His title is *Lord of Man.*[4] However, human consciousness still depends on that first principle, and there has been nothing more difficult for consciousness to tear itself away from. It must hold on to that principle because it is that which posits God; consciousness has also not been prompted to abandon this principle absolutely, only insofar as it has real Being outside of itself. But consciousness is afraid to lose the godhood together with reality.

C. *The third epoch* is *the epoch of the battle* between the generally subdued [*allgemein gebeugten*] blind principle and the potence that brings it back into itself. However, this battle can only be fulfilled in several different moments.

The first moment is when the *consciousness* defies or resists as such the workings of the liberating god and the principle that has become complaisant rises up against the higher god at work. It becomes complaisant only toward that which

---

3. Herodotus, *The Histories* 2.145.

4. See Ion of Chios: "Untamed child with a bull-face, new and not new, very sweet shepherd of the Erotes who are letting out heavy sighs, wine, you who frees the mind and governs men" (Phillipe Borgeaud, "Dionysos, the Wine, and Ikarios: Hospitality and Danger," in *A Different God: Dionysos and Ancient Polytheism,* ed. Renate Schlesier [Berlin and Boston: De Gruyter, 2011], p. 162).

was not yet at work. By rising up and pulling itself together anew, it appears as the *god* who in his uniqueness is rigidly closed off. *This strict god, disinclined to freedom, is the god of the Phoenicians, Tyrians, Carthaginians, and Canaanites: Baal.* Originally, he was the lord of the heavens, Uranos. He is the same but in more limited form since he does not allow the other god any influence [Likewise] Moloch and Kronos. He does not give any space to the liberating god; and as long as he jealously guards his uniqueness, the liberating god can only appear as an incomprehensible intermediary between god and humans, as the god in his humiliation, negation, who has yet to acquire divinity.

It is the Phoenician *Melqart,* Heracles. He is a forerunner of Dionysos and appears as Kronos posited outside of his divinity. Kronos is the false god who excludes the son from consciousness (no longer from Being, for that was already done to him by the previous moment). However, he excludes him from lordship and deprives him of the kingdom. Heracles therefore appears as a servant, not as the son, just as he is also called *the suffering servant* in the O.T.[5] Heracles is the demon who is benevolent toward mankind, always alluring and laden with hardships. Thus, he appears in Phoenician mythology. In Greek mythology, he is finally transfigured into a god. Just as the exclusivity of the king of heavens was previously followed by a moment where his rigidness subsides, so Kronos also becomes feminized.

The second moment. It falls into the consciousness of those peoples who succeed the Phoenicians historically. This female figure is Cybele, who appeared first with the Phrygian-Thracian tribe. From there, she advanced all the way to Greece and Rome, where she became a *religio licita* [permitted religion]. Just as Urania lay the first ground for mythology, so Cybele lay the second ground. With Urania, the mythological succession, or the *process,* became *possible*; with *Cybele,* it became *actual.* The decisive transition to polytheism lies in her.

---

5. Isaiah 53.

Before we move on to the actual polytheism, just a general remark. The principle from which mythology progresses is that of a successive emergence of the potences that were united in the originary consciousness but which, after their division, can only reunite themselves successively. First, it was only *a single potence* that held sway over consciousness, *Uranos.* It subsequently gave room to another potence. *The first victory over the exclusionary **B**, its first καταβολή* [seed or foundation], *is the appearance of Urania.* Until the moment of the second καταβολή, when it becomes the object of an actual overcoming, *until Cybele,* we were dealing with just two principles. Now the overcoming of the first by the second is occurring. However, it also becomes the throne of the highest in the same proportion as the first is being everted [*umgewendet*].

From here on, we are dealing with the totality of potences. *The entire mythological process revolves around just those three potences; all else is more or less coincidental.* Until we reach the point where the first mythologies arise, we can follow *the thread of the potences.* In period B, we see the coming of the second god. Our period C will therefore be the period of the coming of the third potence.[6] *The καταβολή of the first principle in Cybele is the coming of the third potence. The spirit can come only when the un-spiritual* [*Ungeistige*] *has given way.* As long as Kronos refuses all, the third potence cannot come. First, the rigid must decide to soften.

D. The period of the actual overcoming of the first principle and the actual coming of the third potence. In this process, the potences are the genuinely effectuating causes from which the other types of gods need to be distinguished—those I call the material ones. They are only created alongside the genuine causes. The Greeks, therefore, regard them merely as θεοὶ γεννητοὶ [created gods].

One additional remark about the difference between those and the genuinely causative or formal gods: in the first period, when the ensuing principle asserts its centrality

---

6. KG11:37, p. 360: "In A (First Epoch), it is the excluding god; in B, the coming of the second god, his birth; in C, the coming of the third potence."

in the battle between the material and the immaterial, consciousness *is split into the Siderian gods.* The astral gods are merely the effectuated, the material, the ones begotten first. When the subordination of the first principle begins, Dionysos and Urania are the only two effectuating gods. As Herodotus (III.8) has said about the *Arabs,* they regard Urania and Dionysos alone as gods. The material gods during that period are indeed material; they are the gods of the stars who in consciousness are identified more with that which is corporeal.

In the third period, Kronos and Heracles alone appear as effectuating gods. Kronos himself is the god who corresponds to the non-organic time of nature; only non-organic masses are worshipped. The religion has descended from the heavens to the concrete, to earth. Even the Hellenic consciousness seems to have gone through this non-organic time before the decisive Hellenic character came to the fore. The memory of the θεὸς ἀργούς [idle god] (Pausanias) stems from this pre-Hellenic time.[7]

From the time of Kronos only the *fetishism,* the stupid adoration of the non-organic, remains. By no means is it the most ancient religious practice. Fetishism occurs only since that moment. No material gods are yet present when Cybele and Dionysos—the god to whom the proud powers of the exclusionary system have now become more acquiescent—oppose each other in consciousness, when Dionysos appears only as δαιμων [daimon] in Cybele's company. The material gods emerge only when the opposed principle has become Dionysian. Arguably, *Cybele* is called the *Great Mother* of the (material) gods[8] who emerge as the process rises. Here they are moments of a dwindling real god who increasingly retreats into himself, *i.e.,* re-spiritualizes himself. It is the

7. *Cf.* SW XII, p. 293: "Older than all images [...] is the reverence for masses that are unformed, non-organic, and unworked by human hand [...] To these belong the λίθοις ἄργοις, *i.e.,* unhewn stones that are untouched by human hand, which were still held in reverence in prehistoric Greece."

8. KG11:37, p. 360: "Cybele is *magna deorum meter.* She is the mother of the material gods."

god-plurality [*Göttervielheit*][9] posited by Dionysos, in which the overcome principle appears. *The material gods now form a god-plurality.*

This [god-plurality] is posited only in order to be ruled *by the third potence.* In all three potences, the esoteric is in mythology, not in those material gods. We have already anticipated this esoteric understanding of mythology, which

---

9. *Ibid.*: "*Göttervielheit* (god-plurality) is a simultaneous polytheism; *Vielgötterei* (plurality of gods) is successive polytheism." See also *SW* XI, pp. 120–21: "Here, then, we wish to draw attention to a distinction within polytheism itself, which has been passed over in all the explanations up to now [...] It cannot escape anyone who has been made aware of it that there is a great difference between a concept of polytheism that arises from a greater or lesser number of gods being *subordinated* to *one and the same god* as the supreme and reigning one among them, and one where *multiple* gods are assumed, but each being the *supreme and dominant* one a time, and who, therefore, can only *succeed* each other. If we were to think of the history of the Greek gods as having had, instead of *three* succeeding races of gods, only a single race, that of Zeus, for instance, then it would have known only of contemporaneous and co-existent gods, all resolved in Zeus as their common unity. It would have known only of *simultaneous* polytheism. In fact, though, it has *three* systems of gods, and in each of them, only one god is the highest: Uranos in the first, Kronos in the second, and Zeus in the third. These three gods cannot, therefore, exist at the same time but are *mutually exclusive* and therefore *succeed each other in time.* As long as Uranos reigns, Kronos cannot, and for Zeus to grasp power, Kronos must retreat into the past. Therefore, we shall call this polytheism *successive.*

But now the following, too, also becomes evident: [...] only successive polytheism is *true* polytheism. For as far as those gods who are jointly subordinated to one supreme god are concerned, they exist simultaneously with the latter but are not therefore equal to him; they exist in him; he exists apart from them; [...] here there is no *actual* polytheism, for in the end everything is again resolved in unity, or a polytheism only in the sense, perhaps, in which Jewish theology calls the angels Elohim (gods), without being concerned that the uniqueness of the god whose servants and instruments they are might thereby be infringed upon. Here there is indeed *god-plurality* [*Göttervielheit*] but no *plurality of gods* [*Vielgötterei*]. The latter arises only when *multiple supreme* and equal gods succeed each other who cannot be resolved again into a higher unity. We must, therefore, hold fast precisely to this distinction between god-plurality and the plurality of gods."

it grasps for itself only at the end, and right away have seen in mythology the three potences.

To the same degree that the second potence subordinates the first, the first again posits the third. In Cybele, the third approaches. Even if the process from here on passes through different moments, the mythologies do not differ by potences; rather, the potences are contained within them. How then can [the mythologies] be distinguished from each other? Even though the allness of the potences is in each, they are nevertheless different, each according to which principle(s) dominate in a given mythology: one of the two, none of the two, or a third—whereby the third principle again grants the first the right to be the quintessence and root [*das Ansich und die Wurzel*] of all religious consciousness.

There are only three mythologies: the Egyptian, the Indian, and the Greek. The ancient Italian and Etruscan mythologies are but parallel forms of the Greek. All related mythologies, namely the *Tyrrhenian,* require the same past, the *Pelasgian.*

1. *The Egyptian* is the one in which *the fiercest battle against the blind principle* persists. Even while being combatted, it exerts all of its power. *Typhon* has the nature of an all-consuming, free potence especially averse to organic life (Plutarch, *Isis and Osiris*). *The Egyptian mythology is the mortal combat of the real principle.* Typhon is opposed by Osiris, the good god, but the victory is undecided, so that to the consciousness it seems as if now Typhon is *torn apart,* and now Osiris. Only with the appearance of Horos (τὸ ωρισμένον καὶ τέλειον [perfected and complete] in Plutarch)[10] is Typhon fully defeated. *Horos is the third principle.* Osiris is the *god-wedded consciousness* that sways between Typhon and Osiris and is only steadied by the birth of Horos. Typhon, subjected under the higher potence, becomes Osiris after he has been actualized in the latter. Thus transformed, he is the god of the invisible realm of the underworld and re-posited into his essential being [*Ansich*]. The second potence, Osiris, is *that which purely has Being* [*das rein Seyende*], Horos, *he who ought to have Being* [*der Seynsollende*], the actual god as

10. Plutarch, *Isis and Osiris,* 55.1.

spirit. The material gods arise only from the battle; they are the still twitching limbs of the torn-apart *one* reluctant god.

2. *Indian mythology* appears to be the complete opposite of Egyptian mythology. While in the Egyptian [mythology] consciousness holds fast to the real principle—seeing itself being painfully dissolved and transformed into a spiritual [principle], yet holding fast to that center point that must be adhered to—the Indian consciousness, in contrast, is the eccentric one. *In the Indian consciousness,* that principle of creation [*Prinzip des Anfangs*], which is the ground and the hold [*der Grund und der Halt*] of the entire process, is overpowered by the higher potence. The one who corresponds to the principle of creation is *Brahma,* who, however, is lost in a manner that to many seems wondrous and who is worshipped, if at all, without images and temples. He is the god of the lost past. As a bygone god with no relation to the present, Brahma does not enjoy devotion. In his stead rules *Shiva,* the god who brought about the complete destruction of Brahma and dissolution of consciousness. While there is also a third potence, as *spirit, Vishnu,* the following will illuminate how far this *Trimurti* is from the Christian triune doctrine.[11]

Those three Indian deities are not combined into a single entity in the *Indian consciousness,* as the Egyptian deities in the *Egyptian consciousness* were. Subsequently, Vishnu has his special worshippers. However, these exclude Shiva and *vice versa.* While the masses are devoted to Shivaism, the noble classes are devoted to Vishnu; and since Vishnu excludes his precondition, the Indian consciousness could not keep itself at the height of spirituality. Thus arose the legends of the incarnations of Vishnu, which are more or less invented and not part of the mythology. *Vishnu* is allegedly worshipped as *Krishna,* but this is no longer a true product of the mythology but rather a spawn of the imagination.

Buddhism is alien to Indian mythology and can only be explained as a reaction against the mythological process. Buddhism—as well as the *mysticism, idealism, and spiritualism*

---

11. The divine triad in Hinduism—Brahma the creator, Vishnu the preserver, and Shiva the destroyer.

that are inspired by it and have developed especially under the Vishnuites—only serves to complete *the confusion of the unhappy consciousness.*[12]

3. Greek mythology, which does not exclude the declining god but retains him, leads back *to the true center.* Thus, it is the end of the mythological process. In the Indian consciousness, there is also a crisis of the mythological process; however, it does not lead to restoration. The crisis ends in decay; thus in India, no result of the mythological process remains in consciousness. Confabulations, instead of actual mythologies or an exorbitant strive for unity, since the unified consciousness, which was retained in Greek mythology, perished in the [Indian] mythology.

The internal destruction of Indian mythology is also reflected in the deformed [*verzerrte*] essence of the Indian gods. *The Greek gods emerge from the Greek consciousness, which releases itself gently and lawfully from the violence of the real principle, as blessed visions* [*selige Visionen*]. The real principle still plays a part in its decline in order to impart reality to that which is in the process of being created, whereby the latter are eternal and lasting moments. It is the gentle death, *the euthanasia of the real principle,* which upon its decease leaves behind a beautiful world in its stead. *However, the Greek gods are nothing more than appearances.* The Greek gods are not corporeal; they are like entities of pure imagination, yet they are of the most real significance for the consciousness. (The unification of the ideal and the actual.)

This also speaks for the *necessity of such a real process,* one *that is not grounded in fantasy or any other psychic effect.* The Greek gods are humanoid and in the history of the mythological process represent the moment of nature itself, when it dies for mankind the reconciling death after the horrific battles in the animal kingdom.

The secret of mythology lies in the causative potences. At the same moment that the real principle, the singular cause

---

12. *Cf.* Hegel's notion of the "unhappy consciousness" in *Phenomenology of Spirit,* par. 206 (trans. A.V. Miller): "The unhappy consciousness is the consciousness of self as a dual-natured, merely contradictory being."

of the tension [*Spannung*], expires, the potences that are kept apart have to sublate their tension against one another and also touch each other unmediatedly and unite in the consciousness. Once there is a complete god-plurality [*Götter-vielheit*], the potences will collapse out of the tension into the unity of the consciousness.

The first of the potences is the principle that is outside of itself and compounded in its deity, Ἀιοες, Hades, the god who has become invisible. He can be considered in two ways. After the defeat of Kronos in the Greek mythology, he appears among the three gods as the god of the underworld. As such (as the deepest point of the material gods), he is the *ground* for the entire material god-plurality, wherein Zeus occupies the summit. That material god-plurality can only come about by [Hades] being overcome in his rigid resistance against the second potence; the entire Olympus is resting on his becoming invisible and latent. It is he who has become invisible in the material gods, even in Zeus. About the abode of this god, it is said in the *Iliad* that even the gods abhor it.[13]

For if he were ever to rise again from this place, the entire external world of gods would perish, just as in nature, when its *prius,* its countenance that is now faced away, would turn around and the entire manifold world of nature would be annihilated.

Thus the horror before Typhon chased the gods in animal shapes.[14] However, Hades, as the descending god, was also the one who was in place of all those material gods, who in itself was matter. Consciousness becomes aware of itself as the general ground of all gods, not merely that of the gods with Zeus but the gods in the eras of Kronos and Zeus. Uranos, Kronos, and Zeus are but different forms of the One, with Hades as the last. Consciousness

13. Homer, *Iliad,* Book 20: "The houses of the dead—the dank, moldering horrors that fill the deathless gods themselves with loathing" (trans. Robert Fagles).

14. In Greek mythology, Typhon is the youngest son of Gaia and Tartarus. He was described as a serpent-footed giant who was cast into the underworld by Zeus.

becomes aware of itself as the real god, and he retreats into himself, as pure cause, pure potence, which underlies the entire process.

Consciousness attains the general concept of this god who, in his being outside of himself, becomes the substance for all material gods. Thus, he is now a general god, no longer confronted by any of the material gods but only by a formal god, initially A^2.

Since the latter has retreated into himself, he no longer excludes other potences, and these now also appear to him as causes, next to which the other gods are only accidental. These now appear to consciousness in the same way as, for us, the natural things relate to the three creative causes. It is thus understandable how the consciousness of those spiritual or causative gods awakens in the last confrontation, where the full polytheism comes to the fore.

The consciousness for which the most pure god-plurality created itself and which has freed itself from the tension of the real principle in the partial gods *now turns to the consciousness of the spiritual, general gods. The material plurality of the gods is the exoteric, while the unity of the spiritual gods is the esoteric—the mystery cults in mythology.* Thus, it can be explained how the inner theosophy of the Greek mystery cults appears along with the most completed mythology. Both are simultaneous manifestations. For the esoteric, the true *mysterium,* comes about from the real principle being brought back into concealment. If the *resisting* god were not brought back into his *mysterium,* the exoteric plurality would not be possible. Were the exoteric not to be, then the esoteric would also not be. The spread-out plurality would always be pulled into the Cronian indifference.

The inner meaning of mythology is found in the mystery cults; it is therefore the supreme affirmation for the philosophy of mythology. For that and the following reason, I will linger a moment longer on the mystery cults. Since the accomplished revelation can only occur at a certain time and, as it were, was waiting for the end of the merely natural development, the distinction between mythology and revelation can only be explained if we go back to the deepest meaning of mythology and see how the religious consciousness has been restored in paganism. The Greek mystery cults have therefore been considered to be closest to Christianity. Even Paul has alluded to the expressions and customs of the Greek mystery cults.[15]

---

15. See *SW* XII, p. 638: "When Paul, alluding to the seed grain, says, 'What is sown is perishable; it is raised imperishable' [1 Corinthian 15:42 (BSB)], then this was perhaps an allegory he was led to by his acquaintance with the Hellenic teachings (especially also the mystery cults), perhaps an allusion to a similar idea in the Eleusinian Mysteries."

XX. The Greek Mystery Cults

[PL, pp. 575-89]

Transition

Within our development of mythology, there are *two large transitory moments* where the real principle makes itself only *superable* and then when it is *actually overcome.* Each moment was identified with a female deity. Should there not be a third moment where that principle is actually overcome and consciousness comes to a stop in the middle between the past of which it frees itself through the god-plurality and the rise of the spiritual potences?

If there are always two things posited in the process, the god of a particular moment and the corresponding consciousness, then one notices that *the female deity behaves like the consciousness of that god.* The god himself is, in each moment, only a particular god who is destined to be succeeded by another. Furthermore, the consciousness is that which posits the god as such and, to that extent, goes beyond the particular god. Gaia sees further than Uranos, Rhea further than Kronos; both female figures are inclined toward the future. In the second, the consciousness that resigns itself to the overcoming is represented. Thus here, at the end between mythology and the mystery cults, stands a figure of the consciousness that is represented by Demeter, who belongs as much to mythology as to the mystery cults.

Demeter is the consciousness that stands in the center, halfway between the real and the liberating god—a consciousness that still adheres to the first but is in the process of transitioning to the second.[1] It adheres once more to the real god. The female deity is either always the consciousness of the god parallel to her or of a higher, just emerging god. In the first case, she is the wife; in the second, the mother.

---

1. *S*WXII, p. 628: "Demeter becomes [...] the center point, the hinge on which everything turns."

Demeter first appears among the Kronian gods as the spouse of Poseidon. Therewith her nature is already turned toward the higher principle, Dionysos. Where Kronos jealously rejects everything from himself, consciousness cannot have an unmediated relation to Dionysos. There, consciousness sides with the third son of Kronos, who is the material ideal [*Vorbild*] of Dionysos. Further on, Demeter is the consciousness that is unmediatedly turned toward Dionysos; in the end, she is that which is actually overcome by Dionysos. In this last form, she constitutes the καταβολή [foundation], which is simultaneous with the last of the completed formation of the gods.

Now, however, consciousness cannot succumb to the plurality without, at the same time, parting with the exclusive god. However, since the first unforethinkable act, consciousness is attached to this god by a magic power; now it becomes aware of this side of its essence, the one that hangs on to the real god, as one merely contracted by accidence, and differentiates it at the same time from the essential (the essential, positing god; the accidental, positing the real god). It becomes conscious of having to separate from the real god, and thus it separates from that principle through which it is attached to the real god.

It steps out of it through a kind of birth, as *Proserpina.* By loosening the magic bond, the beginning becomes clear to consciousness as well, and thus the first cause of the process comes about—*Persephone.* However, Demeter cannot separate from that which belongs to her from her past without positing it as belonging to the past and perceiving it as such. She has to sacrifice it to the past god in the form of a rape. Naturally, that part of consciousness must follow the god to whom it has fallen from the beginning. Consciousness, together with its god, also becomes the past. Yet even now, this separation is painful for the consciousness—thus it is represented as rape; and Demeter is the irate mother who at first does not want to know about the Dionysian god-plurality, which has taken the place of the real god. (See the Homeric hymns to Demeter.)

The second god actualizes itself in that plurality by positing the real god as past. (Pausanias mentions an ornate sculpture by Polykleitos that shows Zeus as the head of the god-plurality with the attributes of Dionysos). Demeter must first be reconciled with this god-plurality. The exoteric mythology does not go any farther than the rape of Proserpina. But now begins the appeasement of those who mourn, which only happens by their becoming part of the supreme god, he who ought to have Being [*der seyn-sollende*], as substitute for the perished god who can no longer step up to that outward plurality but is celebrated only in a consciousness that goes beyond that plurality in the mystery cults.

The violated consciousness is appeased through *the third god.* This is the essential content of the mystery cults. Thus the ancient Eleusinian Mysteries were also called the Mysteries of Demeter.

Among the preceding explanations, only this is true: that *Demeter* is the *divinity of agriculture.* However, she is also the founder of agriculture and therefore is often commemorated as such. This is not only meant in a physical sense but also because with the installation of agriculture the nomadic life disappeared. Custom and law came into effect, and this moment relating to customs is sanctified in Demeter. She was the θεσμοφόρος,[2] and it was in this sense that Isocrates could say: we received both agriculture and the mysteries as a gift from Demeter.[3]

Sabianism is the natural religion of all tribes not bound to agriculture. Caesar said that even of the Germanic peoples worship only visible gods: sun, fire, moon. He subsequently said of the same Germanic people, *agriculturae non student,*[4] and none of them had borders. Thus, *pure Sabianism* is older than all peoples and civilized societies. As long as humans attach themselves to the general god who is enclosed by neither temple nor walls, the fields are their abode and the heavens their roof. As humans turn away from this general god,

2. The Thesmophoria was an ancient three-day Greek festival celebrated by women in honor of Demeter.

3. Isocrates, *Panegyricos,* 4.28.

4. Caesar, *De Bello Gallico,* 6.22: "They do not study agriculture."

they go from vastness to smallness. Yet they still carry with them a memory of the divine satisfaction they left behind.

On the other side, it seems that after the human race has experienced the *evils of the civilized condition,* they longed to return to the free life of the Golden Age. In later memories, Kronos and Uranos were blended together, like distant objects are to the eye; thus, they became the gods of the Golden Age for the Greeks and Romans. There were no confined fields. *Ante Jovem nulli subigebant arva coloni.*[5] As long as the god of the undivided consciousness ruled, the earth was still a communal heritage. Even the narrative of Genesis (11:1–9), where the thought of having a permanent residence was punished with the confusion of the races, shows some attachment to that first unbounded era.

In the Phrygian mythology, *Cybele* is considered the founder of agriculture. Moreover, earlier, with the Babylonians, it was *Urania.* It is curious that after the founding of large cities was first attributed to the Babylonians, it was then the Kronian races, namely the Phoenicians, that navigated the Desert by the Sea.[6] The Egyptians hate the sea as being Typhonian and cover the land with the golden seed of Isis. With Kronos, the astral principle is restored, while with Cybele, the religion descends from the astral to the earth; thus, Cybele is the founder of permanent cities (Lucertius).

Kronos is credited with introducing *coins* as a symbol of private ownership, insofar as he regarded as the god of the transition. To the Greeks, as the youngest of the mythological races, it is *Demeter* who introduced agriculture. The connection between the decline of the Siderian religion and the introduction of agriculture is the reason for Demeter introducing both fruits, which nourish humans, and the mystery cults.

The first transition to agriculture has long been considered a riddle. None of our types of grain have been found

---

5. Virgil, *Georgics,* 1.125–26: "Before Jove took power, no settlers broke the fields with their ploughs" (trans. Janet Lembke).

6. The biblical name for Babylon. See Isaiah 121:1: "This is an oracle concerning the Desert by the Sea" (BSB). Schelling has "Desert *of* the Sea"; *cf.* also *Philosophie der Offenbarung,* SW XIII, p. 418.

growing wild [*wildwachsend*];[7] one could almost believe that in the mythological process a development of nature occurred that was parallel to the development of the consciousness.[8] The living together has changed the shape of nature; the presence of humans or even four-footed animals seems to have brought about (*e.g.*, in the desert) a modification in the plant life (*e.g.*, mallow springing up in the desert). What the Hellenes, and other races, have said about nourishing fruits having been a gift from Demeter seems to be taken literally. On the premise that the forms in the animal and plant kingdoms evolved, one can presume that nourishing fruits originated by metamorphosis from plants that are no longer known to us.

Persephone is no more a symbol of the physical world than Demeter. It would be absurd to conceive of that lofty spirit as a symbol of visible objects. Rather, the visible is a symbol of the invisible. *Persephone* is the mere potence of positing a god in consciousness; she is the originary possibility because she can also be the opposite. Like a seed of grain, she originated from a seed. *In Persephone, there is only the seed of the god-consciousness,* which, if it does not fall onto the soil, *i.e.*, is not subjugated to a process, remains alone. The quiet insight of the originary consciousness must become loud and pronounced. *In the originary consciousness, the true monotheism was posited, albeit only potentially,* since its opposite was equally possible. For everything that has a possible opposite is posited *in potentia.* This opposite must step forward in the

---

7. See also *Philosophie der Offenbarung*, SW XIV, p. 3, where Schelling calls the mythological religions *wildwachsend,* in contrast to the revealed religion. And SW XI, p. 246, where he compares it to Paul's calling paganism "the wild olive tree" (Romans 11: 17).

8. KG11: 38, p. 364: "A Spanish author who traveled widely in South America points out that certain plants, otherwise not found there, appeared on their own when humans dwelled there." The work by the Spanish military officer and naturalist Félix de Azara (*Voyages dans l'Amérique Méridionale depuis 1781 jusqu'en 1801* [Travels in South America between 1781 and 1801], 4 vols. [Paris: Dentu, 1809]) is highly praised and referred to several times by Schelling in the corresponding passage in SW XIII, p. 419, and throughout his *Historical-Critical Introduction in the Philosophy of Mythology.*

relative monotheism so that through its destruction by polytheism *a spiritual monotheism* is posited.

Persephone is the seed of the god-consciousness; as the one who posits god she ought to remain deep below and not emerge. However, by emerging, she becomes subjugated to a necessary theogonic process. She emerges from deep below with the sole intention of causing the potential monotheism in the originary consciousness to become an actual one, even though this monotheism, coming into its highest form, remains merely a natural one and cannot be compared to the divine one by revelation.

The main content of the Greek mysteries has already been described as the *conciliation of the consciousness that was wounded by its separation from the real god* (the conciliation for Demeter as expressed in the Homeric hymn: I will install the cults so that my heart is conciliated [*ich werde die Orgien einsezen, dass ihr mein Gemüth versöhnet*]).[9] But how was this conciliation achieved? The mystery cults are also called the Mysteries of Dionysos. Until now, we have known Dionysos only as the liberating god, the second potence. How does he now connect with the mystery cults?

A few preliminary remarks in general about the appearances whose cause within the mythological process is Dionysos. In the older religions, *the effect of Dionysos* is generally expressed as senseless enthusiasm; the consciousness must sway in order to free itself from the power of the real god. This explains the exuberance that accompanies his earliest appearance. He first appears simultaneously with Urania. The Sabians ascribe their origin from that time, when the liberation from the oppressing power of the real god was celebrated through wild, immoral acts. According to Livy ([*History of Rome*] 39.8-20), an inquiry initiated by the senate sheds light on the content of the Sabians.[10] Even the

9. "And I myself/will inaugurate/the mysteries,/so that/in doing them piously/you will please/my heart" (Homer, "Hymn to Demeter I" trans. Charles Boer).

10. The inquiry into the Roman Bacchanalia led to the Decree of the Senate concerning the Rites of Bacchus (*Senatus consultum de*

name σαβός, the exclamation εὐοῖ σαβοὶ [Euoi Saboi!] [11] indicates that these rites belong to the first transition out of Sabianism. The Sabians never gained a foothold in Greece. According to Cicero—in (*De Legibus* [2.15])—Sabazios was banned in one of Aristophanes's comedies from the stage on order of the State. The Greek national Dionysos festivals had nothing in common with the Sabians.

In Egypt, where the emancipation from the real god was perceived by some as a victory and where consciousness was divided (Typhon was derided for half the year, then worshipped), those triumphal processions of the *Phallagogia* were celebrated. The victory of Dionysos was here celebrated with festive parades and phallic processions. According to Herodotus ([*History,*] II.49], the ἑορταὶ [festivals] and πομπαὶ [processions] were reintroduced with the Hellenes, and Melampus is supposed to have learned this from the Egyptians (according to a passage from Cadmus). That state of Dionysos, wherein he still excites swaying [*Taumeln*], belongs to a moment earlier than the one represented by the Hellenic consciousness; that animosity had already been customary in Egypt. In Greece, there were at first only imitations of oriental customs. Dionysos is by no means alien to them; rather he is a necessary idea. However, standing in opposition and tension, he was already subordinated in the Hellenic consciousness; the completed Dionysos idea goes beyond that state.

Herodotus says that Melampus did not embrace the whole of the Dionysos idea. This was articulated only later. *Melampus* most likely is Egypt (= black land). That these festivals were not old during the time of the Greeks can be deduced from Greek mythology. The Dionysos talked about here is the son of Semele, a mother whose mortal part was consumed as soon she conceived Dionysos with Zeus. For Zeus is only recognized by the consciousness when the entire plurality of gods is recognized. Semele is the consciousness that is consumed as it approaches Zeus.

---

bacchanalibus) in 186 BC.

11. "Euoi" or "evoe" was the cry used in the Dionysian worship, and "saboi" was used to invoke Sabazios, the Phrygian god of harvest; see Demosthenes, *De Corona,* 260.

However, *the thus-born Dionysos* is still concealed; he remains concealed in the consciousness until the last crisis. His earlier emergence is full of contradiction. He is in the care of a wet nurse; he is fleeing from the threatening voice of the cruel king of the Edonians into the water (since this is the first expression of the feminizing of the rigidity; the water conceals an approaching god with whom only now the freedom and diversity of life begins). Another adversary is Pentheus of Thrace, pursuing the female servants of Dionysos (Euripides, [*The Bacchae*]).

The most famous adversary, however, was Orpheus, who, like Pentheus, was torn to pieces by the maenads. For that reason, Orpheus is set against Homer. He is the representative of the consciousness that defies the liberating god, but this consciousness is torn to pieces by the Dionysian polytheism.

Homer is the last manifestation of that crisis of consciousness, through which the exoteric plurality emerged. In this sense, it is to be understood that in the famous passage in Herodotus ([*The Histories,*] II.53) about the newness of the Greek theology, it was Hesiod and Homer who created the Hellenic theogony. The Pelasgians still display this crisis of the preceding state, where the darkening principle impedes the distinction of forms in the plurality. Homer himself is but a product of the last crisis of the entire mythological process, of which, however, there is no longer any thought in him; and therein lies the beauty of his poetry. *Homer is who he is* because there is no longer any trace of the profound crisis of the mythological process; his poetry gives us only the pure result.[12] The power of any life is to be able to exclude one's past. The child filled with the first awareness of life knows nothing of the process by which he was miraculously conceived. Just as after a storm and rain the sun shines more gloriously, so Homer's youthfulness steps before us; all of its power is derived from the universal validity of the Greek gods.

---

12. KG11:39, p. 365: "Homer himself is the final consummation of exoteric mythology. Homer's power consists precisely in the force with which he excludes the past."

Ever since Wolf[13] destroyed the individual unity of Homer, this poet has become a problem the solution to which cannot be found in the ideas that have held true until now; thus, many wish for the return of the *one* Homer (Voss).[14] *But Homeric poetry is not the work of a single man or the product of a single people. Rather, it is a work of all of humanity, the result of a collective process.* Homeric poetry belongs to an era before the Hellenic people decided to separate themselves from the general humanity as a people; they are not yet a people but humanity. It is humanity that gathered at Troy, and *the* Iliad *does not yet recognize the difference between Hellenes and Barbarians.* The decisive transition to Occidentalism, with its complete overcoming of the Oriental, takes place in Homer.

Opposite him stands *the dark figure of Orpheus.* If, according to etymology, Homer is *the one who speaks out* [*der Aussprechende*], then Orpheus is the *dark one,* from ὄρφνη [darkness].[15] If one assumes an Oriental origin for that word, then he is, according to the Arabic language, an astrologer and mystic. Orpheus appears in the earliest legends as the one in whom the power of the old Sabianism still endures. He is a follower of Sabianism; he refuses to recognize Dionysos by declaring Helios or Apollo to be the mightiest god. However, the Dionysian swaying prevails over the principle of retardation [*retardirende Princip*], which, because of its reluctance, is *torn to pieces, e.g., transposed into the plurality.* However, just as that which is overcome and low is raised

---

13. Schelling refers here to the German classicist Friedrich August Wolf who had proposed (falsely), in his *Prolegomena ad Homerum*—which prefaces his edition of Homer's works (Homerus, *Opera Omnia* [Halle: E Libraria orphanotrophei, 1795])—that Herodotus's claim is to be understood in the sense that Hesiod and Homer were the first to put the theogony into verse but did not invent it and suggested that Homer's works were authored by more than one poet.

14. The classicist Johann Heinrich Voss, known primarily for his translation of Homer's *Odyssey* and *Iliad* into German, was a contemporary of Friedrich August Wolf but disagreed with Wolf's suggestion of a *Vielhomer* (Homer-plurality) or *Flickhomer* (patch-Homer).

15. See KG11:39, p. 365: "Dionysus is Occidentalism; Orpheus is still Orientalism (perhaps Orpheus is related to ορφναιος (the dark)." This is Kierkegaard's last entry on Schelling's Berlin lectures in his notebook.

up for glorification, it is not surprising that, according to Pausanias, images of Orpheus were hanging next to those of Dionysos. Indeed, he is praised as a founder of the mystery cults. But originally, he was the adversary of the Theban Dionysos or Bacchus, the son of Semele.

Orpheus was also celebrated with festivals in Greece, but according to a passage in Herodotus, he was introduced late in Greece, only after the Dionysos idea had evolved to a higher level. Only then did the Bacchic ceremonies enter, but they differed distinctly from the mystery cults as they were completely public. The Dionysos who appears still *in tension,* the raging one, inciting lust, was not the object of these ceremonies; the festivals, whereat the phallus was presented, were public.

The transformation that takes place in the consciousness with the entrance of Dionysos, who is released from strict necessity and agrees with the free life of nature, is analogous to the moment when, after the originary state of the desolate and empty Being of the Earth during its purely astral era, the manifold things began to emerge.

Thus, *the second potence* is not, like *Shiva,* the power that sublates that which is material unmediatedly; rather, it is the opposing god who devours life and all that is concrete wherever he is not being refused. The second potence is the liberating one, Λύσιος, since he is released from the strict power of the first principle.

Even though Dionysos is the bestower of *wine*—as Demeter is the bestower of *seed grain*—the wine is the esoteric; it is a secret, a spiritualization [*Vergeistigung*] of that which was at first material. Eudoxus writes that the Egyptians did not drink wine and make sacrifices until the rule of Psammeticus. Previously, they regarded wine as the blood that was shed during the battle of the gods against the Titans (the Titans are the unspirited [*das Ungeistige*]). Wine is not an unmediated fruit; it has to be pressed. It gains spirited life by dying, and it continually asserts its individual character in a sealed state, like a secret. (During the flowering of the vines, the lesser spirited wines become heavier again and long to return to the material state.) Wine is a gift from the spiritualized god.

The Bacchic festivals were characterized by a kind of drunkenness. Bacchus was accompanied by the *Tityrs* and the *Satyrs,* goat-like human figures. They represented the animal-like life from which humanity had been *freed* by Dionysos. Also to that point, the fawn hides were worn as clothing (as they were in the mystery cults).

Silenus is the oldest and wisest of the Satyrs. He represents the undomesticated and even ironic principle of the originary era (with Plato, its fundamental feature is *irony*). His unconstraintness [*Unbefangenheit*], his banter, takes the place of the old constraint [*Befangenheit*]. *Originally, in contradiction to Dionysos, he was, in his blindness, mindless and stupid*; now, transformed into a friend of Dionysos, he is the cleverest, most experienced among the Satyrs and also the one who can see into the future. In his exterior appearance, he shows slackening and negligence, therefore χάλις, from χαλάω [to slacken]. Just as the Satyrs carried spears wrapped in ivy leaves and vines as a symbol of peace and peaceful conquest, so Silenus is carried by an ass, an animal of peace, not by a warhorse.

What Silenus is in relation to humankind, *Pan* is as *the universal principle of nature*: goat-footed, rough, hairy, a veritable nature god in the now calmed nature, the invisibly acting force in the silence of the forest and open fields. He is no longer feared but has become mild-tempered; with facetious irony compensating for his wildness, he becomes visible, appearing as a philanthropic [*menschenfreundlicher*] god. In fact, he is now the averted force of nature that has become invisible [and] no longer faces Man. If that force turns around, it becomes the cause of groundless horrors incited by the universality of nature. Pan was also made the caregiver of Dionysos's first childhood.

Until now, however, the Dionysos of whom we spoke was not the subject of the mystery cults; the festivals celebrating him were public. Also, Bacchus could not conciliate Demeter. *The conciliation of Demeter* was the main subject of the mystery cults. These are a result of the mythological process and could not precede him. They do not sublate the god-plurality, but they contain its sense the secret that this plurality enfolds.

The mystery cults were of a kind that had to be experienced. One must thus distinguish the mystery cults themselves from the knowledge they generated. As far as what happened at the mystery cults, it could only have been representations of the suffering, the battle, and the crisis of the mythological consciousness. This is neither a wisdom brought about mythologically nor a revelation made conscious by mythology; the process of mythology relinquished all the ideas held in consciousness. The mystery cults contain the esoteric doctrine of mythology, as we have presented it philosophically, in scenic form and as φαντασματα [apparition] first all the horrors of real principle and its death, the actual τελετὴ [rite][16] bound to the dying away of consciousness, and the ἐπόπτεια [revelation],[17] to complete bliss. ἐποπτεύειν μοι δοχῶ proverbially meant: I seem to be in the heavens. I cannot go into what happened at the mystery cults, as described by the writers of old.

---

16. Telete was the goddess or spirit of the initiation rites of the Eleusinian Mysteries and a daughter of the Dionysos.

17. Epoteia was the highest level of initiation in the Eleusinian Mysteries.

XXI. The Subject of the Mystery Cults

[PL, pp. 589-606]

The word δεικνύναι [bring to light, show] has been used in the doctrines of the mystery cults; thus history was demonstrated through scenic arrangements. ὁρᾶν [showing, demonstrating] = to learn. Whether these *demonstrations* included actual *speeches* cannot be ascertained. I conjecture this from a passage by Pausanias who says about the Eleusinian τελετή: "For the Greeks of an earlier period looked upon the Eleusinian Mysteries as being as much higher than all other religious acts as gods are higher than heroes"[1] Accordingly, the deities worshipped in Eleusis stand as high above the other deities as the gods do above the heroes, those mortal gods who are enclosed in a material body. The purely spiritual, causative gods are the content of the mystery cults. They are the *deorum deii* [the gods of the gods], as the gods of the Samothracian Mysteries were called.

The Romans called them *dii potes,* pure potences, in contrast to the material gods. Hence, they were often depicted only as masks; these gods to whom Dionysos belonged, were, according to Pausanias, depicted as προσωπα [masks]. Thus, in a chapel dedicated to Dionysos in Athens, only a πρόσωπον was worked into the wall,[2] as well as on Lesbos. The *dii potes* were furthermore thought of to be indissolubly connected.

This is consistent with our positioning of the three potences. In my treatise on the deities of Samothrace,[3] I believe I have demonstrated that the overarching name for these deities, καβειροι, designates their indissoluble unity. M. Ter. Varro declared the Cabeiri as identical with the Roman *diis penetralibus* [Penates].[4] However, those are the

---

1. Pausanias, *Description of Greece,* 10.31.11 (trans. W.H.S. Jones).

2. *Ibid.,* 1.2.5.

3. *Ueber die Gottheiten von Samothrake* (On the Deities of Samothrake), in SWVIII.

4. The Penates or innermost gods belonged to the *dii familiares* or

esoteric gods, *qui sunt introrsus et in coeli penetralibus*:[5] "they are those who the Etruscans call *consentes* and *complices*" (Varro).[6] They are those, such as our three potencies, who only jointly have Being [*nur zusammen-Seyenden*]. The mystery cults are nothing more than the higher, comprehending consciousness of mythology itself, and its content [are] thus the potences.

However, the deities of the mystery cults are not only indissolubly connected but *in the end are also* one *god or successive personalities of the same*. [They are] only different forms and moments of one and the same god.

Having been fully overcome by Dionysos and brought back in itself, the blind and real god henceforth becomes the same as that by which he has been overcome. Now he is the Dionysos of the first potence. Separated from Being [and] overcome by the Dionysos of the second potence, he leaves behind the Dionysos of the third potence. For consciousness to be completely appeased over the vanishing of the god, it must become convinced that the spiritual one and the material one are one and the same.

Thus, all are Dionysos; the potences differ only in *tension*. According to Herodotus,[7] it was Melampus who introduced the (second) Dionysos of the Thebans (Bacchus) to the Greeks, but he did not teach them every aspect of him. Those who came after him did so more comprehensively.

If we place the triune female deity alongside the triune Dionysos, *i.e.*, the stages of consciousness (more on that later), then we have the most complete content of the highest doctrine of the mystery cults. Aside from the passage in Herodotus, we do not yet have any explicit evidence of this Dionysos-idea in this locality. So far, it has been a necessary philosophical conclusion for us.

---

household deities. According to Cicero (*De natura deorum* 27.68), they reside in the recesses of the house and are also called *penetrales*.

5. "Who are within, and in the inmost recesses of heaven" (Arnobius, *Adversus Gentes*, 3.40 [trans. Hamilton Bryce and Hugh Campbell]).

6. *Ibid.*; so called, according to Varro, because "they rise and fall together." They are said to be the twelve gods who make up the Roman council of gods.

7. Herodotus, *The Histories*, 2.49.

As has been said, the proceedings were shown [scenically]; the last spiritual unity, wherein all tension is dissolved, had come into Being and thus could only be presented as such. The last unity, which no longer contained anything material, is based on the fact that the first Dionysos stepped back into himself. He was the god who first came into Being and then withdrew from it; thus, it was a historical event. He is Dionysos only as one who is already spiritualized; as this invisible one, he was also called Hades. As Heraclitus said: Hades and Dionysos are one and the same.[8]

The other side must be designated by a different name. In the mystery cults, he was called ζαγρεὺς [Zagreus]. That he was the first and oldest is elucidated by the fact that he was called so expressly, commonly, and regularly in the *Nonnus Dionysiaca* (full of scholarly knowledge about the mythology and the mystery cults). He was called παλαιότερος [old in years] ἀρχιγενής [causing the first beginnings of things], in contrast to ὀψιγενής [late-born]; then in Herodotus, he was called διόνυσος χθόνιος [Chtonian Dionysos], and he even appears as such in a fragment of Aeschylus (= the great Zeus of the departed).[9]

As the oldest Dionysos, Zagreus is further identified by his birth to Zeus and Persephone. For the consciousness, the causative gods are but the last result of the theogonic process. *They must always originate from the theogonic process for mythological consciousness.* Since the cognition of the causes is mediated out of it, they originate in the consciousness only at the end of the process, and this end is in Zeus. Through Zeus, the consciousness becomes conscious of those potencies; thus, Zagreus is introduced to Persephone as son of Zeus and the one subjugated by him to the theogonic process. For at the end of the process, the ill-fated possibility that posits the process by entering actuality is recognized in the latter. She is the inward, subjective beginning of the mythological process and therefore the one who posits that

---

8. Heraclitus, Fr. 15.
9. Aeschylus, *The Suppliants*, 154.

which is the objective beginning of the entire process. The unapproachable Persephone is stalked by Zeus in the form of a serpent, and she receives the older Dionysos to whom, having become invisible, as Hades, she becomes betrothed. As mother of Zagreus, Persephone belongs to the doctrine of the mystery cults that continues to speak of procreation and birth in the language of mythology. One of the epithets of Zagreus is ὠμηστής [savage, cruel], another ἀγριώνιος,[10] but in a later moment he is μειλίχιος καὶ χαριδώτης [gentle and joy-giving]; for as the real god, he is hostile toward all that is concrete. Stepping back into himself, he is the mild and charitable god. He is also called ἰσοδαίτης, he who grants everyone the Being that pertains to them. He who was first the exclusionary one foregoes Being and instead makes himself the ground of Being. He is the opposite of the singular, concrete one, and he must perish in order for the singular one to live.

This now amenable [*holdgewordene*] god is the *second Dionysos;* thus, the second Dionysos vanishes in the mystery cults and is thought of in the first one who has been overcome. But the real god steps aside only to be the spirit that is elevated above transformation and decline. His glory is to have been overcome into pure soul. *Soul is the real brought back into itself* [*Das Reale in sein Ansich zurückgebracht, ist Seele*]. In nature, the things in which the blind Being is extant appear soulless. *Soul* is the principle that has been completely brought back into itself; where it is entirely soul, it has the spirit as its fruit and completion [*Frucht und Vollendung*]. The second principle acts as the mediating one [*das Vermittelnde*]. The soul that is able to mediate the spirit is blessed [*selig*], the other unblessed [*unselig*]. Thus, in the mystery cults, that god is thought of as dying in order to reach a higher Being.

We have now developed the *complete Dionysos-idea*; anyone to whom this is told without the striking testimonies it is based on might take it *for something made up.* It has been shown: *firstly,* that the god who was the cause of the tension

10. Agrionios (epithet of Dionysos).

is overcome by the second potence, the only one called Dionysos until now, and becomes Dionysos as the lord of the departed [*Herr der Abgeschiedenen*]. It was him to whom Themistocles had to sacrifice three Persian youths[11] to turn that god of the past favorable toward him. In Pelopidas, on whom something similar was later imposed, the Hellenic consciousness had become so strengthened that he said: I do not worship Typhon but rather the father of gods and men (in him, all three potences meet for the first time, also materially).[12] Plato already emphasizes the *νοῦς βασιλικὸς* [regal mind] of Zeus.[13] *Secondly,* how the god who alone was called Dionysos originarily after overcoming the un-spiritual [*ungeistige*], now himself as a god, appears only in different form. The real one cannot perish in the consciousness without constituting himself in it as the one who has Being and the remaining one. The *third* form of the god is the Ἴαχος [Iacchos] of the mystery cults. He is different from the second Dionysos. Arrian says that the mystical Bacchus-song is chanted not to the Theban Bacchus but to another Bacchus.[14] He is named expressly as the first. the one who has returned.

One should not, however, mistake the first for the third, as some of the ancients have, since they also thought of Iacchos as the son of Zeus and Persephone. If Zagreus and Iacchos were the same person, then there would have been only two Dionysoses, but the tradition speaks of three. Diodorus Siculus says (3.63): some teach that there is only *one* Dionysos, others that there are three.[15] Those who only knew the *one* were those who only knew the Theban one (the exoteric [Dionysos]). That the mystical Iacchos is different from Zagreus is elucidated by the fact that he is not listed (or only in dubious sources) as the son of Persephone but rather as that of Demeter. By way of explanation, Suidas adds: the Dionysos at the mother breast. In Lucretius, Ceres is the

---

11. See Plutarch, *Life of Themistocles,* 13.2.
12. See Plutarch, *Life of Pelopidas,* 21.4.
13. See Plato, *Philebus,* 30*d*.
14. Arrian, *Anabasis of Alexandria,* 2.16.3.
15. Diodorus Siculus, *Library of History,* 3.63.2.

one who breastfeeds Iacchos. Therefore, Demeter is called κουροτρόφος [child-nurturer]. Everywhere, Nonnus distinguishes Zagreus from Iacchos; the nymphs of Marathon perform a dance around the newly born Iacchos.[16] Then he describes how they worship the god Iacchos *after* (μετα) the son of Zagreus and after the son of Semele (*i.e.,* Zagreus). Furthermore, how they employ sacrifices and chant hymns to the third-born Iacchos.

There are, on the other hand, passages where *Iacchos is mistaken for Zagreus*; for he is only the returning *first* one, as in Arrian, who carefully distinguishes him from the Theban one, making him the son of Zeus and Persephone. A scholium to Aristophanes's *Frogs* says: Some say that he is an Other than the son of Semele, others that he is the same. A scholiast to Pindar: Zagreus, born to Semele, who according to some is Iacchos. In fact, Iacchos already exists in Zagreus; hence the mix-up. Thus, according to some Egyptians, Osiris is torn to pieces and, according to others, even Horus (the third Dionysos); but it actually is Typhon who is torn to pieces. In Plutarch and Nonnos, it is Zagreus who meets that fate; in Clement of Alexandria (*Protrepticus*), it seems to be Iacchos. The end is the exposited [*herausgesezte*] beginning, while the beginning is exposed [*ausgesezt*] to the overthrow.[17] Dialectically, the third part takes up the first again; the third concept is the potence that remains as potence. Hence, Iacchos is the restored Zagreus.

What then is the significance of *Demeter*? She is the doubtful [*zweifelhafte*] consciousness that stands midway between the real and the liberating god.[18] According to one side, she must follow the real god. She seeks her daughter, *i.e.,* the god who fills her consciousness and of whom she

16. Nonnus, *Dionysiaca,* XLVIII.948.

17. *Cf. Philosophie der Offenbarung,* SW XIII, p. 482: "The last has led us back to the first because he was considered identical with him and in part was confused with him in a way that the end always again is equal to the beginning and actually is only the beginning exposited and declared as that which has been posited."

18. *Philosophie der Mythologie,* SW XII, p. 628: "Demeter becomes [...] the center point, the hinge on which everything turns."

catches sight of only fragmentarily in the god-plurality. Since she has separated herself from her accidental [nature], she is genuinely the one who posits God [*Gott-Sezende*]. She cannot recognize either Aides or Dionysos until they are joined with the third one, until the first is posited as not having Being but as spirit. In the same act, she becomes that which (fittingly) posits the god who is the spiritual unity over the plurality and as such is the actual spirit; for it to be appeased, the spiritual one must be the same as the lost substantial one.

According to Plutarch, the disappearance of the first god in the Egyptian and Hellenic mystery cults was followed by a resurrection of that same god. In Diodorus Siculus, there is also the thought that the third potence is actually the returning first one. The one who is torn to pieces by the Titans (from τείνειν [stretched, extended]; thus the *tension* of the potences) is reborn anew by Demeter. She becomes conciliated by the birth of Iacchos; her gaze brightens only when a servant reminds her that she will give birth once more. The public events taking place during the processions, mentioned by Clement of Alexandria and translated by Arnobius into crass verse, also point to that.

Already the first organizers of the mystery cults added something for the masses, and therein is expressed the inner sureness of the religious disposition, which can also tolerate the opposite of that which is the purely inward. Such safety is granted in the mystery cults by the last unfolding [*Aufschluss*], which was given with the appearance of Iacchos. The expression of the feeling of being liberated from the oppressive force of the real god is the jubilation of Iacchos; ὁ μυστικὸς Ἴαχος [O secret Iacchos] (as well as the words related to Ἴαχος) signifies first the jubilation, then the celebrated god. It is comparable to the Christian joy in the Holy Spirit.

The second Dionysos is the guide of the souls in death. The present life is the unaccomplished work of the second god; it is only accomplished in death, in order to become conversant with pure potences. In the N.T.: "Blessed are the dead who die in the Lord."[19] Only in the third is the Dionysos-idea brought to completion. In it, the first becomes χθονιος [Chthonian], and the whole history of the god is thus narrated as the history of Iacchos.

The triad of Dionysos has now been joined by Persephone, wedded to Hades, and Demeter. The latter, after having been reconciled by the third Dionysos, now belongs fully to the second Dionysos as his *πάρεδρος* [assistant, advisor]. Adjoined to him, she is reconciled with Zeus and the plurality. Originarily midway between the real and the liberating god, she was the seed of the third god, the collective potence, the still substantive consciousness, the three forms of Dionysos. The development of the substantial begins as Persephone is set apart, and it ends when that which belongs to the third Dionysos is set apart. She then steps into the center, with the same rank as the second Dionysos. A female figure has to correspond to Iacchos, if only, as a moment of consciousness. This is the resurrected Persephone, returned to a virgin state, the higher heavenly one, the *κόρη* [young girl, maiden], adjoined to the *κοῦρος* [youth, boy] Ἴαχος. Her wedding was the highest celebration, the bridal bed on the third day of the Eleusinian Mysteries. *Thus the Church is called the Bride of Christ.* Consciousness became fully removed from mythological process through the *ἱερὸς γάμος* [sacred marriage] (*κόρη* and Persephone are often confused). In works of art, Demeter is often seen with *κόρε* and Ἴαχος (Pausanias in a temple of Demeter in Attica); both children [are] her delight and pride; Iacchos with the torch. Thus, in Rome, Ceres [is] with *Liber* and *Libera*. *Liber* is explained by Cicero; according to him, *liber* and *libera* are merely translations of *κοῦρος* and *κόρε*. Cicero says: *quo ex nobis natos liberos appellamo, ita qui ex Cerere nati sunt, liber et libera appelati sunt.*[20] (Liber in singular [is found] still in Quinctilianus and in the pandects.) *Liber* = Iacchos in Livius and Tacitus (*ann. lib.* 3). Thus, one

---

19. Revelation 14:13.

20. Cicero, *De natura deorum,* II.62: "Because we call our children *liberi,* the offsprings of Ceres were named Liber and Libera" (trans. P.G. Walsh).

finds *Libero et Liberae* in inscriptions and on tombstones, whereby the initiation of the deceased was inscribed into the highest level of the mystery cults, most commonly on the painted vases (on grave sites). The mystery cults were the initiation into communication with the intelligible gods.

The main content of the mystery cults was the one *god who, after the sublated tension, had become spiritualized in all his potences.* His retreat from Being was thought of as a dying; the content of the scenic presentations were the deeds, sufferings, and death of the god. The actual secret could therefore not be a so-called refined theism [*geläuterter Theismus*],[21] not rational, torn away from all that is historical. Something needed to be in the mystery cults that could endure in time. It could only be something that actually happened, not merely a doctrine.

The historical content of the mystery cults, which is tied to an originary event, distinguishes itself quite clearly from philosophy. Persephone does not merely signify but *is* the principle. The neo-Platonists have converted the mystery cults into reflections. According to them, Persephone signifies, by and large, the human soul; her abduction into Hades represents her descent into matter. The dead are the lifeless things of nature;[22] Aides only abducts her so that even the τὰ ἔσχατα τῆς φύσεως [the last of nature] is not to be untouched [*unbefleckt*] [by her].[23] These are merely allegorical explanations.

Neither was the content of the mystery cults an abstract monotheism, negative insofar as it did not overcome polytheism. As a historically mediated unity, which had passed through plurality, it could not have been hostile toward polytheism. Since Warburton's *On the Divine Legation of Moses,*[24]

21. See "Spirit of the Ancient Mythology," in Leigh Hunt, *The Indicator* (London, 1822), p. 113: "A system of refined theism is understood to have been taught to the initiated in the celebrated Mysteries."

22. *Philosophie der Offenbarung,* SW XIII, p. 501: "Persephone is not actually the Queen of the Dead; the dead are rather to be understood as the dead and lifeless things of nature, which she ensouls."

23. *Cf. ibid.*: "Aides only abducts her so that even the τὰ ἔσχατα τῆς φύσεως, the lowest part of the material world, is not without ensoulment [*Beseelung*]."

24. William Warburton, *The Divine Legation of Moses Demonstrated*

it has been assumed that the actual secret was the unity of the godhood. Those who were initiated into it were told that the many gods originated only *euhemeristically*. Rather, it was a reverse euhemerism, *e.g.*, Remus = Remulus, the impeding, resisting one, Romulus (the younger brother because of the *diminitivum*), and Numa (the spiritual potence)—these three Etruscan Cabeiri brothers reinterpreted as Roman kings. Or ought they be personifications of natural forces? How then could mythology have subsisted alongside enlightenment. Yet they stood side by side for almost a millennium. Monotheism recognizes the plurality as a path to itself; the rise of plurality was but the decline of the substantial one, the agony of the un-spiritual principle (as nature in general can be viewed). The history of the gods became the story of the gods in the mystery cults.

In that history of the god, the *doctrine of immortality* was also given. Everything difficult that human life had to overcome was also overcome by the god. It was the inevitable path trodden by the god toward glory. Through pity and fear, says Aristotle, tragedy *purifies* these same passions. What Aristotle said could be accomplished to an even higher degree by the mystery cults. Greek tragedy itself arose out of those choruses, which were sung in celebration of Dionysos. Aristotle uses the same image of purgation (κάθαρσις [katharis, purification]) in his *Politics* for the chants performed in preparation of the orgies.

However, something remains unexplained in all this: *while the mystery cults did indeed contain the secret of mythology, why did they contain it formally as a secret* when the Rape of Proserpina was sung of in the hymn to Demeter and elsewhere publicly; when the spiritual gods were otherwise generally known as the *dii potes* and *consentes*; when the seafaring people of Themistocles demanded the sacrifice of the youths for the wild Dionysos; when everyone knew the Iacchos chant, and even on the stage the poet did not hesitate to let people hear the chants of the initiated? The *Antigone* celebrated Bacchus, the son of Semele, and Iacchos quite openly. Even the suffering and death of the god could

---

in Nine Books (first published between 1738 and 1741 in London).

be sung of by anyone at their pleasure (although only the Orphics did so in their poetry) without being persecuted for it. But what hatred was raised against Alcibiades when he was accused of celebrating mystery cults in his house and against Aeschylus when he revealed some of it incautiously. The latter had to take refuge at the altar of Dionysos in the orchestra section, and he was not saved by his bravery in the Persian battles but rather by the fact that he had never been initiated. The death penalty was not severe enough; confiscation of property and defilement of one's name on publicly displayed tablets were added to it. A scholiast[25] says: Aeschylus spoke incautiously of Demeter. Isocrates says: nothing more enraged the people of Athens than profanities against the mystery cults.[26] The mystery cults celebrate the decline of the Siderian religions and their wild state. Cicero even describes it as if the mystery cults liberated mankind from it; yet this benevolence of Demeter was also celebrated during the public Dionysos festivities (crowns of acorns were worn during the festivities, and similar symbols were found even at weddings, where a child carrying with it symbols from the wild era spoke the words: ἔφυγον κακὸν, εὗρον ἄμεινον).[27]

Plato put words in the mouth of *Socrates* (*as a quasi initiate*)[28] to elevate the mystery cults: that the uninitiated will lie in the mud while the initiated will dwell with the intelligible gods.[29] Clement of Alexandria *et al.* are well informed of sayings, events, etc. But the mystery cults must have contained something whose publication was prohibited and that—admittedly not unmediatedly—was in contradiction to popular belief. Something that was conformable with the public system and yet could not take its place.

---

25. Clement of Alexandria, *Stromata,* 2.14: "Aeschylus, who divulged the Mysteries on the stage."

26. Alcibiades was famously accused of profaning the Eleusinian Mysteries.

27. "Here I leave my sins behind, Here the better way I find" (Demosthenes, *Orationes,* 18.259 [trans. C.A. Vince and J.H. Vince]).

28. *Cf.* Plato, *Symposium,* 209*e* (trans. A. Nehamas and P. Woodruff): "Even you, Socrates, could probably come to be initiated into these rites."

29. Plato, *Phaedo,* 69*c*.

We still have *one* side of the triad of Dionysos that has been less emphasized. The three potences are simultaneous in this consciousness insofar as they are moments of *one* consciousness, but by this its position within the successive potences is not sublated. It was probably also possible that in that coexistence in the last consciousness the first Dionysos was regarded as the ruler of the *past*; the second, of the *present*; the third, of the *future*. The present is filled with the material plurality of gods [*Göttervielheit*]. Even though the third Dionysos was also in that last consciousness, he could only be contained in it as the god of the future. However, if the third was designated as future, then the second, and thus the plurality of gods in general, was meant to retreat into the past. Already the first Dionysian world, along with the Titans, saw consciousness sink into the Tartarus. *It was [the knowledge of] what was yet to come* [das Zukünftige] *that kept the mouth of the initiate sealed,* a knowledge one would have rather kept even from oneself, which one dared to reveal only to the eye but not [confide] to the ear. Thus, the nocturnal celebrations of the highest festivities, just as the first persecuted Church observed its rites at night in the catacombs.

Stepping out of this nocturnal ecstasy back into the light of day, the initiate had to turn ever so tenderly toward daylight, so that the mystery cults themselves would increase the affection for the gods. This secret was of a kind that, if spoken out loud, would quickly spread general horror. *It was an allusion to the future world with which Aeschylus incited the mob.* Prometheus says: "I care less than nothing for Zeus. Let him rule for his little day. He will not hold sway over the gods for long."[30] To Hermes, he says: "High-and-mighty is our speech, but you new rulers will rule only briefly. Have I not seen two rulers cast out already? I shall live to see this one cast out even more shamefully."[31]

Here one ought to speak of the idea of Prometheus within our exegesis [*Entwicklung*]; however, I will move on.

30. Aeschylus, *Prometheus Bound,* 938ff.
31. *Ibid.,* 954ff.

There are analogous ideas [to be found] in Scandinavia, just as there are among the heavy-hearted Etruscans. Only with that last thought of the Hellenic consciousness—which, the less it was expressed, the more it became entrenched in the heart [*Gemüth*]—can the *tragic trait, the heavy heart* [*Schwermuth*], *which pervades the plastic arts* [*bildende Kunst*], be explained. The greatest joy of life converges with a trait of internal pain to [create] the beauty of Greek formative education [*Bildung*]. The tragic, which lies within the religious sentiment of the Greek, is derived from the intermediate position it occupies, between the sensual and the purely spiritual (= future). This intermediate position grants it—in all dependence on a religion that has emerged by inevitable necessity—infinite freedom, whereby it is now directed against the mythological religion and treats it with free irony and could make itself independent from that spiritual religion of the mystery cults. In Greece, religion was by no means compulsory, nor was anyone forced to join the mystery cults. (Neither Socrates nor Epaminondas were initiated.) However, that which was yet to come [*das Zukünftige*] could not be asserted in contrast to the still ruling gods opposite the public life and the State.

Were the causative potences indeed thought of as (successive) world rulers [*Weltherrscher*]? Three are mentioned as belonging together as world rulers, as ἄνακες (alter plur. of ἄναξ [lord, master, king] in the *Iliad* for Zeus), among the deities of the mystery cults. Cicero names the three ἄνακες that were worshipped in Athens: Εὐβουλεὺς, Τριτοπατρεὺς, and Διόνυσος.[32] The last name indicates in which circle we find ourselves. Hesychius names Εὐβουλεὺς = Hades. That would therefore be the name of the first Dionysos. After his overcoming, the wild one (Zagreus) becomes the benevolent one. Dionysos is the second, and Tritopatreus the third Dionysos, the third world ruler. If they are to be regarded as three rulers, then they are rulers of three different epochs.

But should one not be able to find in the Eleusinian customs indications of the concept of the third Dionysos as

32. Eubuleus, Tritopatreus, and Dionysos.

the actual world ruler? Iacchos is introduced as a child to Demeter. Thus, Zeus lay in the arms of Fortuna Primigenia, and the second Dionysos in the arms of Pan. One can see three male youths (representing Aides, Poseidon, and Zeus) on one of the Pompeiian wall paintings under the throne of Kronos during the moment of his fateful nuptial to Rhea.[33] Just as these three beardless youths are thought of here as future rulers, so Iacchos is represented as a child. The *vannus mystica* was an important object in the processions;[34] Iacchos was carried in it. It describes the inconspicuousness of his birth and the peace in which he arrives. *Through a miraculous* πρόληψις [anticipation], *the vessel* [*Wanne*] *later became the crib for the Holy Birth.*

The fact that [Iacchos] was thought of as playing with balls and spheres also points to the above. On the sixth day of the Eleusinian mystery cults, Iacchos appears as a boy,

---

33. Schelling is referring here to one of the frescoes discovered in the Casa del Poeta Tragico (House of the Tragic Poet) in Pompeii in 1825. His reading of the painting as a depiction of the nuptials of Kronos and Rhea and the three young male figures at the bottom right of the painting as being the still unborn sons of Kronos was pivotal to his theory of mythology with respect to the philosophy of revelation. His reading was supported by the German archaeologist Karl Otfried Müller but later disputed by others. Since Wolfgang Helbig's *Wandgemälde der von Vesuv verschütteten Städte Campaniens* (Leipzig: Breitkopf und Härtel, 1868, p. 34), it has been largely interpreted to depict the presentation of Hera to Zeus on Mount Ida, and the three male figures as dactyls. The painting is now in the Archaeological Museum in Naples, Italy. Schelling discussed the painting at great length in his two-part essay "On the Significance of One of the Newly Discovered Wall Paintings in Pompeii," published in 1833 in the art supplement to the *Morgenblatt für gebildete Stände*. (See below, pp. 345–54, for a full translation of the text). Schelling's treatise was accompanied by a lithographic line drawing of the painting (fig. 1). Both the treatise and the image were reprinted at the end of the *Philosophy of Mythology*, SW XII, pp. 675–85. See also Kurt Hildebrandt, "Schellings Deutung des Wandgemäldes der Hochzeit von Kronos und Rhea," *Zeitschrift für philosophische Forschung* 17/1 (1963): 141–46.

34. Virgil, *Georgics* 1.165: "the mystic fan of Iacchos." The "fan" was most likely a wicker vessel used for winnowing grain. It was also called a *liknon*, a wicker-work cradle like the one Dionysos was placed in after his birth. See Jane E. Harrison, "Mystica Vannus Iacchi," *The Journal of Hellenic Studies* 23 (1903): 292–324.

his head wreathed with myrrh (not laurel or acorn), and is brought to Eleusis accompanied by shouts of joy. Even the name Eleusis means *coming* [*Kunft*], *the advent of the god*; the public interpretation was probably referring to the first arrival of Demeter.

In the mystery cults, *Iacchos* is thus *the ruler of the future era*. The ἐποπτεία [epopteia][35] also falls on the sixth day in Eleusis. In the chorus of the Antigone, Iacchos is called ταμίας [lord, master][36] (in Homer, Zeus is also called that, the one who rules over the war of men). So also in Pindar, ταμίας as lord. Iacchos is also called αἰσυμνήτης [someone who gives everyone their fair share], one who gives everyone their share, thus a judge in the fighting games, also ruler as such (in Euripides and Aristotle).

Proper polytheism could only enter humanity in intense fighting, and the pain caused by the lost unity could only be reconciled if polytheism were recognized as a mere transition, so that a future religion could restore the lost unity. The future religion should be a general religion, beyond mythology, bringing together the entire human race divided by polytheism.

When Valentinian I prohibited nocturnal ceremonies, the proconsul in Greece submitted to him that this law—according to which they were not allowed to celebrate the holiest part of the mystery cults, the one that hold the human race together—would make life unbearable for the Hellenes. This caused a postponement for the Eleusinians until Theodosius the Great. Similarly Cicero: "mitto Eleusinem illam ubi initiantur gentes," *etc.*[37]

In all religion, there is a *spes temporum meliorum* [hope for better times]; even Christianity had its Chiliasm. Such consolation was even given—under the pressure of its religious customs and sacrifices through the mystery cults—to the fully achieved paganism. The mystery cults existed therefore mostly in opposition to Christianity.

---

35. The epopteia was the public stage of the initiation during the mystery cults.

36. Sophocles, *Antigone*, 1151.

37. Cicero, *De Natura Deorum*, 1.42 (trans. Horace C. P. McGregor): "Eleusis, / Where all the peoples of the earth / Are made partakers of the mysteries."

The last content of the mystery cults is the complete overcoming of polytheism and the future religion that is common to all. Thus, the mystery cults contained a *revelation,* as it were, about the future of the human race.

In his highest potence, Dionysos was the meaning [*Sinn*] of the doctrine of the mystery cults. They pertained to the past and the future, to the potence underlying the current order (Persephone) on the one hand and to the general future of the religious consciousness, as well as the human race, on the other. Demeter, as the mother of both Persephone and Iacchos, stood in the center. Thus, they are also called the Mysteries of Demeter. It is easy to explain why these deeper gods are less prevalent in poetry, which turned toward those gods that were, in a narrower sense, historical or poetic gods.

The mystery cults were called τέλη, τελεταὶ [far off, at a distance], probably because they showed the end or the future completion; originarily, only the Greater Mysteries were likely called τελεταὶ, but the mystery cults also pertained to the beginning and the past, whereby *initia* only expressed the other side. The difference between the Lesser and Greater Mysteries may lie therein. All Hellenes and even the Barbarians were admitted the Lesser Mysteries, where Persephone seemed to be the focus.

The *Orphics* appear to have greatly striven to join the mystery cults. They probably had no influence on its inner workings, and the reports of later mythographers (Apollodorus) about the mystery cults being founded by Orpheus are certainly apocryphal.[38] The mystery cults emerged from a natural development of mythology. First, what later became mythology was esoteric (Zeus at Knossos and in Dodona). However, just as consciousness grappled with polytheism, so the pure principals, the causative forces, remained behind in the consciousness, and thus the mystery cults were the result of a necessary process. The *Orphics* could only initiate μυστηρία *privata* [private mystery cults]; they had no influence on the national mystery cults. They

38. Apollodorus, *Bibliotheca,* 1.3.2.

also spread cosmogonical-philosophical statements, especially since the *Pythagoreans* began hiding among them.

Only in the mystery cults does mythology come to an end; every life concludes with conceiving its end, its death, and positing the concept of a future. *The conciliation of mythology* lies not in the frenzy of Bacchanalian processions but in the stillness of that grave night when the Hellene becomes conscious of the necessity of the present reality. But now—— *we are approaching the absolute conciliation.* The same causes that in their natural, external position explain the mythological process now explain, in their higher, personal relation, the revelation.

To understand revelation, we had to first understand the principles that make it possible; otherwise, something bad [*ein Uebel*] arises. If, in the traditional presentation, the belief in revelation cannot be substantiated, it is because revelation does not recognize anything outside of itself. From our knowledge of mythology, we are already certain of the reality of the principles of revelation.

XXII. The Difference between Revelation and Mythology

[PL, pp. 606–22]

The principles of mythology are necessarily also the principles of the revealed religion because both—are religions. The major difference is that the ideas of mythology are the result of a necessary or natural process of a consciousness left to its own devices over which no free causative agent exerts any influence, while *revelation is thought of as something that has an* actus *outside consciousness and presupposes a relation that voluntarily has given over to Man the freest of all causes, God.* Thus, science enters here into a completely new realm.

If by philosophy one understands, as most do, a science that generates reason purely out of itself, then a philosophy of revelation would be an attempt to trace the truths of a revealed religion back to those that reason generates out of itself. However, believers in revelation consider their subject matters to be those that cannot be reached through reason. And to be honest, one has to agree that there *must* be certain truths that not only are not known but can never be known except through revelation.—For why else *would there be revelation*?

If those who want to reduce the truths of revelation to mere truths of reason—if only by force, similar to certain explanations of mythology—were asked what purpose these works of providence served, and if they at least acknowledge the founder of Christianity as a highly talented teacher [chosen by providence],[1] would they only be able to respond that by choosing such a path, mankind could gain possession of these cognitions *earlier*? On the other hand, they deny this advantage again by asserting that it requires centuries to strip away the [unessential and][2] darkening wrappings; indeed, this contriving [*Veranstaltung*] needs to be given as

1. *Philosophie der Offenbarung,* SW XIV, p. 5.
2. *Ibid.*

the reason the development of mankind was halted so much. Therefore, either the concept of revelation has no meaning, or one must concede that the content of revelation cannot be known without it. Here revelation becomes its own source of cognition.

But shouldn't there also be a general concept under which to subsume it? Anyone who strives for the highest possible unity of cognition confesses to there being more than one source of cognition; pure reason is set alongside experience. Revelation is but one of the many kinds of knowledge imparted to us. There are other things that we know about from experience, *a posteriori.*

In what way philosophy finds God and how it discovers the possibility in him to be the free Creator of Being [I do not wish to repeat here].[3] We know that such a philosophical path exists. We only know that God wanted to be Creator by virtue of the fact that he actually created. The reasons we then found—why God made what is possible into something actual—are there, but these reasons are in part taken from attributes that we could only learn *a posteriori. The tendency to be cognized is a moral attribute.* The *a priori* attributes, however, are negative ones; the positive [attributes] only let themselves be apprehended *a posteriori.* On the other hand, these moving causes provide no certainty; only facts can do that.

From this point on, we find ourselves once again formally on the path of necessary progression. Once the *tension of the potences is posited* through that decision toward Creation, we are in the realm of a necessity that is always hypothetical, yet in a necessary progression. Posited once as process, it no longer could develop other moments; from the standpoint of the general idea of the process, our knowledge is a *priori,* foresighted. However, with the achieved goal—where it is in Man's control to forever connect Being with the divine or to take it for himself and alienate it from the divine—something happens that could be known *a priori.*

The mythological process proceeds once again according to objective laws, provided that the mediated potence

3. *Philosophie der Offenbarung,* SW XIV, p. 6.

holds out and remains within it. Without it, human consciousness would have been consumed [*verzehrt*].[4] The fact that it remained can only be seen out of the movement itself. Mythology points to a higher order with the question about why the mediating potence remains in the movement. *Mythology* can certainly be comprehended out of itself by virtue of its content but *not by virtue of its existence.* The philosophy of mythology is encompassed by the philosophy of revelation like a concentric circle. There is no (*a priori*) necessity for human consciousness to assert itself during its coming apart [*Auseinandergehen*]; this can only be the decision of a free will, and this free will can only be sought in that which, at the risk of upheaval, willed the world. Mythology can only be an accidental consequence of this will, never its purpose. God has overlooked the times of ignorance, *i.e.*, while he did not want it as purpose, he did not exclude it either; he tolerated it as something that happened concurrently [*als etwas Mitgeschehendes*].[5]

Mythology is therefore the consequence of a divine will, not its revelation. That [divine will] will only be revealed after or beyond [mythology]. One can extrapolate it from mythology, but it is not the effect of this divine will. *How now can this will be cognizable?*

After having cognized that *the catastrophe through which the dark force that had been defeated in nature rose* and took possession of the human consciousness occurred against the divine will, it is only natural to assume that God conceived the thought to restore this system. He foresaw [the Fall of Man] before the founding of the world. Furthermore, this thought had to be adequate to the extraordinary events that, when seen from a human standpoint, no reason could have considered as possible, that *the Creator would give his Creation the power to question his own work.* Reason can admit

4. *Cf. Philosophie der Offenbarung,* SW XIV, p. 13: "a consumption of spirit [*Verzehrung des Geistes*]." See Ecclesiastes 1:17: "And I gave my heart to know wisdom, and to know madness and folly: I perceived that this also is vexation of spirit" (KJV).

5. Acts 17:30: "Although God overlooked the ignorance of earlier times, He now commands all men everywhere to repent" (BSB).

to the latter only after a deeper experience in and outside itself. However, anyone who admits to this should not be in disbelief of the former and should not be surprised by *the extraordinariness of the divine plan.*

One can get this far *a priori,* so to speak, if one admits to the Creation and the catastrophe. In this case, the astounding virtue of the divine plan can be apprehended. That this plan has actually been executed, however, is not cognizable without revelation. This will, as an actual will triggered by the catastrophe, is the mystery [*Geheimnis*] κατ' ἐξοχὴν [*par excellence*], and the last, highest revelation is the revelation of this will. The revelation of the will is, however, the deed. As long as a will is only a will, it is a mystery; the deed is its manifestation.[6] It can now be not only cognized but also comprehended through reflection and combinatory logic. Once truths have been revealed, they are no longer mysteries; to claim otherwise would be a contradiction.

Paul speaks of a plan of God that had been kept secret for ages but is now revealed in Christ—that the mystery of God and Christ has been revealed through the appearance of Christ to the entire world.[7] Here one can explain how a philosophy of revelation is possible. It is not, like mythology, to be understood as a necessary process. Instead, posited completely freely, it can only be grasped out of the decision and the deed of the freest will. Through revelation, a new, second Creation has been initiated as an entirely free act.

But while revelation is not a necessary process, the philosophy of revelation nevertheless will not let it stand as something incomprehensible [*Unbegreifliches*]. Even if it is acknowledged that the Creation can only be a free act, it is nevertheless possible to conceive of a philosophy that can, in part, comprehend and, in part, explicate the will once it has been revealed. That decision of revelation exceeds human

---

6. *Philosophie der Offenbarung,* SW XIV, p. 11: "As long as a will is only a will and has not passed over into deed, it is a mystery. The deed is the manifestation by which it ceases to be mystery and can not only be cognized but, through reflection and combinatory logic, even be *comprehended*!"

7. Romans 16:25–27; Ephesians 3:5.

concepts, yet it is comprehensible insofar as the magnitude of the decision equals the magnitude of God; all that Man can do in this respect is to broaden the narrowness of his concepts toward the magnitude of the divine concepts.

If *the affect of the philosopher is wonder,*[8] then philosophy will have the drive to progress from that which is only visible *a priori* with necessity to that which lies outside and beyond all necessary insight. It will have no rest until it arrives at that which has the most wondrous virtue, at that which sublates the activity of thought itself. Everything that happens without a definite goal [*Ziel*] is vain. The activity of thought must accomplish something whereby it is put to rest. There will be *doubts* within that movement. What is only a moment contains doubt; it progresses but not into infinity. Only in the last thought or event is doubt defeated.

If one wants to call this condition of rest from the activity of thought *faith,* then one may do so; but then one must *not* regard faith as *an ungrounded cognition.* The Last, wherein all knowledge comes to rest, *cannot be without ground*; but it cannot again become the ground for progress. In the line of progress, every point is a last point, but as soon as one sets one's eyes on what has been found, *dialectics* discover a negation that can only be sublated by the subsequent position, which in itself contains a new possibility that may not conceal itself. *All that is possible must become actual in order for all to be revealed.*

Right after the *overthrow,* there would be a tendency for reason to let the Creator *intervene*; but God is greater than our activity of thought. He knows how to counter the utmost [*Aeussersten*] that can occur with another utmost. *Since the world could not be produced by a creaturely* [*creatürlichen*] *will, it will be produced by the undoubtable deed of a supra-creaturely* [*übercreatürlichen*] *and yet human will.* The certitude that sublates all doubt is *faith,* and the latter is therefore *the end of knowledge.* First the Law,[9] then the Gospel [*Evangelium*]![10]

---

8. Plato, *Theaetetus,* 155*d*.

9. The Torah of the Old Testament. *Cf.* Romans 10:4: "For Christ is the end of the law" (BSB).

10. *Philosophie der Offenbarung,* SW XIV, p. 15: "Reason = the Law, Faith = the Gospel."

Thus, the strict discipline [*Zucht*] of science must precede faith.[11]

All the treasures of cognition are concealed in Christ,[12] i.e., *comprehended in him*. They must be fathomed along with him; otherwise, he is not comprehended. The faith at the end of the seeking does not preclude the seeking. The still-seeking science sees that all that it finds sublates itself again. *Ubi finis quaerendi, ubi statio inveniendi? Christum scire est omnia scire* (Tertullian).[13] [*Christ*] *is the end of knowledge; whoever has him truly and cognizes him fully has with him and in him all knowledge!* Faith, therefore, is not the beginning of knowledge, except in the sense that every beginning is faith in an end, but this belief itself drifts toward knowledge and proves itself in the actual knowledge.[14] When we say that the Last no longer contains doubt, it is not said therewith that there could not be any subjectively lingering doubts. For it takes *heart to grasp the supra-abound* [*das Ueberschwengliche*]. Here doubt arises out of the magnitude of the matter and the narrowness of the soul. "Believe, what your small soul allows you

---

11. 1 Corinthians 4:15: "For though ye have ten thousand instructors in Christ, yet have ye not many fathers: for in Christ Jesus I have begotten you through the gospel" (KJV). In the Lutheran Bible, the ten thousand instructors are translated as *Zuchtmeister* (disciplinarians). See also *SW* XIV, p. 15: "But as the apostle says, just as the law of the disciplinarians [*Zuchtmeister*] were in Christ, so the strict discipline [*Zucht*] of Science must precede Faith."

12. Colossians 2: 2–3: "So that they may know the mystery of God, namely Christ, in whom are hidden all the treasures of wisdom and knowledge" (BSB).

13. See Tertullian, *De praescriptione haereticorum* 10.7: "Ubi enim erit finis quaerendi? ubi statio credendi? ubi expunctio inveniendi (Where will be the end of seeking? Where the stopping place in believing? Where the expunction in finding?)" and 14.5: "Adversus regulam nihil scire, omnia scire est" (To know nothing in opposition to the rule [of faith] is to know all things) (trans. Rev. Peter Holmes [modified]).

14. *Philosophie der Offenbarung*, *SW* XIV, pp. 15–16: "So far there is thus a faith as *beginning* (which is itself only a faith in *knowledge*) and faith at the end, which, however, is only knowledge come to rest."

to believe."[15] Thus, the Scripture calls out to us: Believe only if the extraordinary presents itself to you.

Here shall be shown how this faith can be brought into connection with our science of other things—divine, natural, and human.

One can easily see that this connection cannot be found in every philosophy. It is impossible to mediate between nature and grace for a philosophy that excludes all actuality [*Wirklichkeit*] from its reflection. During *Fichte's* time, philosophy was at the aphelion [*Sonnenferne*] of revelation; even though he had to re-introduce the non-I [*Nicht-Ich*], the retired Kantian thing-in-itself [*Ding-an-sich*], into the practical part [of his philosophy]. Then a time arrived when one began to realize that philosophy can only develop in *actuality*. First, *nature* was included. Even then, some instinctively foresaw that *history* had to be involved as well, which previously had been regarded only as a work of arbitrariness. Then, however, it also had to turn toward *the earliest beginnings of history—mythology.*

A philosophy that is insensitive to the actual fabricates its own history. Christianity should not really exist. But it does, and it demands an explication, just like any natural formation has a right to. If *paganism* is an intentional deception, then Christianity must be treated the same way. But if paganism contains a real principle, then such a principle must also be contained in Christianity. I do not want to talk about those for whom God exists only through reason having Being. If reason is all Being in everything that has Being, then where does unreason, which is admixed with all Being, come from?[16] Reason, however, can never be anything but reason; it is that which remains the same.

---

15. From Goethe's 1815 collection of rhymed distichs, "Gott, Gemüt, und Welt" (God, Soul, and World), in *Goethes Sämtliche Werke,* 36 vols. (Stuttgart: J.G. Cotta, 1893), 4:21: "Wo ist der Lehrer, dem man glaubt?/Thu, was dir dein kleines Gemüt erlaubt" (Where is the teacher who one believes?/Do what your small soul allows you to do). In *Philosophie der Offenbarung,* SW XIV, p. 16, Schelling attributes this slightly paraphrased quote to Schiller ("if I am not mistaken").

16. *Philosophie der Offenbarung,* SW XIV, p. 23: "If we say that reason is *all* Being (and therefore, *vice versa,* if all Being is reason), it presents a not negligible difficulty to come up with the unreason that is required to explain the actual world."

Others want to at least have a reasonable God—*a God that does nothing beyond reason*; but even we concede that humans can act beyond reason. To be a reasonable person is not saying much. Everyone has reason. *But to love your enemies is beyond reason.* God's will, with respect to the human race alienated from him, is a mystery and goes beyond reason. One may well say that without unreason. Therefore, however, that decision is not incomprehensible; it is in relation to the extraordinary event to which it refers and to the magnitude of God.

Nothing is sadder than the business of rationalists who want to make those things rational that go beyond all reason. Paul speaks of the weakness and foolishness of God, which is stronger than the strength of Man.[17] Only the strong may be weak. Hamann asks: did [those rationalists] not know that *God is a genius who cares little about whether something is considered rational or irrational*?[18] It is indeed not given to each and every one to comprehend *the deep irony of God in the creation of the world*, as well as in each and every one of his acts. *He is the Other who posits* **B** *and the Other who*

---

17. 1 Corinthians 1:25: "For the foolishness of God is wiser than Man's wisdom, and the weakness of God is stronger than Man's strength" (BSB).

18. Schelling seems to be paraphrasing from Hamann's *Biblische Betrachtungen eines Christen* (Biblical Observations of a Christian) and his *Aesthetica in nuce: Eine Rhapsodie in Kabbalistischer Prose* (Aesthetics in a Nutshell: A Rhapsody in Cabbalistic Prose), in *Hamann's Schriften*, ed. Friedrich Roth (Berlin: G. Reimer, 1821). See also Renate Knoll, *Johann Georg Hamann und Friedrich Heinrich Jacobi* (Heidelberg: C. Winter, 1963), p. 108. On Schelling's high regard for Hamann, one of the most ironic, erudite, and unconventional religious writers of his time—highly appreciated by Kant, Jacobi, Schelling, and Kierkegaard alike—see his tribute published on the occasion of the first edition of Hamann's collected writings, in *Zur Geschichte der neueren Philosophie*, SWX, p. 171: "*Hamann* had no system and did not propose one; yet whoever could be conscious of a whole that would unite all of Hamann's sayings, the coherent [*gereimt*] and the seemingly incoherent [*ungereimt*], the most liberal and, on the other hand, the crassly orthodox ones, would be able to say that he had attained *some* measure of insight, inasmuch as Man can presume to understand anything at all."

overcomes it, but he is not another God. God's freedom consists in the absurdity of this cohesiveness.[19]

Even in Man! The apt expert recognizes whether or not a work of art is sprung from the balance of productive force and abundance in order to put an infinite content, which resists all form, into finite form, which is [true] *poetry.* To be both drunken and sober is the secret of inspiration [*Begeisterung*].[20]

God reveals himself as an artist [*künstlerisch*] insofar as he seeks out the finite and brings everything into the most comprehensible, finite form.[21] The boundedness [*das Beschränkte*] of Christianity is his very purpose. One could perceive the fact that God was not simply satisfied with the possible world as divine foolishness. God's weakness reveals itself in his weakness for humanity. *In the Creation, God shows his spirit; in the Salvation, his heart.* The more powerful the spirit, the more impersonal it is. The most personal deed of God is the revelation. There he has become, in the highest sense, the most personal with Man. A great deed is not diminished by saying that it is beyond all human concepts. There are human deeds that not everyone comprehends. Alexander said: I would do it too (accept Dareius's peace proposals) if I were Parmenio.[22] And God's personality transcends his doings even more than human concepts—not that they were unfathomable, but we must have a measure that transcends all usual measures. Here is something,

---

19. *Philosophie der Offenbarung,* SW XIV, p. 25: "The deity (*i.e.,* the absolute freedom) of God consists precisely in the power of this contradiction—this absurdity, if you will, of being both affirming and denying and yet not therewith to come apart but to remain who he is." *Cf.* also Hamann's famous statement: "*The folly of Christianity* is entirely suited to my taste" Johann Georg Hamann, *Briefwechsel,* ed. Walther Ziesemer and Arthur Henkel, 8 vols. (Wiesbaden/Frankfurt: Insel Verlag, 1955–1975), 5:275.

20. *Philosophie der Offenbarung,* SW XIV, p. 25: "To be drunken and sober at the same moment, not at different moments, is the secret of true poetry."

21. *Cf.* also Hamann: "God reveals himself—the Creator of the world is an author" (*Biblische Beobachtungen,* p. 56).

22. *Philosophie der Offenbarung,* SW XIV, p. 27: "Et ego si Parmenio essem." See Plutarch, *Life of Alexander,* 16.

quo majus fieri non potest [that cannot be greater]; here is the *finis quaerendi et inveniendi* [the end of the search and discovery], where human knowledge must avow to not being able to move any further.

The true objective of a philosophy of revelation can only be, first and foremost, to raise [its content] above and beyond all necessary knowledge; then, not to give reason for the decision that is the true subject of the revelation *a priori* but rather make it fathomable in general terms and in regards to its execution after it has been revealed.

The main presupposition for this philosophy is not an ideal relation to God, one mediated by reason and free cognition, but rather a real relation. For there is an earlier relation of God to Man than cognition, one, that traces back to Being itself. Otherwise, revelation could only be instruction. But instruction is only about something that already exists. It cannot change anything about the relation of Man to God. If it purported to introduce a new relation, it would have to occur through an expressly solemn act before any instruction would even be possible. This act is then the purport of revelation in general.

Revelation has a real purpose. However, this purpose presupposes an originarily real relation of Man to God. Were Man not connected to God in a way that is different from a connection through reason and cognition, the real relation, which is in the revelation, would be unthinkable. Such a real relation is already demonstrated before all revelation by the philosophy of mythology. This basis is unshakable.

Thus, a revelation would not be incomprehensible at all. However, even specifically, *i.e.,* in execution, it is comprehensible since the originary relation of Man to God is already mediated; the Father created Man not unmediatedly but through the Son. The Being created by the Son can only be reconstituted [*wiederhergestellt*] by the Son. This Being, created and to be recreated by the Son, is now, however, already given through that which came earlier.

The mythological process shapes the presupposition; Christianity itself is an event that one has, for eons, known and prepared for. The content of revelation is a history that goes back to the beginning of all things and forward toward their end. The philosophy of revelation wants to trace this history back to its principles, which are known to it from elsewhere. It does not want to be speculative dogmatism; it only wants to explain it, with no concern for conforming to dogmatism. *It does not want to be a doctrine and therefore does not intend to be the antithesis of any dogma.* The matter, revelation, is older than any dogma, and we are only dealing with the matter, not with subjective rules.

Anyone familiar with the circumstances that *compelled the Church toward formulas* knows that this did not occur during the happiest time of the Church. They were in accordance with the scientific consciousness of their time, but how could they be binding for all time? Revelation presupposes a real relation of God with the world, with Man, as no philosophy had done before. When the supra-abound is reduced to finite concepts, then the matter becomes distorted and incomprehensible for other times. It doesn't help to pass the matter off as a mystery. For if it actually were that, then we could ill afford to clothe it in fixed formulas; but if it were a revealed mystery, then it must be comprehensible to us.

The science of the earlier time could not put itself in a different relation to revelation than it did to nature and actuality. It handled the external forms and sought the means to make revelation comprehensible apart from it within each respective philosophy. *Scholastics* had torn Christian theology away from the natural soil of history. With the *Reformation,* the historical spirit awakened but could not rid itself of the Scholastic forms. As the historical spirit awakened and unleashed itself, theology was brought to the extreme of a merely external historical method of treatment.

In addition to those two approaches, there was a third, the mystical, which sought out the heart [*das Innere*] of the matter itself but largely did so not by way of scientific cognition but by arbitrary illumination and unclear feelings. Instead of being objectively explanatory, its utterances were unclear, parochial—not universally persuasive. Mystical theology neglected the external historical analysis.

But *Christianity* is first and foremost *a fact*; only after reviewing the criticism, without excluding any hints but gathering all of them together, can one reach the true system, which underlies the Scriptures themselves *as presupposition. Christianity cannot be proven; it comes to us as a fact and phenomenon, which I will explain as much as possible out of its premises.*[23]

---

23. *Philosophie der Offenbarung*, SW XIV, p. 34: "I want to consider Christianity in the same way that I considered mythology, namely, as a phenomenon, which I want to make as intelligible as possible out of its own premises. I want to let it be self-explanatory.

XXIII. The Exegetical Proof for the Extra-Divine Logos-Christ

[PL, pp. 622–29]

Unlike mythology or paganism, *Christianity* is defined by *revelation*. In the O.T., revelation is only a premonition and prophesy of Christ, only comprehensible through Christianity. The actual content of the N.T. is Christ. He is the bond between the O.T. and the N.T.

A philosophy of revelation is solely about explaining the person of Christ. He is not the teacher or founder but the *content* of Christianity. His significance is greater than any common historical one. It is hard for anyone to attribute a pre-human, indeed pre-worldly, existence to a personality that one does not know until it appears in human form. One regards this only in the form of mental pictures—only during the further course the person is being glorified. Indeed, *he who knows nothing about supra-historical history* has no room for this either.

However, we have known for ages about *a potence that mediates the Creation* and at the end of Creation actualizes itself *as divine personality.* It became actualized through Man. In fact, it cannot be *de-actualized* [*entwirklicht*] in itself; it is negated opposite the newly activated potence. It is no longer lord, but is at first merely a naturally acting potence. The principle that was not to be is subjected to a process that it cannot refuse since it is in the power of Man. Then comes the moment when it makes itself again lord of that Being in human consciousness. *Now it is divine personality as lord over Being, which it possesses independently of the Father; now it is the "extra-divine" divine personality.* It can possess Being independently of the Father, as its own world. Therein lies its freedom. The obedience of Christ is to be understood in this way. *The Son could exist independently of the Father in his own glory.* He could not be the true God, however, outside the Father; he could be God *in actuality* but not essentially—a glory he disdained. He emptied himself of this, and thereby he is *Christ. This is the overall idea of revelation.*

The relevant passage is in the Epistle to the Philippians: ὅς ἐν μορφῇ θεοῦ—ἴσα θεῷ, "to be on an equal footing with God."[1] According to the traditional explanation, this passage is about the Being of Christ—from being the true God to his Becoming Human. However, what one possesses one does not need to seize (ἁρπαγμὸν [grasp]). Where Paul touches on the most profound things, he usually expresses himself sharply (Tiber. Hemsterhuis).[2] Why else, when talking about the essential unity until the time of the Becoming Human, would he have used the expression μορφὴ θεοῦ [form, outward appearance of God],[3] which normally means the opposite. According to what follows, Christ could just as well had to have been *in essence* a servant (μορφὴ δούλου [in the form of a slave or servant].[4] Just as this *servant form* covers up his true being [*Wesen*], so that μορφὴ θεοῦ covers up his true godhood. *In that unclear state, where he is, independent of the Father, lord of a Being alienated from God,* nothing could be said about him other than: while he was not God according to his essence, he was so *in specie, actu*; he had God's externality, the sovereignty over Being. However, he was not one with the Father.

The word ὑπάρχων [to be], which Paul[5] and Luke[6] understand to mean actual, arbitrary Being, never essential, goes with that (*e.g.*, arbitrary attributes like χωλὸς ὑπάρχων [to be lame],[7] Ἕλλην ὑπάρχων [to be Hellene, Greek]. Of himself, Paul says ζηλωτὴς ὑπάρχων [to be zealous].[8] This

---

1. Philippians 2:5-12. On Schelling's nontraditional translation of this passage, see Julius Kögel's discussion in *Beiträge zur Förderung Christlicher Theologie.* Zweites Heft: *Christus der Herr* (Gütersloh: C. Bertelsmann, 1908), p. 72.

2. Tiberius Hemsterhuis, *Orationes, quarum prima est de Paulo Apostolo* (Leiden, 1784).

3. Philippians 2:6: "existing in the form of God" (BSB) or "being in the nature of God" (NIV).

4. Philippians 2:7: "taking the form of a servant" (BSB).

5. Philippians 2:6.

6. *Philosophie der Offenbarung,* SWXIV, pp. 41-42: "Christ in Luke 9:48 says: 'he who is the least among you shall be the greatest' (ο μικροτερος εν πασς νμιν ὑπαρχων, dwells not in temples made by hands."

7. Acts 3:2: "And a man who was lame [...]" (BSB).

8. Acts 22:3: "I am just as zealous for God as any of you here

always expresses a transitional state: ὁ γὰρ μικρότερος ἐν πᾶσιν ὑμῖν ὑπάρχων οὗτός ἐστιν μέγας, *etc.*[9] However, Paul says of God in his sermon to the Athenians: a lord of heaven and earth,[10] ὑπάρχων, but *the relation of God to the world is not essential but rather actual, accidental.*

Christ could have seized this *accidental* state as a lasting, essential one, but he did not desire to: οὐχ ἁρπαγμὸν ἡγήσατο_[not consider to grasp a windfall].[11] One could understand this in a general sense—when one says that a person is witty and full of spirit [*geistreich*], but does not seize the latter! However, it is always in need of what is only accidentally offered. In Heliodorus, it is written that a wise man did not consider his reputation as a ἁρπαγμὸν [windfall] or as a ἑρμαῖον [piece of luck].[12] Thus, it also says: he considered the μορπὴ θεοῦ, wherein he found himself arbitrarily, not as something to take advantage of.[13]

εἶναι ἴσα θεῷ [to be equal with or like God] can just as little be understood of the essential godhood. The Apostle felt that even when the Son had the glorification independent of the Father, he was still not ἴσος τῷ θεῷ but only as

today" (BSB).

9. Luke 9:48: "For whoever is the least among all of you, he is the greatest" (BSB).

10. Acts 17:24: "The God who made the world and everything in it is the lord of heaven and earth and does not live in temples made by human hands" (BSB).

11. According to Hoover, both *harpagma* and *hermaion* were often used synonymously by the Greek Fathers. Roy W. Hoover, "The Harpagma Enigma: A Philological Solution," *Harvard Theological Review* 64 (1971): 107.

12. In his *Ethiopia,* Herodotus speaks of a handsome young man in his prime who rejects the advances of a similarly endowed woman because he does not regard his "endowments" as a "windfall" or as a "piece of luck." Quoted by Johann Jakob Wettstein in his *Novum Testamentum Graecum* (Amsterdam 1751–52) as a footnote to Philippians 2:6.

13. Philippians 2:6: "Who, while living in the sphere of God, did not consider to be like God something of which to take advantage" (trans. John Reumann). See also the exhaustive commentaries on the much debated use of *harpagma* in Philippians 2 in the new translation by John Reumann, *Philippians* (New Haven and London: The Anchor Yale Bible/Yale University Press, 2008), pp. 333ff.

ἴσως, *i.e.*, possessing an external equality with God. Even though this passage cannot mean an essential equality with God, there are those who have related it to the [godhood] having become human. However, the same one cannot be in both divine and servile form. [Some have wanted to translate the ἐν μορφῇ θεοῦ ὑπάρχων (existing in the form of God) as: *cum in forma Dei esse* ***posset***, since even as Man he could have shown his divine glory (*divinitate prae se ferre potuisset*), but did not want to and instead took on the form of a servant].[14] However, even though verbs that designate an act can at times imply potentiality, this is surely not the case here. ὑπάρχων is used for an arbitrary Being. How would it even make sense? That *potuisset* [could have] is entirely deceiving. If he wanted to contradict himself, he could have done so but not as a reasonable being. Evidently, one understood in this passage the middle state—the one separated from us—of Christ.[15]

Hebrews 12:2 can be understood similarly: ὃς ἀντὶ τῆς προκειμένης αὐτῷ χαρᾶς ὑπέμεινεν σταυρόν.[16]

Now many other passages can be explained as well: δόξασόν με—τῇ δόξῃ ᾗ εἶχον πρὸ τοῦ τὸν κόσμον εἶναι παρὰ σοί.[17] "Since the world (κόσμος, our present world) is, Christ has no longer had the glory [*Herrlichkeit*]" (which he had παρὰ σοί = before the world was). When Christ says

---

14. *Philosophie der Offenbarung*, SW XIV, p. 44. Paulus has: *cum in dei forma potuisset*. See Novatian, *De trinitate*, 22: "Who, although he was in the form of God, did not think it robbery that he should be equal with God; but emptied himself, taking up the form of a servant, being made in the likeness of Man [...]?"

15. *Philosophie der Offenbarung*, SW XIV, p. 45: "The highest self-emptying (*Entäußerung*) of Christ consisted in the fact that he decided to become human."

16. "Let us fix our eyes on Jesus, the author and perfecter of faith, who for the joy set before him endured the cross, scorning shame, and sat down at the right hand of the throne of God" (BSB). *Cf. Philosophie der Offenbarung*, SW XIV, p. 45: "Instead of the joy that lay before him (which he could chosen if he wished), he endured the cross."

17. John 17:5: "And now, Father, glorify me in your presence with the glory I had with you before the world existed" (BSB).

that he is in control of his own life, he stands freely opposite the Father.[18] One has to think of him outside of God. This Being-outside-of God he has from Man. Thus, he is called the Son of Man: πρὶν Ἀβραὰμ γενέσθαι ἐγὼ εἰμί.[19] Being must have the same meaning in both sentences. With Abraham, it is less about eternal Being and more about Being within the κόσμος, just as it is with Christ. We must therefore also *speak here of his middle state*: αὕτη δέ ἐστιν ἡ αἰώνιος ζωὴ ἵνα γινώσκωσιν σὲ τὸν μόνον ἀληθινὸν Θεὸν καὶ ὃν ἀπέστειλας Ἰησοῦν Χριστόν (Jesus, as Christ).[20] Opposite him, who is designated to be the Lord of the extra-divine Being [*aussergöttlichen Seyns*], is the invisible Father, ὁ μόνος ἀληθινός [the only true one].

All these passages refer to a Being of the second personality that has been posited by the Fall. This explains why the Father is greater than I![21] Furthermore, the passage in Mark (who I consider the most originary and first author of the Gospels): ὁ οὐρανὸς καὶ ἡ γῆ παρελεύσονται οἱ δὲ λόγοι μου οὐ μὴ παρελεύσονται· περὶ δὲ τῆς ἡμέρας ἐκείνης ἢ τῆς ὥρας οὐδεὶς οἶδεν οὐδὲ οἱ ἄγγελοι οἱ ἐν οὐρανῷ οὐδὲ ὁ υἱος εἰ μὴ ὁ πατήρ.[22] *After all, the Son who is equal to God should know this.* It cannot be in reference to the human Christ. This is already made impossible by the increasing ascension from the angels to the Son. Evidently, it relates *to the Son in his extra-divine state*; the conclusion can only be leading the extra-divine back to the Father.

In order to comprehend the N.T., one must attribute an extra-divine existence to God. Only in this way does the account

---

18. John 10:18: "I have [the] authority to lay it down and the [authority] to take it up again. This charge I have received from my Father" (BSB).

19. John 8:58: "'Truly, truly, I tell you,' Jesus declared, 'before Abraham was born, I am!'" (BSB).

20. John 17:3: "Now this is eternal life, that they may know you, the only true God, and Jesus Christ, whom you have sent" (BSB).

21. John 10:29: "My Father who has given them to me is greater than all"; John 14:28: "The Father is greater than I" (BSB).

22. Mark 13:31-32: "Heaven and earth will pass away, but my words will never pass away./But as for that day or hour, no one knows, not even the angels in heaven, nor the Son, but only the Father" (BSB).

of the Temptation [of Christ][23] become illuminated. Even if this *factum* were invented, it would at least be consistent with the Christian view. The adversary is the *representative of that dark power, the God-negating principle that has again been activated by Man* and concludes his temptation by showing Christ all the kingdoms of the world and their glory. He wants Christ to seize power from the hand of the power that is alienated from God. This presupposes *the possibility that Christ could take Being for himself, independent of the Father.* Had Christ done this, the unity of the world with God would have been torn apart. For the mediating personality was, after all, the only bond. *With the Fall, Man made himself three lords out of the* one *lord*: the first one being the blind power, which brought it as far as offering Christ, the second lord, the power over All if he was willing to tear himself away from God. In his response, Christ described the task of leading the fallen Being from the many lords back to the *one* lord: *Κύριον τὸν θεόν σου προσκυνήσεις καὶ αὐτῷ μόνῳ λατρεύσεις.*[24] So much about existing independent of God, which he forfeits by becoming Man. Only the extra-divine existence enables him to be the mediator.

---

23. Matthew 4:1-11.

24. Matthew 4:10: "For it is written [in Deuteronomy 10:13]: 'Worship the Lord your God and serve him only'" (BSB).

XXIV. The Mediation of the Extra-Divine Potence

[PL, pp. 640–48]

By virtue of his indissoluble life, having let the process of Creation become actuality, *God was entirely in command of the contrary Being* (**B**). That which ought not to be, the anti-divine, was elevated again by Man. God is not in it by his will but rather by his unwill [*Unwillen*] (as the theologians teach, God is also the material cause of sin or the force by which the sinner operates: "With the froward I shall show myself froward."[1] *God is froward in the froward potences themselves. Without mediation, human consciousness would have become devoured* [*verzehrt*].

However, could this mediation not lie in the initial potence (**B**)*? No!* For according to its substance, this principle, which is not meant to be, is *the divine unwill* [*göttliche Unwille*] and thereby once again that which ought to have Being [*das Seyn-sollende*] (like the death penalty, which as the unwill of the law is that which ought to have Being) and is thereby a divine right. God has the right to sublate it forcefully since by *overcoming* it, his glory becomes that much greater. What God has made for himself into a law to overcome, he wants to overcome in such a way that it cognizes itself as having been overcome.

However, in order to carry out the mediation, *the mediating potence* has to *renounce God externally.* Then, however, that contrary principle or un-principle [*Unprincip*] has a right to be as long as *the mediating potence asserts itself in the extra-divinity and alienation from the divine unity, in the tension that is against the divine will.* Thus, the originary principle [*Urprincip*] is only overcome in the mythological process externally, not by law, since the mediating potence is itself extra-divine and only works naturally.

---

1. Psalm 18:26: "with the froward thou wilt shew thyself froward" (KJV).

Within this process, even the highest religious consciousness is, with respect to its content, idle because it tarries in place in the separation from God. In the mythological process, consciousness is stuck in a necessary process.

As different as Judaism and paganism are, they are both under the law. Everything until Christ is contained in the law. The Jews also had no childlike relation, no access to the spirit of the Father. In paganism, the mediating potence overcomes the *contrarium* [opposite] only insofar as it becomes negated by the latter, and it does so only by virtue of its natural will according to each *natura*. *Now it must, however, sublate itself within its extra-divine Being, its μορφὴ θεοῦ.* Only by giving itself up can it also sublate the power of the originary principle. *Therewith the innermost thought of Christianity is articulated. In that sacrifice [Aufopferung], it ascends from potence to personality, thereby becoming* Χριστός [Christ]. To give oneself up [*Sich-selbst-aufgeben*] can only be willed freely because the mediating personality has become free through the Fall. On the other side, it can actually make this freely-willed decision because it is not altered [*alterirt*] by the tension, because it is posited into the tension merely passively against its will and [thus] without guilt into the tension, whereby the unity of God is sublated.

Because it reached this state passively, its will remains untouched by that catastrophe that first gave it its own will. Since the *μορφὴ θεοῦ* is something done to it externally, it remains the consciousness of its originary, untainted [*unbefleckten*] relation to the Father; it cannot have a will other than the one to restore this relation. Thus it is, according to its will, one with the Father, and all of its doing is aimed at that. The will to not only sublate the contrary Being but, after its external glorification, also sublate itself is no longer merely a natural will; rather, it stems from its originary divine nature. It is the will of the true Son in the lap of the Father who has come down from Heaven. He owes his life to God; the originary divine Being [*urgöttliche Seyn*] is but the form to this substance. This will remains one with the Father even during the separation from the Father.

In the foresight that the Son will not only sublate the contrary Being but also himself, the Father cedes Being to the Son since the overthrow. God has made him his heir, as it were. According to 1 Corinthians 15:24, "εἶτα τὸ τέλος, ὅταν παραδιδῷ τὴν βασιλείαν τῷ θεῷ καὶ πατρί, *etc.*,[2] it seems that the Son is not going to keep the dominion. We cite this passage here as proof that for the duration of the world the entire dominion was given over to the Son in order to return and reconcile the extra-divine Being.

Returned by the Son, Being will once again be within the Father at the end of the world. However, since Being will never be within God except through the Son, it is not associated with a surrender of his dominion; rather, the Father possesses it as something handed over [to the Son] continually. *Thus, they are taking it over as a joint possession; it simply indicates the end of the exclusive dominion of the Son over the world.*[3] Once the Son has overcome all that is anti-divine [*Widergöttliche*], his dominion is no longer exclusive. First, all must be subordinated to him, *i.e.*, he must have become God and lord of all things.

However, the subordination of the Son to the Father is different from that during and at the end of the Creation; he returns to the Father as an autonomous personality. *The same is true of the Spirit.*

Thus, we now see *the completion of the trinity—into three persons who are independent from each other.* First, there is ἕν τὸ πᾶν [One is All], then, in the end, there is the reverse, πᾶν τὸ ἕν [All is One]. Each is One, God; as its own, standalone personality, each potence is God. Then God is All in all things [*Alles in Allem*]. Even the Son is not extinguished by virtue of his specialness. Rather, *this Christian pantheism is the most complete form of monotheism.*

Thus, that highest idea of the Trinity is not just logical but also historical; the mediation from beginning to end belongs to it. It may not be expressed in rigid form but progresses from Tautousia (wherein only the Father is the demiurgical cause) through the Heterousia (during the tension up to the

---

2. "Then the end will come, when he hands over the kingdom to God the Father" (BSB).

3. *Philosophie der Offenbarung*, SW XIV, p. 61: "Here thus is indicated a *terminus ultimus* of his dominion."

final reconciliation) to Homousia. The heresies are therein sublated as necessary moments, Sabellianism, Arianism (the Son as extra-divine personality—just not as one who was created! That last one was entirely wrong!).

Only for the sake of the will of the second personality—to follow Being into the alienation in order to sublate itself in the extra-divine in the end—did Father take on the mediation and *give him power* over the anti-divine Being. Only in that way did he want the originary principle [*Urprincip*], the organ of his wrath, to be overcome. It was this consideration that made paganism possible. The true Son was already in the natural potence and therefore also in paganism. As such, it was Χορις Χριστοῦ; yet it was the same natural potence, which according to its naturalness ought to die in Christo, whereby the Pagans would be enlightened.

The Father retreated into the consciousness of a limited [*beschränktes*] people and appeared here also only in his unwill and wrath. Christ was the light, the potence of Paganism, just as the Father was for Judaism. There, Christ prepared the soil since Judaism was too limited. Paganism and Judaism had separate ecumenisms that were to flow together in Christianity. According to Psalm 94, all pagan knowledge is derived from God.[4] The pagans even called the mythological gods σωτῆρες [saviors]. But since that natural potence, the actual effect [*Wirkende*] of mythology, gained power over humanity in order to let the divine break through in the end; thus in paganism, Christ was continually coming, even though he did not actually come until time was fulfilled.

Christ was tempted in all things.[5] He lived among pagans. He was already then the *suffering Messiah*; he was tempted by all aspects of the human consciousness, without becoming tainted by them. He has brought his work to conclusion only through his personal apparition. *He is the anointed, Christ, by virtue of his dominion over the extra-*

4. Psalm 94:10: "He that chastiseth the heathen, shall not he correct? He that teacheth man knowledge, shall not he know" (KJV).

5. Hebrew 4:15: "One who has been tempted in all things as we are, yet without sin" (NAS).

divine Being. Christianity is eternal and the true religion only because it already existed in paganism.

The mediating potence has to make itself the lord of the opposing potence, become the μορφὴ θεοῦ, [and] sublate the opposing principle in its *actus*. Once this happens, *the time* has come for *the great sacrifice, wherein the mediating potence sublates itself together with Being as extra-divine in one and the same deed and thus foments [stiftet] the true reconciliation*. Only then, when it has become lord of the antagonistic Being [*widerstreitenden Seyns*], can the decision [*Wille*] become revealed, which it has made [*gefasst*] from the beginning. ὁ Χριστὸς ἐφανερώθη [Christ was revealed][6] Christ is Christ only by virtue of that decision and as revealed in the deed of the eternal, *i.e.*, lasting, reconciliation.

There was also reconciliation in Judaism and paganism, just as *sacrifice* played an essential part. Both, however, go only as far as an external reconciliation of the opposing principle, which was the cause of the tension. The originary principle [*Urprincip*] is not overcome and reconciled in its right over Man, only in its execution of that right. That sacrifice, therefore, had to be repeated because it only sublated the opposing principle externally. In the great sacrifice, all tension is resolved and its ground sublated. He who, in divine form, was like God, in place of God, empties himself of his godhood [and] subordinates his extra-divine Being to God as a creatural (*creatürliches*) (Becoming Human). The divine sublates its extra-divinity (death); the natural potence dies. By taking on a Being of its own opposite the Father, following the extra-divine Being, it could not remain with the anti-divine Being without incurring the wrath of God, making itself an accomplice and, being both innocent and guilty, drawing the penalty of this Being to itself.

Therewith I have held to the precise meaning of those doctrines, which in common theories have been understood

---

6. See 1 Timothy 3:16: "By common confession, the mystery of godliness is great: He appeared in the flesh, was vindicated by the Spirit, was seen by angels, was proclaimed among the nations, was believed in throughout the world, was taken up in glory" (BSB).

only improperly. The philosophy of revelation widens the meaning of the Scripture. *We can understand Christianity much more properly and rationally than the semi-orthodoxes [halb-Orthodoxen].*

It is said in the N.T.: Christ took on our debt [*Schuld*]; for us, he has made himself the guarantor [*Bürgen*] of a new unity with god,[7] for the mediating function of Christ has been operative since the Fall. Who provides a guarantee for another is responsible for the wrong done by the other. He is not the culpable one, yet he is culpable. The second potence cannot administer to the needs of the anti-divine Being without partaking of its debt. The human race could be preserved by it but not protected from the sin; having made itself a guarantor for its preservation, he has taken on all the sins as well. Thus, he became the eternal conciliator—admittedly, in paganism only as a cosmic potence. In his death, this cosmic potence dies as well. The divine of the conciliator breaks through the natural and reconciliates it in his death.

The tension is therewith *sublated.* Tension is discord; only through this great sacrifice is the entire tension in the human consciousness sublated, and therewith the entire divine unity is restored as well.

The tension also extended to the third personality. Just as the spirit is not negated directly, *i.e.,* posited out of the divine Being, neither can it restore itself directly, affect directly; thus, the third potence also here appears only as a driving [*antreibende*] cause. The prophets, says the Apostle, have spoken, driven by the divine spirit (as that which ought to have Being [*Seyn-Sollende*], the spirit is the potence of the future). [The third personality] is the interweaving [*durchwirkende*] final cause that penetrates to the end. Even in nature, it is the cause of everything that appears purposive; in it alone lies the purpose and goal.

7. Hebrews 7:22: "Jesus has become the guarantee of a better covenant" (BSB).

[The spirit] has also become a *cosmic potence.* The N.T. very clearly distinguishes between the spirit of the world (all that is naturally ingenious and senseful [*Kunstreiche und Sinnige*]) and the spirit from God. We have not received the spirit of the world but rather the spirit from God[8] and do not speak with the natural arts of persuasion. That which the world spirit does not reveal, the latter reveals, *etc.* It is called the *Holy Spirit* in contrast to the cosmic one. Therefore, he is also introduced as supreme teacher,[9] guiding [us] into the whole truth.[10] The spirit cannot come until the entire work of Christ has happened. *Until the originary potence, the second potence is subjugated and has to maintain the tension opposite the third.* Therefore, Christ had to be anointed first by the Holy Spirit, at the baptism. Where that which was previously the extra-divine was declared the true Son of the Father by a voice from Heaven, the spirit descends visibly onto the Son. Only from this moment on does the godhood establish itself in Christ; but now he is εἰκὼν τοῦ θεοῦ τοῦ ἀοράτου[11] since he represents *the entire godhood in physical form* (σωματικῶς,[12] *in the third dimension as well*).

In relation to the human race in general, the spirit can only come after the Father has been reconciled [with the Son].[13] The Father only dwells in Man at the same time as the Son. God stays in us; this we cognize from the spirit he has given us. The spirit is mediated by the Father and the Son. In general, the spirit comes only after the glorification of Christ, having rid itself of the extra-divine Being, after he has been taken from judgment[14] (from the *tension*).

---

8. 1 Corinthians 2:12: "We have not received the spirit of the world but the Spirit who is from God" (BSB).

9. John 3:2: "He came to Jesus at night and said, 'Rabbi, we know that You are a teacher who has come from God'" (BSB).

10. John 16:3: "He will guide you into all truth" (BSB).

11. Colossians 1:15: "The Son is the image of the invisible God" (BSB).

12. Colossians 2:9: "For in Christ all the fullness of the Deity dwells in bodily form" (BSB).

13. The German *versöhnen* (*to reconcile*) and *Versöhnung* (reconciliation) carry with them the untranslatable association to *Sohn* (son).

14. Isaiah 53:8: "He was taken from prison and from judgment" (KJV).

It is for your benefit, says Christ, that I am going away; otherwise, the παράκλητος [helper, advocate] will not come to you.[15]

Until Christ was posited out of the tension, the spirit could not come. Only in death was the unity with the Father restored and the spirit able to come, *in locum Christi quasi succedens* [in the place of Christ as his successor]. *For when one potence has completed its work, another follows. Thus, it was important to conceive of the potences as successive.* In paganism, only the external unity was established, not the relationship to the true God. However, since this tension is sublated externally, the spirit cannot come; it remains *mysterium.* Paganism concludes with something that it posits into the future and does not have in itself. It ends with a prophecy of Christianity; *the third potence becomes present only through Christ.*

All the earlier moments and relations have become enhanced and more fathomable by this mediation and reconciliation. *Because Christ is Christ only through the Father who is in him,* the divine is revealed in the Son; *but he who is declared the Son is not the same as he who has Being in the Father before the Creation. Now a much higher, more apprehensible unity is posited.* The same one who places his will into B, as the irreconcilable one, places his will into the Son and reconciliates the Being in the Son with itself; in this mediation is established the highest unity of God with himself.

Herewith I believe to have *articulated the fundamental idea of revelation.*

What has been presented in general terms is now to be examined in detail: (1) Christ's work before his Becoming Human; (2) his Becoming Human; (3) the subsequent mediation.

---

15. John 16:7.

XXV. Christ's Pre-Existence

[PL, pp. 648–59]

The beginning of John's Gospel has accurately described *the periods of Christ's pre-existence.* First, in regard to the interpretation of the word ὁ λόγος [word, reason], Philo[1] speaks of a θεοῦ λόγος [the Word of God], which he understood to be *an exemplary draft of the world in God, a principle,* δἰ οὗ [by whom or through which are] all things.[2] In this respect, it seems to be identical with the demiurgical potence. But how did Philo arrive at this expression? The answer does not seem difficult. All things, says the O.T., are made through the word of God. This was soon thought of as self-dependent. Philo remarked that λόγος also signified reason and thus could be identified with the Platonic νοῦς [mind, intellect]. To him, the λόγος was the divine reason, with whose intermediation he could keep God as far away from the world as possible. But Philo never speaks of this λόγος as an absolute; rather, he calls it ὁ θεῖος λόγος or θεοῦ λόγος; besides, the expression is not ever used in Alexandrian philosophy.

What is doubtful with Philo, *the personality* of the λόγος, is decided with John, its signification of *demiurgical personality.* However, how could John have presumed Philo's expression to be known? According to another explanation, λόγος = reason = σοφια [wisdom]! Of this, it has already been said in the O.T.: the Lord possessed me before all his works, *etc.*[3] But both explanations presuppose a genitive that is simply not there. John makes use of this word

---

1. *Philosophie der Offenbarung,* SW XIV, p. 90: "I am mentioning Philo because he is currently much in fashion."

2. On Philo's use of "the Word of God" as an instrument through which the world is produced, see Carl Séan O'Brien, *The Demiurge in Ancient Thought: Secondary Gods and Divine Mediators* (Cambridge: Cambridge University Press, 2015), p. 46. *Cf.* also Hebrews 2:10.

3. Proverbs 8:22: "The Lord possessed me in the beginning of his way, before his works of old" (KJV).

only in verses 1 and 14. He intentionally chose the most abstract expression in order to demonstrate it in its various forms. The most abstract explanation would probably be: *the matter of which is spoken here,* like דָּבָר [thing, word]. *The subject of which we are speaking was in the beginning.* (In ancient times, the Jews called Jehovah הַשֵּׁם [name]. Thus ὁ λόγος would be *the word above all,* i.e., *the thing or person that is above all.* Whenever the N.T. intends to be indeterminate, it expresses itself abstractly, impersonally; *e.g.,* the angel says during the annunciation: "The Holy One to be born of you will be called the Son of God."[4] Here also, all is initially in the future, wherefore the first indeterminate subject has yet to become determinate.

The entire prologue adheres to abstract designations. He does not say the "Enlightening One" but rather "the Light." The Epistle of John begins just as abstractly: ὃ ἦν ἀπ' ἀρχῆς.[5] In the same prologue, it says: we are writing περὶ τοῦ Λόγου τῆς ζωῆς.[6] What follows shows that this was simply a more abstract paraphrase of ζωή [life]. The targumim frequently replace Jehovah with "the word of Jehovah." This is merely a paraphrase, as is illuminated by the passage where the King of Judah sends this message to Ben-hadad: "Let there be a covenant between you and me."[7] Here, the targumim translate: "between *my word and yours.*"

In *one* passage in the Apocalypse,[8] where it talks about the secretive name of Christ, it says ὁ λόγος τοῦ θεοῦ. Here, as well, λόγος only means subject, the subject of God. For the Son is the *subjectum primum divinitatis* [the first divine subject]. *God exists first only in the form of that which purely has Being* [*rein Seyenden*], *the* actus purus, *which precedes essence. Later, the same becomes potence but only the second potence.* In the Epistle to the Hebrews, he is called χαρακτὴρ τῆς

---

4. Luke 1:35 (BSB).

5. 1 John 1:1: "That which was from the beginning" (BSB).

6. *Ibid.*: "the Word of life" (BSB).

7. 2 Chronicles 16:3 (ESV).

8. Revelation 19:13: "He is dressed in a robe dipped in blood, and his name is The Word of God" (BSB).

ὑποστάσεως,[9] the marked nature of his ὑποστασις [substance], *i.e.*, the *actus purus*, which, however, is the *prius*, the *primum de Deo intelligibile* [the first understanding of God]. The *actus purus*, set apart, raised to a potence, and objectified, is the *expressa imago* [expressed image].

Before we move on to explain this important passage, one general remark shall be made. *Nowadays, pietist righteousness [Rechtsgläubigkeit] is made dependent on grammatical explication, which constitutes a very weak support.* We are prompted to first seek the realm of God, *i.e.*, the complex of divine activities. Then the divine authority of the Scripture is pointed out, by which only selected passages are meant. It becomes a veritable *hunting-down of passages* [*Stellenjägerei*], which has nothing to do with true reason. (In order to convince oneself of the most important truths, one has to go for the whole.) There is nothing left but the doctrinal concept as it was set down in the sixteenth century. Thus, neither the language nor the explication nor the scholarship has made any progress since the sixteenth century. No more of the Christian spirit can be assembled from this patchwork than can be explained from a philosophy that dismisses all that is historical. One may regard *Fichte's explanation of this* [John's] *prologue* as a monument to such an explication;[10] even the later philosophy cannot say much more.

Now to the *history of the second personality*! ἐν αγχῇ [from the beginning], *i.e.*, *without a potence* or anything else proceeding it. Nothing came before it, not even God. For God himself was in his pure Being, where he is not God. It is called quite simply ἦν [was], in the pure Being; *he was the* actus purus *of the divine Being.* [John's] speech, however, advances *from the unforethinkable Being toward where pure Being is posited* ex actu puro, *potentiated, and has become that which has Being* πρὸς τὸν θεὸν [with God]. That a different moment begins here is shown by the repetition of the ὁ λόγος. It is the same and yet, to some extent, *already a different* λόγος,

9. Hebrews 1:3: "the exact representation of his nature" (BSB).

10. Johann Gottlieb Fichte, *Die Anweisung zum seeligen Leben, oder auch die Religionslehre* (Instruction for the Blessed Life, or also the Doctrine of Religion) (Berlin, 1806).

already distinguished from God, even though it does not have Being outside of him. "πρὸς τὸν θεὸν." For the pure Being stands in the power of God, just as it is *posited* by the initial potence *ex actu*. The subject is with God, *i.e.*, first in God's imagination, prior to the Creation, and in the Creation (really) distinguished from God as demiurgical potence. The Being of the *logos* in the divine imagination and in the Creation are summarized in: "The *logos* was with God."

The Apostle continues, "and the same subject was God," *i.e.*, at the end of Creation in possession of a godhood, which it does not have for itself but only in the Father; thus it says only, θεός [God].

The moments are therefore as follows: first, the pure A, *eternally having Being;* then posited as A, *before eternity*; finally, as affecting demiurgical potence (since the Creation). [The godhood] is *begotten* at the beginning of Creation, *i.e., compelled to actualize itself.*

How is this view compatible with the *eternal* begetting [*Zeugung*] of the Son? If this is understood as the *absolute starting point,* then it is the thought of a pure *actus,* one that corresponds to each potence—a thought wherein nothing that is happening [*Geschehendes*] can be incorporated. It is the simple thought of absolute position. Therefore, it is also passed over by it. He is only moment, the thought of an instant. The thought of eternity is wholly indivisible and has only the content that is God. In this simple thought, there is no room for begetting [*Zeugung*], or in this narrowness, it could only have a logical significance. What follows out of an essence eternally is only what follows out of it logically. 2r in a triangle;[11] here, there is no process [*Vorgang*].

The idea of an eternal begetting (in the more precise sense: *gignere est naturae, creare voluntatis!*) *was one created in the huddle against Arianism,*[12] *which now has pretty much been abandoned and no longer has any importance.* They could only be logical emanations. There is also no basis for it in the N.T. John does not say: in the beginning the λόγος was *begotten,*

---

11. See Euler's theorem for a triangle: $OI^2 = R(R - 2r)$.
12. The dispute between Homoiousianism and Arianism.

but: *it was.* The theologians did not distinguish between that which absolutely is eternal and that which is *from* eternity. Earlier, the entire genealogy of time was undefined and could only be defined through a positive philosophy. *Time has always been the bad conscious of empty metaphysics.*

Pure, absolute eternity is *but an instant thought*; but *from eternity, i.e.,* from when *God is* (*act. pur.*), God represents that *begetting* potence, his means of foreseeing all his future creations. This moment has, without itself already constituting time, a relation to the future time and world. We will call this moment, of proceeding from the absolute eternity onward, *pre-temporal* [*vorzeitige*] *eternity* (the absolute eternity is *supra-temporal*). The absolute eternity is that which precedes according to thought, not according to time. In relation to the succeeding time, the pre-temporal eternity, however, becomes a past, pre-temporal.[13] Even though it is not yet temporal, it is posited through the Creation as past and therefore as time. For *a new time* begins with the Creation, which is only presence.

In general, time begins with the Creation, when past, present, and future are posited. Every time is presumed to have a past. The only way to think of a beginning of time is to posit as *time, i.e.,* as past, that which had not been time. One can only think of it in this way, as a dynamic beginning of time, not as a mechanistic one. Only with the Creation begins the distinction into eons, the pre-temporal eternity (posited through the Creation as the past), the time of the Creation (the present), and the time in which all is to be posited through the Creation (the future eternity). The Creation has not yet arrived at the third; it has become arrested in the second. This [arrested] time—always positing itself, A + A + A into infinity—is not the true time. The

---

13. *Philosophie der Offenbarung,* SWXIV, pp. 108-9: "This pre-temporal eternity, which for itself is not yet *time,* becomes through the Creation a past and therefore is posited *as time.* For with the Creation, a new time (a new eon) begins, whose new time is now the *present,* and thus we can say that time has first been posited with the Creation."

present time has to penetrate into its future; only then does it become true time. *The apparitional time* is the time of this world, which is usually the only one discussed in philosophy. This time does not go beyond this world.

Of the great systems of time that were part of the divine intention, this time is only an image; thus everything repeats within a circle.[14] This time has neither a true past nor a true future. True time is a succession of times that do not continually repeat themselves. With the Creation, a *true* succession of times was posited; the act by which the Creation is posited also posits time. Thus, the act itself is necessarily above all time, πρὸ πάντων αἰώνων [before all eons]; it is the act of Creation that posits the great eons. *Creation begins with the positing of the Son; through him, therefore, the eons are posited, and he is posited or begotten before all eons.*

The ἐν ἀρχῇ [in the beginning] is to be repeated before each of the three moments but with a different meaning each time: (1) *absolute* eternity; (2) *before* eternity; and (3) *before* the present order of things, which is posited by the overthrow. The N.T. thus first asserts *the eternal Being of the subject—the Son.* Thereupon, the Son is also recognized by the Father in eternity προεγνωσμένος πρὸ καταβολῆς κοσμον.[15]

The Paulinian passages are *not as much* a discussion of the eternal begetting as they are of the eternal intent, since God took the Son into his plan. Thus, Paul speaks of the secret that God kept since the beginning of the world. And Christ speaks of the glory that he had with the Father before the world. The son is loved and recognized from eternity.

God is only in the freedom to potentiate and to create *the originary Being by virtue of having a Son, because in him he overcomes*

---

14. *Philosophie der Offenbarung,* SWXIV, p. 109: "Thus the old lament that there is nothing new under the sun, *i.e.,* that in the Creation, one day is like the next, today as tomorrow, tomorrow as today, everything goes around in a dismal circle of monotonous recurring phenomena." See Ecclesiastes 1:9: "What has been will be again, and what has been done will be done again; there is nothing new under the sun."

15. 1 Peter 1:20: "He was known before the foundation of the world" (BSB).

the contrary Being. This God is a God who is free and can do what he wants. He is only God in the Son who is recognized and loved in advance. The Son thus belongs to the essence of God. But the Son is *begotten* before the Creation, at its very beginning, *i.e., posited as a self-dependent potence.* The beginning of Creation is established with the second potence being singled out. Therefore, it says, *πρωτότοκος πάσης κτίσεως.*[16] Therefore, *ἀρχὴ τῆς κτίσεως τοῦ θεοῦ*[17] (both passages speak *against an eternal begetting*). However, as that which posits time, the begetting remains above time. The Father posits tension eternally so that the latter has to be overcome eternally; thus, there is eternal life.

The explanation given in John 1:1 becomes clear from the progression in the three parts of the passage. In the Creation, he was merely *with God,* not God; thus, in Verse 2, he returns to the earlier in order to again take up, in Verse 3, his relation to the Creation, his demiurgical function. In Verse 4, *ἐν αὐτῷ ζωὴ ἦν*[18] is not "the life," not the cause of life, but *in him* was life. Just as the Father had life in him, so he also gave the Son *ζωὴν ἔχειν ἐν ἑαυτῷ.*[19] That is to say, the narration took a further step toward the Son, as he is *self-dependent outside of the Father*; it forms, as it were, an opposite to the *θεὸς ἦν* [God was]. As long as he was God, he had *ζωὴν* [life] not in himself.

It becomes clear that by this is meant the extra-divine Being of the subject: *καὶ ἡ ζωὴ ἦν τὸ φῶς τῶν ἀνθρώπων.*[20] The fact that *the Father gave the Son the ability to exist outside of him* was the salvation of the human race. The human race was therewith declared as that upon which the darkness falls. And this light already shines in the darkness, *i.e.,* in paganism.[21] *Φαίνει* [shines] is a natural effect. Thus, the relation is expressed impersonally; there is nothing personal, nothing yet about a will.

---

16. Colossians 1:15: "the firstborn over all creation" (BSB).
17. Revelation 3:14: "the beginning of the creation of God" (KJV).
18. John 1:4: "in him was life" (BSB).
19. John 5:26: "life in himself" (BSB).
20. John 1:4: "And that life was the light of men" (BSB).
21. John 1:5: "The Light shines in the darkness, and the darkness did not comprehend it" (NAS).

The prophecies of the O.T. agree with that—to be a light for the pagans. The instinctive [*unwillkürliche*] and merely natural in the effect of the mediating potence is expressed in Isaiah as follows: "Who is blind but my servant, or deaf like the messenger I am sending?"[22] "And the darkness did comprehend the light" is just what we have said about paganism. Christ is also in paganism but not as such; he is there only as light.

Now to the historical emergence in the revelation. First, to the precursor. Until now, there was a steady progression. These intermediate states in paganism make Christ's Becoming Human comprehensible. There is no unmediated transition from the divine to Man; the whole of paganism and Judaism lies in between. Now, to the actual coming of Christ. "The true light was coming"[23] The true light is opposed to the natural, shining [light]; the true light is that which gives light to *every human.* Φωτιζει [illuminate], in contrast to φαίνει [bring to light, reveal]—the light that does not only shine but is comprehended by everyone because the personal is no longer hidden under it. ἦν ἐρχόμενον [was coming]—with this expression, the Apostle reminds us that he who came as the true light has always been in the world. "He was in the world." κόσμος is, as in what follows, καὶ ὁ κόσμος δι' αὐτοῦ ἐγένετο.[24] *He speaks here about the cosmogonic demiurgical Being of the second potence.* "For even the world is made through him." He was the demiurgical potence all along. But the world did not recognize him. He came to his own [people], those who knew him already (the Jews are his originary people), who he had already chosen, but they did not accept him. Now that he appeared as a person, the time of comprehension, of free acceptance, had come. The pagans simply did not recognize him.

Those who did accept him, he empowered, *i.e., he gave them the possibility to restore in them the divine birth that had been interrupted by the Fall.*

---

22. Isaiah 42:19 (BSB).

23. John 1:9: "The true Light who gives light to every man was coming into the world" (BSB).

24. John 1:10: "And the world was made through him" (NAS).

Until now, the speech was still focused on the future. Only one last *factum*: the subject, outfitted with all predicates, became flesh and resided among us. We *saw* his glory, which was hidden before, derived from his originary godhood, his being one with the Father. It is a will not just of the potence but also of the Son, who, as having come from Heaven, revealed himself by becoming human. John's narration contains the true knowledge whereby our consciousness partakes in something truly positive and expansive.

XXVI. The Revelation in Judaism

[PL, pp. 659–71]

Once we have cognized the natural history of the mediating potence in all of mythology, it remains to show its personal effect on Judaism and Christianity. What was its mode of action [*Wirkungsweise*] during the O.T.? A mediating potence always presupposes something that demands mediation. Far from considering the originary consciousness of this part of humanity—held back, as it were, from the general fate of the mythological process by the force of the principle to which the consciousness of humanity succumbed in the mythological process—we, in fact, posit the same *terminus a quo* [starting point] for both parts of humanity.

The human race, and thus also the consciousness of the Abrahamites, has an unmediated relationship to the *relatively* one *God*.[1] The unmediated god, including the god of the Israelite people who did not become and was not revealed, is not the true God but rather one whose singularity later presents itself as exclusive, *who later appears to be covetous of the sole possession of Being,* as a consuming fire.[2] However, *another personality* stands beside (rather than opposite) this God, conveys to him the true God, *a [personality] that in the non-truth unlocks the consciousness of the truth.* What is revealed is one that is brought forth; it is not an unmediated [truth]. That which already has Being cannot be the true [Being].

We shall demonstrate the relationship with an event that is archetypal [*urbildlich*], so to speak, for the entire sequence of Old Testament revelations. Abraham is tempted by God to an act that is appalling to the human soul and is one of the most cursed ones.[3] The same [God] who said

1. *Philosophie der Offenbarung,* SW XIV, p. 120: "to the *one-sided,* falsely One God."

2. Hebrews 12:29: "For our God is a consuming fire" (BSB).

3. Genesis 22.

after the Flood: "Whoever sheds Man's blood, his blood shall be shed," [and] "I will avenge your lifeblood, to the betterment of your soul"[4] is supposed to have issued this demand to Abraham? At that time, there were many other peoples who regarded sacrificing their children as a religious commandment. The principle that tempted Abraham to this act was the same as that which misled other peoples to the same action. Abraham's revelation was *tied to,* or presupposed, *a false divine principle.* The *angel of Jehovah* fought back the anti-divine principle. He who is called Elohim is the substance of conscious doing [*Bewusstthuns*]; the Angel of Jehovah is not something substantial but something becoming, merely appearing. He is not here substantively but only *actu.* He is only the appearance of Jehovah and thus always presupposes Elohim as substance, as medium of his appearance. He is not the actual one, for he presupposes the solicitation and its principle itself as a condition of his effectiveness.

Neither of the two is the true God who appears only by sublating the preceding one; rather, *the true God in this narration is mediated by the false one,* and this indicates the limit of the O.T. Revelation is only possible through a medium. This, however, is only given through the *counter-divine* [*gegengöttliche*] *principle.* Here, the higher potence overcomes the lower one not through a natural effect but by willing and thus brings forth the *appearance* of the true God. In the unmediated Being, the true God becomes unlike himself [*ungleich*], mediates himself to himself [*vermittelt sich*], and thus brings himself forth in the consciousness. Otherwise, revelation is not possible; *no consciousness can be infused from the outside,* only by means of a principle that already has Being, that abides as potence in the consciousness.

The Old Testament revelation perpetually presupposes *the tension.* The entire constitution of religion [*Religionsverfassung*] proves the recognition of the reality of the contrary principle, which also underlies paganism and which it has to protect as its presupposition. In the Mosaic religion,

---

4. Genesis 9:5–6.

the pagan principle is that which always becomes limited; therefore, the O.T. is preferably the period of divine revelation. For any revelation presupposes a darkening principle; thus, *Christ is the end of revelation.*

The actual appearance of Christ is more than just revelation because it sublates the presupposition of revelation and therewith [revelation] itself. The revelation of the O.T. is the revelation that breaks through mythology; Christianity has broken through this shell (of paganism). Thus, in one act, Christianity sublates both Judaism and paganism.

The O.T., however, must save its presupposition. Israel derives itself from a race that kept itself apart from peoples, that holds fast to a God who originarily was common to all of humanity. This God is not yet a material god but is spiritually thought of as the lord of the heavens and earth. This unity and spirituality was always the first commandment with the Abrahamites, but it was still a commandment. Strabo says of Moses: "He spoke and taught that the Egyptians [and Africans] entertained erroneous sentiments, in representing God under the likeness of wild beasts and cattle [of the field]; and that the Hellenes still had *θεοὺς ἀνθρωπομόρφους* [gods in human form]. For God [he said] is only One, who encompasses us all, what we call world, or heaven, or the nature of things. Who would then venture to form an image of this [God]? [On the contrary,] we ought to set apart a temple and a shrine and worship God without any similitude."[5]

In Egypt, however, with the progression of mythology, the Jews declared themselves to that one exclusive God (the Kronian moment). Their situation in Egypt and their expulsion from Egypt can be explained by this. While they also remained faithful to the nomadic way of life in Egypt, the pharaohs tried to compel them to work in the fields and in urban construction. In Egypt, the Israelites were regarded as worshippers of Typhon (the remainder of this exclusive, consuming principle that, giving way to the milder principle of Osiris, was worshipped only in limited form and in small

5. Strabo, *Geography,* Book 16.2.35.

temples). The logographers in Plutarch recount how for seven days Typhon, having been ousted from power, fled on the back of a red ass and, after his escape, fathered Hierosolymus and Judaeus.[6] Tacitus referred to Hierosolymus and Judaeus as military commanders who led the Jews out of Egypt.[7]

On the seventh day, Typhon rested. Tacitus also mentions the seventh day, as well as the seventh year. According to some, this was established by Kronos, since the Hebrews were displaced from their seat along with the Kronos. With the Romans, Kronos = Typhon.

Curiously, בַּעַל צְפֹן [Baal-zephon][8] was a sanctuary of Typhon and the first camp of the Jews.

With the prophet Amos, at the time of Jeroboam, Jehovah says: "Did you bring me sacrifices and offerings forty years in the desert, O house of Israel? You have taken along the hut of your king and Kiyyun [Chiun], your idol *etc.*"[9] Kiyyun = Kronos. For the truth could not be torn from falseness and thus had falseness as its presupposition.

In Jeremiah, Jehovah accuses the Jews of burning its sons and daughters, "which I did not command, *etc.*"[10] After all, the Jews regarded it as a divine commandment. In the narration about Abraham, the angel recognizes he who demanded the sacrifice as identical with himself. *The revelation was not allowed to sublate its presupposition absolutely.* The angel of Jehovah is not the second potence, but the second potence is the cause of the appearance of Jehovah in B. However, it is not the appearance itself; *through the second potence, B becomes the medium of its own appearance.*

The preceding potence is always the one that is prophetic of the one that follows. The originary God, who cannot be sublated without touching on the ground of the

---

6. Plutarch, *On Iris and Osiris,* 31.

7. Tacitus, *History,* 5:2.

8. *Cf.* Exodus 14:2: "Tell the Israelites to turn back and encamp before Pi-hahiroth, between Migdol and the sea. You are to encamp by the sea, directly opposite Baal-zephon" (BSB).

9. Amos 5:25–26.

10. Jeremiah 7:31.

consciousness, is the organ of the second God who, throughout the O.T., is a future God. The Father foretells the Son. Even the name "Jehovah" (an archaic *futurum*) means "He will be." The true content of the O.T. is a religion of the future. In the next progression, the second potence becomes the subject of the third; the third foretells the second in the prophets so that even the concept of the "angel of Jehovah" is forward-moving [*fortrückend*]. The successive position of the potences is the key to the ideas of the O.T. and assures its relative truth.

The O.T. has its ground and its unmediated presupposition in common with paganism. This explains the pagan character of many practices and customs, *e.g.,* circumcision.

Circumcision is introduced by Abraham and reaffirmed by Moses. *The most ancient peoples in the mythological process*—the Arabs, Phoenicians, and Egyptians—all have this custom. With Abraham, it is already presupposed as a known practice. It relates to the emasculation of Uranos. Each such transition was linked with an orgy, with the practice of self-injury [*Selbstzerfleischung*]. At the moment of transition from Uranos to Kronos, the oriental practice of circumcising boys is put into the service of deities. *Circumcision is the boundedness to the wildest and most ancient principle.*

In Mosaic law, there are *striking prohibitions of certain foods,* distinctions between clean and unclean animals. *A science dedicated to examining the relation of animal species to the various potences* would provide much insight into this. The pig was abominated by the Phoenicians, Indians, and Ethiopians. In Egypt, it was sacrificed to Dionysos; in Rome, to the mysterious Lares. But since ancient times, it has been regarded as a μιαρὸν θηρίον [unclean animal].

Much of the furnishings of the Tabernacle matches that of the Egyptian temples. In regard to the sacrifices, *the sacrifice of the red bull* genuinely is pagan; red is the color of Typhon. It was burned entirely, and those who dealt with it became unclean.

The furnishings on the Day of Atonement are also superstitious; Azazel, עֲזָאזֵל, from אזל [bring to pass, spend], can be understood as a *fading power.* κεκρατημένον [to be strong] is one Greek translation. The freed [scape]goat was sent into the desert;[11] as for the Orientals, the desert became a place of horrors after they transitioned into civic life. The desert is the habitation of the past, to which the Greeks also expelled Pan. They are the *nostalgic remnants of an earlier, all-prevailing principle.* The Hebrew imagination placed many other adventurous figures in the desert to which some made idolatrous offerings. The open field belongs to the unbounded god; therefore, there are no sacrifices in the open. Thus, the he-goat brought the sin of the people into the land of oblivion.

In ancient times, herds that roamed freely without shepherds (along the Euphrates in Plutarch[12]) were consecrated to the old nature deities, beings of a past still viewed with longing. To these also belong the seven herds consecrated to the sun god in Sicily. According to Suetonius, Julius Caesar dedicated a herd of horses [to the river] during the crossing of the Rubicon and released them to roam freely.[13] Does this hold true only for the nameless, all-prevailing dark forces that Man is reminded of mostly during great dangers or also for the god of the free, natural life?

No people were as subjugated to such servitude as the Jews. The superstitious and irrational, as well as anything seemingly unworthy of God, has always been appalling. One explanation was given by *Spencer*: in some Mosaic customs, God condescended to the mindset of the people and allowed their pagan rites.[14] Another [more generally accepted][15] explanation is the typological [*Typische*], according to which the sacred acts are *types, i.e.,* ideals [*Vorbilder*] that carry the truth not in themselves but rather in what they represent.

---

11. Leviticus 16:8-10: "After Aaron casts lots for the two goats, one for the Lord and the other for the scapegoat [Azalel], he shall present the goat chosen by lot for the Lord and sacrifice it as a sin offering. But the goat chosen by lot as the scapegoat shall be presented alive before the Lord to make purification by sending it into the wilderness as the scapegoat" (BSB).

12. Plutarch, *Life of Lucullus,* 6.

13. Suetonius, *The Life of Julius Caesar,* 81.2.

14. John Spencer, *De Legibus Hebraeorum Ritualibus et Earum Rationibus* (Cambridge, 1685).

15. *Philosophie der Offenbarung,* SW XIV, p. 142.

Spencer does not see paganism as a necessary process, therefore also not in the pagan ground of Mosaism. However, one should not judge the system for excluding all that is prototypical. One could only judge this way if one thinks of Christianity as having no relation whatsoever to paganism. Paganism, however, also contains the prefigurements of a relation that in its truth appears only through Christ. Indeed, the genuinely prototypical of Mosaism is what is pagan in it; any revelation presupposes an originary substantial content of the consciousness. This is the limit of revelation, which does not fall before its sublation.

The law seems to be the ideal of a religious constitution, which never existed in actuality; in practical experience, Jews were, for all intents and purposes, polytheistic. Paganism shapes the substance of their consciousness; what was revealed was the accidental. From the Queen of Heaven[16] to the abominations of the Phoenicians, even to Cybele, the Jews have gone through each stage. The kings, *e.g.,* Solomon, led the way in their disposition toward idolatry. The people perceived it as a severe deprivation that they were not, like other peoples (namely, the neighboring ones), allowed to worship gods. This is the sin of Jeroboam, who (out of political motivation) put up calf idols in Bethel and Dan, thereby revealing the pagan ground. Ahab even erected an altar to Baal, which was removed by Jehoram, but this did not make Jeroboam's [doing] less of a sin, *etc.*

It is said that the disposition toward idolatry disappeared with the Babylonian exile. It occurred at a time when polytheism had reached its goal, having run its course like a disease. To explain the analogy of the pagan and Mosaic furnishings, one does not require any descent of God. Rather, Mosaism is the greatest proof of the true content of paganism. *The desire for sacrifices is not incited by revelation.* The commands of Moses only provide more direct regulations for sacrifices. *The potence of the future already speaks through the prophets*; they are as the mystery cults are to mythology. Here Jehovah himself rejects the idea that he wanted sacrifices.

---

16. *Ibid.,* p. 143: "Malkuth haShamayim." See Jeremiah 7:18.

The prototypical is already found in paganism; only one should not think of it as something that was put into it intentionally, which only yields petty interpretations. Rather, each movement contains the goal as *causa finalis*. *That which ought to have Being* [*Seyn-sollende*] is posited in Being along with it. All sacrifices point to the great sacrifice of the N.T. They brought about external purification. *But the blood of Christ, who on the strength of the third potence offered himself, purges the conscious from the necessity of dead works.*[17] Previously, humanity had fallen under the power of the cosmic potences (στοιχεῖα τοῦ κόσμου), and Paul counts Judaism, as well as paganism, under that.

One could, however, raise the question of why the Israelites, among all peoples, were the chosen ones. Historically, this seems to be attributed to the virtues of their ancestors. But viewed absolutely, [it was] because these peoples were the least capable of founding states in service of the world spirit. They were the bearers of divine history. For the peoples revealed themselves to be so weak that they could not even conquer their land, even under divine command. Its divine service had no religious or moral influence. While they seem to be the favored people, they have expiated this advantage. It was always either potential Christianity or restrained paganism. In Judaism, there was the cosmic hull of that which is in the future, therefore also itself sanctified. That made it all the more difficult for them to tear themselves away from the ritual law, the cosmic elements. And they rejected the human son of God for being a gentile.[18] Wistfully, the Apostle laments the blindness that has befallen a part of Israel, and the Kingdom of God will be closed to them "until the full number of the gentiles has come in."[19]

---

17. Hebrews 9:14.

18. *Philosophie der Offenbarung*, SWXIV, p. 150n: "'You who came out of paganism might worship him,' says the Jew Tryphon, 'but we, worshippers of the God *who made this one* (Christ) *himself*, need neither to know him nor to worship him,' [August] Neander, *Kirchengeschichte* [*Allgemeine Geschichte der christlichen Religion und Kirche* (General History of the Christian Religion and Church) (Hamburg: Friedrich Perthes, 1825)], I.1, p. 380."

19. Romans 11:25 (BSB).

However, to some extent, Christ meant more to the pagans than the Jews. This was also felt by the Jews; they regarded him as a modification of the pagan principle. The Jews were only important as the bearers of the future, and the medium was insignificant, just as the hull is blown away from the seed. The Jews are thus excluded from history. It would have been wrong to give them a merely theistic religion; rather, as long as they are holding fast to the paternal religion, they still have a connection to the true historical process. They are reserved for the Kingdom of God, which they shall enter in the end. The day will come when they are taken up into the Divine Economy. In the meantime, one should grant them the necessary human rights. What remains now is only this wish: *Auferat Deus omnipotens velamen ab oculis vestris* [Almighty God, lift the veil from their eyes].

XXVII. Christ's Becoming Human

[PL, pp. 671-90]

We have now arrived at the moment of the actual appearance. Once the time was fulfilled, this moment was predetermined, for everything had to happen that could happen externally. No revelation was needed *to overcome the opposing principle externally*; this could happen by way of the natural potence. The declared (external) end of the process took place during the time of the Romans who were indifferent toward the process and did not represent any one moment of it; yet all [came] together in it. Even the ancient oriental religions were re-awakened, and a general feeling that something new must come was prevalent. The distinction between pagans and Jews was obscured by the Roman dominance until it was dissolved internally. The Jewish particularism was brought close to its expiration under the Roman yoke.

We have now arrived at the *moment of the revelation of Christ*, the moment of his Becoming Human [*Menschwerdung*]. This is the most important and essential moment in our investigation.

General remark: the Becoming Human of the Son of God is assumed to be a *mysterium imperscrutabile* [inscrutable mystery], inasmuch as there cannot be any scientific explanation for it. However, many things have become accessible to science that had previously been considered inscrutable. *Non omnia possumus omnes* [we cannot all do everything][1] holds true for all ages. One has wanted to dismiss the exploration of the secrets of religion by arguing that even nature holds many secrets (*e.g.*, the fecundity of organic beings). However, this is a comparison of things that are distinctly different. In fact, it is in nature that something unrecognizable could remain.

It is said that *general gravity* is the first negative condition of all material Being, but we cannot not recognize gravity

1. Virgil, *Eclogues*, VIII.62.

in the way we recognize material things. By realizing this, gravity itself is understood as something that cannot be recognized through the senses.

That general prius *of nature,* about which we have spoken earlier, can only be seen by not being seen; for by virtue of its nature, it is unseeable. If we let it be covered up by the attributes with which it appears, then it is invisible—and visible only insofar as it covered up. *It is its character to be something that is invisibly visible* [*ein unsichtbar-Sichtbares*]. During the process of reproduction, we know what goes on even though we do not know the exact chain of all causes. But here it comes down to something that does not fall under sense perception.

Here we are dealing with a *factum,* Christ's straightforwardly [*freimüthig*] considered becoming human. This fact does not fall under sense perception. If we could not link it to any thought, we would have nothing at all. We must first comprehend it, and then we arrive at the point of perception. One must first specify which sense is to be connected to it, and theology has always done so.

The typical way to imagine the matter is this: the Man Jesus was created by the unmediated divine omnipotence; with this, the second divine personality became most intimately connected, up to the identity of the person so that *God and Man are* one *person.* One had to describe it as if the divine person took on or attracted a person independent from it merely in order for the purely divine nature to not have to undergo any change that could make it seem as if the godhood has gone over into humanness. *Vivendum erat, ne pura divinitas mutata fuisse videretur, sed* [*ad eam simpliciter*] *aliquid accessisse* [Being alive did not change his pure godhood, it simply came to him] (Petavius).

But *our view of the preexistence of Christ* removes these difficulties; for we have seen *the Son* in a state in which he is posited without his intervention, merely by the action of Man, *as extra-divine potence, yet in the "form of God." He has emptied himself* [*entäussert*][2] of that form, *not from his godhood but*

2. Schelling uses the Lutheran translation of the Greek *kenosis* (Christ's renunciation of the divine nature) as "Entäusserung"

rather from his extra-divine Being as a divine one, whereby the incarnation emerges only as the highest act of the godhood that remains inside him. For only *the God in him* is capable of emptying himself of the μορπη θεοῦ [form of God], whereby at the same time the originary godhood becomes luminously visible in the incarnated. "We beheld his glory,"[3] *i.e.,* we saw him in the whole truth of his divine benevolent nature. Had he not emptied himself of his true godhood, the Apostle could not have said that the godhood in him had become visible.

We thus have no cause for improperly understanding the [process of] becoming human. There are *no two actions* to be presupposed: an action of the divine omnipotence, whereby the demiurgical *logos* could also not be excluded; and the sublation of the hypostasis of Man. *This concept is much too complicated and forced* and does not accomplish what is pretends to do: to explain *how the* logos *became flesh.* The theologians themselves are saying that human nature never existed separate from the divine. However, therewith the preceding is sublated with respect to time, but in substance. Substantively, Man had to be there before his connection with the λόγος. If Jesus was created by the divine omnipotence, then the origin of Christ's humanity is an event that is physically, though not morally, independent from the will of the *logos* to exist as Man.

However, the Apostle says ἑαυτὸν ἐκένωσε [he emptied himself][4] indisputably of that which was in him. If he only links himself to Man, then he has not taken anything away from him. If the Becoming Human is actually a κένωσις [self-emptying],[5] then Christ's humanity is the pure result of this κένωσις. In the other case, the self-emptying is mere *nonusus* [failure to use]. *γινώσκετε γὰρ τὴν χάριν τοῦ κυρίου ἡμῶν Ἰησοῦ Χριστοῦ, ὅτι δι' ὑμᾶς ἐπτώχευσεν*

(alienation, expropriation, self-emptying); see Philippians 2:7.

3. John 1:14 (KJV).

4. Philippians 2:7.

5. See Bruce McCormack, "Kenoticism in Modern Christology," in *The Oxford Handbook of Christology,* ed. Francesca Aran Murphy (Oxford: Oxford University Press, 2015), pp. 444–60.

πλούσιος ὤν, ἵνα ὑμεῖς τῇ ἐκείνου πτωχείᾳ πλουτήσητε.[6] Here the *πλούσιος ὤν* [being rich] equals the *μορφὴ θεοῦ*. One cannot say of one who is rich and makes no use of his wealth that he became poor. The κένωσις is the forfeiture [*Entschlagung*] of the non-essential *μορφὴ θεοῦ*, accidental in relation to the Son itself, a μορφὴ that he could have taken possession of. That he did not do that is the consequence of his disposition.

In order to be human, the *λόγος* required that no human become other. *ὁ λόγος σάρξ ἐγένετο* [the word became flesh].[7] *The σάρξ* [flesh, body, human nature] *has no starting point other than the* logos. Otherwise, the logos would merely have entered into a relation with something that is human. *The true identity of the subject is only [revealed] if that which is the divine in Christ is also the cause of his humanness. The will to put himself, as a divine Being, in the extra-divine Being is the cause of the Becoming Human.* The Son lowers his extra-divine Being to a historical, human one. [His] humanness has no substance other than the extra-divine Being having been lowered to creatureliness [*Creatürlichkeit*].

If the ordinary imagination [*Vorstellungen*] were to identify the subject of the condescension, it would put itself in the most embarrassing position. If this subject can be neither God nor Man, then it can only be an intermediate: the divine posited outside the divine. Just as the sun is not darkened by the intermediate appearance of a cloud, but only *σχετικῶς* [accidental, non-essential], so the humanness of Christ is imagined only as that cloud. Against this are the clear utterances of Christ and John: "Whoever sees me, sees the Father."[8] The godhood becomes visible precisely in his Becoming Human. The subject that became human is the same subject that, in the form of God, is elevated above all concrete and human Being [and] has ceased

---

6. 2 Corinthians 8:9: "For you know the grace of our Lord Jesus Christ, that though He was rich, yet for your sakes He became poor, so that you through His poverty might become rich" (BSB).

7. John 1:14.

8. John 12:45: "Whoever sees me sees the One who sent Me" (BSB).

to be ἐν μορφῇ θεοῦ [in the form of God] without ceasing to be God. Rather, by ceasing to be ἐν μορφῇ θεοῦ, an essential godhood has become visible. There is no transition from the pure being-God to Man, only from a conditional [*zuständlichen*] Being (ἐν μορφῇ). In his humanness, the subject that has become human now appears as a subject that originated from heaven. Since it is not two [separate] persons but the *one* ἐν μορφῇ θεοῦ, who knows itself in the voluntary self-emptying as being One with the Father and thus divine, we have a perfect identity of the being-God and Man, for Man exists only through the godhood in him in unity with the Father.

One cannot, therefore, speak of God as becoming human, even though the one who became human is God. *The extra-divine of the divine has made itself human or become human.* From the beginning, there is one personality, not two; the human Being is *its Being.* It willed it and has given it to itself, and therefore it is *above* this Being. The identity of the divine and the human is not a substantial one but a personal one, so that the human nature is the impersonal [*Unpersönliche*], the substantial; the divine is *id cuius substet humanitas,* that which posits [the human]. The change affects only the μορφῇ θεοῦ. *The divine does not change;* it only becomes visible.[9] *The extra-divine was the hull of the divine; now that this extra-divine has been deprived of its glory, the true glory of the Son is revealed.*

Our explanation neither tears the natures apart again nor conflates them. We oppose the ecclesiastic opinion insofar as we do not follow the canon it established.

This is the concept of the Becoming Human, its possible concept. *Now to the factual explanation.*

First, the moral side. What is actually to be achieved with the Becoming Human? It is not about the *logos* or *the mediating personality* relinquishing its extra-divinity. For to be the mediating potence, it must be relatively independent from both sides! Rather, *it relinquishes the extra-divine*

---

9. *Philosophie der Offenbarung,* SW XIV, p. 165: "With regard to the divine that remained in the extra-divine, the Becoming Human is not a becoming Other but simply a becoming visible."

as a divine. Nor does it relinquish the essentially divine of its nature. The Becoming Human is about forfeiting the divine μορφῆ in the extra-divinity; the product of this self-emptying is humanness.

However, what is the basis for this purely moral necessity? This mediating that was already operating in paganism was the dominating principle, but paganism only got as far as *externally overcoming the principle that divides us from God.* (In paganism and Judaism, it is sublated merely *actu,* not with respect to its potence, its essence.) It was imposed on Man for separation from God, for penalty and discipline: sublating its effect, however, did not help anything. *The will of the Father had to be sublated.* God could not sublate it; neither could Man, for the latter was powerless against him, as was the mediating potence through an external natural effect. Will can only be sublated by will. An *internal principle of will,* a will stronger than death, had to be overcome. Here a physical overcoming of the will was not possible, only a moral one, through the most freely willed [*freiwilligste*] submission under the godhood, a submission that is accomplished in place of Man.

The most freely willed submission would not actually have been freely willed; the mediating personality, however, was without guilt [*Schuld*], independent against the Father. It was also important for that personality to be independent. It had to have submitted itself fully under the human consciousness in the mythological process in order to become a substitute [*Vertreter*] for this consciousness. The world of Man, where it was subjected to the powerful pull [*Zug*] of the cosmic principle, was its world. It would not have withstood that pull had it not received divine disposition. After all, it was still subjected to great temptations after becoming human. In the Epistle to the Hebrews,[10] the Being in temptation also references the pre-human Being. However, it wanted to sacrifice the dominion [*Herrschaft*], and therewith itself, in its extra-divine glory.

---

10. Hebrews 5:2: "He is able to deal gently with those who are ignorant and misguided, since he himself is beset by weakness" (BSB).

The last is the sacrificing of the extra-divine personality, which takes the place of guilty Man. The decision to make this sacrifice is *a miracle of the divine disposition.* It is the revelation that breaks through nature, and this act is the last: *quo nil majus fieri potest* [nothing more can be done]. It is the ultimate miracle of the divine disposition.

Now to the physical side of the Becoming Human! As I said, it is indeed a miracle, a miracle of the absolute divine disposition. However, once the exalted sacrifice was decided, the execution could go on in a natural way, as is commensurate with the higher potence. If there were no mediation for the transition of the potence into humanness, then this would indeed be a *miracle, more curious than Ovid's* Metamorphoses.

First, we realize is that just as the free will of the mediating potence is the sole cause of the Becoming Human, so it must equally have the material possibility of the Becoming Human in itself.[11] *It has emptied itself of the divine form.* The mediating potence—namely, *its extra-divine substantial Being, not its actual self*—has made itself into the material.

I cannot accept as explained, as I have in previous lectures, or argue that *materiality* and *immateriality—just as,* in a higher meaning of the same concept, *that which has Being and that which does not have Being*—are not absolutely opposed to each other. That which *immaterially* has Being opposite one subordinated to it can appear material in relation to a higher [potence]. A materialization of that which in itself is immaterial can therefore only take place in relation to a higher [potence], which, having come about through the materialization of that Other, is above it. That which was once immaterial can become material opposite a higher one. The principle that dominated the consciousness in the beginning was an immaterial one, consuming all that is concrete; but in certain moments, B takes on a material relationship against A^2 or materializes itself n the moment represented by Urania. Thus, the higher potence ($A^{2)}$ can in turn materialize itself against a higher A^3 (*the spirit*), subject

---

11. *Philosophie der Offenbarung,* SW XIV, p. 170: "It is for itself the material, just as it is for itself the cause."

its Being likewise to the higher [potence], and position itself against the latter in a passive state.

Just as the principle that, in the beginning, relinquished its destructive properties has made itself into the material of what will be concrete in the future, so the higher [potence], whose Being in itself was a glorious one, made itself, opposite that which in turn is higher, into a material for what will be concrete in the future. *The higher potence is the third, which, as long as the tension lasted, also stood in tension opposite the second* and was excluded from it. Sublating the tension against the hitherto excluded third [potence] makes it possible for it to subsequently identify with the third, as it happened during the *baptism of Christ.*

As in the first καταβολή [conception, founding], the fiery principle made itself the foundation of that which is concrete and of a subsequent process, and therewith the water appears (in mythology as well), so *the water* that *Christ is immersed in during the baptism is but the external sign of the inner materialization,* whereby the substantial principle makes itself accessible to the Spirit. The second potence materializes itself against the higher one. It is not the personality but the potence, the natural, the substantial of the personality, the Being, that which is independently kept and which it materializes.

But with the mere materialization it is not yet *stripped it of its extra-divinity as a divine entity;* this only occurs *with the assumed divine form.* It thus materializes, *i.e., it makes itself the material of the highest organic process.* Since it now makes itself into the material of an organic process, against a higher one that competes with it, *it can choose the location of the materialization.* It can choose a human being, whereby it only now acquires *a right to be extra-divine.* It is precisely this [right] that has to be confirmed for Christ to be the eternal mediator.

He committed himself to the extra-divine Being through the Becoming Human; therewith his mediation is complete. The subject, which was the ἐν ἀρχῇ [in the beginning] actus purus *of the godhood, through which everything was subsequently made—which, since the Creation,*[12] *was* ἐν μορφῇ θεοῦ *and then made itself the*

---

12. *Philosophie der Offenbarung,* SW XIV, p. 173: "since the Fall."

lord of the human consciousness—was born at a specific time as Man and entered the circle of other events as a final external *factum*. This *factum* no only had to have merely subjective-objective truth but also *absolutely objective truth,* independent from the human consciousness. In paganism, the reconciliation was merely external, *i.e.,* merely subjective since it did not overcome the divine unwill [*Unwille*], only its consequence [*Folge*] in the human consciousness. There, subjective *facta* sufficed; the reconciliation could be only subjective. Now, however, *the cause of the divine unwill* needs to be sublated; this can only happen through an objective event. That which there has only subjective truth must here happen objectively. That which the pagans formed only imaginatively [*sich einbildeten*] was here touched with one's hands,[13] and a history, such as the one we have been traversing, could only be concluded through such a *factum*.

With this appearance, the *ecstatic* history passes over into actual history. The ecstatic state, which was at the same time an inner history of the consciousness, could not have concluded through a more transcendent, more objective *factum,* an external fact with which the ecstatic consciousness arrives on the soil of actuality. Only an actual, which, however, was so extraordinary that nothing greater could happen, could conclude paganism. The one who was ἐν μορφῇ θεοῦ could be called *the god of paganism* but not the one who appears ἐν μορφῇ δοῦλον [in the form of a servant][14] and is obedient unto death. Since he empties himself of that μορφῇ θεοῦ (the Hellenes frequently speak of μορφαὶς θεοῶν [in the forms of the gods]; Socrates, according to Xenophon, said, "before the gods appear to you *in bodily presence,*

13. 1 John 1:1: "That which was from the beginning, which we have heard, which we have seen with our own eyes, which we have gazed upon and touched with our own hands." *Cf. Philosophie der Offenbarung,* SW XIV, pp. 173-74: "That which the Pagans only believed, only, as the German language aptly says, *einbildeten* [formed imaginatively], that the gods existed in human form, that became here the visible truth, to be seen with human eyes, even, as John says, to be touched with one's hands."

14. See Philippians 2:7.

content yourself with their works"[15]) unto the death on the cross, *all of paganism died.* The external actual history begins with Christ.

Now to a few *specific* points. In its substantial Being that is independent of God, the second potence makes itself the material one against the higher one. The pure godhood is restored in the Becoming Human so that the spirit can connect to it. *το γὰρ ἐν αὐτῇ γεννηθὲν ἐκ πνεύματός ἐστιν ἁγίου.*[16] Here the *ἐκ* [from] is not to be understood *sensu materiali* [in a material sense] but *potentiali* [in a potential sense], in the sense that the Holy Spirit made it possible. Only by virtue of the higher potence could the lower one materialize itself. *πνεῦμα ἅγιον* [Holy Spirit] should not be translated as divine omnipotence, as this would sublate the deeper sense, that of successiveness.

I do not claim that the *Evangelists* thought about this as we do; but *they write about things whose connection they did not perceive* and behave in part like the mythological consciousness. In that sense, they were guided by *inspiration.*

It has been dogmatically established that Jesus was not begotten by the Holy Spirit *σπερματικῶς* [germinally, by seed], but rather *δήμουργητικῶς* [demiurgically][17]—not as the Son of the Holy Spirit! The demiurgical function passes over into A^3 since A^2 is matter. But it is not an absolute creation of the Man Jesus. The second potence is the matter. From the moment that A^2 is made into the material basis of the future human Being of Jesus against A^3, the Man Jesus *comes into being by a merely natural process.* According to the Church Fathers, the Holy Spirit has operated only *οἰκονομικῶς* [economically].[18] The Church Fathers understand the relationship, the order of the divine personalities, as successive potences. The utterances found in Luke also

15. Xenophon, *Memorabilia,* 4.3.13.

16. Matthew 1:20: "for the One conceived in her is from the Holy Spirit" (BSB).

17. Greek: "demiurgically."

18. Schelling refers here to the notion of the Economic Trinity (what God *does*) versus the Ontological Trinity (what God *is*).

speak about the workings of the Holy Spirit.[19] Now, interpretation (time and consciousness are conditions that one must subtract) should always be separated from the matter itself. In Luke, we find poetic embellishment.

We thus see that the *logos* does not require any other matter since the former has *a Being that has befallen him,* which it at first materializes and surrenders to a further process in order to be creaturalized. Thus, the entire process cannot be explained by the principles of the material world. To understand it, one must ascend to the supra-material causes.

If Christ created the first matter out of itself, then this cannot be detrimental to his descent from the forefathers; he only descends from them by his maternal lineage. As that [material] basis, on the progression of which I will not declare myself further, must be incorporated into the organic process of the mother, the one who has become human is the son of his mother, all the way back to David, indeed, all the way back to the progenitor of the human race.

While the prevalent theory does not assume a *creatio ex nihile* for the complete Man, it does assume a supra-naturally animated matter in the human mother; but there one encounters an objection about *the contagiousness of the original sin.* The mediating potence, which by virtue of the divine hidden in it, subjects its extra-divine Being under the higher one, is, however, not merely a hypothesis invented *ad hunc actum* [as of today] but a consequence of the progression through all intermediate parts, which rests on the fact that the preceding subordinates itself hereafter to the subsequent one as matter for actualization. If the first matter was not of this world but has only become matter for his purpose, then it makes sense that the principle that materializes itself can attract [*anziehen*] the matter of this subordinated material world without which a complete Man would be impossible and beget a perfectly unsinful [*unsündlicher*] Man. For through the Becoming Human, the divine personality sanctifies this matter as if it itself had been unholy, all the more so as one can assume this submission to be the transition to

19. Luke 1:35: "The Holy Spirit will come upon you, and the power of the Most High will overshadow you."

the third potence, which, after the sublation of the tension, is the Holy Spirit. (The Holy Spirit acquired Christ for us and restored the interrupted divine birth—thus, the baptism in [the name of] the Father, Son, and Spirit.)

One cannot compare our assumption that the *logos* has taken the *material* for his Becoming Human *from his [own] substance* with the assumption of the *Valentinians* and other sects that impart a physical or pseudo-body to Christ. He took the matter for his Becoming Human from his own substance since *the substance of the divine in him was lowered to the potence of Man* and subordinated to an organic process.

With [Christ's] Becoming Human a substantially new principle came into the world. This new element did not come into the world as one that was excepted from the laws of the world, but its *de-glorification* [*Entherrlichung*] consisted precisely in its being completely analogous to *that which has Being in the world.* However, *an element that was not of this world underlay his corporeality.* Although an otherwise true and complete Man, *he was, by virtue of his corporeal condition, raised above the exigency of earthly matter.* Because a miraculous force emanated from him, the people gathered around to be able to touch him. His early childhood progression and his untimely death on the cross point to this as well. Christ's flesh and blood were praised by him as heavenly bread.[20]

Just as the theologians hovered between too much and too little in the doctrine of the Trinity, so this doctrine also hovers between Eutychianism and Nestorianism.[21] Before the union, says Eutyches, there are two natures, and one after the union.

1) Christ consists of *two natures* but not *in* two natures (Eutyches).

2) Christ consists of *two natures* and *two persons* (Nestorius).

3) Christ consists of *two natures* but *only one person* (orthodoxy), whereby this union of the person arises only from the violent sublation of the human personality.

---

20. John 6:51: "I am the living bread which came down from heaven."

21. *Cf.* Boethius, *Contra Eutychen et Nestorium* (Against Eutyches and Nestrius). In Boethius, *The Theological Tractates* and *The Consolation of Philosophy* (London: William Heinemann, 1918).

None of these three notions can satisfy us. Our notion denies the presupposition of all three, namely, that Christ consists of two natures. Even though he is *in duabus naturis* [in to natures], he is not *ex duabus naturis* [from two natures]. Our notion is that Christ is not *ex duabus naturis*! by conceiving the *subjectum incarnationis* before becoming human to be neither God nor Man but *natura sui generis* [nature of its own kind]. Instead, according to our development, it is this subject that posits itself as both divine and human. For as soon as the *μορφῆ θεοῦ* is divested of its godhood, the truly divine appears. His absolute unity notwithstanding, Christ actually exists in two natures. Christ is God and Man in *one* person only in the act of the Becoming Human. The Becoming Human is the condition for the liberation of the divine in him; therefore, the divine cannot sublate humanity. The appearing godhood cannot sublate the condition under which it alone appears.

The Being that has become independent of the Father lowers his second personality to the human one. In relation to the divine, Christ regards himself entirely as Man. "The words I say to you I do not speak on my own; the Father dwelling in me performs the works."[22] The Father is in him only because of his Becoming Human. Only because he has made himself entirely human, *i.e.,* has made *all* that is substance in him [human], is God truly in him. The deprivation of divine attributes [*Entgottung*] took place before, but he did not make himself into an extra-divine; therefore, the divine remained in him as a divine constitution [*Gesinnung*], which is only revealed in his Becoming Human.

What he says with respect to *his miracles, which, on a higher order to which only Christ belongs, are only natural,* he also says with respect to his teachings. The fact that one balks at the notion of miracles stems from the two known points of view. *If God is completely outside of the world,* then the overreaching transgression [*Uebergreifen*] seems somewhat petty [*hat etwas Kleinliches*]. If he is in the world, then it is merely as a necessary consequence of his nature. He is in it *only as blind substance.* If God were in the world with

---

22. John 14:10.

his will, then there would not be as much division and discord. It is for this reason that we say that God is in it with *his unwill.* Therefore, the world in which he could be with his will is *potential,* or according to the matter always there. Therewith the possibility of the miracle is given whereby God is with his will in any one point of the world.

Christ says that he heals the sick ἐν πνεύματι θεοῦν [by the Spirit of God],[23] through the willing, the spirit of his Father, whom he therefore invokes in order to glorify him through the miracle.[24]

Differentiating among the miracles would lead to instructive remarks; there are also some among them that reveal, more certain than others, the thought of paganism, *e.g.,* the wedding at Cana. Paganism partakes in Christ as much as Judaism; the partition between the two had to be sublated. Judaism is but the matter of his appearance; *he himself is the potence of paganism that is alien to Judaism. He is the pagan's savior* [*der Heiden Heiland*] and thus hated so that this potence can be freed completely. Thus, according to the Gospel of John, he tells the Hellenes that the seed falls onto the ground, [and if it dies], it bears fruit.[25] *During the course of his human life, he becomes more and more conscious of himself as the potence of paganism.* What a path from saying that he was only sent to the lost sheep of Israel to his demand to baptize all peoples! *He was indeed worshipped by the pagans as the merry giver of wine and breadfruit. Several of his miracles refer to this fact.*

I will *add one more detail. After the overthrow of the originary Being,* God pulled his true will away from the world; *God is no longer in the world with his personality; he is* only present in person in his guidance of the Israelite people. That which by his nature is unbounded has pulled back into a narrow circle. He effects the universe only according to his nature, *the demiurgical potence;* in person, he is only the Son of Man. Without the enduring effect of the demiurgical potence, the world could no longer exist. However, it endured. Thus, one should conclude that the extra-divine mediating potence had demiurgical power even in the becoming human.

---

23. *Cf.* Matthew 12:28.
24. John 11:40–42.
25. John 12:24.

However, the logos has also exerted *the demiurgical power in his Being that is independent from God,* but only *natura sua.* But this natural reference, because it is natural, cannot be sublated with humanity, just as humanity cannot draw the same toward it. (Even when God effectuates *in person*—since he has turned away from the world and only effectuates it according to his nature—then this is a miracle, for it is not according to the existing order, in which everything happens by a will-less, uniform operative principle.)

Does the Son of God now also exert the demiurgical function? This is at odds with the boundedness of humanity. However, if he were to stop exerting it, then the world would cease to exist and could no longer sustain itself. The natural relation to the world, because it is natural, could not be sublated with his Becoming Human, any more than humanity can posit this relation as its own attribute. The demiurgical cause is not being sublated since it does not adhere to the condition, only to the subject. The subject remains the same, even if its form is another.

The response to the dilemma is this: the demiurgical effect does not cease because its subject has become human, nor has the subject this effect on humanity *as* Man. This is impossible because the demiurgical attribute does not adhere to the form of Being but only to the subject. Without his will, the demiurgical effect is an *actus naturae suae, irreflexus* [an act of his own nature, irreflexive]. It is an old canon: *actus naturae non ingreditur actum voluntarium* [an act of nature cannot initiate an act of will]. Equally, no *actus naturae* can be sublated by an *actus voluntarius.* That someone is heavy is an *actus naturae suae* and cannot be sublated by any *actus voluntatis;* the heaviness remains *modo irreflexo. If God is somewhere in nature with his will, then this is a miracle.* Therefore, when a miracle is supposed to happen, Christ says: "You will see the glory of God."[26] Then the Son is also in nature with his will, and there the demiurgical potence becomes the leader again, *i.e.,* with the *actionibus in distans.* The condition for miracles is that the Father is in nature

26. John 11:40 (BSB).

with his will. Therefore, the glorification of the Son through miracles depends on the Father.

I believe I have *sufficiently demonstrated how an originary godhood could persist with the complete humanity of Christ.* I will add only that the humanity of Christ can only be conceived as an *actus involuntarius* of self-emptying. For Christ says explicitly: "I have authority to lay down [my life] and authority to take it up again" (*i.e.*, precisely that *μορφῇ θεοῦ*).[27] The human life of Christ is only sustained by the continued will to be obedient to the Father: "This is my food."[28]

---

27. John 10:18 (BSB).

28. John 4:34: "My food is that I should do the will of the One having sent me, and should finish his work" (BSB).

XXVIII. Christ's Death

[PL, pp. 690–96]

The greatest evidence of Christ's obedience to God is his death, which he freely accepted for the human race—the last and greatest act of the human life of Christ. The death of the one who became human was decided by him before his Becoming Human and condoned by the Father.

This death was not an accidental event like, say, when another human perishes during a great undertaking. This is evident from the prophecies. It was a sacrifice *that was demanded by divine disposition, that is, by God himself.* God is just by nature, and *in his eyes, the mediating potence, as a natural one, is not worth more than that principle,* even though it negates God. It would be against his nature to sublate this principal one-sidedly. *He is the God of this principle as much as of the other.* In fact, he yields the second potence only out of love to that initial principle. He is the *All-One* and cannot give up any of potences one-sidedly. *The absolute impartiality* is the expression of his sublime all-oneness. It does not allow for *one* principle to be broken for itself. Should this occur, the potence whose nature and will is to overcome that contrary principle must itself lead by example. *That potence, whose nature it is to return that which has been lost, has to subject itself to its extra-divine Being for the very reason that God did not permit* one *principle to be defeated one-sidedly.*

This occurs first through the Becoming Human. But this was only the transition to the true act of reconciliation. *For immediately after the Fall, the Son of Man took upon himself the divine unwill [and] put himself between the unwill and the apostate Being.* Even in paganism, he was the only savior and preserver of human nature. However, by entering into a relationship with the Being alienated by God, he positioned himself on the side of the enemy, although he did not substantialize himself. He is thus not outside of God with his knowledge. But it was his free will that made him persevere and persist in it in order to bring it back. He has put himself through this relationship on equal terms with the apostate

Being. By taking our place, he took our debt upon himself, and thus also the penalty, so that we could have peace. Whoever takes the debt of another upon himself becomes the debtor and must suffer the other's penalty, death.

One could object that humans are still dying, as before. But they are dying by a completely different death. He died in our stead,[1] for us, his enemies, the enemies of his originary godhood, because Man has posited him outside the unity with the Father. He has *redeemed* our life with his death *from the power of the principle in which Man was caught.* Only through such a miracle of love, larger than the one that moved the Creator to create the world, was there salvation for Man.

As far as the *external circumstances* are concerned, there is nothing to add other than that all of humanity had gathered at his cross, Jews as well as pagans. The former were only the instrument, only had the power, but the latter had the will. The pagans are closer to the mediating potence through the experience of its effect since the Jews were kept away from those natural experiences by the strictness of their laws and their obdurateness. Those to whom the Messiah first and solely was announced had to be the cause of his death.

As far as the *shameful circumstances* under which Christ died, only his divine disposition puts this in a better light. Death by crucifixion was introduced by the Romans for the Jews. *The pagan principle had to die a pagan death. The extension [Ausspannung] on the cross was but the last appearance of the tension [Spannung] wherein the mediating potence was posited throughout.* Through death, he is removed from the judgment and the anxiety, *i.e., from the tension.*[2]

Had there not been a principle independent from God opposing reconciliation, then, of course, no such sacrifice would have been needed; the Father could have granted a pardon simply out of love. If one still wanted to preserve the necessity

---

1. *Philosophie der Offenbarung,* SWXIV, p. 197: "paid the *ransom* for us." Mark 10:45; Matthew 20:28; *cf.* 1 Peter 1:18–19.

2. *Philosophie der Offenbarung,* SWXIV, p. 198n.1: "Anxiety, Judgement = Tension."

of reconciliation,[3] then one would say: God is but the executor of the moral law. Were it not postulated by our reason that happiness is bound to the fulfillment of the moral law, there would be no need for a God. God would thus have been able to forgive the transgression unmediatedly.

Why then did he demand the *sacrifice*? He did it, it is said, to dispel any and all doubt about the mercy befallen to humanity. The death, therefore, was not required for an objective reason but for our own needs [and] merely served a pedagogic purpose. However, if one cannot find an objective reason, then it would be better to abandon altogether the notion of reconciliation through the death of Christ. In the Scriptures, it says that Christ died *in our stead,*[4] not for our benefit [*zu unserem Besten*].

If one says: God might have been able to temper justice with mercy unmediatedly, but then doubt on the sanctity of God would have risen. Such a notion is pharisaic and anti-Paulinian. In order to gain an instance that is independent from God, the moral law becomes personalized here. However, this idea reveals *the insight that a principle independent from God is needed* to explain why reconciliation ought not to occur unmediatedly.

That Christ died for us would then be, according to such modern-orthodox notions, a *fiction*; and there would be a pardon from God. Then, Christ would have endured the punishment for our benefit, not in our stead. *However, the latter is the decisive message of the revelation.*[5] An injury that can be healed presupposes a real injury.

---

3. *Philosophie der Offenbarung,* SW XIV, p. 199: "as some newer theologians since Kant have done."

4. Romans 4:25.

5. *Philosophie der Offenbarung,* SW XIV, p. 201: "If one wants to really explain it, one must not begin by falsifying what needs to be explained to make it easier on oneself. The harder, the more incomprehensible something is [...], the more it challenges our thinking. For me, it is not about agreeing with some ecclesiastical doctrine. I have no interest in being orthodox, or whatever it is called, just as I would have no problem with the opposite. For me, Christianity is merely a phenomenon [*Erscheinung*] that I seek *to explicate.* Whatever the sense, the actual meaning of Christianity has to be judged based on authentic documents, just as,

The principle incited by the overthrow is *the divine unwill itself,* in which resided not just the natural potence but the divine potence itself; the latter attains its own godhood by subjecting its ownness [*Eigenes*] to the godhood. Being divine itself, it now stands opposite the contrary essence (*i.e.,* the divine ground) of the concrete principle. The divine ground of that principle is the divine unwill itself.

However, why did it not remain with the Becoming Human? In the mediating principle, we presuppose the will to subject oneself to God; however, that simply means *to give power over oneself to the divine unwill.* The principle showed its might in the power of death. The complete subjugation for the mediating potence had to be a subjugation unto death; otherwise, it would only have been a conditional subjugation. Only hereby was the power of that principle broken. By sacrificing itself, the mediating potence made all further exclusion impossible for another principle, for it has succumbed completely. That contrary principle consists, however, only in the exclusion of the mediating potence. If the exclusion is made impossible for it, then its own power is broken. +A and -A (*e.g.,* as opposing electrons) have reality only by mutual exclusion. If one gives up its selfhood, then the other can no longer be what it is either. The contrary principle consists in that way, in the exclusion of the mediating potence. *But if it gives up all tension,* then the contrary principle loses its power.

Christ has partaken of human flesh so that by his death he takes away the power of death.[6] In another passage, this victory is presented as a swallowing up of the opposing principle.[7] *B is swallowed up by A when B is robbed of its self-dependency. The exclusion on the part of B was insublatable* [*unaufhebbar*].

---

e.g., we sought to determine earlier the meaning of the Dionysian doctrine or any other mythological idea through the writings of established authors."

6. *Philosophie der Offenbarung,* SWXIV, p. 203: "that is, the devil." *Cf.* Hebrews 2:14: "Now since the children have flesh and blood, He too shared in their humanity, so that by his death he might destroy him who holds the power of death, that is, the devil" (BSB).

7. 1 Corinthians 15:54: "Death has been swallowed up in victory" (BSB).

This is the explanation of the objective of Jesus's death! That Christ of Christianity has to be judged based on authentic documents, dies for humans, *for their redemption* and *in their stead,* now presents no difficulty. It was not a necessity for him to die. While he was excluded through that principle of divine unwill, it was only his divine disposition that made him feel the exclusion as such. He himself could not be reached by the power of death; indeed, *even though he was outside of God,* he could not take this exclusion as exclusion, and be above that feeling of abandonment. On the other hand, Man could not acquire redemption through his own death. For Man was beholden, once and for all, to that principle of the divine unwill. Through the death of Christ, Man could find his reconciliation with God. Before, any unmediated relationship with God was denied to him. "But to all who did receive him [...] he gave the right to become children of God."[8] What Man could not do for himself, Christ did not need for himself; Christ died in Man's stead and for him. Christ is accepted, as taking the place of Man opposite God, covering for him so that God sees the Son, not Man, in Man's place.

---

8. John 1:12 (BSB).

XXIX. Christ in the World of Spirits

[PL, pp. 696–98]

One wonders what *change* has taken place now in the *person of Christ* through this death.

Generally speaking, what happens to Man in death? *Two ideas* [*Vorstellungen*] can be offered. The first is that the two parts of Man are separated in death. But it would be unnatural for only one part to endure in death. It would be more appropriate to assume a second one (namely, to be, in different ways, one and the same subject). Otherwise, not even the *identity of the consciousness in both states* would be ensured. Were death to be taken as the cause of the separation of those two parts, then the body would be comparable to a layer of ore, wherein the precious metal is enclosed.

With the second idea, death is rather compared with extracting the *spirit* (*or essence*) *of a plant,* whereby the power passes over into the oil even though the form is destroyed. Etheric oils, like wine, become tough when the mother plant grows green again. On the oil of Melissa, one can see the form of the plant's blossoms; equally, the camphor reveals a peculiar inner life in the conflict with water, not a dead one but a spiritualized inner life. Thus, one can think of an *essentification* wherein the accidental perishes, but the essence is preserved. This essentified part of Man, wherein the physical is also preserved along with it, is an actual entity, more actual than the current body, which is subjugated to destruction during the separation of its parts.

The subject in the different states is the same. After death, the same subject lives, as spirit, "put to death in the body but made alive in the spirit."[1]

Related to that is the *descensus Christi ad inferos* [the descent of Christ to the dead].[2] The passage in Peter is very important in this context: τοῖς ἐν φυλακῇ πνεύμασιν

1. 1 Peter 3:18 (BSB).

2. The Harrowing of Hell.

πορευθεὶς ἐκήρυξεν, etc.[3] Those who did not believe are *the ones who perished in the Flood.* The Flood is the appearance of the transition from the oldest human race, which did not yet have a consciousness of the second potence, wherein only a consciousness of this second potence arose. This was the first transition to the revelation. *Those who did not believe in the times of Noah did not want to enter into a relationship with the second potence and were therefore excluded from all mythology, as well as all revelation.* It is this perished race, which lived on freely and proudly, that was visited by the spirit of Christ. Φυλακῆ [detention, custody] is not precisely a prison, as that ancient race was granted an *intermediary state,* in which it was, so to speak, deposited, *kept safe* [*aufbewahrt*].

---

3. 1 Peter 3:19: "He went and preached to the spirits in prison" (BSB).

XXX. Christ's Resurrection

[PL, pp. 699-702]

The Redeemer traversed *two stages* of the general human life cycle, from *conception* to *death,* and life *in the spirit world.* However, he was to be equal to us in all aspects. *He was also to represent visibly the third potence of human existence.* For after Man separated his life from that of God, he could reach that unity again only by going *through three stages. The first stage* is the current life, full of free movement. *The next is the life of the Being that is bound to itself, of necessity [Müssen], where faculty [Können] has been extinct,* the night when nothing more can be done. *The third stage is the resurrection of the flesh,* where faculty is restored. The human life cycle is based on these three stages; the present life is the one-sidedly natural. That many humans now live spiritual lives is only subjective; they are still under the potence of the natural life. Even the highest spiritual life is subjected to the exponents of the present life. As a necessary supplement, a second life follows the one-sidedly spiritual life; finally, there is a third potence of life, wherein the natural and spiritual are reunited.

It is only because of this—through Christ's return to the visible world in transfigured human corporeality—that the human life of Christ became completely human. Of the three days, the first still belonged to the life in this world—the third, to the Resurrection. It is the decisive *proof of the irrevocability of his human appearance,* and of his retaining only the divine mindedness [*göttliche Gesinnung*] of his godhood. "The reason the Father loves me is that I lay down my life, etc."[1] Only because of this did he prevail upon God to let him re-assume human form. *This re-assumption of human form in Christ mediates the general resurrection.* We have all died with him and thus will be resurrected with him. *However, for those who do not die with him, the moment of death will be enduring; it will become an eternity.*

---

1. John 10:17 (BSB).

In facts like the Resurrection—without which there would be external memorative knowledge of the events but never a true understanding of the history—*transcendent history makes its entrance.*[2] Anyone who looks upon history from an external position regards it in the same way that the great masses judge any major event. The impetus of the philosophy of revelation should be not to dissolve the external history in that internal one but rather to preserve its connection with the latter That such facts are few in number should not be a reason to doubt them.

Much can be asked about *what happens between the Resurrection and Christ's Ascension.* There are, however, details about which one should refuse to speak because that for which there is no human analogy can never be completely comprehensible, even though it can be described. But this would mean to get head of our own experience, since *our bodies must first become transfigured in order to be like Christ's body.*[3]

Questions should first be asked about the *nature of matter* and its relation to the higher potences, but there is *no space* here to answer these. After an extra-divine world is bettered in Christ, the goal can only be to represent and make externally visible the internal world, as it was originarily intended to be. Therein the Christian view distinguishes itself from all rational philosophical views, which do not know of any true goal or appeasement [*Beruhigung*] for the more distant Being.

After passing the first test, Man—compared to today—would have been *supra-human*; as Man, he shall now partake, without forsaking himself, in the joys that were meant for him originarily. Only in the expectation of such an end is there appeasement. This is promised by Christ, and, according to

2. *Philosophie der Offenbarung,* SW XIV, p. 219: "Facts like the Resurrection are like lightning flashes in which the higher, *i.e.,* the true, inner, history breaks into and enters the merely external history."

3. Philippians 3:21: "who, by the power that enables him to subject all things to himself, will transform our lowly bodies to be like his glorious body" (BSB).

Peter,[4] we can expect a new heaven and a new earth after the last κρίσις [crisis].

In death, in Christ's sacrifice of his self-hood, the Holy Spirit becomes the spirit of Christ himself. He is thus the one who is awakened during the Resurrection, "by the power of the Holy Spirit."[5] The full godhood, ἡ δόξα τοῦπατρός [in the glory of the Father], has awakened him. Thus, Christ had to be brought into the state of *expiration* of all self-hood. After the Resurrection, he is equal to the full godhood and at the same time a representation of the originary Man who had lost the δόξα [glory]. Restored in Christ, the latter is also returned to Man.

According to the authentic Christian view, it is not individual human actions but rather the entire present condition of Man that displeases God's eye. Because Man carries this consciousness in himself, this leads to that *unbelief* in which he becomes indifferent to everything he does. First, all of the human condition needs to be *justified because our entire existence is reprehensible.* Only Christ can make us just. By Christ's resurrection, by his continually and eternally being human and having led the extra-divine Being back into itself, into God, our condition, separated from God, is justified and one in which we can now be with joy and comfort. "If Christ has not been raised, […] your faith is also in vain."[6]

---

4. 2 Peter 3:13: "But in keeping with God's promise, we are looking forward to a new heaven and a new earth, where righteousness dwells" (BSB).

5. Romans 1:4: "who through the Spirit of holiness was declared with power to be the Son of God by his resurrection from the dead: Jesus Christ our Lord" (BSB).

6. 1 Corinthians 15:14 (NAS).

XXXI. The Lasting Condition of Christ's Exaltation

[PL, pp. 702–4]

According to a passage in the Epistle to the Philippians, God exalted the one who emptied himself of the *μορφῆ θεοῦ* and bestowed on him a name above all names.[1] With regard to this exaltation, the prevalent explanations meet with the same difficulty as those of the descension. *What is the actual subject of the exaltation?*

Since the godhood is as incapable of exaltation as of descension, Man is decreed as the subject. The descension was to consist of the non-use of the divine attributes and the exaltation therein that Man has entered into the full use of the same. Aside from numerous difficulties, the word *ἐχαρίσατο* [granted, bestowed] speaks against this, since one cannot bestow the use of something to someone who already has it. The meaning of the exaltation is instead as follows: *the subject—which before the Becoming Human was neither God nor Man and subjects itself to God in its substantiality and proper essence [Eigenheit]—is exalted in its propriety by God, i.e.,* recognized by God the Father as Lord, as Son of God 'εν δυνάμει [in or with power], since (ἐξ) the Resurrection (Epistle to the Romans 1:4). It is precisely this subject, which in human form tarried in obedience and subjection until death, that *in its extra-divinity* is declared the actual heir to God, to whom the Father leaves Being in order to rule over it as extra-divine personality.

This is Christ's reward, that he has a right to be outside of God in his own form; he is outside of God with God's will. Peter says to the Jews: "Therefore let all Israel know with certainty that God has made this Jesus, whom you crucified, both Lord and Christ!"[2] He did not cease to be Man.

1. Philippians 2:9: "God highly exalted him, and bestowed on him the name which is above every name" (NAS).

2. Acts 2:36 (BSB).

We are in need of such an mediator, for he is the eternal mediator. Christ is outside of God by virtue of his eternal humanness, and he is outside of Man by virtue of his godhood. He became elevated toward dominion, which he did not greedily seize for himself. He who has been made Lord could not substantially be God; he could only be made perfect through suffering.[3] Did Christ not have to suffer to be brought to glory? Only he who was *ἐν μορφῇ θεοῦ* could be exalted to be at God's right side, *i.e.,* acknowledged by God himself. Only he who was independent of God could surrender himself to glory in order to reach the glory with god. "All authority in heaven and on the earth has been *given* to me."[4]

Herewith we have arrived at the point of present human life.—By God's reconciling the world with himself in Christ, *the mystery of Creation, which only the highest thought could reach, has become comprehensible,* tangible, and concrete for all Men.

---

3. Hebrews 2:10.
4. Matthew 28:18 (BSB).

XXXII. Concluding Remarks

[PL, pp. 704-10]

Now it has become evident *that Christianity is not a doctrine but a matter* [*Sache*]. Its true content is Christ himself and his history, not just the history of his deeds and sufferings during his humanness but the higher one wherein his life as Man is only a transition, a moment. Christ is indeed the unmediated object in his historical appearance, but this can only be explained by a connection that extends to the end of time.

The last task of these lectures is to provide *the* [*objective*][1] *explanation of Christianity.* Let's take another look at this explanation. Imagine how someone *brought up in a strictly rationalistic way,* after being confronted with Christianity, would be inclined to explain its appearance just as he would mythology. With regard to mythology, nothing is historical other than that it is believed to have occurred at a certain time; however, no historical truth is to be ascribed to these [mythological] figures themselves. Because they are *the actual theogonic potences, we assume actual appearances of gods,* but this does not make the gods into [actual] persons.

Christ, however, is not merely an appearance. His historical existence is authenticated [like that of any other historical person].[2] The appearance of Christianity falls so clearly within the authenticated history that [to my knowledge][3] no one has denied Christ's existence. If they had, one could attempt to present Christianity as [merely the continuation or][4] the necessary end of the mythological process [without making a distinction between mythology and revelation].[5] In that case, one could say that after the earlier time had been concluded with the suffering and the death

1. *Philosophie der Offenbarung,* SW XIV, p. 229.
2. *Ibid.,* p. 230.
3. *Ibid.*
4. *Ibid.*
5. *Ibid.*

of the real principle, the second God had to necessarily also become a past for the human consciousness through suffering and dying, so that the third potence could emerge in the consciousness. This part of the process can be understood as having to fall into the part of humanity that remained unmingled with paganism, and that this higher mythological scene attracted paganism with irresistible power.

Even though never proposed, this would have been an explanation; but it is impossible for the reason that Christ is a historical personality. Here [the realm of imagination [*Vorstellung*] ends and] truth and actuality [*Wahrheit und Wirklichkeit*] take its place.[6] By mentioning this subterfuge [*Ausweg*],[7] I hope you will trust that I have not learned of this only through the most recent attempts at it.[8] *The philosophy of revelation, which I first presented in 1831–32*[9] *and have lectured on frequently,* is based on an expansion of philosophy and the philosophical consciousness, which was only possible by repeatedly going back to the principles. How could I deem those worthy of consideration who presuppose a given philosophy as irrefutable and completely misapply its propositions?

The question concerning the meaning and reality of revelation depends on a *crisis of philosophy, which had to arise necessarily.* The *failure* of the before mentioned, as well as the *impotence* of what they call philosophy *to understand Christianity,* need not be explicated for those who are knowledgeable. **My** [lectures on the] *philosophy of revelation* have been distributed widely.[10] It would be surprising if expressions and thoughts of it were not known. *The lectures on the philosophy of mythology go back even further.*

---

6. *Ibid.,* p. 231.

7. *Ibid.*: "which has found so much acclaim in recent years."

8. Schelling is referring to the controversial critical study of the life of Christ by David Friedrich Strauss: *Das Leben Jesu, kritisch behandelt* (The Life of Christ, Critically Discussed), 2 vols. (Tübingen: C.F. Osiander, 1835–36).

9. His Munich lectures ("*Urfassung*").

10. *Philosophie der Offenbarung,* SWXIV, p. 232: "They were audited by a great number of people and, to my knowledge, distributed through transcribed notes far beyond Germany."

Concerning that hypothesis [of Jesus's mythological glorification],[11] which so many have considered during the past forty years, it is evident that the life glorified through legends and myths was already on a higher level [through deeds or otherwise distinguished].[12] A Jewish country rabbi [named] Jesus is supposed to have become glorified through his *teachings*! His morals were already anticipated in the Jewish Scriptures; however, his own words about himself[13] were greeted by the Jews with stones raised against him when he declared, "I was before Abraham was born, *etc.*"[14] Likewise, the claim that he was the Messiah was not believed by the majority of the Jews. Moreover, even if one presumes all this [and] proposes that he was deemed among the Jews to be the same man we are taking him for, it does not explain all of the traits and stories. Christ's majesty is completely independent from these more or less incidental stories. They are not necessary to recognize Christ's majesty; rather, Christ's majesty is necessary to comprehend the stories. Those who use mythological explications should consider this.—By the way, we have given only one explanation of Christianity. We do not have dogmatic intentions. In this regard, we invite anyone who does not favor this explication to propose another. An explication is not necessary, however, since Christianity is an undeniable fact.

Nothing can be said to those who believe that one *simple-mindedly should be content with the grace of Christ,* if they are personally satisfied with that. At most, they may be reminded that *all treasures of cognition are buried in Christ* but *not in such a way that they should be left unretrieved.* Such people should not desire to be taken as a measure for others. *In humans, cognition and understanding go above all.* Moreover, Christianity does not want to be recognized merely by single individuals, but universally, which it can only achieve scientifically. This unifies even the most diverse Men.

---

11. *Ibid.*, p. 232.
12. *Ibid.*
13. *Ibid.*: "how he was sent by God and God's son."
14. John 8:58.

We have explained Christianity purely out of itself. Like any significant phenomenon, it contains the key to its understanding within itself. That [key] lies in the relation of the succession of the highest causes. If Christ is the true content of Christianity, then according to the above, we may very well have reached the end of our *explication.*

We have not touched on his Ascension from earth. We could give some explication for it; however, the necessary insights cannot be deduced from the above. *One would need to deal with the matter of infinite space,* as well as that of infinite time. The doctrine of space is in no less a sorry state [than that of time].[15] The doctrine of the world system, from the physical extension beyond that which is meaninglessly unmeasured, rests on presuppositions that, viewed more closely, cannot withstand criticism. If space is the necessary form of existence in one single point in the universe as a whole, then it does not necessarily follow that distances that appear spatial to *us* do not express merely ideal [relations and] differences.[16] If Man posited the spatial world, one cannot conclude that this effect extends beyond his reach. Heaven is precisely that from which Man, through his present existence, is separated.

If one now asks why it should be assumed that God nevertheless would partake more in a limited part of the universe, I can only answer [with the words of Christ][17] that there is more joy in heaven about one penitent sinner than about the many that are just.[18]

---

15. *Philosophie der Offenbarung,* SWXIV, p. 235

16. *Ibid.*: "If space has become at any one point of the universe as a whole a necessary form of existence, and thus also a necessary form of intuition, then *from this point,* that is, *relatively,* the entire universe will appear in space, but it does not follow that the whole [universe] is therefore *actually* in space and that distances that appear to us as spatial can not merely express ideal relations and differences."

17. Ibid., p. 236.

18. Luke 15:7.

XXXIII. Christ's Work

[PL, pp. 710-13]

Aside from the person of Christ, we now have to consider the *Work of Christ,* which, however, is *continual.*

We are given *only the possibility to become children of God.* It was only the potential to attract the spirit that Christ acquired for us. Without his leaving, the second παράκλητος [advocate, prophet, angel][1] (mediator) would not have come. Only therewith is the true spirit posited in us. Before Christ's appearance, Man was ruled on the one side by the real principle and on the other by the merely cosmic potence. After the sublation of the tension, the third potence is given space. Now the Holy Spirit can actually enter (no longer as a cosmic potence). Here, in its last and highest appearance, *the succession of personalities* comes forward. Because of this relation, Christ could become human only by virtue of the Holy Spirit [and] only die by virtue of the same (Epistle to the Hebrews, αἰωνίου [eternal])[2]. After Judas left, Christ says: "Now the Son of Man is transfigured."[3]

The first effect of Christ is the outpouring of the Spirit mediated by him. Only then, after the power has been taken from the cosmic potence, does the religion of freedom and spirit begin. He has stripped the ἀρχὰς καὶ ἐξουσίας,[4] *i.e.,* the cosmic potences [of their power]. Christ has been elevated to be the head over all ἀρχῆς καὶ ἐξουσίας [ruler and authority].[5] He was elevated above all names,[6] above all power, not only in this eon, which ends with Christ, but in any future eon.

---

1. See John 14:16: "And I will ask the Father, and He will give you another Advocate to be with you forever" (BSB).

2. Hebrews 9:14.

3. John 13:31: "When Judas had gone out, Jesus said, 'Now the Son of Man is glorified, and God is glorified in Him'" (BSB).

4. Colossians 2:15. Schelling uses the Lutheran "hat ausgezogen" (has stripped) for ἀπεκδυσάμενος rather than the Anglican "has disarmed" of the KJV and others.

5. Colossians 2:10.

6. Philippians 2:9.

Any powers that might still arise will be equally subordinated to him.[7] Ἀρχαι are principles; ἐξουσίαι correspond to the potences. They are to be understood in their cosmic form. Thus, Christ put an end to them.

However, it is not *only the three potences* that are meant by this. *Each province in the realm of nature has its own ruler, and the human consciousness is thereby placed in a [state of] tension with numerous such rulers, which are at any one point of the human consciousness.* The meaning of the powers and potencies contained therein changes from moment to moment. For that reason, a myriad of such powers can appear that can assert a claim in any area of the consciousness. Christ has liberated Man from them, *i.e., he took their insurmountability, but he did not sublate their Being.* The latter will only occur when Christ gives the realm back to the Father.

Consciousness exists only in the freedom against the extra-divine powers. God has redeemed us from the external world, μετέστησε[ν] [remove, transfer][8] The Gospel is the law of freedom. In Christ, *the whole of cosmic religion* died, *for it rested on the tension in which he, as natural potence, still stood with the principle of the Father.* When the tension was sublated, paganism began to approach its downfall at a rapid pace. It only exists now as the *caput mortuum* [worthless remains] of a non-existing process.

The Scriptures call paganism the Power of Darkness.[9] In other passages, it speaks more specifically and personally: you used to walk [...] *according to the prince of the power of the air*[10] (the astral potence, elsewhere called *Satan*), who was regarded as a principle of evil and paganism. Here begins *the chapter on Satan,* which we will treat as a supplement in

---

7. Romans 8:38–39: "Neither death nor life, neither angels nor principalities, neither the present nor the future, nor any powers, neither height nor depth, nor anything else in all creation, will be able to separate us from the love of God that is in Christ Jesus our Lord" (BSB).

8. Colossians 1:13.

9. Luke 22:53; Colossians 1:13.

10. Ephesians 2:2 (KJV).

a separate lecture.[11] *Everything has now been said about what can be demanded, in material and formal ways, from a philosophy of revelation. There is no need to go into a discussion of morality, as this is but an unmediated consequence of it.* For dogmatism, it provides the means to consider scientifically every dogma not taken into account.

What remains to discuss is *the complete transition of this internal history into the external history by the Church.* Thus, the development of the history of the Christian Church has to be the final task. But we can only address *the leading ideas,* and herewith the principles established until now will explicate the course of the fates of the Christian Church.

---

11. See *Philosophie der Offenbarung,* SW XIV, pp. 256–78 (Lecture 34).

XXXIV. Leading Ideas in the History of the Christian Church

[PL, pp. 713–30]

Christ told his followers that a time such as the one when he was walking on Earth would never come again. Even though extraordinary gifts were supposed to continue *until paganism was completely dissolved,* Paul predicted a time when the prophecies, *the gift of language,* the γνῶσις [knowledge][1] would end—namely, that special knowledge that is not universal but is directed only toward a part of consciousness (ἐκ μέρους γινώσκομεν [we know in part]).[2] However, when the complete one comes, then all that is partial will end. *With the end of the tension is supposed to come the end of the supranatural,* which Christianity has adopted in opposition to paganism. The *ecstatic* states were based on the tension, which, in their fight against the Christian principle, incited the cosmic powers. Everything ought to finally enter into the completely free, self-conscious, and human cognition.

That Christ was to be with them until the end of days[3] did not mean that therewith the natural development of Christianity entering into the world should be sublated. Rather, Christ compared himself to a sower and the Gospel to a seed. The fruit grows αὐτομάτως [of or by itself].[4] After Christ has planted the germ of a life that would grow all the way to eternity through his life, suffering, and death, he entrusted that germ to develop successively [but irresistibly][5] in the storms of this world. Christ himself says that the enemy will come and sow weeds among the wheat.[6] [It will, therefore, be subject to][7] the same inhibitions to

---

1. 1 Corinthians 13:8.
2. 1 Corinthians 13:9.
3. Matthew 28:20.
4. Mark 4:26–28.
5. *Philosophie der Offenbarung,* SW XIV, p. 295.
6. Matthew 13:19.
7. *Philosophie der Offenbarung,* SW XIV, p. 296.

which all natural developments are subjected. [Christianity must advance],[8] in part through general expansion and in part through internal growth, especially in its knowledge. While no one should lay a foundation other than the one already laid,[9] *the spirit should led to all truth.*[10] In addition, not *all sides of the consciousness* were enlightened yet. A structure that should gradually embrace all that is human was to be erected and grow into a spiritual house of God,[11] wherein all striving, thinking, desiring, and knowing is unified. Not cognition through revelation but cognition that under any circumstances, at all times, and in all places [would be possible and accessible to Man][12]—thus free but scientific cognition.

The Apostles were still under the influence of the processes initiated by Christianity. Thus the great discrepancy between the first beginnings of free Christian cognition and the scriptures of the Apostles. *The large* [and] *divine excitation was followed by the deepest de-tension* [*Abspannung*], *if one considers* [the weakness of the Christian consciousness in most of the so-called Apostolic Fathers, such as] *Clement or Ignatius.* The Kingdom of God is meant to be there externally. Here it had to counter the effects of the internally defeated spirit cast out into the external world, which here, in the external [world], sought influence under a changed form and, openly or masked, faced off against Christianity.

In its ideal purity, the oldest state of the Church was not what it was meant to be. Since the *Lord of the Church* let it be entangled with other issues, it must have been his intention that we think of this prehistoric age as one of innocence or potentiality. We do not need to discuss either the pre-historical or the post-historical age (except for this one).

However, how are those ages of the Church different from each other? It would have been most desirable if the Lord had pronounced those differences himself.—*I will not move forward*

---

8. *Ibid.*

9. 1 Corinthians 13:11.

10. John 16:13.

11. 2 Corinthians 5:1.

12. *Philosophie der Offenbarung,* SW XIV, p. 296.

by way of an a priori *rationalizing but by following the thread of historical development.*—I find the views I now present, as well as their applications, to be *strikingly consistent* with the thoughts of *Abbot Joachim of Fiore,* which are discussed—for the first time, among the numerous church histories I have read—in the newest volume of Neander's church history.[13]

Christ always assembled three of his followers around him on festive or important occasions: Peter, James, and John. Peter was the first he called for. While he designated twelve Apostles, those three had been singled out beforehand and been given special names.[14] He took them with him to see Jairus's daughter,[15] to the Mountain of Transfiguration,[16] and up to the Mount of Olives.[17]

Among those three, Peter [Simon] was undeniably the First. About Simon, it is said expressly in Matthew: *ὁ πρῶος* [first].[18] He talks often in place of the others: *Σίμων Σίμων, ἰδοὺ ὁ Σατανᾶς ἐξητήσατο ὑμᾶς τοῦ σινιάσαι ὡς τὸν σῖτον· ἐγὼ δὲ ἐδεήθην περὶ σοῦ ἵνα μὴ ἐκλίπῃ ἡ πίστις σου· καὶ σύ ποτε ἐπιστρέψας στήρισον τοὺς ἀδελφούς σου.*[19] These words speak most decisively for Peter: "Blessed are you, Simon son of Jonah, for this was not revealed to you by flesh and blood but by my Father in heaven."[20]

Admittedly in favor of a one-sided system, very different notions of *priority* and *superiority* have been confused with each other. *The primacy of Peter* implies nothing less than lasting and permanent domination. Christ compares

---

13. Augustus Neander, *Allgemeine Geschichte der christlichen Religion und Kirche* [General History of the Christian Religion and Church], vol. 5.1 (Hamburg: Friedrich Perthes, 1841), pp. 423–37.

14. *Philosophie der Offenbarung,* SW XIV, p. 299: "Simon was given the name Peter; James and his brother John, the name Boanerges, meaning Sons of Thunder" (Mark 3:14–17).

15. Mark 5:22ff.

16. Mount Tabor (Matthew 17:1–8; Mark 9:2–8; Luke 9:28–36).

17. Mount Olivet (Matthew 26:30).

18. Matthew 10:2.

19. Luke 22:31–32: "Simon, Simon, Satan has asked to sift each of you like wheat. But I have prayed for you, Simon, that your faith will not fail. And when you have turned back, strengthen your brothers" (BSB).

20. Matthew 16:17 (BSB).

Simon to a rock—a foundation. The foundation of a building is above him. The First of the Apostles is the beginning and the foundation of a succession, wherein something truly new follows him; therewith for this entire development, a historical succession is achieved. The *foundation* always remains but this does not exclude a new principle.

James was the first to be carried off. This position may have significance in itself since he was called the Second, irrespective of the brevity of his life. Who could occupy this position other than Paul, who was elected to replace James when he died? It is even possible that it was for that very reason that his life was taken so early. This position came with a mission, which could not have been carried out by Peter.

Peter, Paul, and John: in this succession, they are the *representatives of the ages of the Christian development,* like Moses, Elijah, and John the Baptist for the O.T. *Moses* represents the principle of permanence and substantiality; *Elijah,* comparable to fire, quickens and urges on toward the future; *John* [the Baptist] concludes the O.T. and [with it] the age before Christ. *Peter* is the lawgiver, the grounded and stable one. *Paul* broke forth like a fire; he is Elijah, representing the development, movement, and freedom of the Christian Church. *John is the Apostle of the future.* Peter's state of mind, as demonstrated in his rock-like and undivided nature, speaks of his substantial character. Like no other, he contains information about the oldest times. An earlier race that regarded itself as equal to the gods perished in the Flood (parallel to the baptism). *There the real principle died; from then on, the second potence gained dominion.* It died naturally in Christ; we die together with the natural potence in baptism. In their significance, baptism and the Last Supper go beyond Judaism.

Christ instituted the *Last Supper* before his death being mindful of all the earlier relations. Just as *the gift of bread and wine* was once regarded as a pledge of a καινὴ διαθήκη [covenant or testament], in contrast to the abolished earlier relation, so in a new relation to God it once again becomes a διαθήκη.

Peter sees as far into the past as *John* [sees] into the future. In *Paul* lives the dialectical, moving, scientific, argumentative principle. He represents the new [testament] while Peter represents the old testament. For the ground not to remain infertile, it has to be cultivated. With Paul, a principle independent of Peter arrives, and James was perhaps only called away because, having originated from the same circle, he was not sufficiently independent.

In the Epistle to the Romans, Paul recognizes the ground (the foundation of the community), which he had not prepared. In substance, the community was thus *pre-Paulinian, i.e., Petrine.* However, in this regard, he says that he enjoys a special freedom as the Apostle of the pagans and is not bound by any human authority. He declares expressly, in the Epistle to the Galatians, not to have received the Gospel from a human being.[21] Paul opposed Peter decisively when he came to Antiochia.[22] Paul acted as a new principle. (In Corinth, the disciples of Paul and Peter are divided.[23])

Peter's second epistle mentions [that] Paul's letters *ἐν αἷς ἐστιν δυσνόητά τινα* [are hard to understand].[24] Since all subsequent [relations] are *pre-formed* [*vorgebildet*] in this first relation, one could find here, already pre-formed, the future ban on reading the Bible.[25] For the Church to gain historical ground, Peter had to rule first. In him was steadiness and firmness; in Paul was eccentricity. First the body, then the ideal, the spirit. Indeed, Paul has long held an eccentric position in the Church. For whenever his words, with their stirring power, were heard, commotion was the result. So still, much later, in *Jansenism*; so also do the animated ideas of the *Methodists* have their origin in Paul's writings. In the Middle Ages, countless victims shed their blood because

---

21. Galatians 1:11-12.
22. Galatians 2:11-17.
23. 1 Corinthians 1:12
24. 2 Peter 3:16.
25. In 1199, Pope Innocent III spoke out expressly against reading Paul's epistles, and in 1229 the infamous Council of Toulouse forbid any lay persons to possess and read in translation any books of the Old or New Testament.

of this new principle. It was the basis for Paul's rebellion against Peter's unbounded authority. Galatians 2:11-15 is the *Magna Carta* of Protestantism.

The true Church is not the one of those two but rather the one that moves from the foundation laid by Peter through Paul to the Church of John. It was not in the power of the Roman Church to occupy or not occupy that great position in the world. *The Church had to occupy the empty place of the necessary political power.* "I have not come to bring peace, but a sword."[26] *The same sword* killed the Manichaens, the *fratres spirituales,* the Spiritual Franciscans, *etc.* These therefore led to the view that the Pope was the true Anti-Christ. *Everything one can accuse the Roman Church of is preformed in the mistakes of Peter.* When Peter took Christ aside, rebuking him to save himself, Christ says: "Get behind me, Satan! [...] *For you do not have in mind the things of God, but the things of men."*[27] Thus, we see in the Roman Church a persistent faith with the most disdainful discernment about the world. "If anyone wants to come after me" (and Peter was supposed to succeed him), "he must deny himself and take up his cross and follow me [...] What will it profit a man if he gains the whole world, yet forfeits his soul?"[28] The triple denial is no less significant. *For in the denial, the Roman Church has pursued a gradual evolution* when striving for political omnipotence. It made these into instruments to execute blood orders only to, in the end, itself become an instrument of political power. However, three times Peter was also told: "Feed my lambs."[29]

Despite all this, the Roman Church is for all times foundation and real hold; without that, the Church would have been lost in the political storms and contradictions of thought. *Perhaps the moment is not far away when even this Church* may weep in the face of God, as Peter once did.[30] Despite the repeated denials of his Lord, Peter was appointed the direct successor of Christ in the last chapter of John's Gospel. Three times: "Feed my lambs." There is

---

26. Matthew 10:34 (BSB).
27. Matthew 16:23 (BSB).
28. Matthew 16:24-26 (BSB).
29. John 21:15-17 (BSB).
30. Matthew 26:75.

not a mere πρωτοστασία [leader, principal] here but rather a *πρωτοστασία* without authority—not because he was the Lord's favorite but because his talent made him adept at being the beginning. If anything were to develop, the foundation had to be preserved, and the Church had only just accomplished this.

The Church of Paul remained hidden and secluded for a long time. The more the *real* [principle] contained itself, the more it had to posit the *ideal* [principle] outside of itself. This was, however, the principle of the second and new era. *Reformation is to be explained by higher laws of a divine reason,* not by instrumental and concurring causes, which compete with everything. Each thing requires a beginning, which ought not to be for its own sake; it requires a higher potence to liberate the development from its presupposition. Thereby, however, the First is not denied its right to remain that which is firm [*das Feste*]. It had to break with the newly emerging principle, which the old Church could no longer keep hidden.

The Church of Peter represents strong lawfulness; but a church that is free and independent from the exclusionary Petrine Church was intended through the calling of Paul. The independence, which the new community adopted opposite the others—which had become narrow—was not a separation from the Church itself. Rather, both are, as it should be, mediating members of the Church. *The priority* remains on the side of the Roman Church. Having come from the outside, the new Church is founded in the Germanic nations; in the Germanic nations, it is practically their nature. Germany is the desert into which the woman fled.[31] To the Neapolitans and Paduans, Christ is at too great a distance; St. Januarius or St. Anthony are much closer to them (modern mythology).

The Greek Church made the same claims as the Roman Church but, inundated by Mohammedanism, it remained in a living contradiction to the Roman Church; the Greek Fathers understood the *Confession of Peter*[32] as the foundation on which the Church was built.

---

31. Revelation 12:6.
32. Matthew 16:13-20; Mark 8:27-30; Luke 9:18-20.

Except for the *Epistle of Jude,* there are no didactic writings other than those by the three aforementioned Apostles—a distinction that is relevant also in the far future.

Paul, the first Apostle to write, was the reason for the Epistles of Peter. However far the criticism extends, I will note that if, in our developments, we make use of the N.T., then these are considered as *documents, wherein inspirations of Christianity are perceived.* The particular question about the author of this or that scripture is secondary and only of dogmatic interest. *For dogmatism possesses truth only because it is laid down in the Apostolic scriptures.* However, we consider to be *true,* i.e., *to be necessary in the greater context, that doctrine out of which Christianity is to be understood*; we therefore consider those scriptures to be authentic [and] infused *by the spirit of Christianity.* It is not the external testimonies but the content that makes them authentic, and those who doubt their authenticity (*e.g,* the Epistle to the Philippians) should first seek a true understanding (of, *e.g.,* that *extra-divine* state). *The fate of Christianity shall be decided in Germany.* The German people are the most universal people. For a long time, they also counted as the most truth-loving, sacrificing even their political stature for the truth. Both Churches stand opposite each other with equal rights—the sign of a forthcoming new development. *Even Protestantism is only a transitional form.* **My** view of Christianity is within the totality of its historical development; **my** goal is that a truly universal Church (if Church is still the correct word here), to be built solely in the spirit and only *in a perfect fusion of Christianity with general science and cognition.*

As long as Christ is treated like a mystery by the Church and the Church considers it its task to present Christ in a closed shrine, Protestantism will not reach its goal. ἐκκλησία [gathering, assembly, church] implies a boundedness; they are the ones that are summoned out of this world. It means that the ἐκκλησία has the world outside of itself. In that sense, Protestantism does not object to being denied the name Church. It can say with Paul: "By the grace of God I am what I am [...] I worked harder than all of them."[33]

---

33. 1 Corinthians 15:10 (BSB).

Protestantism could also be accused of being a principle of destruction. This could also be said of the mediating potence, which, however, also brings forth a free and tolerant [*bewegliches*] life. Protestantism is but an intermediate in relation to a higher [goal]. Thus, it alone has a future. *The rigid Papism* can only get to that future with its help. As the Church of Christ, *Catholicism owned the matter and still does*; its merit is to have preserved the historical connection with Christ, but it has no understanding of it. Its unity was external, blind, not understood. Once Catholicism has found its historical opposite, the latter can only be the transition to a fully apprehended, free unity.

Once this goal were achieved, then Christianity might remove, in reliance upon the now gained necessary cognition, the barriers of the intermediate stage. Only then would Reformation be complete, and the Roman Church could no longer accuse it of inconsequence—that it opposes materialism and other excrescences only with human opinion. Science is the greatest power. Nothing can be scientific without it passing into the world and realizing itself. What the Petrine Church could only reject would then have prevailed in an open battle. Since the emancipation from authority, even the most external principle, atheism, could not be prevented. However, since the free spirit has found a way back, not to a universal religion but to *Christianity in its truest determinateness*, only true Catholicism is the achievement of the Reformation.

The Paulinian principle liberated the Church from blind unity. *The third period, the Church of John,* is the unity that is willed resolutely and is therefore eternally lasting. Just as *Jehovah* manifested himself by Elijah *in three forms,*[34] so Peter is the one who violently moves forward, the beginning; in Paul, we see the thunderclaps of genius that at the same time up-heave and make an entire related territory fertile; and John is the gently waving spirit, like an already transfigured spirit, while we can still hear the thunder rolling up in the sky. John has both Peter's simplicity and Paul's

34. 1 Kings 19:11-12.

dialectical acumen. He approaches on the Paulinian Gospel of Luke.

In an attempt to explain the difference between the fourth Gospel and the three other ones, it has been pointed out that *Socrates's thoughts were expansive enough to bridge the distance between the systems of Xenophanes and Plato.* The secret of the descension of Socrates lies in the consistently moral significance of Socrates's deepest speculations. *Only morality can reach up to the highest level and down to the lowest.*

Mark, in his modest and simple narration, matches Peter (Matthew is only an explanation of Mark). There, the spirit of the first Christian community wafts. *Luke* matches Paul. *The Gospel of John* is written for the distant future. Paul and John are in close accordance as to their relation to Christology. Their accordance lies less in the divine effects ascribed to Christ than in the precise *knowledge of the intermediate state of Christ.*

Just as *there are three distinctions in God,* so the Church is only completed in the three Apostles. Peter gazes most deeply into the past; he is the Apostle of the Father; Paul, of the Son; John, of the Spirit. He alone has the words of Christ about the *spirit of humanity* that is to be delivered. With the decision in Jerusalem[35] that divided up Jews and pagans between Peter and Paul, John is designated the Apostle of the final unity. John, whom we find again as bishop of an already existing parish in Ephesus (made up of pagans and Jews) and whose impact as Apostle we know little or nothing about, seems to have been poised to found a church composed of pagans and Jews—as a *church of the future.* For they are not yet separated.

The pagans could not turn to *their works.* They became blessed *χωρίς ἔργων* [apart from works];[36] the Jews did not accept undeserved grace[37] (James spoke antithetically against Paul). Thus, all later divergences are *preformed* in the N.T. Thus one recognizes the pagan element in the one church and the Jewish one in the other. John himself—thus

---

35. The "Incident at Antioch" described in Galatians 2:11-14.
36. Romans 4:6.
37. Acts 15:11.

the condition of his life in comparison to the deedful [*tatenreich*] one of Paul—was to be the evangelist of the New Jerusalem, chosen to be the head of that church, which opens itself for the second time to take in those who were still pagans and have them join those who were still in it as Jews. He was chosen to be the Apostle of the non-exclusive city of God, wherein pagans and Jews are at last received in the highest sense (see, *e.g.*, the antagonism between worldly and Christian science at that moment), and to which each belongs of its own conviction. It was John whom the Lord loved.[38] The last chapter of John's Gospel hints at all that. Christ asks Peter: "Do you love me **more** than these?" Peter answers simply: "Yes, Lord, you know I love you." The second time, the Lord releases him from his painful memory and simply asks: "Simon son of John, do you love me?" Questioned for the third time, Peter becomes saddened and says: "Lord, you know all things [...] You know I love you." *Each time,* Christ says: "Feed my *lambs.*" And the last time, he adds: *ἀκολούθει μοι* [follow me].[39]

What follows in *John*[40] cannot be understood to refer to John's death; rather the μένειν [remain] refers to the preceding *ἀκολούθει μοι*. For the *μένειν* does not directly follow what is said about the future death of Peter since the *ἀκολούθει μοι* is in-between. Christ says: "Follow me." Now one must think that Christ actually leaves. The invitation to follow him represents a symbolic segregation. Now John, who had never seen himself left out, also follows him. Peter, who sees this, says: "Lord, what about him?"[41] *μένειν* is in relation to the previous = *μὴ ἀκολουθεῖν*. *Peter is Christ's direct successor; John, his successor at the time he comes.* (It is precisely the misinterpretations, given to the words

38. John 21:20.

39. John 21:15–19 (BSB).

40. John 21:22–23: "Jesus answered, 'If I want him to remain until I return, what is that to you? You follow me!' Because of this, the rumor spread among the brothers that this disciple would not die. However, Jesus did not say that he would not die, but only, 'If I want him to remain until I return, what is that to you?'"

41. John 21:21 (BSB).

in this chapter that show that Christ's words are authentic [*Christiächt*]).

I am of course aware that since Grotius, this chapter has been regarded as an addendum;[42] however, the fact remains that the prevailing opinion among Christians, as a consequence of Christ's words, is as follows: John will not die. *The speech referred to John's mission, since the later potence only emerges in the last era of the Church.* John's function only begins *when Peter's exclusionary function is completely destroyed,* and when "there will be *one* flock and *one* shepherd" (John).[43]

The Church of John in the Lateran, the world's oldest church, is, in its most ancient part, only a *baptisterium*; only one chapel is dedicated to John. The Church of Paul in Rome, destroyed by fire under Pius VII, is located on the outskirts of the city. The one [dedicated] to Peter stands in the center of the city. However, [one day] a church will be built as a pantheon of Christian ecclesiastical history that will unite all three Apostles.

I believe to have now surveyed the path that the philosophy of revelation has to traverse. Christianity has been prepared since the beginning of the world; it is the execution of the thought embedded in the world principles themselves. There is no salvation aside from those principles; we are bound to them. There is no other ground to be laid. We are not in a universal, abstract world. We cannot sublate an infinite past in which the presence rests. The present state is highly contingent. Those who relish universal and abstract principles may find this order limiting; [but] the world is not boundless. While we ought to worship God in spirit and in truth, the *revealed God,* in order to be the true God, *must not be an abstract idol.*

Paul has designated the era that ends this external contrivance as the last era, the one that began *with the Son being posited outside himself*; however, the Apostle posits this time

42. *De veritate religionis christianae,* in Hugo Grotius, *Opera omnia theologica,* vol. 3 (Amsterdam, 1679).

43. John 10:16 (BSB).

as the Last. This will *not be a pure theism but one that presupposes the entire previous path of God.* The older theologians distinguished between the ἄορατος θεολογία [unseen theology][44] and the οἰκονομία [economy, administration]. They belong together.[45]

Reformation, which the speculative dogmas left undiscussed, turned to the internal process and the *soteriological doctrine,* which, by gaining exclusive importance in the end, generated *Pietism.* Everyone must go through the internal process on their own. What is common to all is the *historical path,* which is described by doctrine, cult, and the cycle of festivities. Only through it can the internal process be kept alive, and only through the cognition of the historical course of events can the Church sustain its objectivity and keep itself from being dissolved into pious subjectivity on the one hand and *empty* rationality on the other.

---

44. *Cf.* Exodus 33:20-23.

45. *Philosophie der Offenbarung,* SWXIV, p. 333: "Thus Basil the Great says in his letters: Our intelligence must be preserved through the Holy Spirit, so that we don't favor theology over economy, the abstract doctrine of God over the historical."

Introduction to the Philosophy of Revelation, or Grounding of the Positive Philosophy

First Lecture

(Berlin 1842-43)

[*SW* XIII, pp. 3-17]

It seems neither inappropriate nor inopportune to begin with a general word about philosophy before turning to the particular subject of these lectures. There is probably no one among *you* who has not come with some idea, or at least an apprehension, of philosophy. *Here,* those questions will be answered for which—as even a novice would say—no answers are given in any of the other sciences and which, sooner or later, would disquiet any upright spirit. Here, we will lift the veil that has concealed until now—not only its particulars but this *entirety* itself of which I feel to be a part of and which becomes more inconceivable the more I seek to educate myself about it. Here also, convictions of great magnitude are to be gained, those that uphold human consciousness, those without which life would have no purpose and would thus be deprived of all dignity and independence. All the sciences I once occupied myself with rest on presuppositions that are in themselves not justified. The mathematical disciplines progress without any significant impetus [*Anstoß*]; however, mathematics does not comprehend itself since it provides no account of itself or of its own possibility; were it to attempt to justify itself, it would go beyond itself and abandon the only grounding on which it can achieve its results. Aside from mathematics, I preferred to occupy myself with the study of classical languages. I am indebted to these studies for that exercise of the mind that, more than any abstract logic or rhetoric, enables me to notice and express the most subtle gradations or distinctions of any thought. I am also indebted to this study for the invaluable advantage it has given me of being able to draw directly from the great works of antiquity and be elevated and refreshed by their spirit. Yet the more deeply I grasped these languages and studied their construction, the more I felt the need to penetrate the very nature of this wonderful tool that, when properly used, expresses *thoughts* with infallible certainty and is delicate enough, in regard to *sentiment,* to render its most gentle whisper but strong enough to reproduce the most violent passions. Where does language come from? How did Man come into its possession? What is the origin of the power created by this tool, not *before* it is implemented but *while* it is implemented—a tool not mediated by my hands or any other external organs but by the spirit I inhabit, and which I ensoul by moving freely and without any resistance?——Next I looked at the manifestations of nature around me. I acquainted myself with the rudiments of physics, acquired the elementary ideas and concepts of the most universal natural phenomena, learned about the laws of gravity, pressure, and kinetics, and observed the effects of light, heat, magnetism, and electricity. I also listened to explanations of these phenomena. Some, such as the laws of gravity, are attributed to immaterial causes; others, to certain imponderable substances. But even if I were to go as far as to concede that these substances and forces actually explain the phenomena—something I am not fully convinced of—*one* question remains: From where do these substances come from and what purpose and necessity do they have to exist? Why are there such things? I admit that light originates from or consists of the oscillations of the ether, which fills outer space—but what of the ether itself? What is the reason for its existence? It seems so random that I cannot comprehend it and therefore cannot consider any phenomena caused by it as explained. I also looked into natural history, and while this inexhaustible diversity of colors, forms, and shapes—wherein organic nature appears to play—excited already my childish sensibilities, and while I would later believe to sense an unstated law that would guide my spirit through this labyrinth, showing me the path of the creative nature itself, nevertheless, *one* question remained unanswered: Why are there such things at all? Why are there plants, why animals? The answer I received was that they are but stages through which nature ascends in order to arrive at mankind. Thus it is in Man that I am meant to find the answer to all questions, the solution to all riddles; for this reason, I am inclined to agree with those who long ago declared the sole subject matter of the final science that answers all questions—that is, philosophy—to be Man. But if Man is the *end,* insofar as he is the *goal* of all becoming and all creation, am I justified in pronouncing it the *ultimate purpose* as well? I would be so justified if I knew how to state what any creature, by passing through every stage of becoming as its effecting cause, *desired* of him. But am I able to do so? I could think of that creature as, having been blind originarily, struggling for consciousness throughout every stage of becoming. Man would then be that moment—the point wherein the hitherto blind nature would attain self-consciousness. But this cannot be, for our self-consciousness is in no way the consciousness of that all-pervasive nature: it is only *our* consciousness, and by no means does it encompass a science of all becoming. This universal becoming remains just as foreign and obscure to us as if it had never born reference to us at all. If, therefore, any purpose is to be achieved in this becoming, then it is *through* Man but not *for* Man; for the human consciousness is not = the consciousness of nature. One might reply, however, that the ultimate and highest purpose does not lie in the human faculty of cognition; if nature is impenetrable to Man and, conversely, Man is foreign to nature—a nature that indeed progresses beyond it and its works—then it has no significance for it. The reason for this lies in the fact that Man has *broken away* from nature and, as experience has shown, has not been destined to be merely the goal or end of a process independent from him, but was rather meant to be himself the originator and creator of a new process, of a second world that would rise above the first,—and thus the actual purpose of Man lies in what he, through the freedom of his will, ought to be in this other world. He was the goal of nature only to the degree that he was destined to *sublate* [*aufzuheben*] nature within himself, to step beyond nature and begin a new sequence of events. But far from arriving at the *true* ground of the world through this postponement of the ultimate purpose, this freedom of the will—which I have conceded to Man and from which I now expect the solution to this great riddle—becomes itself a new riddle, indeed the greatest of all riddles, and throws Man back into an even deeper ignorance than that in which it previously found itself with respect to nature. For when I consider the actions and effects of this freedom by and large—and having taken at least a general look at history before I turned to the study of philosophy—then this world of *history* presents such a desolate spectacle that I doubt that there is even a purpose and thus a true reason for the world. For if every other creature of nature, in its position or at its stage, is what it should be and thus fulfills its purpose, then Man, who can attain what he ought to be only with consciousness and freedom, as long as he remains unaware of his purpose, is swept along by this enormous and never-ceasing movement we call history toward a goal that he does not know. And since he is supposed to be the purpose of everything else, then through him everything else becomes without purpose. All of nature struggles and is engaged in continuous labor. Man also does not rest, and as an old book says, everything under the sun is full of struggle and labor, yet one does not see that anything is being furthered or truly attained that one could believe in. One generation vanishes, and another emerges until it is its turn to vanish.[1] We expect something new to happen and the unrest to finally end to no avail; everything that happens only happens so that something else can happen, which in turn becomes the past to something else. Basically, everything happens in vain, and there is in every action, in all the struggle and labor of humanity, nothing but vanity: *everything* is vain, for every-

1. Ecclesiastes 1:1–4: "The words of the Preacher, the son of David, king in Jerusalem. / Vanity of vanities, saith the Preacher, vanity of vanities; all [is] vanity. / What profit hath a man of all his labour which he taketh under the sun? / [One] generation passeth away, and [another] generation cometh: but the earth abideth forever" (KJV).

thing that lacks a true purpose is vanity. Thus, far from making the world comprehensible through its actions, Man himself is that which is the most incomprehensible, and this inevitably compels me to believe in the unblessedness [*Unseligkeit*] of all being, a belief that is reflected in many bitter pronouncements made in both ancient and recent times. It is Man who compels me to the final question, which is laden with despair: Why is there anything at all? Why is there not nothing?[2]—

Unquestionably, there is a compelling, indeed necessary, longing—not of this or that individual person but of human nature itself—for a science that answers these questions and wrests us from this despair. What other science is capable of this if not philosophy? For each of the other sciences invented or developed by humanity has its specific task, and none answers this final and most universal question. So there can be no doubt that philosophy is, in itself and at all times, the most desirable of sciences, since only through it does all other knowledge gain its highest reference and final hold. If I cannot answer this ultimate question, everything else sinks into the abyss of a bottomless void. But it is not in our time alone that these questions have been raised and the need for philosophy has arisen. What Horace said about heroes—*Fuere fortes ante Agamemnona* [They were strong before Agamemnon][3]—applies equally to explorers of wisdom. Philosophical spirits have wandered not just under the plane trees of Thyssus but also under the palm trees along the Ganges and the Nile, even if no perceptible or definitive words, except for some nondescript utterances, have reached us. But the Greek philosophers—from Pythagoras to Plato—already had questions they deemed worth traveling to the ends of the known world in search of answers, as, for example, when the dying Socrates challenged his

2. *Cf.* Leibniz: "The first question we have a right to ask will be, *why is there something rather than nothing*?" "The Principles of Nature and Grace, Based on Reason" (1714), in G.W. Leibniz, *Philosophical Essays*, ed. and trans. Roger Ariew and Daniel Garber (Indianapolis and Cambridge: Hackett Publishing Co. 1989), p. 210.

3. Horace, *Odes*, IV.9.25: "Vixere fortes ante Agamemnona" (Brave men lived before Agamemnon).

pupils to even ask the barbarians about their wisdom. In the meantime, how many momentous centuries have passed over the human spirit! The Orient and the Occident have not only made contact with each other but felt compelled to penetrate one and the same consciousness (which for that reason alone should have been expanded into a world consciousness!)—all on account of Christianity being transplanted to Europe and, in more recent times, through the almost unrestricted expansion of world relations. Since the Middle Ages, so much has been effected and accomplished for philosophy by the German spirit alone! Nonetheless, there has never been a time when a philosophy that takes on the great subject matters—not just deals with them formulaically—was more urgently and universally needed and perhaps no other time when we have been so astray from philosophy's true goal. If human affairs have, for many years, asserted themselves on a certain uniform course, then the convictions necessary for life, which have acquired validity independent of all philosophy through that very necessity, become a kind of sweet habit. In such times, one does not easily think of an investigation of these principles, and while these long-held tenets and doctrines have long since, and inevitably, loosened and essentially lost their originary power, this very fact is treated as a mystery. For fear of ruining a state of comfort, one avoids trying to get to the bottom of this or pronouncing that the moral and spiritual powers by which the world is still held together, if only in a merely habitual sense, have long since been undermined by the progressing science. Such a state can last astoundingly long, most likely because the untenability of the earlier belief (according to the previous concepts) is so apparent that the more powerful intellects do not deem it worth the trouble to expose. Instead, they leave the business of publicly pronouncing what for every profound observer is no longer a secret—namely, that there is no longer a place for truths considered sacrosanct in the consciousness of the present time—to less competent minds, those incapable of doing anything on their own. Then, a great clamor typically arises, less about the matter at hand, which one has long since been unable to hide and also now cannot deny, than about the unseemly cockiness with which it is pronounced. Those more farsighted, however, will recognize in this simply a desire to become aware in a new way of the principles that hold human life together—the consciousness itself, not the truths that can no longer find a place in it, is antiquated and should make room for a different, expanded consciousness. The transition to this new consciousness, however, *cannot* occur without a disruption, a momentary sublation [*Aufhebung*] of the earlier state. In this general commotion, there will be *nothing* for quite some time that is solid, that one could attach oneself to and build on; the beautiful and elating illusions of a past age vanish before the unrelenting truth. Truth, *pure* truth, is what one demands and alone desires in all relations, in all institutions of life, and one can only be pleased when it is time to openly declare war on every lie, every deception, when it is pronounced that truth is sought at *any* price, even the most painful. Ever since publication of Kant's *Critique of Pure Reason,* more than half a century ago, the German spirit, in particular, has initiated a methodical examination of the foundations of all knowledge, indeed of all foundations of human existence and life itself. It has fought a fight the likes of which have never been fought with such persistence, in so many changing venues, and with such sustained fire; far from deploring this, one should spur the Germans to hold their ground in this fight and not let up until that great reward is won. For the more glaringly one portrays the phenomena of our present time—unrest, discord, and dissolution—the more certain it is that the truly learned will see in this the harbinger of a new creation, of a grand and enduring restoration that, of course, would not be possible without the pains of labor, preceded by the heedless destruction of all that has become foul, brittle, and faulty. Nevertheless, there must be an end to this fight since there cannot be the endless, *i.e.,* purpose- and meaningless, progress that some imagine. Man does not progress into infinity; mankind has an goal. Therefore one must expect to reach a point where the pursuit of knowledge *arrives at* its long-sought end, where the millennia-long unrest of the human spirit is at ease, when Man finally takes hold of the proper organism of his knowledge and learning, where the spirit of all-sided mediation pours over the previously divided and mutually exclusive parts of human knowledge like a balm healing all the wounds that the human spirit inflicted on itself in its zealous struggle for light and truth—and from which our time still partially bleeds.

"But this would be too much to expect of philosophy," one might reply, if one deems possible a restoration of the time through it, since philosophy itself has fallen into disregard, and there is no longer a general interest or apparent enthusiasm for philosophy. It may be that over a longer period of time, and with the favor of fortuitous circumstances, a manner of philosophizing has asserted itself that in some honorable men leads to a certain aversion to philosophy. An entire class of respectable scholars who come from such a time may believe—and make no secret of it—that they can do away with all philosophy, whereby then the absence of a more profound culture would soon become palpable if pure historical knowledge were not complemented with an understanding of the ancient classics and were instead used as its replacement. But when I see in philosophy the means for healing our tattered time, I am not talking about a weak philosophy, a mere artifact. I am talking about a strong philosophy, one that measures up to life and—far from feeling powerless in the face of life and its monstrous reality or being confined to the sad business of mere negation and destruction—takes its power from reality itself and thereby brings forth something productive and enduring.

One might then say, "It is not at all the task of science, and thus not that of philosophy, to bring the shrill discord of this time back into harmony. Would not poetry be more likely to heal and put our time right again?" But history shows us that a happy time, one appeased and satisfied with itself, drowns itself in poetry and pronounces it to be the natural product of a time that has appeased all its essential interests. On the other hand, history has not shown us examples of a time deeply tattered, gone astray, and doubtable of itself having been healed, made right again through poetry. "Secrets," says Friedrich Schiller, "are for the happy ones."[4] One could as well say that poetry is for the happy ones. But where are those happy ones in a time that has fallen out with its past and present, that cannot find its way to a different time, to the true future? A true poet—should one be found in such an time—would be able to gather the discordant notes of the time into his spirit and combine them into an artful but supremely subjective totality, like Lord Byron; lesser spirits would have to reach for appalling and even abominable material for their poetry to nevertheless appear to be something opposite reality. But I need not comment on this. By all accounts, as far as poetry is concerned, the judgment on our time, at least in Germany, has already been passed by another, indeed by one who does not think much of philosophy but expects a fresh and healthy poetry to arise from political upheaval.[5] Now this may well remain *his* opinion, and I have no reason to touch upon it. I would, however, like to pose the following question: How can someone who pays no attention to an element of German literature as essential as philosophy claim the ability to foretell the future of German literature? Philosophy has engaged so deeply with the affairs of this time, and its literature in particular, and has developed such a deep and inward relationship with poetry that henceforth, or at least for now, the destiny of both can only be a common one. Just as in earlier times, poetry preceded philosophy and had a truly prophetic relationship to the latter, especially in Goethe, so a revived philosophy is destined to bring about a new age of poetry by returning to it, at least as its necessary foundation, those grand themes in which our time has lost faith and which for some time it has failed to understand.

To be sure, a true teacher of philosophy should not expect objections to the effects he hopes for to come only

---

4. Friedrich Schiller, *Wallensteins Tod* (The Death of Wallenstein), III.18.2051-52.

5. A reference to revolutionary movement *Junges Deutschland* (Young Germany), which existed from about 1830 to 1850, and to one of its main proponents, the German poet Georg Herwegh (1817-1875).

from others. Once he has shown the uplifting side of philosophy, it is his duty to sweep forth [*hervorzukehren*] the dismal and daunting side so no one is deceived. A glimpse into its recent history provides plenty of material for melancholic reflections on philosophy because until now no manner of philosophizing—or the different philosophical systems—has been able to hold its ground. It is also the duty of a teacher to put forth the side of philosophy that repulses rather than attracts, to consider the many who have shipwrecked in these rough waters—those who with no calling for philosophy have devoured the marrow of their life and hollowed out their inner self in the futile and wrongful pursuit of philosophy, who then wander about the weatherworn tombstones of former systems of theory, not to mention the deserted halls of the ancient schools of wisdom. Closer to our time, some have taken note of how scholasticism—which reigned almost exclusively throughout the Middle Ages and was still favored by the heads and teachers of both churches during the Reformation—suddenly and completely succumbed in the seventeenth century (if not in the schools then in popular opinion) without much resistance from Cartesian philosophy (which in comparison could be called well-nigh underage [*unmündig*]) and how this brought about a lack of gratitude that required nothing less than the stature of a Leibniz to bring philosophy back into reasonable repute. No less than the spirited Leibnizian system, in the form given it by Christian Wolff, dominated the German schools for a long time but eventually nearly vanished, numbering only a few scattered followers by the time Kant's *Critique of Pure Reason* scientifically put an end to it, as indeed it already earlier had given way to a shallow popular philosophy without principles or an intellectual lodestar.—As again, the last-mentioned philosophy, the so-called critical philosophy [*Kriticismus*], which for a time enjoyed a nearly absolute, one might even say tyrannical, reputation, is today barely known and even less understood by many who boast about philosophical studies and knowledge and has lost any influence on the great questions of life.—As thereupon the vigorous Fichte, the founder of transcendental idealism, whose appearance had the effect of a bolt of lightning and who for a moment more or less inverted the poles of thought but, in another bolt of lightning, vanished, would barely find within the *present* consciousness of the Germans the spot on which he constructed his system and would find it difficult to make clear to his successors the fundamental thoughts of his doctrine;—anyone who subsequently has taken note of how after a period of joyful movement, when with the accomplished sublation of the opposition between the real and the ideal world all the barriers of knowledge seem to have fallen, *one* single law was being threaded through the world of nature and spirit and how in those days nature itself appeared to comply with this new cognizance through a series of dazzling and illuminating discoveries following the first observation of galvanism, as if, to use an expression of Goethe, a very heaven of knowledge upon earth appeared to descend;[6] anyone who has taken note of how after such a time a new darkening set in and how what began on a grand note ended small—anyone who truly contemplates and regards all of the above may be wistful about the vanity of all human efforts toward that highest knowledge, which is demanded in philosophy, and in the end may find only a profound, albeit bitter, truth in the words that Goethe put in the mouth of the negating spirit in his *Faust*:

O trust me, who for many a thousand year
Have chewed the same hard fare
That from the cradle to the grave
No one could digest the old sour dough!
Trust the likes of us: all this
Is made only for a god!

---

6. Goethe to Schiller, 28 September 1800: "Ritter was with me yesterday; he is a very heaven of knowledge upon earth." *Correspondence between Schiller and Goethe,* vol. 2: 1798 to 1805, trans. L. Dora Schmitz, vol. 2: 1798–1805 (London: George Bell and Sons, 1890), p. 342. Johann Wilhelm Ritter (1776–1810) was a German chemist and physicist who in 1798 became the first scientist to establish an explicit connection between galvanism and chemical reactivity. He later discovered the ultraviolet end of the spectrum and the first dry-cell battery.

He dwells in eternal splendor,
Us he brought into the darkness,
And for you there is but day and night.[7]

In any case, this diversity, this alternation of systems that are not merely different from each other but oppose each other, is a phenomenon that heralds a nature entirely unique to philosophy; and if we do not forego to fully recognize this nature, then this very phenomenon must also be considered and, where possible, comprehended from the nature of philosophy itself.

One cannot disregard this diversity of philosophical systems by saying that every philosophy is philosophy just as every kind of fruit is fruit. How odd it would be if someone rejected grapes or some other fruit because, although he asked for just fruit, he did not ask for this kind of fruit.[8] The objection to the diversity of systems in philosophy used against philosophy itself can be dismissed with this simple comparison. First of all, it is not clear that someone who asks for fruit must accept any kind of fruit; if, for example, one offered him woody wild pears [*Holzbirnen*] or sour grapes [*Heerlinge*], he would be justified in saying that they are not what he asked for, since in asking for fruit he was asking for something edible; just as someone who is thirsty and asks for water would not be obliged to drink strong water [nitric acid] since he craves something drinkable, not just something that is just physically or mechanically drinkable, *potile* [merely drinkable] but something that to his taste is drinkable, *i.e., potabile* [drinkable and agreeable to human taste]. Second, it is not clear that we have ever asked for

---

7. Johann Wolfgang von Goethe, *Faust,* I.1776–83.

8. *Cf.* G.W.F. Hegel, *The Encyclopedia Logic.* Part I of the *Encyclopedia of Philosophical Sciences,* trans. T.F. Geraets, W.A. Suchting, H.S. Harris (Indianapolis and Cambridge: Hackett Publishing Co., 1991), §13: "If someone who wants fruit, for instance, were to reject cherries, pears, raisins, etc., because they are cherries, raisins, but not fruit. But in the case of philosophy we allow ourselves to justify the rejection of it by pointing out that philosophies are so diverse and that each of them is only *one* philosophy, not the philosophy, just as cherries were not fruit."

philosophy *in general.* This would be like those fathers or guardians who direct those under their care to study some philosophy, regardless of what kind, since knowing something about philosophy is part of a proper education—or, at the very least, to receive some practice in logical and dialectical argumentation so that, as they say, the head will get cleared. After all, everyone wants to know something about philosophy. Even those with contempt for philosophy—who probably would not resent being told that they do not know how to compose a march or write Latin verse—would nonetheless resent being told that they do not have a philosophical mind.

But *if* someone were to announce that he is not merely asking for or intending to lecture on philosophy in general but on *the* philosophy, on the philosophy that *is* and also endures, then such a person would be most inclined to give credence to the preceding developments since they all must find their goal in the true philosophy. Such a person would be reluctant to incite the opinion that his listeners should be instructed in a particular system and intentionally left in ignorance as to other viewpoints or should only be told of them in a partisan manner. Nothing would more outrage a youthful and fiery spirit, one burning with desire for truth, than the intention of a teacher to instruct his audience in just one particular system, in this way underhandedly removing or conjuring away [*escamotiren*] the freedom of inquiry. Consequently, I have preceded all my other lectures on philosophy with a genetic exposition of the systems of philosophy from Descartes to modern times. Since then, a great many expositions have been presented and written about, but sadly in much of it the partisanship stood out all too glaringly; unfortunately, in some circles philosophy has increasingly become a partisan issue, whereby it is not about truth but about upholding an opinion. This time, I am limiting myself to Kant, or rather, the old metaphysics that serves as the foundation of the Kantian philosophy, which was not a system in the way one speaks of philosophical systems since Descartes. But just as in Germany, for example, one speaks of a common German law, to some extent the former metaphysics constituted the common German philosophy, which prevailed in the schools and held its ground even after the appearance of those philosophical systems, since the systems, *e.g.*, the Cartesian, were never incorporated in their entirety into the common philosophy of the time but at most only as individual components. For this reason, I will begin with the former metaphysics in order to demonstrate how, as the consequence of necessary developments, philosophy had to reach a point where it differentiated itself into negative and positive philosophy and at the same time recognized that only if both were combined would it find its perfect and satisfying conclusion. I will take up this point, which I touched upon in an earlier lecture that dealt with the presentation of positive philosophy itself, here in order to substantiate it and expound on it further.[9] Yet, since the negative or rational philosophy will only come up this time with respect to its general foundation, ideas, and methods without itself being explicated, I swill attempt for this purpose a different deduction of this science that for some of *you* may be more comprehensible.

---

9. See Schelling's 1833–34 Munich lecture, *On the History of the Newer Philosophy* (*Zur Geschichte der neueren Philosophie,* SW X).

Appendix

On the Significance of One of the Newly Discovered Wall Paintings at Pompeii

(With a lithographic line drawing)

(Munich 1833)

[*SW* XII, pp. 675–85]

I wish to call the kind attention of the class[1] to one of the recently discovered—in 1825, as far as I know—paintings in Pompeii. At the time of their first publication, the opinions of the expounders on the meaning, or actual content, were not just divergent but, as far as an important aspect is concerned, completely uncertain and undecided. Having seen some recently obtained images of the painting after having come across earlier, by happenstance, a description of it in no. 8 of the *Kunstblatt* from the year 1826, I am now able to present its meaning with great probability, not only in a general sense but also in regard to the previously unexplained part. After my return to Munich, I sought more information about the nature of this painting from the eminent scholar of antiquity, Prof. Gerhard, who is with us today, but I received nothing more than what is contained in the aforementioned article. This convinced me that neither Prof. Gerhard nor any others had gained any further insight into its meaning. I later was fortuitous to obtain a sketch of the picture in question through my friendship with Prof. Schorn, and it is this scholar, whom I am especially happy to see in our assembly today and to whom I am particularly

---

1. This paper was first presented during a meeting of the philosophical-philological class of the Royal Academy of Sciences in Munich and first published in the *Kunstblatt* 14 (1833). Today, the scene interpreted by Schelling is widely considered to depict the wedding of Zeus and Hera, not Kronos and Rhea; see Bettina Bergmann, "The Roman House as Memory Theater: The House of the Tragic Poet in Pompeii," *The Art Bulletin* 76, no. 2 (1994): 225–56. See also above, p. 232n.33.

pleased to share, with his approval, my own interpretation. This sketch, which I am submitting here, enables me to present my interpretation of the picture visually.

Since it would be impossible to describe the picture with more clarity than has already been achieved in the *Kunstblatt,* I content myself with repeating the description given therein and adding that the picture is located on the wall of one of the courtyards in the newly discovered Pompeian building that has been named *House of the Poet.* It is by far the most richly decorated of all the houses discovered until now.

"On the transverse wall," as is written in the aforementioned description, "to the right of the entrance is an image of a mythical wedding. With his right hand, a seated bearded man holding a scepter touches the left arm of a partially veiled woman who wears a richly ornate dress, headband, and bracelet. Each of them wears a wedding band on the fourth finger of their left hand. The movement of the woman is as coy as the expression of her exceptionally beautiful head is fiery and full of life; this and the winged female who appears behind her as guide and who might represent Victory,[2] may have contributed to the initial identification of this composition as depicting the remarriage of Menelaus and Helena after the Trojan victory—an interpretation no less inauspicious as a more recent one, as Peleus and Thetis. The column in the background, standing erect between trees and decorated with three lions at the top as well as with flutes, cymbals, and a tympanum would indicate an Asian locale; but in the case of Menelaus, this interpretation would be a stretch. The costume of the bearded man, with the back of his head veiled by his red coat, seems out of place for a Greek. I would not be averse to thinking of this as the betrothal of Saturnus to Rhea were it not for the three youths seated beneath and engaged in hearkening conversation, whose identity has remained unexplained. This picture has suffered much before its recent discovery, but the brilliance of its original glory cannot readily be obliterated."

---

2. Nike, the winged goddess of victory.

The distinguished gentlemen may have noticed from this description—which, according to the initials placed at the end, has as its author the aforementioned Prof. Gerhard—that there has been much division and indecision among the interpreters as to the meaning of the two main figures. Some wanted to see Helena after she had been returned to Menelaus through the victory of Troy—others, even less likely, the betrothal of Peleus and Thetis. Conversely, there is no doubt that Prof. Gerhard's supposition that the two main figures depict Kronos and Rhea is the correct one; the back of the head covered by a red veil, which, as everyone knows, is an attribute and symbol in the iconography of Saturnus, speaks to this.[3] The wildly beautiful facial features of the female figure and the severe ones of the male speak no less in its favor. The scene belongs to the age of Kronos's rule. Prof. Gerhard hesitates to advocate conclusively for this interpretation because, as he has written, the three youths sitting together underneath the seat in hearkening conversation have thus far eluded identification. However, it is precisely these three youths and their possible signification, as suggested by the description, that persuaded me to agree with the identification of the main figures as Kronos and Rhea. Only that the description of the three youths was too vague: one has to assume that the artist had somehow differentiated them individually, but there is nothing about that in the description. I was therefore even more eager to see an actual reproduction of the painting—an advantage granted to me, as mentioned earlier, by Prof. Schorn. Having now seen that the characteristic position and designation of each of the three youths agree perfectly with my preconceived notion, I no longer doubt the correctness of my explanation; and its having stood this test gives me the courage to present it to this distinguished class.

According to Greek theogony, Kronos fathered three sons with Rhea: *Aides, Poseidon,* and *Zeus.* But, as told by Hesiod, the great Kronos devoured each of them as soon as Rhea bore them so as to prevent the prophecy of *Gaia* and *Uranos,* the older gods he ousted, that he was destined to be

3. The Roman name for Kronos.

defeated and overcome by his own son. Rhea suffered inconsolable pain over the deaths of her children. Deceiving Kronos, she does, however, succeed in saving their youngest son, Zeus, who then, as is known, defeats his father and sets free and brings back to light his devoured brothers. From then on, the three sons share the dominion of the world; instead of the one and exclusively ruling Kronos, three gods rule. Zeus stood out as the highest among them, but each was allotted his own kingdom. *Aides* received the lowest part, the Underworld, as his dominion; *Poseidon,* the middle, or the deepest of all that is overground—the sea; and *Zeus,* the highest that is overground, the ether.

As long as Kronos still ruled, the three gods were against him with respect to being future world rulers, but as such, they were still hidden in the background of the future. I am now stating, for the first time, that the three youths in our painting are none other than the three sons of Kronos. If one inspects the drawing closer, one finds that each is depicted sitting higher than the next; thus I declare the figure sitting lowest, turning its back to us, to be Aides. I also notice his right hand placed on the back, whose fully open palmar surface faces the viewer and may point to *Aides* being the god of the past turned away from the present. With this painting, we most certainly have a copy of a Greek work, and the great significance of this composition shows that this must be a picture from the most beautiful Greek period. Thus, I declare the figure sitting lowest, his face almost entirely turned away and his back and the palmar surface of his hand facing the viewer, to be *Aides.* The second figure, sitting higher, I declare to be *Poseidon,* whose consistent characteristics, his being broad-chested for instance, were never missing in poetry or in art and are expressed here most distinctly. The third figure—the slimmest, the most youthful, attentive, and thoughtful, and sitting highest—is Zeus, who, according to the *Theogony,* is the *youngest* of the three and had been praised for his older age in the *Iliad* because he was the first to be withdrawn and rescued from the child-devouring father, while the others therefore only came to light after him.

If, in this way, the characteristic position and the otherwise signified do not contradict but rather affirm the supposition that the three youths are the sons of Kronos, then this question arises: What is the meaning of their position under the throne, which hides them from both their father and their mother? I cannot provide an answer other than that it is precisely this position that signifies them as the future gods hiding in the background. I have persuaded myself that these three figures were also treated differently from the two main figures in a painterly respect. I hope the painting is sufficiently preserved to confirm this point during an analysis of its condition. I do not know whether Prof. Gerhard's observation that the condition of the painting has suffered greatly before its rediscovery refers to that part of the picture.

If one wished to give this position another daring interpretation, it would not be the first time that we learned through a work of antiquity of a different perspective, namely, one that deviates from an earlier one but is an equally old interpretation of a mythological narrative. As is well known, the same catastrophe—namely, that a ruling god or race of gods is ousted by a subsequent one—is repeated twice in the history of the Greek gods. First Gaia and Uranos rule, the latter hiding his defiant sons in the depths of the earth (*πάντας ἀποκρύπτασκε καὶ ἐς φάος οὐκ ἀνίεσκε, Γαίης ἐν κευθμῶνι*) as soon as they are born.[4] The expression for the same deed with Kronos is already different. It says, *καὶ τοὺς μὲν κατέπινε μέγας* Κρόνος.[5] An even more precise variation is found in the story of what takes place *subsequently*; the monstrous Gaia sighs deeply about the fate of her children and procures a great, sharp sickle with jagged teeth, which she hands to her youngest son, who had hidden so as to ambush his father and castrate him with the sickle the moment he approached his mother

4. Hesiod, *Theogony*, 156: "And he used to hide them all away in a secret place of Earth as soon as each was born" (trans. Hugh G. Evelyn-White).

5. Hesiod, *Theogony*, 460: "These great Kronos swallowed as each came forth" (trans. Hugh G. Evelyn-White).

(εἷσε δέ μιν κρύψασα λόχῳ: ἐνέθηκε δὲ χερσὶν ἅρπην καρχαρόδοντα[6] and later: ὃ δ' ἐκ λοχέοιο πάις ὠρέξατο χειρὶ σκαιῇ[7]). Hence, the son attacked from an ambush. This ambush can only be thought of as the same place that all of the sons, and with them also Kronos, were hiding. The overthrow of Kronos now occurs in an altered way: to save Zeus, Kronos is handed a stone wrapped in swaddling clothes to be devoured. Thus Zeus can grow up until he is strong enough to overtake the father, which this time takes place without castration. The sense of poetry alone would not have allowed the author of the *Theogony* to tell the same story twice. However, we cannot know if in other myths, especially popular legends, the two events were not told much more similarly. According to one other documented legend, Kronos was castrated by his son Zeus. At Zancle,[8] whose name means "scythe," a *drepanon* [*sickle*], allegedly used by Zeus for this deed, was shown publicly even in much later times. It would not then be impossible that, according to this or some other version, Kronos was also attacked by Zeus, from the place where he was hiding with his brothers. If this were more than just a possibility, then one could claim that the spot under and, so to speak, behind the throne in our picture could be the place where Kronos held his sons captive. We could not conceive of this without the presupposition of a myth having been altered in such a way because, according to the story known to *us*, Zeus is *not* devoured along with his brothers, *i.e.*, returned into his hiding place. For now, I cite this second explanation merely as a possibility, as the highly symbolic character of the entire picture presents no reason for me not to think of this position of the three sons as the symbolic representation of a *general* notion of gods still hidden in the background of the future and not yet having come into actuality.

---

6. *Ibid.*, 174-75: "Set and hid him in an ambush, and put in his hands a jagged sickle" (trans. Hugh G. Evelyn-White).

7. *Ibid.*, 178-79: "From his ambush stretched forth his left hand" (trans. Hugh G. Evelyn-White).

8. Ζάγκλη, the ancient Greek name for Messina.

This symbolic designation of what lies in the future of the three figures can be discerned not only by their being smaller in scale than the main figures but by their depiction as youths without beards, *i.e.,* as adolescents, as future world rulers. My interpretation of this youthful appearance is supported by examples of similar symbolism. Thus, Jupiter, the future world ruler, lies in the arms of Fortuna Primigenia at Praeneste as a *child.*[9] Similarly, in Egyptian sculptures, Horos appears at the bosom of Isis, designated as future world ruler by the solar disk on her head. Likewise, the world ruler Iacchos is shown in the mystery cults as an infant at the bosom of Demeter, whereas in other images, he is presented as a child with the attributes of the future world dominion and as a boy (*kuros*) who joins the festive Iacchos procession to Eleusis on the sixth day of the Eleusinian Mysteries. We should therefore recognize the same naive symbolism in our picture. I will offer an opinion about the three myrtle wreaths later.

Concerning the overall expression of the position and faces of the three male youths, the earlier quoted description assumes that they are engaged in conversation; most likely, they are not listening to each other but rather to the conversation of the parents and are expressing themselves to one another about it. Were one able to clearly discern therein an expression of listening, then this would speak for the second view, namely, that they are at the very place where their father is keeping them captive. I will, however, leave as undecided the question of whether the alleged expression of listening could not also be understood as an expression of the tension and the expectation by which again the general notion of that which lies in the future is hinted at. For that which is not yet but only is to be is in a natural tension with that which is now. Undoubtedly, this tension, which one *can* consider an attentive listening, is related to that which happens above them.

Now it is time to focus on the two main figures. The overall movement is clear: grabbing her left arm with his right

---

9. The statue of Fortuna Primigenia at Praeneste is described by Cicero in *De Divinatione* 2.85.

hand, Kronos pulls Rhea, who is, if not resistant, certainly hesitant and expressing doubt toward him. The previously mentioned description finds the movement of the female figure to be coy; however, it is less a coyness of virginal bashfulness than a cautious shyness, which the consciousness of an ominous occurrence inspires, that is especially visible on Rhea's face. Those who claimed to recognize Helen having been brought back to Menelaus in the figure saw in her expression, indisputably, the sentiment of the injustice committed against her former husband. However, an injustice was also committed by Rhea against her husband, insofar as she knows that the children who will spring from this union will one day overtake their father and rule in his place. If one had to think of the three sons, inclusive of Zeus, according to the second view, as already born and still hidden and banned from the light, then one must discern in Rhea's face an expression of resentment over the fate of her children and her refusal to give birth again. If the artist wanted to express this, he would have selected a subordinated and more common representation instead of the grand, originary one. The quality of his work does not suggest such a choice; the juxtaposition of the virginal and the highly ominous in Rhea's face leaves no doubt that the first contact between Kronos and Rhea is depicted here. One believes to see Rhea in the way Hesiod describes her:

Ῥείη δὲ δμηθεῖσα Κρόνῳ τέκε φαίδιμα τέκνα.[10]

Rhea, as Kronos first conquers her. This certainty, even independently of the bridal struggle, which here is depicted as the first contact between Kronos and Rhea, is also decisive in regard to the other [depiction], which until now has remained questionable—that the three sons are not already born and merely hidden from the light but that they are the ones of the future, still hidden from the present, which are destined to be borne from this still evolving union. The painting thus takes on the same sublime symbolic character that we find in the most grandiose depictions of antiquity. It

---

10. Hesiod, *Theogony*, 454: "But Rhea was subject in love to Kronos and bore splendid children" (trans. Hugh G. Evelyn-White).

is therefore not completely set above the common historical perspective and appears as the work of not only a skilled hand but a bold spirit, one who, by showing us the future side by side with the present, elevates us from the present moment with a liberating gesture and, rather than showing us an individual event, lets us see the entire depth of the fate that prevails throughout the history of the gods at once. If the future itself is to be depicted, then it cannot be depicted any other way than as a tarrying and waiting for the decision that allows it to come to light.

Now I want to mention the winged female being who gently drives the hesitating, unwilling Rhea forward with an evidently prophetic gaze. No one would object to our declaring this figure to be Nemesis, who here, where it is about a grand fate, would fully belong. After all, Nemesis is none other than the invisible power that brings about everything that is to happen and is the adversary of that which has Being insofar as it prevents that which ought to be from completing itself. She drives forward the one who hesitates, toward the fateful union, not with force but with gentle motion, as is her way everywhere. If I, however, consider the highly symbolic representation on the opposite side of the picture, then I might be more inclined to see in the winged figure a notion that is *universal* yet related to Nemesis. The wings themselves suggest motion: the winged figure is the power of time itself driving forward because that which in the present is striving and driving constitutes the future that is still concealed in it, the power of the future itself, through which the hesitating present is driven forward, i.e., toward that which is still concealed in the womb of the future time (which here are the three male youths). What is in the center represents the present that gently resists Rhea's moving forward [*Fortschreiten*], with foresight of the future (for the foreseeing prophetic [ability] is always placed in the female deities). Kronos, the god who makes a stand against the forward movement, nonetheless draws in Rhea, the future, to himself by thinking that he could subsequently shackle her and hold her up by violent force.

I have neglected to mention Rhea's gesture of [holding] one corner of her peplos, which is wrapped over the arm seized by Kronos [in front of her]. This gesture is obvious enough and does not require any explanation; it is both a [gesture] of warning and resistance aimed at Kronos, of opening her fateful womb to the ominous births.

To complete the interpretation of the picture, a word about the column visible in the distance between the trees and centered between Kronos and Rhea is necessary. The column is adorned on top with three mythical lions and at the front with two flutes, two cymbals, and timpani. These instruments are known to be associated with orgies or orgiastic rapture. Less remarked on, but no less certain, is that orgiastic behavior involving wild, uncontrolled, and, as it were, tumbling rapture is regularly manifest at moments of mythological forward stride, where a previously oppressive force loses its power over consciousness and a new principle, not yet comprehensible to it, assumes control. Such an oppressive force will also come to an end with Kronos because of this unfolding union. A gentler time will arrive with Zeus's reign. This transition will also be accompanied by manifestations of orgiastic behavior. I only call to mind Strabo's description of the orgiastic worship of Zeus on Crete, where, as is well known, the *incunabulum* of the service to Zeus, thus also the arena of the transition from a previous wilder religion to the kinder one of Zeus, is to be found.

Thus, the column erected in the distance points toward the time in a distant future of a necessary and inevitable transition set in motion by the union of Kronos and Rhea.

The myrtle wreaths placed on the pates of the three young men also point toward the gentler future, while Kronos, as the wilder, more inhuman god, is still crowned with oak leaves. Similarly, in the Eleusinian procession, the boy Iacchos was garlanded with myrtle.

Glossary

Abfall	falling-away
All-Einheit	all-oneness
Allesseynkönnende	that which has the ability to be All
Allheit	allness
Anschauung	intuition
an sich	by itself
Ansichseyende	that which has Being by itself
aufheben	sublate
Aeusserlichkeit	externality
Bildung	formation, formative education
Blindseyende	that which blindly has Being
Einbildung	imaginative formation
Einheit	oneness
entäussern	self-empty
Entäussern-könnende	that which has the ability to empty itself
Entäusserung	self-emptying
Erkennbarkeit	cognizability
Erkenntnis	cognition
Erscheinung	apparition
Existirende	that which has existence
für sich	*for itself*
für sich Seyende	that which has Being for itself
Geisterwelt	spirit world
Gelassenheit	the state of being left to oneself
geradezu Seyende	that which straightforwardly has Being

Gleichwirklichkeit	equal actuality
Gottheit	godhood
Gottvielheit	god-pluratlites
Grund	ground
höchstes Wesen	highest essence
in sich	within itself
intellectuelle Anschauung	intellectual intuition
Menschwerdung	Becoming Human
Mysterien	mystery cults
Nachbild	afterimage
nach der Hand	afterhand (antiquated for afterward)
Nicht-Absolute	non-Absolute
Nicht-Seyn	non-Being
Nichwahrhaft-seynkönnende	that which genuinely does not have the ability to be
Notwendigseyende	that which necessarily has Being
Potenz	potence
Realität	reality
Reflexion	reflexion, reflective cognition
reines Seynkönnen	the ability to purely be
rein Seyende, Reinseyende	that which purely has Being
relative Nichtseyende	that which has relative non-Being
Seyendes	that which has Being
Seyn	Being
Seynkönnen	the ability to be
Seynkönnende	that which has the ability to be
Sinnenwelt	sensate world
Sprung	leap
That	deed
Thätigkeit	activity
Thun	doing

Uebergang	passing-over
Uebermaterielle	the supra-material
uebernatürlich	supra-natural
Ueberschwenglich(e), Ueberschwänglich(e)	the supra-abound
Ueberseyn	supra-Being
Ueberseyende	that which has supra-Being
Ueberwesentliche	the supra-essential
Ueberwindung	overcoming
unmittelbar	unmediatedly
Umsturz	overthrow
Unbeschränkt-Seyende	that which unboundedly has Being
Unendlichseynkönnende	that which has the ability to infinitely be
Unphilosophie	unphilosophy
Unseligkeit	unblessedness
Unvordenkliche	the unforethinkable
unvordenklich Seyende	that which unforethinkably has Being
Ur-	originary
Urbild	originary image
Urmöglichkeit	originary possibility
Urprincip	originary principle
Urstand	originary standing
Urzufällige	the originary accidental
Verhältnis	relation
Verwirklichung	actualization
Vorbild	ideal
Vorsehung	providence
Vorstellung	imagination
Vorwelt	prehistoric world
wahr, wahrhaft	true, genuine
Wesen	essence
Wirklichkeit	actuality
Wirklichseyende	that which has Being in actuality
Wahrhaftseyende	that which genuinely has Being